THE CHURCH IN THE BIBLE AND THE WORLD
An International Study

*This book is sponsored by the Theological
Commission of the World Evangelical Fellowship*

Titles in this series produced by the Faith and Church Study Unit of the Theological Commission of the World Evangelical Fellowship:

BIBLICAL INTERPRETATION AND THE CHURCH:
Text and Context

THE CHURCH IN THE BIBLE AND THE WORLD:
An International Study

TEACH US TO PRAY:
Prayer in the Bible and the World

RIGHT WITH GOD:
Justification in the Bible and the World

WORSHIP:
Adoration and Action

THE CHURCH IN THE BIBLE AND THE WORLD
An International Study

edited by
D. A. CARSON

Published on behalf of the
World Evangelical Fellowship by

BAKER BOOK HOUSE
Grand Rapids, Michigan

THE PATERNOSTER PRESS
Carlisle UK

Unless otherwise stated, Scripture quotations in this
publication are from the Holy Bible, New International
Version. Copyright © 1973, 1978, 1984 International Bible
Society. Published by Zondervan and Hodder & Stoughton.

British Library Cataloguing in Publication Data
The Church in the Bible and the world.
1. Mission of the church
I. Carson, D.A. II. World Evangelical Fellowship
266   BV601.8

ISBN 0–85364–421–7

Library of Congress Cataloging-in-Publication Data

The Church in the Bible and the world : an international study /
edited by D.A. Carson.
    p. cm.
    Originally published: Exeter, U.K. : Paternoster Press :
Grand Rapids, U.S.A. : Baker Book House, 1987.
    Includes bibliographical references and indexes.
    ISBN 0–8010–2526–5
    1. Church. 2. Church–Biblical teaching. 3. Mission of the
church.
BV603.C4645 1993
262—dc20
                                        93–16687
                                        CIP

Typeset by Photoprint, Torquay, Devon
and printed in the UK by
The Guernsey Press Co. Ltd., Guernsey, Channel Islands
for the publishers.

Table of Contents

Preface

This is the second volume to be produced by the 'Faith and Church' study unit established by the World Evangelical Fellowship. The first, *Biblical Interpretation and the Church: Text and Context* (also published by The Paternoster Press), attempted to probe some of the hermeneutical problems relevant to understanding the nature, scope and mission of the church in various cultures. The members of the study unit then decided that it might be wise to put some of that study to use in a second volume that would try to formulate some biblically informed and hermeneutically sensitive statements on the doctrine of the church. This book is the result.

The contributors to this volume were part of a larger group that met in Cambridge, England, in November of 1984. That larger group included Satoru Kanemoto from Japan; Pablo E. Pérez, now from Texas; and for at least part of the time, Sue Brown of England. Another member, Tite Tiénou, was unable to come, owing to passport difficulties; yet another, Emilio Nuñez, was prevented from coming because of severe illness in his family. For these and other reasons, a number of important topics we had originally planned to treat in this book fell by the wayside. These include: The Nurture of the Church; The Church and Social Responsibility (a subject whose omission from this volume is particularly regrettable); Church and Churches; The Marks of the Church. One contributor, Ronald Fung, was unable to come, but interacted with members of the group by means of extensive correspondence.

But regardless of what has been omitted, the essays printed here deal with some of the most sensitive subjects relating to the doctrine of the church that are discussed in many parts of the world. Most of the treatments are fresh and probing, and therefore valuable enough to warrant publication without further delay.

Members of the study unit did not of course agree at every point; but it was both humbling and encouraging to observe how much unanimity of interpretation could be achieved if sufficient time and good will were invested in discussion of particular points. As was the case with the last book produced by the study unit, each of the chapters was studied and discussed at some length at the conference, and the author then revised the work and sent it back for final editorial touches. In that sense, each contributor has had the benefit of many Christian minds from widely scattered countries and cultures contributing to his thinking. The result, as the subtitle suggests, is a truly international study.

Once again the members of our unit are indebted to Tyndale House for excellent facilities and warm hospitality, and to the families of Eden Baptist Church that hosted us in their homes and went out of their way to welcome, feed, transport and generally serve us. One of the elders in particular, Mr Stan Blake, competently looked after the logistics and made our comings and goings remarkably smooth. We are very grateful.

The members of the study unit decided to pursue the topic of prayer at the next meeting, which took place in November 1986.

Perhaps it should be made clear that if there are any Christian organizations, especially in poorer parts of the world, that would like to translate and publish one or more of the essays in this or the last book from the study unit, but lack the financial resources to do so, application may be made to the editor for financial assistance. Any profits from these volumes are directed toward meeting such needs.

Soli Deo gloria.

D.A. CARSON
Trinity Evangelical Divinity School

Abbreviations

(Names of certain journals are shown in full, and are therefore not listed below.)

AB	Anchor Bible
AV	Authorised Version
BibThBull	*Biblical Theology Bulletin*
BJRL	*Bulletin of the John Rylands Library*
BNTC	Black's New Testament Commentary
CBC	Cambridge Bible Commentaries
CBQ	*Catholic Biblical Quarterly*
CBR	*Christian Brethren Review*
CD	Barth, *Church Dogmatics*
CH	*Church History*
CT	*Christianity Today*
EBC	Expositor's Bible Commentary
EMQ	*Evangelical Missions Quarterly*
EQ	*Evangelical Quarterly*
ERT	*Evangelical Review of Theology*
ExpT	*Expository Times*
HTR	*Harvard Theological Review*
IBD	*Illustrated Bible Dictionary*
ICC	International Critical Commentaries
IDB	*Interpreter's Dictionary of the Bible*
IDBS	*Interpreter's Dictionary of the Bible Supplement*
Int	*Interpretation*
Inst.	Calvin, *Institutes of the Christian Religion*

IRM	*International Review of Mission*
ISBE	*International Standard Bible Encyclopedia*
ISBER	*International Standard Bible Encyclopedia Revised*
JAAR	*Journal of the American Academy of Religion*
JBL	*Journal of Biblical Literature*
JETS	*Journal of the Evangelical Theological Society*
JTS	*Journal of Theological Studies*
KD	*Kerygma und Dogma*
KJV	King James Version
MNTC	Moffatt New Testament Commentary
NASB	New American Standard Bible
NBCR	*New Bible Commentary Revised*
NBD	*New Bible Dictionary*
NCB	New Century Bible
NICNT	New International Commentary on the New Testament
NIDNTT	*New International Dictionary of New Testament Theology*
NIV	New International Version
NLC	New London Commentary
NovT	*Novum Testamentum*
NTA	*New Testament Abstracts*
NTS	*New Testament Studies*
RefThRev	*Reformed Theological Review*
RevExp	*Review and Expositor*
RSV	Revised Standard Version
RV	Revised Version
SE	*Studia Evangelica*
SJT	*Scottish Journal of Theology*
Str-B	Strack/Billerbeck, *Kommentar zum Neuen Testament*
TDNT	*Theological Dictionary of the New Testament*
TNTC	Tyndale New Testament Commentaries

TOTC	Tyndale Old Testament Commentaries
TrinJ	*Trinity Journal*
TWNT	*Theologisches Wörterbuch zum Neuen Testament*
TynBull	*Tyndale Bulletin*
WBC	World Biblical Commentary
WEF	World Evangelical Fellowship
WTJ	*Westminster Theological Journal*
VE	*Vox Evangelica*
ZNW	*Zeitschrift für die neutestamentliche Wissenschaft*
ZPEB	*Zondervan Pictorial Encyclopedia of the Bible*
ZTK	*Zeitschrift für Theologie und Kirche*

I

The Biblical Theology of the Church

EDMUND P. CLOWNEY

Do Christians need to think again about the doctrine of the church? Many would answer, 'No!' Mention the church and they begin to smell the musty odour of churchianity. It rises from the crypts of institutional religion, and permeates the seat-cushions of formal traditions. Martin Luther thanked God that even a child of seven knows what the church is. 'Let the church focus on the gospel, preach Christ and him crucified, and the church will become part of the answer instead of the problem'. That is the way Luther's point is often made today.

Others would add that Luther's child of seven has had plenty of help in the last few years. If the teaching of the Bible about the church has been neglected in past centuries, that neglect has certainly been more than remedied. Few cathedrals have been constructed in the last half century, but theologians have launched a building boom of their own. The publishing skyline is full of books about the church.[1]

Not all of those books are theological, to be sure. Some writers assume that we cannot expect Scripture to answer the problems of the computer age. The Apostle Paul did not have to face Marxism nor deal with the problems of colonial exploitation and its aftermath. He was not troubled with the internecine warfare of rival denominations and non-denominational agencies. Nor did he have to plant churches

13

in a tribal cultural setting. He worked within his own culture and could ordain as leaders, even in the Gentile churches, men who had been instructed in the Scriptures as adherents of the Jewish synagogues. With such considerations the contemporary ecclesiastical pundit eases the Apostle to the Gentiles into his place back in the Hellenistic age. He is then free to display his own grasp of sociometrics, group dynamics, structuralist anthropology, and political hermeneutics.[2]

It would be foolish, of course, to suggest that the behavioural sciences should be set over against Biblical understanding. In applying the teaching of God's Word, we must surely understand as fully as we can the circumstances to which it is applied. Yet even in that understanding, we seek to manifest the mind of Christ. Certainly we cannot begin our understanding of the church with sociological analysis. We must begin with the teaching of the Bible, and return to the Bible again and again to deepen and renew our understanding. Theology is reflective; we do understand God's revelation better as the context of our own experience widens and varies our perspective. But the church rests upon the foundation of apostolic teaching. The authoritative words of the inspired witnesses chosen and endued of the Spirit communicate to us the full and final revelation of Jesus Christ (Acts 10:39–42; Heb. 2:2–4; Rev. 22:18, 19).

The doctrine of the church is not the most fundamental doctrine of Scripture. J.C. Hoekendijk may be right in saying, 'In history a keen ecclesiological interest has, almost without exception, been a sign of spiritual decadence . . .'[3] At the Third World Conference on Faith and Order held in Lund in 1952 the conferees acknowledged: 'In our work we have been led to the conviction that it is of decisive importance for the advance of ecumenical work that the doctrine of the church be treated in close relation both to the doctrine of Christ and to the doctrine of the Holy Spirit'.[4]

Indeed, the doctrine of the church is not only closely related to the doctrine of the Trinity, it flows from it. The promise of God's covenant is, 'I will . . . be your God, and you will be my people' (Lev. 26:12; 2 Cor. 6:16). God's people are his own possession, those whom he has formed for himself that they might set forth his praise (Is. 43:21). The focus of Scripture is on the living God, of whom, through whom, and unto whom are all things, not least the people he has redeemed and claimed as his own.

It is not surprising, therefore, that the Biblical doctrine of the church is directly related to God's revelation of himself. As we trace the history of redemption recorded in the Word of God, we find that the church comes into view as the people of God, the disciples of Christ, and the fellowship of the Holy Spirit. Yet these views of the redeemed do not simply succeed one another; far less do they exclude one another. The Apostle Peter, writing to Gentile Christians in Asia Minor, calls them 'a chosen people, a royal priesthood, a holy nation, a people belonging to God' (1 Pet. 2:9). To be sure, they were once 'not a people', but now they are 'the people of God' (v. 10). The language that described the calling of Israel in the Old Testament Peter applies to the New Testament people of God. On the other hand, Christ is central for the Old Testament as well as for the New, and Paul, reflecting on the experience of Israel in the wilderness, affirms that 'the Rock that followed them was Christ' (1 Cor. 10:4). That same leading of Israel through the desert is ascribed by the prophet Isaiah to the Holy Spirit (Is. 63:9–14).

To gain the richness of biblical revelation, we do well to trace the unfolding of the theme of the church through the history of God's saving work. In doing so we are instructed by the transformations of that theme as well as by the underlying unity of the purpose and work of God. To focus our consideration, we may reflect on the *calling* of the church. The church is called to God, called to be his people. By that relation to God the being of the church is defined. The church is also called, by that very relation, to a bond of life together. It ministers not only to God, but also to those who make up its company. The church is also called in the midst of the world. Its ministry is therefore threefold: it ministers *to God* in worship, *to the saints* in nurture, and *to the world* in witness.

In systematic theology the doctrine of the church is often

presented under the rubrics of the Nicene Creed: the church
is one, holy, catholic, and apostolic. Yet these attributes of
the church flow from the more fundamental teaching of the
Bible regarding the nature of the church as it is related to
the Lord himself. Ecclesiology is part of theology. We gain
the clearest light on the issues that the church now faces
when we reflect on the calling of the church by the Father,
the Son, and the Holy Spirit. This trinitarian approach to
the doctrine of the church may then be structured in relation
to its calling to minister in worship, nurture, and witness.

I. THE CHURCH AS THE PEOPLE OF GOD

A. God's Worshipping Assembly

Matthew's Gospel reports the words of blessing that Jesus
spoke to Simon Peter in response to Peter's apostolic confession. Jesus then said, 'And I tell you that you are Peter,
and on this rock I will build my church, and the gates of
Hades will not overcome it' (Mt. 16:18). Matthew uses the
common term for 'church' in the New Testament, the term
ekklēsia. It was once the habit of critics to question the
authenticity of Matthew's report. Jesus spoke of the kingdom, and knew nothing of the church, they said.[5] Since the
discovery of the Dead Sea Scrolls there has been a belated
acceptance of the genuineness of the saying. The scrolls are
full of the concept of the community, understood as the
congregation of the saints awaiting the coming of the Lord.
Further, the thought of the congregation being established
upon the confession of the truth is also prominent in the
Dead Sea writings.[6] So is the figure of the rock, and of the
building established upon it.[7] The parallels between the
language of the Dead Sea sectaries and the words of Jesus
do not, however, indicate that Jesus was dependent upon
the Essenes. The background to both is the Old Testament.

1. The People of God Constituted as God's Assembly

The concept of the people of God as assembly has its Old

Testament roots in the gathering of Israel before the Lord at Mount Sinai. God had demanded of Pharaoh, 'Let my people go, so that they may worship me in the desert' (Ex. 7:16b). That service was to be a specific gathering for worship ('a feast unto me', Ex. 5:1). Of course there were further implications of that demand. Pharaoh regarded the Israelites as his slaves, subject to his own divine claims. His lordship was directly challenged by God's claim. The worship, the service of the Lord on the part of Israel, would mark them as his people, his sons (Ex. 4:22, 23). It would be a covenant-making ceremony in which the claim of God upon his people and the claim of the people upon God would be ratified in worship.

The term *ekklēsia* describes an actual assembly, a gathering of people together. The same is true of the Old Testament term *qāhāl* that is translated by *ekklēsia* in the Septuagint version of the Old Testament.[8] The words themselves do not have the restricted meaning of our word, 'church'. Yet, when Jesus said, 'I will build my church' (whether he spoke Greek, or used in Aramaic a word that could be so translated), he was not simply saying, 'I will bring together a gathering of people'. Rather, he was using a well-known term that described the people of God. The 'assembly in the desert' (Acts 7:38) was the definitive assembly for Israel, the covenant-making assembly when God claimed his redeemed people as his own. In Deuteronomy it is spoken of as 'the day of the assembly' (Dt. 4:10 LXX; 9:10; 10:4, 18:16).

The key to the meaning of 'assembly' is found in God's command to Moses: 'Assemble the people before me to hear my words so that they may learn to revere me as long as they live in the land and may teach them to their children' (Dt. 4:10). The assembly is a gathering to meet with God. God declares, 'You yourselves have seen what I did to Egypt, and how I carried you on eagles' wings and brought you to myself' (Ex. 19:4). God's deliverance of Israel from Egypt is indeed an act of liberation. God strikes off their yoke and enables them to go upright (Lv. 26:13). But liberation from slavery in Egypt is not the final purpose of God's saving work. God brings them out that he might bring them in, in to his assembly, to the great company of those who stand before his face. The Lord who assembles the people to himself is the Lord of hosts. His heavenly assembly is composed of the mighty ones (*'elohim*), the holy ones (*qedoshim*), the sons of God (*benei ha'elohim*) over whom he reigns as King (Jb. 1:6; Ps. 82:1; 1 Ki. 22:19; Dn. 7:10). When the Lord descends at Sinai, the tens of thousands of the heavenly holy ones are assembled with the congregation that is gathered at his feet (Dt. 33:2; Ps. 68:17). The earthly assembly, too, is composed of the saints of the Lord (the same term can describe saints or angels). The Dead Sea community had a vivid awareness of this Old Testament panorama. Those who were added to the community became members of God's eternal assembly. They gained a place with the holy angels (1QS 2:25; 11:7–9; 1QH 3:21; 11:11, 12).

God's assembly at Sinai is therefore the immediate goal of the exodus. God brings his people into his presence that they might hear his voice and worship him. 'I am the Lord your God, who brought you out of the land of Egypt, out of the land of slavery. You shall have no other gods before me' (Ex. 20:2, 3). Standing in the assembly of the Lord, hearing his voice, the people gain their identity from the self-identification of the Lord.

Later Assemblies

The assembly at Sinai could not remain forever in session, however. It was succeeded by other covenant-making assemblies. Deuteronomy, the second giving of the law, provides the account of the renewing of the covenant in another great assembly before the death of Moses. When Joshua brought the people into the land, he convened a great assembly between Mount Ebal and Mount Gerizim, and read the blessings and curses of the covenant from the law (Jos. 8:34, 35). David convoked an assembly to secure the succession of Solomon (1 Ch. 28:2, 8; 29:10, 20). Jehoshaphat, Joash, and Hezekiah summoned assemblies of covenant renewal (2 Ch. 20:5, 14; 23:3; 29:23–32; 30:2–25).

After the exile, the great assembly under Ezra and Nehemiah was gathered to hear the Word of God (Ne. 8). This assembly was regarded in later times as the prototype of the synagogue. The reading of the law in the synagogues and the prayers that were offered found their precedent in this post-exilic assembly.

In addition to these assemblies of renewal on historic occasions, there were other assemblies of Israel. The law required that the people gather three times a year at the appointed place of worship (Lv. 23). These were festival assemblies: the Passover, Pentecost, and the Feast of Tabernacles. At this last feast every seventh year the law was to be read and the covenant renewed (Dt. 31:9–13).

To be a member of the people of God was to have the privilege of standing in the great assembly before his face. To be sure, worshipping Israelites could rejoice in fellowship with one another as they assembled together. They could sing, 'How good and pleasant it is when brothers live together in unity!' (Ps. 133:1). But even that joy is a blessing that flows down from above, like the dew of Hermon, or the ointment running down the beard of the high priest (Ps. 133:2, 3). Israel is bound together as a kingdom of priests, a holy nation (Ex. 19:6). Israelites are a nation formed for worship, called to assemble in the courts of the Lord, and to praise together the name of the Most High.

The Future Festival Promised

Israel failed woefully in this priestly calling. The unity of worship was broken when Jeroboam set up the image of a calf at Bethel to bar the pilgrimage of the northern tribes to worship at Jerusalem. In the temple at Jerusalem, the whole purpose of the assembly was shattered by idolatry. And so in judgment God scattered the people in exile; yet he did not forget his calling to a priestly nation. The prophets proclaimed a new assembly of the people of God. It would come in the glorious future when God would again manifest his presence. Isaiah pictures a great feast, spread on the mount of God, to which not only the remnant of Israel but also the remnant of the nations would be gathered in (Is. 2:2–4; 25:6–8; 49:22; 66:18–21; cf. Je. 48:47; 49:6, 39). Zechariah sees a new Jerusalem, transformed into a holy city by the presence of the Lord (Zc. 12:7–9; 13:1, 9; 14:7, 8, 16–21).

Pentecost Fulfilment

Jesus promised that he would build his assembly by his death and resurrection. After he rose from the dead, he commanded his disciples to remain together in Jerusalem until they received the promise of the Father, the gift of the Holy Spirit. That gift was poured out as they were assembled together. It was at Pentecost, and the theme of the feast of Pentecost was fulfilled. Pentecost was the time of the first-fruits, the beginning of the great harvest of redemption. Peter preached the fulfilment of the prophecy of Joel. The Spirit had been poured out, the worship of the new age had been ushered in. The church, the assembly for worship, was praising God. The great eschatological feast had begun. Jesus in his parables had spoken of the feast prepared, and of his mission as the Servant of the Lord to call to heaven's feast the host of poor and broken sinners who filled the byways of the earth (Lk. 14:15–24). Now the ingathering had begun.

The gospel call is a call to worship, to turn from sin and call upon the name of the Lord. It is no accident that the New Testament church is formed by the coming of God the Spirit in the midst of an assembly gathered in praise. The church in any city is composed of those who 'call upon the name of the Lord' in that place (Acts 9:14; 1 Cor. 1:2). Peter writes that the church is the people for God's own possession, 'that you may declare the praises of him who called you out of darkness into his wonderful light' (1 Pet. 2:9).

The Assembly on Mount Zion

The picture of the church as a worshipping assembly is nowhere more powerfully presented than by the author of the Epistle to the Hebrews (ch. 12:18–29). He contrasts the worship of God at Mount Sinai with the worship of the New Covenant. The worship at Sinai was an overwhelming experience. Even Moses said, 'I am trembling with fear' (v.21). Yet the fear of Moses was inspired by merely physical phenomena — a fire that could be touched (v.18). In contrast, the church of the New Covenant comes to the full reality: 'our God is a consuming fire'. If Moses feared the earthly manifestation of God's presence, how much more should we be filled with reverence and awe? We do not come to Mount Sinai in our worship, but to Mount Zion. That Zion is not the earthly, but the heavenly Zion, the sanctuary of the eternal city of God. For the author of Hebrews, this is not a figurative way of speaking. The heavenly Jerusalem is not a Platonic abstraction. It is as real as the living God, as real as the risen body of Jesus Christ. In our worship in Christ's church we approach the throne of God the Judge of all. We enter the festival assembly of the saints and the angels. We gather in spirit with the spirits of just men made perfect. We enter the assembly of glory through Christ our Mediator, and the blood of his atoning death. For that reason we must hear and heed the word of the Lord, and 'worship God acceptably with reverence and awe' (v.28).

Just as the great assembly at Sinai defined the covenant people of the Old Testament, so does the heavenly assembly define the church of the New Covenant. The principle is the same, the saving purpose of God is the same. Moses and the other heroes of faith described in Hebrews 11 are among the 'spirits of righteous men made perfect' who gather with us in the heavenly assembly. Yet they without us could not be made perfect (Heb. 11:40). We now enjoy with them the worship for which they longed by faith.

Does the tremendous reality of that heavenly worship make our earthly behaviour irrelevant? Can we think, 'Since nothing can stop the heavenly hallelujahs, our feeble little gatherings on earth are of no consequence'? That argument has often been advanced. 'Since the church invisible is one, earthly divisions are not too serious.' 'Since the heavenly church is holy, we need not worry much about either personal holiness or church discipline.'

The author of Hebrews draws the opposite conclusion. Precisely because we do approach the heavenly assembly in worship, we are not to forsake the assembling of ourselves together (Heb. 10:25). Precisely because we have the faithful promise of the city of God, we are to provoke one another to love and good works (Heb. 10:24).

Reverent corporate worship, then, is not optional for the church of God. It is not a form of group behavior to be accepted just because of its long tradition or its acceptability in many cultures. Rather, it brings to expression the very being of the church. It manifests on earth the reality of the heavenly assembly. The glory of God is that to which and for which the church is called.

The Word in Worship

We may not lose sight, either, of the importance of God's Word in the assembly of worship. The description of the heavenly assembly in Hebrews 12 comes to a focus in the admonition to hear him who speaks. God spoke from Sinai; the worship of the people responded to the Word of the Lord. In the assemblies of the new covenant, the Word of God is no less central. God is not only present in the midst of his people. He speaks. The ministry of the Word of God in worship partakes of the solemnity of the occasion. Solemnity does not mean joylessness, for the Word calls to praise. Yet the authority of the Word of the Lord remains central for Christian worship. This is the Word of him who speaks from heaven (Heb. 12:25). God spoke in many different ways to the fathers through the prophets, but now he has spoken finally and conclusively through his own Son. It is that word of the Lord that 'was confirmed to us by those who heard him. God also testified to it by signs, wonders and various miracles, and gifts of the Holy Spirit distributed according to his will' (Heb. 2:3, 4).

Multi-level Assembling

Another consequence of the definition of the church as a worshipping assembly is the extreme flexibility that the New Testament shows with respect to its use of the term 'church'. On the one hand, the term is applied to the church universal. This is the church which is the people of God and the body of Christ without qualification (Mt. 16:18; 1 Pt. 2:9; Eph. 1:22, 23). It is the church as God alone can see it, the whole company of those who have been, are now, or ever will be gathered to God in Christ. Some who perceive this New Testament concept have gone on to deny that any local gathering can be called in a full and proper sense the church. Such a gathering may form a congregation of the church, no doubt, but the church by definition must be the church universal. On the other hand, there are those who isolate what the New Testament teaches about the local church. Paul does speak of the church at Corinth as the church of Christ. In the book of Revelation, Jesus addresses letters to the seven churches in Asia Minor. Congregational theologians have therefore limited the church by definition to the local assembly. Anything beyond the local assembly, they say, should not be spoken of as the church, but as an association of churches.[9]

In the New Testament, the question is further complicated by the fact that *local* churches are spoken of in more than one sense. At least, local churches come in surprisingly different sizes. The church in Laodicea is a city church, but apparently there was also in Laodicea a house church, meeting in the house of Nymphas (Col. 4:15). So, too, Paul can in one breath speak of the churches of Asia and of the church in the house of Aquila and Prisca (1 Cor. 16:19). The Westminster Divines noted the house churches that existed along with city churches in the New Testament and argued from this evidence for a presbyterian system of government.[10] The city church corresponded to the presbytery, and the house church to the local congregation. This line of reasoning recognized smaller and larger gatherings of the church, and further recognized that one could exist within another. The presbytery, however, was a gathering of the ministers and elders, not of the whole membership of the city church. Another difference emerged from the development of congregational structure in the cities. Village churches were swallowed up in growing metropolitan areas. They became parish churches — gatherings of a size that was larger than the house church, surely, but perhaps smaller than some of the city churches of the New Testament.

We may ask, however, if the full flexibility of the New Testament view of the church is adequately recognized today. Because the church is defined by the heavenly assembly for worship, there is no one size of assembly on earth that is ideal or normative. Those who call upon the name of the Lord together may do so in larger or smaller assemblies. Such a recognition does not mean that smaller assemblies may be disorderly, or that assemblies at any level exist apart from the exercise of gifts of teaching, ruling, and diaconal service. But it does suggest the possibility of fuller expxressions of the worshipping assembly in large city gatherings, as well as the recognition of the important place of the house church, not as a rival form of organization, but as an expression, in a more immediate setting, of the fellowship of those who call upon the name of the Lord in one particular place.

2. The Church as God's Dwelling

The picture at Sinai of the people of God as a worshipping assembly is heightened by God's provision of the tabernacle. God not only met with the people as they were assembled before him. He also came to *dwell* among them. In the wilderness where they lived in tents, God's house would be a tent, too. When they entered the land and had fixed dwellings, God would put his name in a place, and sanctify the temple of Solomon as his dwelling. The figure of the tabernacle made the presence of God more immediate and permanent.

The immanence of God's presence with his people is a continuing theme in the Pentateuch. The Lord who walked in the garden of Eden to talk with Adam and Eve continues to address the patriarchs in the land to which he called them. The altars that they built witnessed to the presence of the Lord. This is particularly dramatic in the case of Jacob at Bethel, where God descends the stairway of Jacob's dream to repeat the sure promises of the covenant to the exiled patriarch. (Genesis 28:13 should be translated, 'And, behold, the LORD stood over him . . .' See Genesis 35:13, where the same preposition is used, 'Then God went up from him at the place where he had talked with him'.) In the morning Jacob marvels at the presence of God: 'Surely the LORD is in this place, and I was not aware of it. . . . How awesome is this place! This is none other than the house of God; this is the gate of heaven' (Gn. 28:16, 17).

How important for the people of God is the dwelling of God among them? Moses gives an eloquent answer in a time of crisis before the tabernacle was built in the wilderness. While he was in the heights of Mount Sinai receiving the law of God and the plans for the tabernacle, Israel at the foot of the mountain committed idolatry before the golden calf. When Moses came down from the mountain and was confronted with the sin of the people, God proposed another plan for his relation to Israel (Ex. 33:1–3). God was too holy and the people too sinful for God to dwell among them. His presence was too great a threat. Surely, as the Holy One, he must consume them in a moment to remove their iniquity from his presence. God proposed, therefore, that the tabernacle not be built. God would not dwell in the midst. He would go before Israel in the angel of his presence, drive out the Canaanites from the land, and give them the inheritance he had promised. But instead of living among them, he would meet with Moses in a tent set up outside the camp (Ex. 33:7–11). The elaborate plans for the tabernacle would not be necessary, since God would not have his dwelling among the people.

The reaction of Moses to that alternate plan shows how crucial the dwelling of God in the midst of Israel really is. Moses was distraught with grief. He mourned, and Israel mourned with him. Moses cried, 'If your Presence does not go with us, do not send us up from here!' (Ex. 33:15). God's presence among the people was the whole point of the exodus deliverance and of the inheritance of the land. Significantly, Moses prayed for God to reveal his glory. What Moses asked was the very blessing that the alternate plan would have removed: the immediate presence of the living God and the vision of his glory. God did appear to Moses, and proclaimed his covenantal Name (Ex. 33:17–34:7). Although Moses was permitted to see only God's back, he did see the glory of the Lord. His request was granted. God did make his dwelling among Israel, and Moses could pray that God's presence in the midst would bring not swift judgment, but the forgiveness of sins. He could pray, too, that God would not simply give the people their inheritance in Canaan, but that he would take the people as his inheritance, claiming them as his own (Ex. 34:9).

Moses' prayer was answered and the tabernacle was built. It symbolized both the threat of God's dwelling in the midst of Israel and the grace by which God's immediate presence was possible. The tabernacle was a dwelling in which the presence of God was both screened off and revealed. The curtains of the holy of holies, of the holy place, and of the tabernacle enclosure screened off the Holy One from the camp of sinful Israel. The curtains insulated, as it were, the holy presence of God. But the plan of the tabernacle also symbolized a way into the holiest place, an avenue to the throne of God. After the blood of atonement had been shed at the sacrificial altar, the priest could wash at the laver, enter the holy place, and present the prayers of the people. Once each year, on the day of atonement, the high priest could enter even the holy of holies to sprinkle the ark of the covenant with blood.

Christ the True Temple

The New Testament presents the fulfilment of this symbolism in Jesus Christ. He is Priest, Sacrifice, and Temple. 'Destroy this temple', he said, 'and in three days I will raise it up' (Jn. 2:19). The temple that he spoke of was his own body. 'The Word became flesh and made his dwelling among us. We have seen his glory, the glory of the One and Only, who came from the Father, full of grace and truth' (Jn. 1:14). The outward picture of God's dwelling among his people becomes a reality in the incarnation.[11] Further, since God is present in Christ, and Christ is present among his people, they, too, become a dwelling for God. Christ, who promises to prepare a dwelling place for his disciples, promises also that both he and the Father will come and take up their dwelling with the disciple that loves him (Jn. 14:2, 23). Both the individual believer and the church are spoken of as the temple of God because of the presence of the Holy

Spirit (1 Cor. 6:19; 2 Cor. 5:1; Eph. 2:13–22; 1 Cor. 3:16–17; 1 Pet. 2:5; 2 Cor. 6:16).

The coming of the Holy Spirit fulfils the promise of the Father and makes actual the presence of God. The spiritual relationship portrayed by the temple figure includes *permanence* as well as intense immediacy. The epiphany of Pentecost was not a passing phenomenon, but the advent of the Spirit, no less central for the understanding of the church than the advent of the Son. Through the finished work of Christ the hour came when neither Mount Gerizim nor Jerusalem were holy places any longer (Jn. 4:21). In his words to the Samaritan woman, Jesus does not deny the legitimacy of the temple at Jerusalem. Salvation, he says, is of the Jews. Nor does Jesus simply state that because God is a Spirit, he cannot be worshipped at a holy place. Jesus cleansed the temple, called it his Father's house, and violently affirmed its sanctity. What changed everything was the fulfilment of the temple symbolism in Jesus himself. Worship in truth could begin. It would be 'true' worship in the sense of being *real*, unobscured by the shadows of symbolism, as the Jerusalem temple worship had been. The coming hour of which Jesus spoke was the hour of his death, resurrection, and return to the Father. True worship is not templeless: it is worship at the true Temple, the One raised up on the third day. Because the reality has come, the symbols are fulfilled. Worship is now spiritual — in the Holy Spirit (the living water promised by Jesus). Worship is now true — in Jesus Christ the Truth (Jn. 14:6).

B. God's Chosen People

1. The Election of Israel

The church, then, is both the assembly of God and the dwelling of God. God leads his people from the convocation at Sinai to the land of their inheritance, where God will dwell in the midst of them. In addition to these great figures, God speaks directly about the people as his own. The covenantal affirmation 'I will be your God, and you shall be my people' makes explicit this relation. The prayer of Moses,

'Take us for your inheritance', is inspired by the Lord who claims Israel for himself. 'The LORD your God has chosen you out of all the peoples on the face of the earth to be his people, his treasured possession' (Dt. 7:6). God purposes to make his people 'in praise, fame and honour high above all the nations he has made' (Dt. 26:19).

God's election of Israel follows upon his election of the patriarchs. It is God who calls Abram out of Ur of the Chaldees; it is God who chooses Isaac, not Ishmael, and Jacob, not Esau (*cf.* Rom. 9:11–13). Yet God's choosing was not only an expression of his purpose of blessing toward his elect. God promised not only to bless Abraham, but to make him a blessing. In him all the nations of the earth would be blessed (Gn. 12:3). The table of the nations in Genesis 10 prepares for the call of Abraham in Genesis 12. So, too, Israel is called to be a light to the nations: 'May God be gracious to us and bless us . . . that your ways may be known on earth, your salvation among all nations' (Ps. 67:1, 2).

It would be a serious mistake, however, to deny the *status* of Israel in order to affirm the *mission* of Israel. Israel is called first to fellowship with God, to be his treasure people; and only as that people does Israel witness to the nations, that they, too, might be drawn into the worship of the true and living God. God does not choose Israel just in order to use Israel. Certainly Israel is not chosen for its utility. 'The LORD did not set his affection on you and choose you because you were more numerous than other peoples, for you were fewest of all peoples. But it was because the LORD loved you and kept the oath he swore to your forefathers . . .' (Dt. 7:7, 8).

Election in Love

Here is the language of love: 'The LORD set his love upon you, because . . . the LORD loves you'! The Lord pours out his love for his people in rich language. Israel is God's son (Ex. 4:23; Ho. 1:10; 11:1–3; Is. 45:9–11), God's bride (Ho. 1–3; Is. 50:1; Ezk. 23). God's consummation joy over Israel will be like the joy of a husband over a bride (Zp. 3:17). Israel is God's vineyard (Je. 12:7–9), the apple of his eye

(Dt. 32:10). They are a people near to him (Ps. 148:14), borne on his shoulders (Dt. 33:12), engraved on the palms of his hands (Is. 49:16).

Yet God's delight in Israel is of his sovereign good pleasure, the 'favour of him who dwelt in the burning bush' (Dt. 33:16). God's people are *chosen*, not *choice* (*bachir*, not *bachur*).

Sadly, the chosen people prove themselves unworthy of God's favour. God's judgment is immeasurably more severe because of the privilege that Israel despised and forfeited. The adulterous wife will be stoned (Ezk. 16:40); the rebellious son will be cast out (Ho. 11:1, 8; 12:14; 13:1); the pleasant vineyard will be laid waste (Is. 5:5, 6); the planted vine will be uprooted and burned (Ezk. 19:10–14; Ps. 80:12–16). Redemptive history in the Old Testament is full of the realization of these dire predictions. The temple itself, where Israel had worshiped idols, is destroyed by the armies of Babylon. The people are carried into exile. Ezekiel sees the hopelessness of the exiled nation in his vision of the valley of dry bones (Ezk. 37).

Grace in Judgment

Yet that same vision is the Lord's message of hope. 'Son of man, can these bones live'? Well does the prophet answer, 'O Lord Jehovah, you know'. God's promises will not be void, his purposes will not be frustrated.

Two great principles are given to the prophets: first, the destruction is not total. God has preserved for himself a remnant. Even if the remnant is as hopeless as dry bones in a valley, or as the scraps remaining from a lion's kill (Am. 3:12), a remnant nevertheless it is. The second principle is that of renewal. To the dry bones life will be given. If the glory of Israel is like a cedar that has been felled by the axe of Gentile powers, nevertheless a stump is left in the ground. God promises that the stump will send forth a shoot; that shoot will be an ensign to which the nations will be gathered (Is. 10:33–11:5).

The remnant will be the faithful people of God, the true Israel. By God's renewing grace, their hearts will be circumcised. They will know the Lord. God will make with them a new covenant (Je. 31:31–34). Paul explains this theology of the prophets. As the doctrine of the remnant shows, there is an election within the election of Israel. 'For not all who are descended from Israel are Israel' (Rom. 9:6). The true and spiritual seed are the heirs of the promise. Further, the new Shoot that grows from the felled cedar is the Messiah. He is God's servant Israel, in whom God will be glorified (Is. 49:3). In him the mission of Israel will be fulfilled and the status of Israel will be established in a way that surpasses all imagining. Not only will he restore the remnant of Israel, he will also be a light to the Gentiles, 'that you may bring my salvation to the ends of the earth' (Is. 49:6). The prophets describe the ingathering of the preserved of the nations along with the remnant of Israel (Je. 48:47; 49:6, 39; Is. 66:19–21). Paul explains how Christ fulfils the ministry of the circumcision: 'For I tell you that Christ has become a servant of the Jews on behalf of God's truth, to confirm the promises made to the patriarchs so that the Gentiles may glorify God for his mercy . . .' (Rom. 15:8).

Jesus Christ indeed comes to gather the remnant, the 'little flock' of God's good pleasure who are given the kingdom (Lk. 12:32). But Jesus is more than the Sent of the Father. He is the Son of the Father. He is the Vine as well as the Shepherd, and he brings salvation in himself. The people of God are claimed at last by God himself, coming in the person of his Son. He claims them by joining them to himself as their Lord and their life. Both the status and the mission of the people of God are therefore now defined in Christ. In his Sonship they are made sons of God; as the Father has sent him into the world, so Christ has sent them into the world (Jn. 17:18).

C. God's New Nation

1. The Bond of God's Covenant

The tie that binds God's people to their Lord binds them also to one another. The bond of Israel's nationhood was not ethnic but religious. It was the covenant at Sinai that forged Israel into unique nationhood. Strangers and sojourners could be admitted to the assembly and people of God. They could gain an inheritance in Israel (Ex. 12:47–49; 23:9).

On the other hand, to reject God's covenant was to be disinherited from Israel. Not only did God judge covenant-breakers with death; the Levites were commanded to execute God's judgment upon their brethren (Ex. 32:26, 27). If a son in Israel blasphemed the name of God, his own father was to denounce him (Dt. 13:6–11). For apostasy a whole generation could perish in the wilderness, and all Israel be driven into exile. The promise of the prophet Hosea recognizes the justice of God's disinheriting judgment. Those who once were the people of God have become *Lo-ammi*, 'no people' (Ho. 1:9). If they are again to be called *Ammi*, 'my people', it can be only by the mercy of divine re-adoption, not by the claim of ethnic nationhood. For that reason, Paul can appeal to Hosea's language to defend the inclusion of Gentiles among the people of God (Rom. 9:24–26). All were disinherited by sin; all were *Lo-ammi*. But by the grace of God in Christ, those who were no people have been made the people of God.

2. The Church of the New Covenant

In Christ the New Testament church is the new and true Israel, one with the Old Testament saints in the spiritual ethnicity that defines the people of God in all ages. When Peter calls the Gentiles of Asia Minor the *diaspora* (1 Pet. 1:1), he is viewing them as the true people of God scattered in the world.

The Apostle Paul in the same way claims that Gentiles are made members of the people of God. Writing to Gentiles as the 'uncircumcision', Paul says, 'At that time you were separate from Christ, excluded from citizenship in Israel, and foreigners to the covenants of the promise, without hope and without God in the world' (Eph. 2:12). Note the parallels from which the Apostle argues. To be separate from Christ is to be outside the commonwealth of Israel and strangers to God's covenant. But Christ has broken down the middle wall of partition that preserved the distinctiveness of the circumcised.

What, then, is the situation of those who are no longer separate from Christ? 'But now in Christ Jesus you who once were far away have been brought near through the blood of Christ' (Eph. 2:13). Christ has brought them within the community from which they were once excluded by the wall of separation. In Christ they have the same access to the Father as do all the true people of God. They are no more strangers from God's covenant promises; they are his covenant people. They are no more aliens from the commonwealth of Israel; instead, they have been made fellow-citizens with the saints of that commonwealth (Eph. 2:19).

Indeed, if the Apostle to the Gentiles had not taught this, the circumcision controversy described in the New Testament would never have taken place. Paul's Judaizing antagonists would have had no objection to Paul's organizing a church that was quite distinct from Israel. The rabbis were already making provision for the 'God-fearers' who had attached themselves to the synagogues but who did not wish to be circumcised or to become Jews. If Paul had merely been organizing such devout Gentiles, there would have been no objection from the zealous Jews. But what infuriated even many Jewish Christians was that Paul was claiming to bring Gentiles into the covenant, into the number of the people of God, without circumcising them. It is notable that Paul never dropped or lowered his high claim in order to meet Judaizing objections. He never said: 'Of course I am not circumcising these Gentiles. I am not adding them to Israel, but to the church. They are therefore being baptized into a proselyte status, but not added to the covenant people'.[12]

Instead, Paul said the exact opposite: 'For it is we who are the circumcision, we who worship by the Spirit of God, who glory in Christ Jesus, and who put no confidence in the flesh' (Phil. 3:3). Paul could say nothing else, because of his glorying in Christ Jesus. If Jesus is the true circumcision, the heir of all the promises of God, and if we by faith are united to Jesus, then in Christ we are Abraham's seed, heirs according to the promise (Gal. 3:29).

3. The Church as a People: Spiritual Ethnics

The new Israel of God is not less a nation because it is spiritually constituted. Jesus said to the Jewish leaders who rejected him, 'The kingdom of God will be taken away from you and given to a people who will produce its fruit' (Mt. 21:43). Like Israel, the New Testament church is a theocracy, subject in all things to the word of the Lord. But unlike Israel of old, God's people are no longer to bear the sword to bring God's judgments on the heathen, nor to defend a territorial inheritance in the earth. Jesus commanded Peter to put away his sword, and declared to Pilate, 'My kingdom is not of this world. If it were, my servants would fight to prevent my arrest by the Jews. But now my kingdom is from another place' (Jn. 18:36).

To this church Christ gives, not a sword, but the keys of the kingdom. The authority so sanctioned is not less, but greater than the power that the state exercises with the sword. Not temporal, but eternal judgments are pronounced in the name of Christ. Those who are judged by Christ's word on earth are judged by that same word in heaven. On the other hand, penitent sinners who are welcomed in his name have heaven opened to them (Mt. 16:19; 18:18–20; Jn. 20:22, 23). It is because the church invokes eternal rather than temporal judgment that the sword cannot be its instrument. The day of judgment has not come, but the longsuffering grace of God is revealed. Although the sentence of the church is so solemn, it is not final. Church discipline is to be exercised with a view to the reclamation of the offender, as well as for the vindication of the name of Christ, and the holiness of his church (1 Cor. 5:5).

4. Church and State: the Power of the Sword

The sword that is given to the state is not that which is denied to the church. That is, we may not suppose that Christ denied to his apostles the right to bring in his kingdom with the sword, but conceded that right to Pilate. Pilate is

a ruler. He has authority given to him by God (Jn. 19:11).
But Roman power does not continue the theocratic authority
that was Israel's and which now passes in spiritual form to
those who are the servants of Christ ('my officers', v.36).
Nor is the church denied the sword because its concerns are
more limited: the conduct of public worship, for example.
God's kingdom of salvation is not administered in different
departments, of which the church is one and the state
another. To be sure, the new humanity in Christ is to serve
him in all the spheres of human life. Christ is Lord of all;
we must do all to the glory of God. But the church is the
form that Christ has given to the people of God in the world.
They may not reincorporate and take up the sword to
anticipate his judgment or to see that God's will is done on
earth as in heaven.[13]

Worldly power, enforceable by the sword, is associated
with territory. But the church is catholic, universal. It cannot
be confined to any area nor defend boundaries. 'Here we do
not have an enduring city, but we are looking for the city
which is to come' (Heb. 13:14). It is of the very nature of the
New Testament church to be scattered among the nations of
the world. We are pilgrims and strangers, the new *diaspora*
of God. The relation of the church to the state therefore
resembles that of Israel in dispersion. The exiles were warned by Jeremiah to realize that their captivity would be the
length of a generation. They were not to look for a speedy
return, but were to settle down in the land of their dispersion. 'Also, seek the peace and prosperity of the city to
which I have carried you into exile. Pray to the LORD for
it, because if it prospers, you too will prosper' (Je. 29:7).
The words of the prophet are echoed by the Apostle. He
exhorts Timothy to encourage prayer for kings and all in
high place 'that we may live peaceful and quiet lives in all
godliness and holiness' (1 Tim. 2:2). He adds that this is
acceptable to God, 'who wants all men to be saved and to
come to a knowledge of the truth'. As C. E. B. Cranfield
has pointed out, such prayer is not only a Christian responsibility, but can even be said to have an evangelistic outcome.[14]

The church, then, may not use the sword, but it is not
without a weapon. Paul says, 'The weapons we fight with

are not the weapons of the world. On the contrary, they have divine power to demolish strongholds. We demolish arguments and every pretension that sets itself up against the knowledge of God' (2 Cor. 10:4, 5). The Word of God is the Sword of the Spirit, and the truth of the gospel can accomplish what no sword can achieve, the turning of men's hearts to God. The enemy of the church is the Devil and the spiritual hosts of wickedness. No sword can strike Satan but the sword of the Spirit.

The temptation to repeat the Crusades remains with the church. Others would create another Geneva, or gather another community in the wilderness, or perhaps even, one day, in literal world-flight, colonize another planet. Still others would seek to capture some political state and make it a new Israel, the earthly political form of the kingdom of God. It seems difficult to accept a calling for the state that is so limited: to preserve peace and order, to protect and support human life. Many rightly recognize that the expression of God's saving kingdom must go beyond personal piety, and they look to the state (or to a new revolutionary order) to crush social evil and bring in divine justice. But the state is not called to bring in the kingdom, nor to enforce the rule of God's absolute righteousness. Yet there stands another nation, the church of Jesus Christ, to be not only a witness and a refuge, but a *people* among whom the power of the kingdom is already at work, and Christ's final salvation already realized. Until the church manifests in corporate form the meaning of the coming of the kingdom in the Spirit, its witness will be hindered. It will not appear as a city set upon a hill. Not only will it fail to manifest the social dimensions of God's saving righteousness: it will diminish the gospel message that it seeks to proclaim.

5. The Fellowship of the Covenant

The church, then, is a 'new nation under God', and the bonds that unite it are God-given. Clearly, God did not bring Israel out of Egypt to give them the opportunity to become acquainted with one another so that the social graces could flourish. He brought them to himself, and claimed them as his sons and daughters, so that their relation to one another might be grounded in their relation to him. Hittite treaties of the period required that vassals of the same suzerain refrain from hostilities against one another.[15] Certainly the servants of the Lord, joined in covenant with him, must live at peace with each other. But the God-centered character of covenantal religion required much more. Because God was the Father of Israel, the people were also a family, a 'fatherdom' (Eph. 3:14, 15). The electing love of God made Israel his people. They, in return, must not only love the Lord their God with heart and soul, they must also love their neighbour as themselves (Lv. 19:18). They are not free to enslave their brothers or sisters; they must not hate them in their heart (Lv. 25:35, 55; Dt. 15:12; Je. 34:8–22; Lv. 19:17). The underlying motive for that respect and affection was the joy of sharing together in the redeeming power and love of God. The Psalmist put it eloquently: 'I am a friend to all who fear you' (Ps. 119:63).

The Israelites were neighbours geographically because of their shared possession of the land of promise. Each man had his inheritance within the bounds of the tribal allotment, and the whole land was an inheritance received from the Lord. To belong to the people of God is to have a share in the inheritance (Dt. 10:9; 12:12; 14:27, 29; 18:1). The New Testament concept of 'fellowship' (*koinonia*) contains this same thought of sharing, of having in common the blessing, the inheritance given by God. God himself is the inheritance of Israel, the portion of his people (Ps. 16:5; 73:26: 119:57; 142:5: La. 3:24).

The prophets denounced the sin of Israel in the breach of love within the family of God's people. Those who oppress the widow and the orphan or defraud their neighbours are not merely guilty of anti-social conduct. They have broken God's covenant. No one who hates his neighbour in his heart can rightly love God. The theme that John expounds in his First Epistle is firmly grounded in the Old Testament teaching regarding God's covenant with his chosen people.

Fellowship and Separation

There is another side to the coin. The bond that joins Israel to the Lord and to one another also separates them from the nations. The people of God are not to be numbered with the nations (Nu. 23:9). They are distinct religiously, for they are to serve the Lord, and no other God. He is their God, and they are his own possession, his inheritance, although all the earth is his (Ex. 19:5). They are also to be distinct morally. They must not practise the abominations of the heathen nations around them (Lv. 18:24–30). That ethical separation is symbolized in the ceremonial distinctiveness of Israel. The motif of cleanness and its opposite enforces the separation. Sources of uncleanness are not only forbidden foods, dead bodies, certain skin diseases, and bodily emissions, but also marital alliance with Gentiles (Ex. 34:12–17; 1 Ki. 11:2). The geographical separation of Israel gave practical support to the concept of Israel's distinctiveness.

In the New Testament the spiritual separation of the new people of God is heightened as the geographical and ceremonial forms of separation are fulfilled and transcended. No longer are the people of God to be barred from certain foods. In the cleansing of Christ's atonement, the ceremonial pictures are realized (Acts 10:9–16, 28; 1 Cor. 8:8; 10:23–27; 7:14). The removal of the dietary restrictions, and of the ceremonial sanctions that separated Jews from Gentiles — even more than the termination of the geographical distinctiveness of the new Israel — opened the door for the mission to the Gentiles. This was the evident effect of Peter's vision on the house-top in Joppa. He was freed to associate with the Gentile soldier Cornelius, to be a guest at his table, and also to baptize him into the membership of the church (Acts 10).

Yet the separation of the New Israel remains, and is intensified. Paul does not hesitate to use the language of separation from uncleanness in quoting from the Old Testament. 'Come out from them and be separate, says the Lord. Touch no unclean thing, and I will receive you. I will be a Father to you, and you will be my sons and daughters, says the Lord Almighty' (2 Cor. 6:17–18). The religious and

moral separation of Israel now has a new depth. All defile-
ment of flesh and spirit is to be cleansed away as the
Christian church perfects holiness in the fear of God (2 Cor.
7:1). The quest for holiness among the New Israel is both
individual and corporate. Not only must each Christian
pursue holiness: the church must grow together in the image
of Christ, and must exclude from its fellowship those who
are heretics or impenitent sinners (Rom. 16:17f.; 1 Cor. 5:9–
13). Paul was concerned not only to present every man
perfect in Christ (Col. 1:8), but also to present the whole
church 'as a pure virgin to Christ' (2 Cor. 11:2). Christ
sought a renewal of love from the church at Ephesus, but
he commended them for exposing and bringing to trial
false apostles. Other churches are warned of the danger of
tolerating the Nicolaitan heresy (Rev. 2:2, 14, 20).

The overflowing love and grace of God radically renew
the community of the covenant. The church that has been
purchased with Christ's blood cannot ask 'Who is my
neighbour?' with a view to limiting the circle of those to
whom the love of compassion must be shown. Yet the love
that reaches out in Christ's name to the lost does not deny
the reality of lostness. It calls men to enter the fellowship
where the love of God is shed abroad in our hearts, but the
bond of that love can be forged only in union with Christ.

A City Set on a Hill

1. Israel's Calling before the Nations

God's worshipping assembly, his chosen nation, is also a
city set on a hill. As we have seen, God calls Israel to bear
witness as well as to worship and to live in brotherhood.
Israel is set before the nations to make known the saving
work of the living God. The whole history of Israel is
interwoven with its calling to witness. God's judgments on
Egypt in delivering the people from bondage are a memor-
able witness to his redeeming power (Ex. 9:16). So, too, will
the conquest of the land manifest to the nations the power
of God (Ex. 34:10). Israel did not enter the land as invaders,
but as inheritors. On the one hand, Israel was commissioned

by God to execute his judgment upon the wicked inhabitants. The Israelite incursion was providentially delayed until the iniquity of the Amorite and Canaanite inhabitants was ripe for judgment (Gn. 15:16; Lv. 18:24–30). God's people were his avenging judges to bring the day of judgment, in a figure, on the rebellious inhabitants of the land. On the other hand, the land had been given by God to the descendants of Abraham; in the sight of the nations, Israel received her inheritance from God.

When Israel rebelled in the wilderness, Moses pleaded with God to withhold his judgment so that the Egyptians would not mock God's deliverance (Dt. 9:28f.). Joshua made the same plea when Israel suffered defeat in Canaan: 'What will you do for your great name'? (Jos. 7:9). When the kingdom had been established through the wars of David, Solomon constructed the temple. In his prayer of dedication, Solomon eloquently acknowledged the blessing to the nations that must flow from the place of God's dwelling on earth. 'As for the foreigner who does not belong to your people Israel but has come from a distant land because of your name — for men will hear of your great name and your mighty hand and your outstretched arm . . . hear from heaven your dwelling place . . . so that all the peoples of the earth may know your name and fear you, as do your own people Israel' (1 Ki. 8:41–43).

The Nations Share in Israel's Blessing

The ingathering predicted in Solomon's prayer did begin in his reign. Indeed, the blessing of wisdom that God granted to Solomon became the catalyst for that ingathering. A passage that describes the depth and breadth of the wisdom of Solomon concludes, 'Men of all nations came to listen to Solomon's wisdom, sent by all the kings of the world, who had heard of his wisdom' (1 Ki. 4:34). The visit of the Queen of Sheba is described as a case in point. The Gentiles are drawn to the king of Israel, and to the God who so richly blessed him and his people (1 Ki. 10:9). The gifts of the queen represent the freely brought tribute of the nations as they see what God has wrought among his chosen people.

2. Judgment and Blessing

From this zenith of blessing Israel rapidly drops into the nadir of apostasy and judgment. Solomon's wisdom becomes folly, for he fails in faith. To gain security and peace for Israel, he trusts not in God, but in marital alliances with the heathen nations. He builds altars for the gods of his wives: Ashtoreth, Milcom, Molech, and Chemosh (1 Ki. 11:1-8). Picture Solomon standing on the Mount of Olives, his back to the glory of the temple of the Lord, dedicating the high place he had built for Chemosh, the god of Moab!

God's judgments begin. Solomon's kingdom is divided; both Israel in the north and Judah in the south refuse the warnings of the prophets, and cause God's name to be blasphemed among the nations because of their apostasy. Eventually both kingdoms are destroyed and the people carried into exile. Yet, even in the midst of judgment, God continues to make his name known among the nations. The very severity of his wrath against Israel is a sanctifying of his holy name, but God will also sanctify his name among the nations by delivering Israel, as he had done in Egypt (Ezk. 20:9, 14, 22, 39, 44; 36:20).

The Nations Blessed in Israel's Judgment

Further, the nations are blessed in Israel's judgment. When God withholds rain from Israel, his prophet Elijah becomes a blessing to a widow in Zarephath (1 Ki. 17; Lk. 4:26). Elisha heals Naaman, a Syrian general whose task it is to fight against Israel. He also prophesies that Hazael will be King of Syria, knowing well that this spells grief for Israel (2 Ki. 8:7-13). The most dramatic Old Testament account of how judgment on Israel brings blessing to the Gentiles is found in the prophecy of Jonah. Jonah's reluctance to go to Nineveh is understandable. Nineveh, under Shalmanezer III, had already subdued Israel, and forced Jehu to pay tribute.[16] Jonah well knows that Nineveh is the great threat to the security of Israel. The message that God gives him is that in forty days Nineveh will be destroyed. God's wrath is about to fall on that savage military power. Only Nineveh's repentance can stop this judgment, and Jonah, knowing

God's mercy, fears that his call to repentance may be all too effective (Jon. 4:2). Since Nineveh cannot hear without a preacher, Jonah flees the scene. He is willing to be accursed so that Israel might be spared. But Jonah is taught that salvation is of the Lord, and that God has determined to bring the promised blessing to the Gentiles not only in spite of his judgment on Israel, but even through it. Jonah becomes a figure of the Servant of the Lord, raised from death to proclaim repentance to the nations.

Israel Blessed by Judgment on the Nations

On the other hand, the nations, too, must be judged. God uses the nations as his axe and saw to cut down the pride of Israel (Is. 10:5, 15). But the nations are not God's obedient servants in accomplishing his will. They trust in their own might, and worship their idols. Their arrogance will be punished. God will deliver the remnant of his people from their power. In the great day of his salvation he will again set his people free (Mi. 7:14–20; Is. 10:5–27; 63:1–6). As judgment on Israel brought blessing to the nations, so now judgment on the nations will bring blessing to Israel.

Blessing Shared: Israel and the Nations

This picture broadens to a vast eschatological horizon. Israel's blessing will be shared by the nations. A remnant of the nations will be saved with the remnant of Israel (Je. 48:47; 49:6, 39), and in that glorious day the enemy nations Egypt and Assyria will be God's chosen people along with Israel: 'Blessed be Egypt my people, Assyria my handiwork, and Israel my inheritance' (Is. 19:18–25).

Consummation Blessing: God Comes!

Such incredible blessing can be given only because God himself will come to bring his promises to fulfilment. The vision of the prophets sees the Lord coming in glory, delivering his people by a second exodus, and so filling his people with his glory that all the nations will be drawn at last to share in the blessing. The first covenant will be transcended in a new covenant, and God will make all things new (Is. 25:6–8; 40:1–11; Je. 31:31–34; Zc. 2:11–13; 12:8; 13:1; 14:20, 21; Zeph. 3:9).

The Psalms had celebrated God's dwelling in Zion, calling on the nations to join in the praises of the Lord (Ps. 57:9; 65:2; 67). With prophetic vision the psalmists also look forward to the day when a new song will be sung, when God himself will come and the trees of the field will sing for joy before him (Ps. 96:12, 13). In that day the peoples of the earth will be gathered to be the people of the God of Abraham (Ps. 47:9). The Lord will write the names of Babylonians, Philistines, Tyrians, Ethiopians among the citizens of Zion (Ps. 87).

God's coming is associated with the coming of the Messiah, through whom all these blessings will be brought. He will not only gather the lost sheep of the house of Israel, but will be a light to the nations, that they may see the salvation of God (Is. 42:6, 7; 49:6).

The witness of the people of God will be restored by the God of their salvation. He must come to deliver them and to make his promises of glory come true.

II. THE CHURCH AS THE DISCIPLES OF CHRIST

A. The Gathering Church of Christ

We have seen the Old Testament people of God first as a worshipping assembly, then as a holy people, and finally as a witness, a city set on a hill. As we turn to the new Covenant, we meet at once the witness and mission of Christ and of those whom he calls. We will first reflect on the witness of Christ's church, then on its worship, and finally on its fellowship as Christ's body.

1. The Lord Comes to Gather

'Today in the town of David a Saviour has been born to you; he is Christ the Lord' (Lk. 2:11). The herald angel announces to the shepherds the long-promised coming of the Lord. He is not only the Lord's Anointed (Lk. 2:26); he is the anointed Lord, the glory of his people Israel (Lk. 2:32). His name is Jesus, for it is he who shall save his people from their sins (Mt. 1:21). The inspired witnesses present him in the Gospels as the Lord of creation, obeyed by winds and waves (Mt. 8:27). He is Master of life and death, of men and demons, with authority not only to heal the sick but to forgive sins (Mk. 2:8–11). He is more than a prophet, for he is the Son of God, the Word who became flesh and tabernacled among us so that we might behold his glory, the light that shines in the darkness (Mt. 16:16; Jn. 1:1–5, 14, 18).

He comes to earth on a mission from the Father, so that he might gather the remnant flock, the people given him of the Father (Lk. 12:32; Jn. 17:2; 10:27–29). He looks with compassion on the people as sheep scattered, without a shepherd (Mt. 9:36; 26:31). Ezekiel prophesied that the Divine shepherd would come to gather his flock and deliver them from the false shepherds (Ezk. 34). Jesus, the Good Shepherd, undertakes that task of gathering. Although he is the Lord, he is also the Servant. He comes as the Sent of the Father, not simply to call the unfaithful stewards of God's kingdom to account (Mt. 21:37, 38), but also to summon sinners to the feast of the kingdom (Lk. 14:16–24; Mt. 22:2–14). He calls first the lost sheep of the house of Israel (Mt. 10:5; 15:24); when Gentiles come seeking him, he views their coming as a sign of his impending death and resurrection (Jn. 12:20–33). When he is lifted up, first to the cross, then in glory, he will draw all men unto him. The gathering work of Christ awaits the glory to be given him of the Father. The Lord who gathers calls his disciples to be gatherers with him. In a solemn saying, Jesus declares, 'He who does not gather with me scatters' (Mt. 12:30; Lk. 11:23). After the resurrection, Jesus calls and commissions his disciples to this gathering task. They are to be labourers in an abundant harvest, praying that the Lord will thrust forth yet more labourers (Mt. 9:37f.). They are to be fishers of men, called by the Lord who commanded them to thrust out into the deep, and who filled their nets to the bursting point with fish (Mt. 4:19; Lk. 5:10).

2. The Church is Called to Gather

Because Christ's church is a missionary church, the order *of* the church serves the order *to* the church to make disciples of the nations. Under the dome of St. Peter's in Rome are inscribed in Latin the words of Jesus to Peter: 'You are Peter, and on this rock I will build my church' (Mt. 16:18). It is not only the church of Rome that has emphasized the building of the church in an institutional sense to the detriment of the mission of the church to the world. It is for this reason, in part, that Ralph Winter has concluded that mission is the function of the church as sodality rather than modality.[17] The missionary orders rather than the ecclesiastical hierarchy promoted the mission of the church of Rome. Among the churches of the Reformation, mission societies rather than denominational organizations have carried the gospel to the ends of the earth. There is no disputing how often this has been the case, although Winter surely goes too far when he tries to represent the Apostle Paul and those who accompanied him as a kind of para-ecclesiastical missionary team. It is clear that Paul looked at the matter quite differently. He argued at length and with passion for his authority in the church as an apostle, and for his calling as the apostle to the Gentiles. In relation to the order of the church, he could not have conceived of his work more centrally. He was fulfilling the gospel, bringing to fruit the promises of the Old Testament. Paul the Apostle was a wise master-builder of the church. Through his ministry, the Gentiles glorified God for his mercy. Paul uses formal language in describing his official ministry as Apostle to the Gentiles (Rom. 15:15–20).

The Apostolic, Missionary Church

Indeed, the fact that the apostolic office is both foundational and missionary has abiding significance for the church. The foundational aspect of the apostles' work was accomplished in the apostolic age. They were witnesses of the resurrection, who had seen with their own eyes the risen Lord (Acts 1:21, 22; 10:41, 42; 1 Cor. 15:8). They were organs of revelation, having received from the Lord what they delivered to the church (Eph. 3:4, 5; Heb. 2:3; 1 Cor. 15:3). But they were also missionaries, sent into the world with the only Name by which men can be saved. The Gospel of Matthew joins the foundational word of Jesus to the apostles (Mt. 16:18, 19), to the Great Commission (Mt. 28:18–20). Mission is not an addendum to the doctrine of the church. It is the calling of the church in the world. If it is neglected or abandoned, the life of the church, not just its work, is threatened.

The Father's Missionary Love

The missionary character of Christ's church does not issue only from the command of Christ. It flows from the revelation of the Father that Christ provided. He sends the disciples into the world as the Father sent him into the world (Jn. 17:18; 20:21). How did the Father send him? With authority, of course, but also in grace and love. In the teaching of Jesus, the astounding love of God is set forth. Jesus is the Beloved Son, but the Father has not spared him; instead he has sent him to give his life a ransom for many. In the parable of the welcoming Father, Jesus tells of the joy that his Father has in receiving lost sinners home again (Lk. 15:11–32). The story shows God's amazing grace, for — as the prodigal confesses — he does not deserve to be called the son of his father, or even to be made one of his servants. But the father receives him as a son and welcomes him with a feast. The older brother is furious because he knows well his brother's sin, but does not know at all his father's love. The key to the parable is the contrast between the older brother and Christ himself. Jesus told the story as one of three parables after he had been criticized for eating with publicans and sinners. In each story he shows the joy, and the feast, that accompanies the finding of the lost. 'There is joy in heaven over one sinner who repents' (Lk. 15:7, 10). Jesus understands heaven's joy, and the love of the Father that rejoices in finding the lost. Jesus is the seeking shepherd of the first parable; he is like the woman of the second parable, who turned her house upside down to find a coin. The shepherd sought one sheep of a hundred, the woman one coin of ten; but the older brother would not seek one brother of one. In fact, not only did he fail to go to the far country to seek him, he even refused to eat with him when he came home. Not so Jesus. He, the true older brother, knows his Father's heart. He goes seeking publicans and sinners. He eats with them, and calls them to come home to the Father.

The gospel is the message of God's redeeming love in sending his own Son into the world. Those who understand that love will be driven to share it. They will not only rejoice to sit down with other redeemed sinners in heaven's feast: they will seek other sinners in Christ's name to call them home. As Christ was sent, so he sends them, and the dynamic of mission is the heart of the love of God. Again we see that mission is not an addendum. Rather, it is evidence that the church understands the gospel. The love that fulfils the law, as Jesus taught in the parable of the Good Samaritan, is the love of compassion, love modelled on the love of God.

Mission: Going Out and Coming In

The witness of Christ's church to the world is not expressed only in the going of Christ's disciples to the ends of the earth. The outgoing, centrifugal mission of the New Testament church does not simply replace the ingathering, centripetal movement of the Old Testament witness. The church is still a city set on a hill. Indeed, even its mission to other lands and cultures is a continuation of the task of calling the nations to worship at Mount Zion. The difference is that the Zion to which people are now called is the heavenly Zion, the Jerusalem above that is our mother (Gal. 4:26). Men and women of every tribe, tongue, people and nation are now called to join the heavenly worship described in Hebrews 12. Because we do not have a continuing city here, we can no longer call men to an earthly centre. Because we do have a continuing city above, our call goes to the whole world. The heavenly centre for the worship of the whole earth accounts for the mission to all the world. On the other hand, we are not to forsake the assembling of ourselves together on earth. Our local assemblies therefore become

Mount Zion in miniature. Israel's calling to show to the world the holiness of the true people of God is maintained and deepened. Paul teaches this when he calls upon the church to 'Do everything without complaining or arguing, so that you may become blameless and pure, children of God without fault in a crooked and depraved generation, in which you shine like stars in the universe' (Phil. 2:14, 15). The Apostle uses language from Deuteronomy 32:5, but with an interesting reversal. Moses, dealing with the perpetual murmurings and questionings of Israel in the wilderness, described them as a perverse and crooked generation, corrupted and blemished. Paul urges the church to forsake the sins of the people of old and to be what Israel was not.

The holiness of the church is to be shown particularly in love for one another (Jn. 13:35). The world will be struck by the changed life-style of the Christian community, and will speak evil of it (1 Pet. 4:4). But the world cannot ignore that love that binds Christ's disciples together in a unity of heart (Jn. 17:23).

B. The Church as the Worshipping Assembly

The worshipping assembly of Christ becomes Mount Zion for those who are drawn in by seeing the lives and hearing the praises of those who know the Lord. Paul says of a well-ordered service of worship that its prophetic ministry will fulfil Old Testament promises, for the stranger who enters will fall down on his face and say that 'God is among you indeed!' (1 Cor. 14:25; Is. 45:14; Zc. 8:22, 23).

Peter emphasizes the place of worship when he writes that 'you are a chosen people, a royal priesthood, a holy nation, a people belonging to God, that you may declare the praises of him who called you out of darkness into his wonderful light' (1 Pet. 2:9). No doubt the praises of God serve as a witness to the nations. Yet praise to God is offered not for the sake of the Lord who is adored.

1. God's Glory Evokes Worship

All worship is qualified by the transcendent glory of God. The Psalms celebrate God's glory in the works of his hands.

The heavens thunder the glory of God's power (Ps. 18:7–15; 19:1; 33; 147). God is also the Governor of men and nations, shaping history by his will (Ps. 145:13; 46:10). Above all God is to be praised for his work of salvation (Ps. 18; 145:7, 8,18–21). His hills skipped like lambs when he led forth his people like a flock (Ps. 78:52; 114:4, 6). But the crescendo of praise builds toward the great work of salvation that God will do in the latter days. God will come and new songs of praise will be sung (Ps. 96:1, 11–13). Isaiah adds prophetic chorales praising the glory of God that will be revealed when all flesh shall see it together (Is. 40:5; 58:8; 59:19; 60:1).

Because worship praises the Lord himself, and does not simply celebrate his works, it moves from thanking God for what he has done to adoring him for who he is. The psalmists sing 'the glory due to his name' (Ps. 29:2). His mighty acts reveal his transcendent power and wisdom. We are called to marvel not only at his wisdom displayed in the cosmos and the ages, but at his wisdom in forming and knowing us personally (Ps. 139:1–18). Just as we praise God most for his deeds of salvation, so of all his attributes we are most overwhelmed by his saving love, the spring of our redemption. There is therefore a climactic and dramatic movement to our worship. Worship spirals upward from the works of God to the attributes of God, from his sovereignty in creation to his sovereignty in salvation. 'For from him and through him and to him are all things. To him be the glory for ever!' (Rom. 11:36).

2. God's Presence Evokes Worship

The supreme heightening of worship is evoked by the very presence of God. The angels who cry 'Holy, holy, holy!' are not reciting a litany, but are responding to the ever fresh and expanding revelation of the *presence* of God as it sweeps over them, wave upon wave. The climax of worship is always found in the immediate presence of the Lord. We have not only heard with our ears of his wonderful deeds and his glorious attributes; our eyes have seen him, and with Job we repent in dust and ashes (Jb. 42:5, 6).

We have seen how central the presence of the Lord was for the worship of Israel: God must dwell in the midst; a way must be opened into his presence. The Psalmist longs for the courts of the Lord, not to enjoy the spectacle of worship, but to meet with God (Ps. 84; 63:1–3; 122:1). 'My soul thirsts for God, for the living God. When can I go and meet with God'? (Ps. 42:2).

3. God's Holiness Demands Exclusive Worship

Because 'our God is a consuming fire' (Heb. 12:29), his own holy nature and will determine all of our worship. The Lord demands exclusive worship: 'Do not worship any other god, for the LORD, whose name is Jealous, is a jealous God' (Ex. 20:5; 34:13). The forms, as well as the object, of our worship must be exclusive. God will not tolerate worship through idols, but insists that he be worshiped in the way that he has commanded (Dt. 12:30–32). All this is to say that worship is total commitment. It is nothing if not extravagant. To withhold anything is to fail to worship (Dt. 6:4–9).

4. Fulfilment in Christ

When we consider the church as the worshipping assembly of Jesus Christ, we see how all these biblical themes for worship are brought to fulfilment. Old Testament prophecy proclaims the great day of worship when the glory of God will be revealed. That climax comes with Jesus Christ. The works of God are manifested afresh in the miracles of Jesus. He shows his power over creation as Lord. But the wonder of worship overflows when the grace of God is revealed. The works and words of Jesus reveal the fulness of that grace. He glorifies the name of the Father as he is brought by the Father's love for sinners to the cross. In Jesus Christ God comes and is present. The extravagance of Mary's worship shows that she perceives his person as well as his work as he goes to Jerusalem to die (Jn. 12:1–8). Jesus shows his zeal for pure worship as he cleanses the temple, but he also announces that he is the true temple (Jn. 2:19–21). Worship in truth is worship of the Father in and through the Son.

The church with joyful worship hails Jesus Christ as Lord. Christians are designated as those who call upon his name (Acts 9:14). The church is the assembly of those who call upon the name of our Lord Jesus Christ (1 Cor. 1:2). This is a standard Old Testament expression for the worship of God (Gen. 4:26). The prayer 'Maranatha', associated with the Lord's Table, reflects the way in which the worship of the church centred on the future coming of the Lord in glory, as well as his presence in the Spirit (1 Cor. 16:22).[18]

The worship of the church is centred on God's revelation in Christ in two ways. First the worshippers enter heaven itself, where Jesus is. The visions of the book of Revelation present the glory of the risen Lord who, with the Father and the Spirit, is the object of Christian worship. As we have seen, Hebrews 12 powerfully presents this access of worship. On the other hand, Christ is also present in the gathering on earth where two or three are gathered in his name (Mt. 18:20). The table fellowship of the upper room is continued with the risen Christ. The jealousy of God that demands exclusive worship now requires that we approach the Father only in and through the Son. The church therefore gathers in the name of the Lord Jesus (1 Cor. 5:4). The mercy-seat in the tabernacle remained empty. No image or likeness could be placed there, because that seat was reserved for the One who is the image of the invisible God (Co. 1:15; 2 Cor. 4:4; Heb. 1:3).

Awareness of the presence of the Lord creates in the church a longing that surpasses that of the psalmist. The fellowship that hears his Word, celebrates the sacraments, and responds to his presence in praise has always marked the true church of Christ. The spiritual mystery of his presence was not heightened but lost in the doctrine of transubstantiation, making Christ physically present in the elements, rather than spiritually present among his people. Yet the reality of the spiritual presence of the Lord has also been lost in Protestantism when social crusades, self-improvement lectures, or camaraderie have crowded out worship.

C. The Body of Christ

Many figures are used for the church in the New Testament. It is pictured as a bride, a flock, a vine, a field, a temple. But Paul emphasizes a figure unique to his writing. The church is the body of Christ. In the Hellenistic world of the Apostle it was possible to speak of any organization as a body of people. Our term 'corporation' means just that: a group of people joined as one body by a legal fiction. But Paul speaks of the church, not as a body of people, but as the body of Christ. Evidently he is not simply saying that the church is a Christian corporation. Certainly we should not be surprised to find Paul joining Christ to the figure of the body. Every other figure for the church is related to Christ. If the church is a bride, Christ is the Bridegroom; if the church is a flock, Christ is the Shepherd; if the church is a temple, Christ is the Builder, the Foundation, or the Cornerstone. The figure of the vine makes the union of Christ and the church even more intimate. In the prophecy of Isaiah, God describes Israel as the vine he planted, 'the garden of his delight' (Is. 5:7). Jesus said to his disciples, 'I am the vine; you are the branches' (Jn. 15:5). Christians are joined together by being joined to Christ. They are a body because they are Christ's body.

1. Representative Union with Christ

To grasp the force of Paul's figure, we must recognize the extraordinary importance the physical body of Christ his Lord had for him. As Saul the Pharisee, persecuting the church, Paul was confronted on the road to Damascus by the risen Lord. He became a preacher of Christ and the resurrection (Acts 17:18). In his First Epistle to the Corinthians, he strongly opposed the Greek denial of the resurrection of the body. When he wrote to the church at Philippi, he said of Christ that he 'will transform our lowly bodies so that they will be like his glorious body' (Phil. 3:21) — the body he had seen on the Damascus road.

Christ's Body on the Cross

But it is not only the risen body of Christ that is important for Paul. Even more frequently he speaks about the crucified body of Christ. In Colossians 1:22 he tells of our 'being reconciled by Christ's physical body through death'. In Romans 7:4 he says that we have 'died to the law through the body of Christ'. As Peter puts it, Christ 'bore our sins in his body on the tree' (1 Pet. 2:24). Our sins deserve the death penalty, but the penalty was paid by Christ who died in our place. Paul reflects profoundly on the *representative union* with Christ that causes his death to have a saving outcome for us. So closely does he identify the figurative with the literal body of Christ that it is sometimes difficult to say which he has in view. In Ephesians 2, for example, Paul writes that Christ in his death broke down the wall of partition between Jews and Gentiles, that he might 'reconcile both of them to God through the cross' (Eph. 2:16). Does 'one body' here mean the one body of the church, into which Jews and Gentiles are joined as they are made one new man (v. 15)? Or does 'one body' mean the one body of Christ on the cross by which they are reconciled ('in the blood of Christ', v. 13)? Either interpretation is faithful to Paul's thought. The unity of the church as Christ's body rests on the unity of the body of Christ on the cross. The church is one body in Christ (Rom. 12:5); it is a body of Christ (1 Cor. 12:27); it is the body of Christ (Eph. 4:12).

Representation: the Church not a 'Continuing Incarnation'

This closeness of identification does not mean that Paul is caught in a naive or mystical realism in which he cannot distinguish between the physical body of Christ and the figure of the body applied to the church. Even less does Paul think that Christ died in the body of his flesh, to be raised in the body of the church. Paul does not think of the church as continuing the incarnation. Paul did, after all, *see* the risen body of the living Lord. He was told, to be sure, that in persecuting the church he was persecuting Christ, but he never imagined that he saw the *church* on the road to Damascus.[19] On the contrary, nothing is more fundamental for Paul's thought than the literal resurrection of Jesus Christ. The resurrection sealed the finished work of Christ with divine approval; he was declared to be the Son of God with power by the resurrection from the dead (Rom. 1:4). But more than that: in both his death and his resurrection, Jesus represented those who are united to him. The identification that Paul sees between Christ and the church is first of all representative.

The Parallel with Adam

The Apostle makes this clear by the parallel that is established between the first and second Adam (Rom. 5:1–21; 1 Cor. 15:22). When Adam sinned, all men sinned in him, and death, the penalty of sin, passed upon all men (Rom. 5:12). Those who are in Christ are related to the Head of the new humanity in the same representative way. When Christ died, they died; when he rose from the dead, they rose with him, and are now in the heavenly places because Christ is there as their great Representative (Rom. 4:25; 6:8, 9; Col. 2:20; 3:1; Eph. 1:3).

Covenantal Headship

The background of Paul's concept of forensic representation is in the covenantal headship of the Old Testament. God makes his covenant with Abraham and with his seed after him (Gen. 12:3; 18:18). God redeems Israel to fulfil the promises he had made to their fathers (Ex. 3:6, 15; Deut. 7:8). The tribes of Israel are blessed in their fathers (Gn. 49). The prophets, priests, and kings that God raises up serve as mediators of God's covenant, representing the people before God, as well as representing God to the people. Israel is called to be God's servant, but Moses also is the servant of the Lord: Israel trusts in the Lord and in his servant Moses (Ex. 14:31). Representative headship is strongly presented in the figure of the suffering Servant in Isaiah. The Servant of the Lord is distinct from Israel, yet can be identified with Israel (Is. 49:3, 5, 6). Because he is the Representative in whom God's covenant is fulfilled, his sufferings are vicarious and redemptive (Is. 53).

It is the concept of covenantal headship that leads Paul
to speak of Christ as the Head, and the body as his members.
Paul does not think of Christ the Head as constituting only
the top member of the body. This is clear from the fact that
when Paul speaks of the members of the body he includes
ear, eye, and nose (1 Cor. 12:16–21). It is also clear from
the fact that Paul uses headship in a way distinct from the
body figure. His usage is shaped by the Greek Old Testament, where *kephale* is associated with *arche* in translating
the Hebrew *rosh*. Primacy, origination, honor, authority,
and summation are signified by headship in the Old Testament.[20] In this sense Paul speaks of the husband as the head
of the wife as Christ is the Head of the church. Christ is the
Head of every man (Rom. 7:4; Eph. 5:25–32; 1 Cor. 11:3).
Christ is the Head of the principalities and powers (Col.
1:22), and has universal dominion as the head of the church
(Eph. 1:20–23). Paul thinks of the church as a body in terms
of one whole new man in Christ, or, alternatively, as the
bride of Christ, springing from him as Eve was taken from
the body of Adam, and united to him as a wife to her
husband (Eph. 1:15; 5:23–32). We would distort Paul's
figure beyond recognition were we to speak of Christ as a
head, helpless without a body. The body of Christ is not to
be divided at the neck! Even when the two figures are put
side by side, as in Ephesians 4:15,16, the distinction remains.
We are not to suppose that Paul is imagining a strange
physiology by which the body grows up into the head and
is nourished by it.

2. Vital Union

When Paul speaks of our union with Christ, representative
union is always in view. Because Christ died, we died. Our
death in Christ has paid the penalty of sin and freed us from
the chains of sin. Because Christ rose, we rose, and we now
enjoy the freedom of new life in Christ. But while this
representative relation is always in view, Paul's understanding of our union with Christ is richer than forensic relation.

Paul's Phrase 'In Christ'

This is apparent from Paul's use of the phrase 'in Christ'. On the one hand, Paul speaks of our being 'in Christ' representatively. When Paul writes, 'Therefore, there is now no condemnation to those who are in Christ Jesus' (Rom. 8:1), he is referring to the representative relation that he has been expounding. 'In Christ' also refers to the representative status of believers in passages that speak of God's saving action or gift to us in Christ (e.g. Eph. 1:3, 6, 11; 2:13, 14; 4:32; Rom. 6:23; Gal. 3:14; 2 Cor. 5:19, 21). This is true also of passages that use 'in Christ' to designate believers as they sustain a saving relation to Christ (e.g. Phil. 1:14; 3:9; 4:21; Rom. 16:7, 11; 1 Cor. 1:30). But in other passages the phrase carries a fuller meaning. Paul speaks of 'the church of the Thessalonians in God the Father and the Lord Jesus Christ' (1 Thes. 1:1). Unless Paul meant more than simply a representative union with Christ, he could not have joined the Father to Christ in the same phrase. Because we are united to Christ, we are not only in Christ representatively, but also vitally. Christ is in us by the presence of the Holy Spirit (Rom. 8:10, 11). The resurrection life of Christ is not only reckoned to our account, it is a living power transforming our existence. We grow up into Christ (Eph. 4:12–16; Col. 2:6, 7), being conformed to his image (Rom. 8:29). Christ gave his body once for all on the cross; in the sacrament of the Lord's Supper, we remember his sacrifice. As we commune with him in the sacrament, however, we also feed upon him spiritually by faith, and our living fellowship with him is sustained (1 Cor. 11:24–29; cf. 1 Cor. 12:13).

This vital union 'in Christ' is mystical in the sense that it far surpasses the relation possible between finite persons, yet it is not an impersonal mysticism. We are not immersed in Christ as in the air that we breathe. We misunderstand Paul's language if we think of our vital union with Christ in spatial terms.[21] Yet Paul does use the language of the temple to describe Christ's dwelling with (in) us, and moves easily to the figure of our dwelling in him as the other side of the personal communion that his indwelling represents (Col. 1:27, 28; 2:9f.).

Fellowship in Union with Christ

Paul's concept of the body of Christ is drawn from his doctrine of our union with Christ. For that reason the fellowship of the body is a sharing together in fellowship with Christ. The fundamental idea expressed in *koinonia* is not the link that joins Christians to each other, but the common bond that unites them to Christ.[22]

At the same time, union with Christ does bind Christians together by the ties of the Spirit. By our union with Christ, we are united to each other. The image of the body is a happy one for this purpose, since it presents a unity that is organic. An organism manifests unity in diversity, and Paul makes powerful use of this metaphor. As an organism, the church is one body. When party strife threatened to divide the church at Corinth under the names of ministers of the gospel who had laboured there, Paul cried out in anguish of heart, 'Is Christ divided? Was Paul crucified for you?' (1 Cor. 1:13). The church of Christ cannot be divided by following human leaders, for the church is one: one in Christ's body on the cross. That oneness is symbolized at the Lord's Table: 'We, who are many, are one body, for we all partake of the one loaf' (1 Cor. 10:17).

Making Church Unity Evident

The unity of the body of Christ is to be evident on earth. To declare oneself to be a follower of Apollos rather than Paul, or of Paul rather than Peter, is to deny the unity of the body. The lowliness, meekness, longsuffering, and forbearance in love that are the fruits of the Spirit enable us to keep the unity of the Spirit in the bond of peace (Eph. 4:3). The mere fact that the church has been divided denominationally does not justify such division. A flat denial that division exists will not help; neither is it a solution to start with a clean slate, as it were, and to create yet another division in the church by establishing a group that will not be followers of Peter, Paul or Apollos, but simply of Christ

(1 Cor. 1:12). Another expedient is to declare one denomination to be the true church of Christ, and all others apostate or schismatic. Such efforts have succeeded only in creating further division, yet they begin from a proper premise. They rightly assume that the church should be one, not just in heaven, but on earth. When the unity that we are zealously to maintain has been broken, we cannot ignore the calamity, but must set about seeking to restore the broken fellowship. We cannot ignore deep and serious doctrinal differences. Neither can we ignore false teaching, and unite a church that is indifferent to creed, or even committed to denying the need for doctrinal discipline. The path to restoring unity requires discipline along with patient instruction and loving admonition. We are not without direction on this path. The writings of the New Testament provide us with an inspired model of how unity in the Spirit is to be sought.

3. Individual and Corporate Unity with Christ

The model of the body assumes that our relation to Christ is both individual and corporate. If the individual relationship did not exist, the differing gifts that make up the body would not appear. The individual saints are chosen and called of God. They have been saved by faith, and their faith stands in the power of God (1 Cor. 2:5). Salvation is an individual experience: 'The man who loves God is known by God' (1 Cor. 8:3). The same affirmations that are made about the church as the body of Christ are also made about the individual Christian. He, too, is a holy temple (1 Cor. 6:19; 2 Cor. 5:1); that temple may be defiled by one member (1 Cor. 6:15). The Christian is joined to Christ, as is the church (1 Cor. 6:15; Eph. 5:30; Col. 1:28; Eph. 5:22–23; 2 Cor. 11:2).

On the other hand, just as there is no salvation apart from Christ, so there is no salvation that does not join us to one another as members of his body. The sanctified in Christ Jesus at Corinth make up the church of God at Corinth (1 Cor. 1:2). Divisions among the saints imply that Christ can be divided (1 Cor. 1:3). There is one Christ; apostles and teachers are his servants, called by him and endued with gifts of his Spirit (1 Cor. 3:5). There is one church — Christ's church; apostles and teachers are given to the church as stewards of Christ (1 Cor. 3:21–F23).

If the church may not be divided by the diversity of its leaders, neither may it be divided by the diverse gifts of its members. The organic figure of the body shows that diversity does not produce division, but unity. Not only do the gifts proceed from one Giver; they are also interdependent. The interdependence applies to both the ministry of the gifts of the Spirit and the benefit from such ministry. If a church had only teachers, the absence of ministries of order and mercy would soon destroy the one-sided fellowship. The body is not composed entirely of the tongue. All ministry in the body is therefore team ministry. We serve together as we minister to one another.

On the other hand, those who receive the ministry of others depend upon the gifts of others for their growth. Growth in Christ must take place in the church of Christ, for it is in the body of Christ that the nurturing gifts are exercised. Christian life 'in Christ' is in the body of Christ. Indeed, the steward of Christ's gifts grows through exercising his stewardship just as the recipient of his ministry grows through receiving it. To deny to a brother or sister the ministry of grace given to one is to be an unfaithful steward of the manifold mercies of God (1 Pet. 4:10). In such ministry, pride cannot say that it has no need of the humblest of ministries, nor can envy refuse to perform the lowliest of tasks (1 Cor. 12:4–31).

III. THE CHURCH AS THE FELLOWSHIP OF THE HOLY SPIRIT

A. Worshipping in the Spirit

In some countries of the world, the church may seem to bear a close resemblance to Ezekiel's vision. Critics picture the church as a dead remainder of another age, the age of faith. They assume that the church survives in a post-

Christian society only until its elderly members are laid to rest and its ancient buildings are torn down or converted into museums. For believers too, the lament of Israel seems sadly appropriate, 'Our bones are dried up and our hope is gone; we are cut off' (Ezekiel 37:11).

Ezekiel's vision, however, is not a picture of despair, but of hope. At the command of God Ezekiel prophesies to the dry bones in the valley. There is a thundering earthquake, and the bones are brought together. Again Ezekiel prophesies and the Spirit of God breathes life in the valley of death.

The church that is the people of God and the body of Christ is also the fellowship of the Holy Spirit. Apart from the Spirit the church can be only an institutional sepulchre organizing the bones of dead men. Indeed, it may organize those bones in surprising ways: in the ecclesiastical catacombs of Lima, Peru, the bones are classified not in skeletons, but by bones!

The vision God gave to Ezekiel is not just a passing image of the contrast between human deadness and the life-giving Spirit of God. No, it presents the central promise of the prophets: God himself will come to bring life from death. In Ezekiel's vision, God's coming is in the outbreathing of his Spirit.

1. The Spirit of the Lord

God's covenant promise is 'I will be your God, and you shall be my people' (Lv. 26:12). That relation means that God claims his people for himself. They become his heritage, his precious possession (Ex. 34:9; Dt. 4:20; Ps. 33:12; Ex. 19:5; 1 Pet. 2:9). It also means that God graciously gives to his people a claim upon himself. He is their God. Christ comes to fulfil the covenant promise. He comes as Lord, to claim for himself the people of God, those that have been given to him by the Father (Jn. 17:2; 15:19). He also comes as the Servant, to be identified with his disciples, and to give himself, not only for them, but also to them. Union with Christ becomes the great theme of the Apostle Paul.

The relation of the Spirit to the church must be understood in the same way. The Spirit is Lord: the coming of the Spirit is the coming of the Lord; the presence of the Spirit is the presence of the Lord. As Lord, the Spirit claims the people of God as his own. But the Spirit also comes so that God's people might possess God as their own. The Spirit seals the relation between God and his people from both sides. In the Spirit God seals his inheritance: his possession of his people. In the Spirit we have the seal of our inheritance: possessing the Spirit, we possess God himself, our Saviour (Eph. 1:13, 14).

2. The Spirit as Possessor

It is the presence of God in the Spirit that forms the church as the worshipping assembly. If we think only of the gifts of the Spirit to be used in worship and neglect the *presence* of the Spirit, we shall lose from view the very reality that makes worship to be worship: the presence of the Lord. The great event described in Acts 2 is the epiphany of the Holy Spirit. James Dunn has pointed out that just as the first chapter of Luke's Gospel prepares for the coming of the Son in chapter two, so does the first chapter of Acts prepare for the coming of the Spirit in chapter two.[23] Indeed, the ministry of Jesus has an aspect of preparation as well as of fulfilment. The coming of the Spirit is the promise of the Father which the disciples are to await in Jerusalem (Acts 1:4). Jesus promised that he would not leave the disciples orphaned, but would come to them (Jn. 14:18). It is better for them that he should leave them in the body of his incarnation in order that he might come again in the power of his Spirit (Jn. 16:7). At Pentecost, Jesus both comes in the Spirit and baptizes with the Spirit. The presence of the Lord the Giver and the enduing of his Gift are not in conflict. In the wonder of worship that crowns our relation to God, we possess him as we adore him.

Pentecost: Continuity and Newness

Pentecost is the coming of the Lord, the Spirit, to fill his temple, and so it marks both the *continuity* and the *newness* of the church. Like Sinai, Pentecost manifests the presence of God in the flame of fire. The promise of the Father is being fulfilled. As Peter says, this is the promise of the covenant: 'The promise is for you and your children and for all who are far off — for all whom the Lord our God will call' (Acts 2:39). Paul identifies the promise of the Spirit with the promise made to Abraham. The blessing promised to Abraham is fulfilled in the coming of the Spirit (Galatians 3:14).

Yet, while Pentecost must be understood in continuity with the promise of the old covenant, it is continuity in fulfilment. The epiphany of the Spirit fills the church of the new covenant with the presence of God. The Christian church is a Holy Spiritual church. After Pentecost, we cannot think of the church in merely Old Testament categories. The church is still the people of God, but it is the Spirit-filled people of God of the latter days. The church is still the disciples of Christ, but disciples who have their Lord in their midst and in their hearts by his coming in the Spirit. Of course, even to say that the church is still the people of God is not enough. Only by the coming of the Spirit is the full meaning of Israel's calling displayed. The new covenant does not destroy, it fulfils; it brings to realization the calling of the Father and the Son.

Fulfilment at the Feast of the First-Fruits

At the command of Jesus, the disciples remained in Jerusalem until the feast of Pentecost. In the divine plan it is appropriate that the coming of the Spirit should be in the setting of the feast of the first-fruits at Jerusalem. Jesus had fulfilled the Passover in the offering of himself; the great harvest ingathering could now begin. Further, the feasts prescribed in the law summoned all God's people to appear before him and to praise his name before the peoples of the world. In Jewish tradition, as early as the writing of the *Book of Jubilees*, Pentecost was associated with the giving of the law at Sinai.[24] Israel came to Sinai in the third month after the Passover, when she left Egypt (Exodus 19:1). It was assumed that this period was equivalent to the fifty days between the Passover and Pentecost, and that the law was

given on Pentecost. The *Book of Jubilees* makes Pentecost
the time of covenant renewal for Noah, Abraham, Isaac, and
Jacob. *Jubilees* adds that it was then forgotten until renewed
again at Sinai. In any case, this feast at Jerusalem marks the
great day of covenant renewal for the disciples. They are
gathered together when the rush of a great wind is heard
and tongues of fire divide to rest upon them. The outward
phenomena link the epiphany of the Spirit at Pentecost with
the whirlwind, the fire, and the earthquake of the divine
epiphany at Sinai (Acts 2:1–3; cf. 4:31; Ex. 19:18; 20:18; 1
Ki. 19:11–12).

Repentance, Covenant Renewal and Praise

As is fitting when the Lord manifests his power and glory,
the people are called to repentance and faith. Peter's sermon
summons the men of Israel to repent of the crime of the
crucifixion, and to acknowledge their Messianic King, now
raised to heavenly glory. The coming of the Spirit is the
fulfilment of the renewal of the covenant that the prophets
have promised. The coming of the Lord in power calls forth
praise from the disciples. The gift of tongues by which they
can utter their praises is not, of course, that which evokes
praise. They are enabled to express their praises in the languages of the many pilgrims gathered at Jerusalem. But they
are not praising simply because they *can* praise in languages
other than their own. They are praising the Lord because
he has come. The greatness and goodness of their God and
Father, of their risen Lord and Saviour are made known to
them. Peter's sermon clearly shows what the subject of his
praise had been: the glory of his risen Lord. The Spirit who
came from the throne filled the hearts of the disciples with
knowledge of heaven's Lord.

In Luke's account, the missionary implications of Pentecost are clear. In their diverse languages the pilgrims in
Jerusalem hear the mighty works of God wrought in Jesus
Christ. The curse of the tower of Babel is reversed in the
outpouring of the Spirit. But the implications for the worship of the church are equally evident. When God comes in
the Spirit, the response is corporate praise.

As we have seen, God is worshipped for what he has done, and for who he is. That worship is elicited and intensified by the awareness of the immediate presence of God. As the Spirit came upon the disciples at Pentecost they were moved to praise God for his mighty works (Acts 2:11). These are, of course, his mighty acts of salvation in Christ, culminating in the resurrection and the ascension. The presence of the Spirit opened the hearts of the disciples to recognize the actuality and significance of the things that they had seen and heard, and of which they were witnesses. A change was wrought in their consciousness; yet it was not such as to focus their attention on themselves, but on the Lord. Peter does not preach his transformed consciousness, but the truth that his transformed consciousness clearly perceived: the risen glory of Christ, and, therefore, the need of his hearers to repent of their sins and be baptized in the name of Christ so that they, too, might praise him in the joy of the Spirit.

The Filling of the Spirit

At Pentecost the Spirit comes to abide, to dwell in the midst of the new people of God. The house is filled with the wind of the Spirit (Acts 2:2) as a sign that the church, the house of God, is filled with the Spirit. If Pentecost is the coming of the Spirit, a coming in which God the Father and Christ the Son also come to dwell in the temple of living stones, then how can impersonal figures be used to describe the coming of the Spirit? The term 'filling' can describe the movement of the wind or of water filling a vessel, but how can it be applied to a personal presence? Jesus compared the Spirit to the wind when he spoke with Nicodemus (Jn. 3:8); he likened it to water when he spoke to the Samaritan woman, and when he called temple worshippers to himself (Jn. 4:13, 24; 7:38, 39). Jesus was to baptize with the Spirit and with fire (Mt. 3:11); when he was baptized, the Spirit descended upon him as a dove (Mt. 3:16; Mk. 1:10; Lk. 3:22; Jn. 1:32).

Such figurative terms do not deny the personal presence of God in the Spirit. Rudolf Bultmann uses unfortunate language when he speaks of the Holy Spirit being conceived of in the New Testament both animistically and dynamistically.[25] But it is true that the Spirit is presented both as the Giver and the Gift. The key to understanding the ministry of the Spirit in the church is to hold together both aspects of his presence: not to forget that even when we speak of the power and enabling of the Spirit in figurative terms, we are describing the work of a Person. The figure of the Spirit as a wind filling the house suggests the overwhelming power of the Spirit's presence, driving out everything else and taking complete possession of the disciples (and, in this case, their entire environment). So, too, the possession of the Spirit can be compared to the overmastering influence of wine (Eph. 5:18). Another contrast is also suggested. The possession of the Holy Spirit may be contrasted with demon possession. The mastery that an evil spirit may have over a man can be only at the expense of his own liberty and manhood. The Gerasene demoniac healed by Jesus was a man who had been brutalized and depersonalized by demonic power (Lk. 8:26–39). Possession by the Spirit has the opposite result. Since the possessing Spirit is the Creator Spirit, his presence does not bring destruction or suppression, but fulfilment and affirmation. The filling of the Spirit is not the invasion of an alien power, but the infusion of the life-giving presence of the Creator who has come as Redeemer.

Filling of Christ and the Father

That the figure of filling does not diminish the personal presence of the Spirit is also clear from the fact that the same figure is also used of the presence of Christ and of the Father. Christ not only fills all things by his divine power (Eph. 1:23; 4:10); he also fills the church in a special sense, for the church is his body, 'the fulness of him who fills everything in every way' (Eph. 1:23). So, too, the Father fills the church. Paul prays for the church that it might be 'filled to the measure of all the fulness of God' (Eph. 3:19). Clearly, the filling of the Spirit, of Christ, of the Father, are not different things. To be filled with the Spirit means to 'know the love of Christ that surpasses knowledge' (Eph.

3:19); it means to have Christ present in one's heart and life. By the coming of the Spirit, the church becomes the church where Christ is present. If the triune personality of God's presence is lost from view, there is danger that the figures for the Spirit's power will be misunderstood and abused. The error of Simon Magus then begins to emerge (Acts 8:9–24). We may erroneously think of the Spirit only as a power, like electricity, perhaps. We may seek the gifts of the Spirit for their own sake rather than for the fellowship with God that they manifest. Jesus was filled with the Spirit in his ministry, and as James Dunn has well said, 'the Spirit fills us with Jesus'.[26]

3. The Spirit as Possessed: Gifts of the Spirit in Worship

The gifts of the Spirit, then, must not be abstracted from the Spirit who gives them. We need to appreciate, however, the New Testament emphasis on the rich abundance of gifts that the Spirit provides for worship, and particularly for the corporate worship of the people of God. Proclamation of the Word of God, prayer, singing of the praises of God, offering ourselves to God, along with the ministry of our possessions: all these elements of worship are enabled by gifts of the Spirit (1 Cor. 12:28; 14:1, 6, 14, 15; 2 Cor. 9:12; Rom. 12:1, 2; 15:16; 1 Pet. 4:9–11). The Corinthian church, as Paul put it rather ironically, did not fall behind any church in the possession of spiritual gifts. The church was the fruit of Paul's ministry and the 'signs of an apostle' continued to be manifest whenever the church met for worship (2 Cor. 12:11–13). The worship of the Corinthian church, however, for all of the miraculous gifts that were evident, was not different in character from the worship of other churches less markedly endued. The miraculous gifts were the heightening of gifts of the Spirit given to all the church of Christ in every age and circumstance. The ministry of the Word need not be the inspired ministry of an apostle or prophet to be carried out by the charism of the Spirit. Paul prays for the Colossians, that they might be filled with the knowledge of God's will 'through all spiritual wisdom and understanding' (Col. 1:9). This is not to ask that they all be made prophets, but that they be enriched in their understanding of how the Word of God was to be wrought out in their walk of obedience. So, later in the Epistle, Paul says, 'Let the word of Christ dwell in you richly as you teach and admonish one another with all wisdom, and as you sing psalms, hymns, and spiritual songs with gratitude in your hearts to God' (Col. 3:16). Under the blessing of the Spirit the richly indwelling word of Christ would yield spiritual wisdom, wisdom that would find expression in songs of worship pleasing to God and edifying to the saints.[27]

We may fully recognize the extraordinary character of the gifts of the Spirit in Corinthian worship. Presumably, if a member of that church 'had a psalm' (1 Cor. 14:26), he or she had it by revelation of the Spirit; it was an inspired utterance. But the charisms, the gifts of the Spirit for worship are not limited to the Corinthian phenomena. It would undercut the worship of the church to fail to understand the illuminating work of the Spirit, granting the gifts of teaching, praise, ordering and caring that must mark the corporate devotion of those who have been gathered by the Spirit into the presence of the Lord. It is in the Spirit that the church is 'built into a spiritual house to be a holy priesthood, offering spiritual sacrifices acceptable to God through Jesus Christ' (1 Pet. 2:5). No greater gift for our worship can be found, however, than the gift of the Spirit's intercession for us. At best, we do not know what or how to pray in accordance with the perfect purpose and will of God, but the Spirit intercedes for us, and in us, with groanings that go beyond words.[28]

B. Nurture in the Spirit

1. The Spirit's Work of Edification

The indwelling of the Spirit of God requires holiness of the church as his temple (1 Cor. 6:19, 20; 2 Cor. 6:16–7:1). That holiness is achieved by the Spirit's sanctifying work, in which he not only cleanses and renews the inward life of believers (Ezk. 36:27), but also uses the communion of the saints to minister to one another (1 Pet. 4:10). The figure of the erection of a building is often used to describe the development of the church in maturity and holiness. This figure has a strong Old Testament background. The building of the people of God is a term for his blessing. It is used in parallel with planting, and both have their opposites in figures of judgment: tearing down and plucking up (Je. 24:6). Israel was judged of the Lord for sin; the house of the Lord was torn down. But through the prophets came the promise of the rebuilding of the house of David (Am. 9:11), and of the temple (Ezk. 40:48). 'The concept of upbuilding thus becomes a symbol of the gracious dealings of God with the remnant of his people, and is found in this sense in later Judaism's expectation for the future.'[29]

Paul shows how closely the thought of building is linked with that of the temple. Jesus Christ, rejected of the builders, is the chief Cornerstone 'in whom the whole building, fitly framed together, grows into a holy temple in the Lord' (Eph. 2:21).

The organic figure of growth and the architectural figure of construction are blended together in those words of the apostle, just as planting and building are used together in the Old Testament. Paul speaks of himself and Apollos as fellow labourers. Paul plants and Apollos waters (1 Cor. 3:6). Alternatively, they can be thought of as builders. Paul works as a master builder, laying the foundation. Other builders add to the structure: they are warned to build in gold, silver, and precious stones, not wood, hay, or stubble (1 Cor. 3:10–15; Rom. 15:20). But while there are many farmers and builders working together, they are all in God's service. The church is *God's* tilled land, *God's* building (1 Cor. 3:9).

God the Source of Nurture

A number of major lessons about the development of the church are drawn from the twin figures of building and growing. One is that God is the source of the nurture of the church. Specifically, it is the work of the Holy Spirit to nurture the church as the body of Christ. God gives the increase (1 Cor. 3:7), and God gives it through the Spirit who gives life to the body and holiness to the temple (1 Cor. 3:9; cf. 3:16; Eph. 3:16–19).

Growth Is Corporate

A second major principle is that growth is corporate. The temple grows as a structure, composed of living stones. It is rare to find the concept of building, of 'edification', used in application to the individual believer (as it is in 1 Cor. 14:4). The same is true of the growth figure in the image of the body. The body grows as a unity; individual members function for the development of the whole body (Eph. 4:11–16). The mature man of full stature is the one new man in Christ, not first the individual believer.

Growth through Mutual Ministry

This leads to a third principle: that growth takes place through the ministry of the members of the body to one another. Every member of the body becomes a 'joint of supply' to contribute to the upbuilding of the whole (Eph. 4:16). The work of the Spirit is therefore not only internal within every believer, providing the fruits of the Spirit that conform the individual to the image of Christ; the work of the Spirit is also to provide the gifts of the Spirit for ministry, so that the members of the body can minister to one another. Since these gifts of the Spirit are varied and of varying importance for the growth of the body, another implication follows: there are those who have special callings to be builders and horticulturalists. Not all are apostles, prophets, evangelists, pastors or teachers. Some Christians carry major responsibility for the ministry of edification because of the gifts they have received (1 Cor. 12:28; Rom. 12:8; Eph. 4:11, 12).

Growth Is Gradual

A fourth principle that appears in the use of these figures is that growth is gradual. Paul labours unceasingly to present every man perfect in Christ (Col. 1:28), and to present the

church corporately as 'a pure virgin to Christ' (2 Cor.
11:2). Sanctification is not instantaneous and complete. The
holiness of the church must be zealously defended and
advanced. As Israel was led through the wilderness to be
tested and proved, so the Spirit guides the New Testament
church along a life-curriculum of testing and growth. When
Jesus was baptized and filled with the Spirit for his ministry,
the Spirit led him into the wilderness. The power and
blessing of the Spirit does not remove us from the world
but leads us in a programme of growth through trial.

The Centrality of Christ for Nurture

A final principle that is emphatic in these figures takes us
back to the first: it is the centrality of Jesus Christ for the
church. Christ is the Builder, the Foundation, the Cornerstone; his is the body; he is the Vine, and the disciples are
the branches. The gifts and nurture of the Spirit are given
in the body of Christ.

As we have seen, the church is missionary in its nature,
and the upbuilding of the church, too, includes outreach as
well as inward development. Paul uses the figure of the olive
tree to describe the ingrafting of the Gentiles into the people
of God (Rom. 11:17–24). He describes his own far-flung
ministry as laying a foundation where none has been laid
(Rom. 15:20). The gospel bears fruit and increases, just as
Christians bear fruit and increase (Col. 1:6, 10). The emphasis of the figures of building and growth, however, is on the
inward edification of the church as the body of Christ.

2. Nurturing by the Spirit of Life

The upbuilding of the church in the Spirit flows from the
nature of the Spirit as the Spirit of life (Romans 8:2), and
the Spirit of Truth (Jn. 14:17; 15:26; 1 Jn. 4:6; 5:7). In the
Old Testament man is given life by the divine inbreathing.
The *ruach*, the breath or Spirit of God, is not an additive,
provided to add rationality to a living animal; no, the Spirit
that gives man life makes him to be *man* in the image of
God (Gen. 2:7). In his vision of the valley of dry bones,
Ezekiel saw God breathe new spiritual life in a people devoid

of life or hope (Ezk. 37:5, 9, 10, 14). Jesus accordingly teaches Nicodemus that entry into the kingdom is by the new birth, the giving of life by the Spirit, who moves with sovereign mystery like the wind (John 3:3–8). After his resurrection, Jesus breathed upon the disciples, and said, 'Receive the Holy Spirit' (Jn. 20:22). Paul continually associates the Spirit with the resurrection of Christ (e.g. Rom. 1:4). He recalls the Genesis passage when the first Adam received life by the breath of God and compares it to the resurrection life of Christ: 'So it is written: "The first man Adam became a living being"; the last Adam, a life-giving spirit' (1 Cor. 15:45).

Apart from the life-giving power of the Spirit, the church remains an empty shell, whatever its form or verbal profession. Paul answers the critics of his doctrine of justification by faith by affirming the new life in the Spirit of those who have been united to Christ (Romans 6:1–11; 8:1–17). The life of the Spirit bears fruit in the Christian graces (Gal. 5:22–24). By the Spirit the love of God is poured out in our hearts: the love in which the Father did not withhold his only Son, but delivered him up for us all (Rom. 5:5, 8; 8:32). The life given by the Spirit is not a mere feeling, but a new realm of existence in relationship to God. Love is the first of the fruits of the Spirit, and the New Testament constantly describes the love for God and for neighbour that fulfils the law. In the church of Christ, life together manifests a love that the world does not know, a love modelled on that love of God imparted by the Spirit. The unity of the church is forged by sharing in the Spirit, and in the love of the Spirit. Paul joins the fellowship or sharing of the Spirit with the encouragement of love, and with tender mercy and compassion (Phil. 2:1). The lowliness of mind that enables Christians to think of the concerns of others before their own is the fruit of the Spirit of Christ, who humbled himself to become obedient to the death of the cross. The life of the Spirit has the power of Christ's resurrection, the power of eternal life already begun (Rom. 8:11; Jn. 4:14; 7:37–39). The Spirit is the Spirit of glory (1 Pet. 4:14). But the Spirit is the Spirit of Christ's glory, glory that he entered by way of the cross. It is precisely in and through suffering that the power of the Spirit becomes manifest (note the context of 1 Peter 4:14). Paul's description of the power and joy of the life of the Spirit leads him to turn again to the theme of suffering. The final triumph is that nothing can separate us from the love of Christ (Rom. 8).

3. The Nurture of the Spirit of Truth

The Spirit of life is also the Spirit of Truth. In the Old Testament, the Spirit as the Breath of God is closely linked with the word of God, since a spoken word is a vocalized breath. The prophets wrote as they were borne along by the Holy Spirit (2 Pet. 1:21). Indeed, it was the Spirit of Christ in the prophets who pointed to the sufferings of Christ and the glory that was to follow (1 Pet. 1:11). The key New Testament term for inspiration is *theopneustos*: it means 'God-breathed', not so much breathed into the prophets (inspired) as breathed out by God.[30] The church spreads as the word of God increases and is multiplied (Acts 6:7; 12:24; 19.20). The letters of Christ to the seven churches of Asia are concluded with the admonition, 'He who has an ear, let him hear what the Spirit says unto the churches' (Rev. 2:7). The apostolic witness is in the power and authority of the Spirit. Jesus promised that the Spirit, sent from the Father in his name, would bring to the remembrance of the apostles all the things that he had taught them (Jn. 14:25, 26). The Spirit would also reveal further things of Christ that the apostles could not receive during Jesus' earthly ministry (Jn. 16:12–14). The apostles and prophets are the foundation of the New Testament church because they are organs of revelation, receiving in the Spirit the mystery of the gospel of Christ (Eph. 2:20; 3:4–6). The church is apostolic because it rests upon that foundation: the revelation of Christ given once for all by the witnesses chosen of God and attested by signs given of the Spirit (Heb. 1:1, 2: 2:3, 4: Acts 10:40–42; 2 Cor. 12:12; Acts 2:42). The church dare not abandon the apostolic witness or seek to build on another foundation. God's own witness to his saving work has been given by the Spirit in his Word. For that reason the Word of God holds authority and priority. Saving truth is not our project, to be wrought out in practice and subsequently given theoretical expression.[31] Only the Spirit of God knows the deep things of God, and these are the things that were revealed to the apostles by the Spirit (1 Cor. 2:6–16). To be sure, we receive the apostolic witness in our own context of thought and life. There exists a reciprocal relation between our practice of the truth and our understanding of it. But the way of life opens to us through hearing the Word of God and believing God's witness to himself.

The Illumination of the Spirit

The Spirit who communicated through the apostles and prophets the deposit of sound doctrine (1 Tim. 6:20, 21; 2 Tim. 1:13) also works to illumine our understanding of the truth. The Spirit uses the Word as a sword to pierce our hearts, and to build us up in the knowledge of Christ (Heb. 4:12, 13; 2 Timothy 3:16). The edification of the church rests upon the work of the Spirit in giving understanding of the truth. The people of God are taught of him, as the prophets promised (Is. 54:13; Jer. 31:34; 1 Jn. 2:27; 1 Thess. 4:9; Jn. 6:45; Ephesians 1:17, 18).

To recognize the authority of Scripture is not to strip Scripture of all but authority. Jesus said that the words that he spoke were spirit and life (Jn. 6:63). Too often we think of written words as 'dead letters', forgetting the meaning of *theopneustos*. The God who speaks by revelation also opens our ears to hear. He discloses a wisdom that is foolishness to men but is his power to salvation. Growth in edification always begins with understanding the Word of God.

The Spirit who edifies is the source of life and of truth. In his work he draws us into a new existence, a new relation to God, to one another, and to the world. He is therefore not only the Spirit of life and of truth, but also the Spirit of sonship and of stewardship.

4. The Nurture of the Spirit of Sonship

As the Spirit of sonship, the Holy Spirit seals the new relation that we have with God through the gift of Christ's righteousness (Gal. 3:5, 4:6).[32] That sonship secures our inheritance (Rom. 8:17). Our status as the children of God is affirmed by the witness of the Spirit (Rom. 8:15, 16). Since the Spirit also renews us in the image of Christ, and leads us as the children of God, he ministers the vital union that we have with Christ as well as the representative union by which we are declared to be children of God. But the renewing of the Spirit that gives us *growth* in Christ rests upon the attesting and sealing work of the Spirit that affirms our *position* in Christ. It is far from being the case that the New Testament church is merely a servant church, differing from the world only in the task it has received. The church differs in status. It is the family of God, sealed by the indwelling Spirit of adoption. The Spirit seals God's claim on us, marking us as his possession (Eph. 1:14; 4:30). We might say that from God's side the Spirit of Sonship is the Spirit of Fatherhood. At the same time the Spirit seals our possession of God (2 Cor. 1:21; Eph. 1:14).

Those who have been sealed as the sons and daughters of God have not only the assurance of their position in Christ. They have also the experience of being children of God, in fellowship with God and with each other. The fruits of the Spirit provide growth in that fellowship. Because the Spirit pours out God's love in their hearts, they are drawn to respond in love for God (1 Jn. 3:1). They also learn to love one another (1 Jn. 4:11). The mind of the Spirit is life and peace (Rom. 8:6). The peace with God that their justification establishes becomes the source of the peace that guards and patrols their hearts in their relations to each other (Eph. 4:3; 1 Cor. 14:33; Col. 3:15; Phil. 4:7). So, too, the joy and hope of the Spirit turn believers toward God and toward the fellowship of the church (Phil. 4:4, 10; Rom. 8:23–25; 12:15; 15:14). Paul emphasizes the hope of the church in the Spirit. We taste now the first-fruits of the Spirit (Romans 8:23). The Spirit who is present in our hearts is the Spirit of Glory. He is the 'earnest', the down-payment of the life to come (Eph. 1:13; 2 Cor. 1:21). That is, in the Spirit we have not merely a sure promise of eternal life, but the beginning of that life. The fellowship with God and with the saints that we now experience is already a taste of heaven. What we will receive in heaven is marvellously greater in degree, but it is not different in kind.

Sonship in Suffering

At the same time, the status and experience of sonship in the Spirit does not remove us from the sorrows and sufferings of our existence in this world. To the contrary, it is the sons of God who are chastised that they might be corrected, and tested that they might be proved (Heb. 12:5–13; Rom. 5:3–4). God proved Israel as his son, leading the nation through selected experiences in the wilderness that he might prove them (Ex. 16:4; Dt. 8:2). This was the work of his Spirit (Is. 63:9–14; Ne. 9:20).

Educational goals are often stated in terms of knowing, doing, and being. The nurture of the church in the Spirit involves knowing the truth and knowing the Lord; it also involves our doing of the truth. The Spirit leads us in paths of proving, corrects us by his discipline, and continually calls us to the obedience of the children of God. The nurture of the Spirit also provides the provision and protection that is necessary for our new being, as those called from darkness into light.

Edification requires that we bring to the test the truth of God as we apply it to our experience. We must prove the will of God as we make decisions and choices (Phil. 1:9–11). Growth cannot be instantaneous; the guidance of the Spirit does not unroll before us the journey that our lives are to take. But the leading of the Spirit develops in us a growing wisdom to discern what is pleasing to God in our daily circumstances.

5. Nurture in the Stewardship of the Spirit

The Spirit of sonship is also the Spirit of stewardship. In claiming us as sons and daughters of God, the Spirit personally possesses us. In providing his gifts for ministry and service the Spirit gives himself to us, is possessed by us. The gifts of the Spirit for the edification of the church are granted toward the goals of the Spirit in enduing us. Since they are given to help us build up the body, they are 'other-directed' gifts. The work of the Spirit enables us to seek, not our own things, but the things of others. Those who seek the things of Christ will seek the things of others (Phil. 2:20, 21). It would be vain and foolish to seek self-fulfilment in bringing to expression the gifts of the Spirit. The steward is a servant. He does not seek to advance his own cause, but the cause of his master. The faithfulness required of stewards is precisely this. When Paul describes the spiritual service that we are to bring to God, he makes continual use of the expression 'one another' (Rom. 12:5, 10, 16; 13:8; 14:13, 19; 15:5, 7, 14; 16:16).[33] The gifts of the Spirit endue a mutual ministry of edification: 'try to excel in gifts that build up the church' (1 Cor. 14:12; Col. 3:16). The members of the church are to be built up so that they may build one another up; this is not an end in itself, since the object is that each brother and sister, as well as the church as a whole, may be presented to God to his glory (Col. 1:28; Eph. 4:12f.; 2 Cor. 11:2). Edification equips for worship and also for witness in the world. Since the church is as light and salt the vocations of Christians must reflect the Lordship of Christ in all the spheres and activities of life. Edification, therefore, includes equipping the saints for their individual ministries in the world.

Gifts and Calling of Stewards

The gifts and calling of the stewards of the Spirit are interrelated. Since spiritual gifts are not to be wrapped in a napkin, but used, the possession of a gift that would make for the edification of the church constitutes a call for its exercise. As the possessor of such a gift seeks to serve Christ by its use, he commends himself to the church so that his or her gifts may be recognized (Rom. 16:1, 2). As Paul was called to be an apostle, so every Christian is called to be a saint, and is granted gifts to exercise in mutual ministry (Romans 1:1, 6, 7). Paul's calling, of course was to a special and foundational office in the church, but the principles are the same. Paul serves as an apostle because of the gift of grace given to him. He sometimes designates his office by the term 'the grace given me' (Rom. 12:3, 6; 15:15, 16).

Individuality of Gift Patterns

Our calling is of one Lord, to one hope, in one faith, but to many individual ministries or functions. Every Christian has a function to perform. Not all functions require public recognition for their proper exercise: a man may show mercy to a sick friend without needing anyone to recognize his ministry, or even to know of it. But if someone is to administer diaconal funds on behalf of the church, or to become a regular hospital minister in the name of the church, public recognition is necessary. Church offices as they are presented in the New Testament require groupings of gifts. A teaching elder, for example, must have gifts to rule as well as gifts to teach. Yet the constellation of gifts that an individual possesses are uniquely his own.

The individuality of gifts implies, therefore, that gifts are granted *in a measure*. No one but Jesus Christ possesses all the gifts of the Spirit in their fulness. Since gifts are measured, a man is not to think of himself more highly than he ought to think (Rom. 12:3). The Christian must judge soberly as to what his or her own gifts are (1 Cor. 7:17; 2 Cor. 10:13). Further, these gifts form a pattern. Paul's analogies to the members of the body suggest that. When Paul tells Timothy to stir up the gift that is in him, he is saying, in effect, 'take care to fulfil your function' (2 Tim. 1:6). On the one hand, the fruits of the Spirit conform us to the image of Christ, and make us *resemble* one another. On the other hand, the varying patterns created by the gifts of the Spirit cause us to differ from one another. We are, therefore, identified by our gifts. What I am to do in serving Christ's body is an expression of who I am in the Lord. A harmony exists in Christian identity and vocation that cannot be found outside of Christ.

It is well to remember that each Christian is a new creation in Christ. It is not merely the gifts freshly granted of the Spirit that are new. One's 'natural' gifts are also new in the Creator Spirit. Since all gifts are granted for service, we discover them not in the abstract, but in use. In the love of Christ, we seek to serve others. To be effective in that service, we may desire greater gifts than we have received.

We may expect to grow in the effectiveness of our own ministries as we seek to build up Christ's church.

When all our gifts are marshalled in the service of the Lord, we will be faithful stewards (2 Cor. 4:1, 2; 1 Pet. 4:10; Eph. 4:1; Col. 1:10). This does not mean that all our gifts, natural and spiritual, will come into full use. The purposes of Christ's kingdom set priorities for us. Since our goal is not self-realization, we need not worry about 'wasted' talents. Heaven offers time enough, in any case!

The case of Samson warns us that spiritual gifts may be misused. Paul knew that some of his opponents were preaching Christ out of envy during his imprisonment in Rome (Phil. 1:15). The Apostle takes pains to warn against both envy and pride in the use of the gifts of the Spirit. Most importantly, all the gifts lose their meaning apart from love, love that recognizes the indebtedness to others of the gift that has been received (1 Cor. 13; Rom. 1:1; 14, 15; 1 Cor. 9:16–23).

Patterns of Gifts in the Ordering of the Church

The pattern of the gifts of the Spirit granted to individuals establishes and supports a pattern in the structure of the church. The church is a body; in an organism there is both life and structure, ardour and order, to use the phrase of J. E. L. Newbigin. Often there has been tension between the advocates of vitality and structure in the church. At times this has been seen as a struggle between the spiritual and the institutional. But it is a mistake to equate the Spirit with life and not also with order. The Creator Spirit moves upon the face of the waters and brings order out of that which is without form and void. Paul must tell the rather frenzied Corinthians that God is not a God of confusion, but of peace. His instructions, he reminds the church, are not lacking in inspired authority, given of the Spirit (1 Cor. 14:33–40). The life of the Spirit is organic life, ordered life, life in the discipline of the family of God, in the structure of the Christian temple.

In particular, the ministry of the church is ordered of the Spirit to the goals that we have been examining: the goals of the worship of God, the edification of the church, and the evangelization of the world. The gifts of the Spirit to these ends are gifts for the ministry of the Word, the ministry of order, and the ministry of mercy. Further, these gifts are granted to some in greater measure; their stewardship needs to be recognised in the church. We may therefore distinguish between the general office of every believer and the special offices recognized for those with outstanding gifts in these areas. The mediatorial office of Jesus Christ is unique, standing above all office in his church. The attached diagram provides a schematic picture of the order of ministry in the church of Christ.

The Means of Ministry: Ministering the Word

The ministry of the Word is committed to every believer in the sense that every Christian must confess Christ before men, and be ready to give a reason for the hope that is in him (Rom. 10:10; 1 Pet. 3:15). This is, of course, a minimum. Christians should seek to be as effective as possible in ministering the Word in their families, and as they have opportunity to encourage their fellow Christians. Paul and the other New Testament writers emphasize the ministry of those who have been called to preach and teach the Word of God (Eph. 4:11; 1 Cor. 12:28; Rom. 12:7; 1 Pet. 4:11). There is danger that the church today, in resisting clericalism, will move to an opposite extreme. A popular exegesis of Ephesians 4:12 explains that official teachers are to equip the saints for their work of ministry. That exegesis may well be correct. Certainly Paul does think of every Christian serving as a joint of supply (v.16). But the structure of the whole passage still needs attention. The risen and glorified Christ gives the special teaching gifts to the church as the means of its growth to maturity in Christ. It is the priority of the Word of God that gives such prominence to the teaching gifts. Jesus Christ is the only Logos; his is the prophetic office that has inspired the Scriptures, through the Spirit. Ministers of the Word are his servants.

The Ministry of Order

The Spirit of truth establishes the ministry of the Word, the Spirit of holiness establishes the ministry of order. It is not enough for the church to know the truth. We must confirm in our lives the confession of our lips. The order of the church is the order of the law of love. Paul is dismayed that the Corinthians are prepared to take financial disputes before heathen magistrates. He argues that if they do not have qualified judges to handle such matters, they should choose unqualified ones. All they stand to lose is money! But, really, no Christian ought to be regarded as without qualifications. Do not the Corinthians know that one day they will judge angels? (1 Cor. 6:3). How much more may they judge the affairs that concern only this life! The life-style of the Christian community must be ordered by love in all things. The hortatory sections of the New Testament epistles regularly recognize that God has appointed authority structures for the ordering of life in Christ's church. Special gifts for governing are given of the Spirit (Rom. 12:8; 1 Cor. 12:28; 2 Tim. 5:17). 'Obey your leaders and submit to their authority. They keep watch over you as men who must give an account . . .' (Heb. 13:17). Rule under the Lordship of Christ is not imperial domination, but self-giving service, yet it does carry authority; Christ has given the keys of the kingdom to establish order in his church. The discipline of government in the church maintains the glory of Christ's name, reclaims the offender, and bears witness to the world.

The Ministry of Mercy

Finally, since the Spirit is the Spirit of glory, the Spirit of the age to come, the ministry of mercy is part of the form of the church. Christ's miracles of compassion were signs of hope; they foreshadowed the final salvation of the Lord when the curse would be removed. The Christian church continues to show mercy in Christ's name in faith and hope given of the Spirit. Every Christian has hope through the witness of the Spirit (Rom. 8:23). The Spirit prays for us and with us, and we find healing and relief from the throne of grace. The Christian reflects the hope of the Spirit in the tenderness of his service to those in need. Every Christian must minister to others, even to the least of Christ's brothers (Mt. 25:31–46). The ministry of mercy is also exercised in a special sense by those whose gifts enable them to bring comfort, hope, cheer and counsel to those in distress (Acts 6:1–6; 1 Tim. 3:8–13; Rom. 16:1, 2).

C. Mission in the Spirit

1. Missio Dei

The mission of the Spirit is the mission of God who draws men and women to himself through Jesus Christ. By the work of the Spirit Jesus was incarnate in the womb of Mary (Lk. 1:35). The Spirit descended upon Christ at his baptism, enduing him for ministry as one filled with the Spirit (Mt. 3:16; Lk. 3:22; 4:14). The mission of Jesus was fulfilled in the Spirit. When the time came for Jesus to leave his disciples, he promised the coming of another Friend and Advocate, who would be sent by the Father and the Son (Jn. 14:16, 16; 15:26). The Holy Spirit would continue the divine mission. After the resurrection, Jesus told the disciples to remain in Jerusalem until they received the promise of the Father. This was the baptism of the Holy Spirit that Jesus alone could provide. It was the blessing that he would send from the throne of glory (Acts 1:4, 5; 2:33).

In the introduction to the Book of Acts, Luke refers to his Gospel, the first volume of his account about Jesus. Luke says that in the Gospel he recounted the things that Jesus 'began to do and to teach' (Acts 1:1). He evidently intends in his second volume to tell about what Jesus continued to do and teach. Jesus no longer appears in his resurrection body in Acts, except for his meeting with Saul on the Damascus road. Instead, Luke's second book is filled with references to the Holy Spirit. From the coming of the Spirit at Pentecost the great movement of the mission of the Spirit is evident. The initiative is always with the Spirit, who calls, empowers, and directs in the spread of the gospel from

Jerusalem (where Peter preaches to the Jews), to Rome (where Paul teaches the Gentiles).

The Spirit uses believers as his instruments, but he shows his sovereignty in the whole mission enterprise. Peter well acknowledges, 'We are witnesses of these things, and so is the Holy Spirit, whom God has given to those who obey him' (Acts 5:32). Peter's own understanding had to be enlarged by a special vision before he was prepared to go to the house of Cornelius (Acts 10:9–16). The leaders of the Jerusalem church were shocked when they heard that Peter had baptized the uncircumcised Gentile centurion and his household. But the Spirit had again taken the initiative. He had fallen on those Gentiles as they heard the preaching of Peter. 'They had no further objections and praised God, saying, 'So then, God has granted even the Gentiles repentance unto life' (Acts 11:18).

The Spirit guides the church in choosing Spirit-filled men for its ministry (Acts 6:3), but the Spirit also intervenes directly in choosing whom he will. Jesus meets Saul the persecutor; Saul is filled with the Spirit (Acts 9:17), and the Spirit commands that Saul and Barnabas be separated as the first mission task-force to carry the gospel overseas (Acts 13:1–4). Luke tells us how Paul's journeys are directed by the Spirit (Acts 16:6, 7). Even through opposition and persecution the Spirit guides in scattering the church and thrusting forth witnesses to Christ.

The Mission of the Spirit for the Glory of God

The Spirit reveals divine power in accomplishing his mission. His task is to exalt Jesus Christ and to glorify the Father. The disciples, as they fulfil the Great Commission, are to baptize into the name of the Father, the Son, and the Holy Ghost. In mission, the Spirit is one with the Triune God.

The work of the Spirit in oneness with Christ is pictured in the Book of Revelation. There John beholds seven Spirits before the throne (Rev. 1:4). But the seven Spirits belong to Christ (Rev. 3:1); they may reflect the seven-fold enduing of the Messiah (Is. 11:2). In the intricacy of the vision, the seven Spirits are also the seven eyes of the Lamb, seeing and directing all things (Rev. 7:5). By the Spirit, Christ's work will be brought to consummation glory.

The Spirit, as the Spirit of glory, leads the mission of Christ's kingdom forward as well as heavenward. Jesus has returned to heaven, as Peter declared, until the 'time . . . for God to restore everything' (Acts 3:21). The outpouring of the Spirit points to the final cosmic renovation that will accompany the coming of the great day of the Lord (Acts 2:19, 20). The fire of the baptism of the Spirit signifies that renovation (Lk. 3:16, 17). If the disciples are endued rather than consumed by the flame of heaven, it is because the fire is the baptism of their Lord. He has borne the searing flame of judgment, having been baptized in that fire (Lk. 12:49, 50). Now his baptism of fire upon them cleanses and renews, but does not destroy.

Vindication by the Spirit's Mission

The Spirit's purpose in glorifying Christ is accomplished in a mission that brings judgment as well as blessing. The Spirit as Advocate brings the case for the prosecution against the world (Jn. 16:8–11).[34] The world stands convicted for the sin of unbelief. The Spirit also brings a verdict against the world with respect to Christ's triumphant righteousness, sealed by his ascension. Satan, the Prince of this world and the Accuser of the brethren, is also convicted and condemned. In Paul's confrontation with Elymas the power of the Spirit in judgment is evident. Ananias and Sapphira are judged for lying to the Spirit (Acts 5:3); Stephen accuses his hearers of resisting the Spirit (Acts 7:51). The mission of the Spirit of glory in a rebellious world brings conflict, as the history of missions after Acts continues to show.

2. The Mission of the Church in the Spirit

The mission of the church is carried out through ministries of the Word, of life (or order) and of mercy. In all of these areas the church witnesses through the Spirit. The witness of the Word is required of every believer, for every Christian must confess the name of Jesus Christ (Rom. 10:9, 10; Mt.

10:32f.). This confession must often be made before sceptical or hostile audiences. Every Christian must be prepared 'to give an answer to everyone who asks you to give the reason for the hope that you have' (1 Pet. 3:15). The questioner in such a case may well be a magistrate before whom the Christian stands accused. In such circumstances, the Holy Spirit will be the teacher of the accused, fulfilling his role as Advocate (Mt. 10:20; Mk. 13:11; Lk. 12:12; 2 Cor. 13:3). The New Testament never suggests that all Christians have the gifts of an evangelist, a pastor, or a teacher (1 Cor. 12:29). Skill in presenting the claims of the gospel, wisdom in expounding the Scriptures to show their testimony to Christ: these are special gifts of the Spirit. But, significantly, no Christian may be ashamed of Christ. The greatest obstacle to the spread of the gospel is not the limits of the believer's understanding or powers of expression. It is the limits of his courage and faithfulness. Faithfulness will often be put to the test in the life of the church and the experience of the Christian. For that reason, the witness of every Christian is put in the context of confession under scrutiny and duress. In the Book of Acts we have records of the witness of gifted men on trial, speaking as the Spirit gives them expression (Acts 4:8; 5:29–32; 22:3–21; 24:10–21). The filling of the Spirit endues Christians to speak the Word with boldness (Acts 4:31).

The Witness of Life

The verbal witness of the church is supported and extended by the witness of the life of the believing community. The apostolic church, 'encouraged by the Holy Spirit it grew in numbers, living in the fear of the Lord' (Acts 9:31). The grace of the Spirit that built up the church became the ground of the growth of the church. Barnabas, 'a good man, full of the Holy Spirit and faith', was called to mission after he had manifested his gifts in encouraging the saints in their walk with the Lord (Acts 11:23f.). As in the Old Testament, the very separation and holiness of the people of God (2 Cor. 6:17–7:1) becomes a witness, like that of a city set upon a hill. Seeing the good works of the Spirit-filled church, the nations will be brought near, will fall down and declare that God is in the midst of his people (Mt. 5:16; 1 Cor. 14:25). As the last cited passage shows, the gifts of the Spirit for worship and for edification have their own attractiveness with respect to witness. The spiritual holiness of the church, by its contrast with the corruption of a heathen world, will shine as a light of witness (Phil. 2:12–18).

As we have seen, the Spirit perfects the church in holiness through a godly discipline. The order of the law of love structures the life of the church. That self-denying love must also reach out to others (1 Thess. 3:12). Christians must be concerned for the peace of the city where they are passing residents. They pray for those in authority to this end, knowing the importance of a context in which the gospel can be spread (1 Tim. 2:1–4). It is part of the mission of the church to witness to God's standards of righteousness in the midst of a world where they are defied. Especially the lay members of the church must penetrate with their witness the spheres of work, government, and leisure where they are involved. The church penetrates like salt or leaven, not with physical force; it is the work of the Spirit that enables this penetration. The weapons of our warfare are not physical, but spiritual, as Paul reminds us (2 Cor. 10:3–5).

Witness of Mercy

The witness of the church is extended through the ministry of mercy. This appears clearly in the ministry of Jesus Christ. The miracles he performed were not wonders of judgment, but of healing and forgiveness. Jesus identified his own ministry in terms of the prophecy of Isaiah 61. He was anointed of the Spirit to preach the gospel to the poor, to proclaim release to the captives, recovering of sight to the blind, to set at liberty the bruised and to proclaim the acceptable year of the Lord (Lk. 4:18, 19). The year of the Lord is God's own fulfilment of the year of Jubilee in the law of Moses (Leviticus 25). It was the fiftieth year in the sacred calendar, the year when all debts were to be cancelled, all Israelite slaves set free, and every man restored to his own inheritance. God's great day of restoration and renewal would accomplish all that was symbolized in the year of Jubilee. Jesus announces the fulfilment in himself, and proclaims that he is the Anointed One who will do all that the oracle promises. In his ministry of healing Jesus revealed the mercy of God's salvation. His miracles were signs of hope pointing to the final blessing in store for those who trusted in him. Again, the work of the Spirit is an anticipation of glory, an intrusion into the present of the joy that will come at last.

In the early church the work of ministering to the poor and afflicted took on such large proportions that the apostles were overwhelmed, and sought relief so that they might give priority to prayer and the ministry of the word. Those who were chosen to assist the apostles were men 'full of the Spirit and wisdom' (Acts 6:3). The involvement of others in the administration of benevolence did not end the ministrations of the apostles themselves. Miracles of healing were performed by Peter, John, and other apostles. The 'signs of an apostle' given of the Spirit were signs that conformed to the ministry of Jesus, who was anointed with the Spirit, and who 'went about doing good, and healing all that were oppressed of the devil . . .' (Acts 10:38; cf. Heb. 2:4; Acts 5:12–16). Peter speaks of the stewardship of the gifts of the Spirit as benevolent sharing of what we have received, shown for example in the grace of hospitality (1 Pet. 4:10). Those who sow to the Spirit will be eager to show kindness to all men as they have opportunity, especially, of course, to the household of faith (Gal. 6:8–10).

3. The Missionary Gifts

The Spirit moves the whole church to witness to Christ in word and deed, but the Spirit also structures the church for witness according to the gifts that he imparts. The gifts and office of the apostle are first in the church, because the apostles, as we have seen, are foundation stones. Inspired apostolic teaching is the foundation upon which the church rests. But the apostles are also those who are sent into the world with the message of the gospel. Barnabas, who shared the missionary task, is called an apostle along with Paul.

Barnabas did not share the foundational calling of the twelve, but he did share their evangelistic labours (Acts 14:14). If the first office in the church, supported by unique gifts of the Spirit, is a missionary office, we are reminded again that the church itself is a missionary organization. Its missionary calling may be blunted by worldliness or smothered by worldly institutionalism, but the gifts of the Spirit do not move it in that direction. Unfortunately, the foundational aspect of the apostolic office, the authority of the apostles in delivering to the church the teachings of Christ, has been emphasized to the detriment of the missionary calling that they fulfilled. This may seem strange in view of the extensive information that we have in the New Testament about that apostolic missionary *par excellence*, the Apostle Paul. Still more unfortunate is the obscurity that has been allowed to surround the New Testament record about the office of the evangelist. At the time of the Reformation, the vast number of clergy at all levels in the hierarchy without pastoral charges was rightly seen as an abuse in need of correction. Appeal had been made to the office of the evangelist to justify ordination to hierarchical position (on the ground that Timothy and Titus were evangelists who ordained elders: 1 Tim. 5:22; Titus 1:5).[35] To avoid this possible conclusion, the Reformers linked the office of the evangelist to the office of the apostle so closely that both were held to have ceased with the apostolic age.[36] As a consequence, the missionary character of the church itself was diminished or lost from view for a large segment of Protestantism. When the church was reawakened to its missionary calling in the latter part of the eighteenth century, much of the organization of the mission was assumed to be unconnected with New Testament teaching regarding office. To this day the tendency persists. Missionary structure has been adapted to para-ecclesiastical forms that may be shaped more in the model of a business or political organization than the order of Christ's church.

Of course, the office of the evangelist is not the only missionary office in the church, although it has a distinctive missionary focus. Pastors and teachers are necessarily involved in proclaiming the gospel. Paul writes to the church at Rome and speaks of his desire to preach the gospel to them: something that he does in his epistle (Rom. 1:15). Deacons, particularly, are involved in witness as they exercise their gifts of helping and healing. As we recognize the missionary dimension of all church office, the outreach of the church can be seen to include not only the evangelist to preach the gospel, but the use of every gift of the Spirit by the widest range of gifted Christians. The fellowship of the Spirit that binds Christians together also calls and equips them to be Christ's envoys to the ends of the earth.

2

The Church as a Heavenly and Eschatological Entity

P. T. O'BRIEN

A. INTRODUCTION

Christians live in the overlap of the two ages, this present
age and the age to come. In Jewish apocalyptic thought the
former was seen as being characterized by plagues, war,
famine and the like. It was an evil time through which even
God's people were called upon to pass prior to the arrival
of God's anointed ruler who would usher in the coming age.
The New Testament teaching concerning the end-time is
not unrelated to these Jewish apocalyptic conceptions, but
it makes two significant modifications: first, the figure who
will appear at the advent is not some unknown entity: it will
be the Son of Man on the clouds of heaven, who is none
other than the crucified and risen Lord Jesus. Second, with
the death and resurrection of the Lord Jesus Christ the
'coming age' has been inaugurated even while the present
age continues; so that we as Christians live in the overlap of
the two aeons. On the one hand, as those who are in Christ
we have already participated in the world to come, the
powers of the new age have broken in upon us and we

already participate in the resurrection life of Christ. On the other hand, we are still in Adam. The sufferings of this present time are still very real, even if they are not worth comparing with the glory yet to be revealed. The warfare between flesh and Spirit still continues until the last day and we long for that final adoption, the redemption of our bodies. We know the tension that exists between the 'already' and the 'not yet', between the life of heaven and an existence that is very earthly.

That tension is brought out in a number of New Testament references to the people of God, and it is the aim of this paper to examine several aspects of it as we focus upon the church as a heavenly and eschatological reality. In the first instance a number of significant references to *ekklēsia* are examined. It is noted that while the term frequently points to a local assembly or congregation of Christians, and on occasion to a gathering that met in a particular home, i.e. a house-church, several important references have a heavenly entity in view. What do these latter instances say about this heavenly reality? And what can we discover about the tension between the 'already' and the 'not yet'?

Secondly, several important metaphors or images used of the people of God are studied in order to determine (i) who or what is denoted by the picture and (ii) what teaching — particularly that bearing upon the major theme of the paper — is being conveyed by the image. The metaphors chosen for study are the *temple*, the *body*, and the *bride*. Finally Col. 3:1–4:6 is examined to determine something of the responsibilities set before the people of God who live in the overlap of the ages, between the first and second comings of Christ, and who already partake of the life of heaven while still dwelling on earth.

B. EKKLESIA AS CHURCH

1. Outside the New Testament

Although more than one hundred[1] terms or phrases in the

New Testament are used to designate God's people with whom he has entered into a saving relationships, an appropriate point with which to begin our specific study of the church as a heavenly and eschatological entity is the Greek word *ekklēsia*,[2] a term meaning 'congregation', 'church', 'gathering' or 'assembly'. Attested from the fifth century B.C. onwards, *ekklēsia* denoted the popular assembly of the full citizens of the Greek city state. This assembly, in which fundamentally political and judicial decisions were taken (cf. Acts 19:39; at vv. 32 and 41 an unconstitutional assembly is also called an *ekklēsia*), was regarded as existing only when it actually assembled (as such it was distinct from the *ekklēsia* 'people', 'populace', 'crowd', which was continuous).

In the Greek version of the OT, i.e. the Septuagint, *ekklēsia* frequently was a translation of the Hebrew *qāhāl*, a term that could describe assemblies such as the gathering of an army in preparation for war (1 Sa. 17:47; 2 Ch. 28:14), or the 'coming together' of an unruly and potentially dangerous crowd (Ps. 26 [LXX 25]:5). Of particular significance, however, are those instances of *ekklēsia* (rendering *qāhāl*) which denote the congregation of Israel when it assembled to hear the work of God[3] on Mt. Sinai, or later on Mt. Zion where all Israel was required to assemble three times a year. Sometimes the whole nation apears to be involved, as when Moses addresses the people prior to their entry into the promised land. Dt. 4:10 describes 'the day when you stood before the Lord your God, in Horeb, when he said to me, 'Assemble the people before me to hear my words' (the Septuagint uses the term *ekklēsia* and its cognate verb *ekklēsiazō*; note also Dt. 9:10; 18:16; 31:30; Jdg. 20:2; etc.). At other times it is only the chief representatives that seem to be present, as with the congregation of tribal leaders, or patriarchal chiefs, at Solomon's dedication of the Temple of Jerusalem (1 Ki. 8:14, 22, 55; etc.).

In the Greek and Jewish world prior to the contemporaneous with the NT *ekklēsia* meant an assembly or gathering of people. It did not designate an 'organization' or 'society'. Although it had no intrinsically religious meaning and could refer to meetings that were quite secular in character, of special significance are those occurrences of *ekklēsia* in the

Septuagint which refer to the congregation of Israel when it assembled to hear the word of God.

2. The New Testament

The word *ekklēsia* turns up over one hundred times in the New Testament and more than half of those occur in Paul (of a total 114 instances sixty-two are in the Pauline corpus, three in Matthew, twenty-three in Acts, twenty in Revelation and in the non-Pauline epistles six occurrences). Since Paul's uses all pre-date the other instances in the New Testament it is important to determine the meaning he attaches to it in various contexts.

a. *A local assembly or congregation of Christians.* The first use is at 1 Thess. 1:1 in his greetings to the Christians at Thessalonica: 'Paul, Silas and Timothy. To the church of the Thessalonians (*tē ekklēsia thessalonikeōn*) in God the Father and the Lord Jesus Christ.' Our term is employed in the same way as in Greek and Jewish circles, that is, like other assemblies in the city it is described as 'a gathering of the Thessalonians'. But it is distinguished from the regular political councils by the addition of the words 'in God the Father', and from the regular synagogue meetings by the use of the term *ekklēsia* and the additional phrase 'in the Lord Jesus Christ'.[4] From the closing remarks of the letter it is clear Paul has in mind an actual gathering of the Thessalonian Christians. So he requests that his letter 'be read to all the brethren' and that they 'greet all brethren with a holy kiss' (1 Thes. 5:26f.).

Other instances of *ekklēsia* (singular) and *ekklēsiai* (plural) in Paul's epistles also denote a local assembly or gathering of Christians in a particular place: it is thus not a metaphor, but a term descriptive of an identifiable object.[5] In the two Thessalonian letters reference is made to 'the churches of God' (2 Thes. 1:4) and 'the churches of God in Judea' (2:14). Other epistles such as Galatians (1:2), the two letters to the Corinthians (1 Cor. 7:17; 11:16; 14:33; 2 Cor. 8:19, 23, 24; 11:8, 28; 12:13) and Romans (16:4, 16) also employ the plural when more than one church is in view (the only exceptions are the distributive expression 'every church', 1

Cor. 4:17, and the phrase 'the church of God', 1 Cor. 10:32, in a generic or possibly localized sense). The term was applied to an actual gathering of people or to a group that gathers as a regularly constituted meeting.[6] Although we often speak of a group of congregations collectively as 'the church' (i.e. of a denomination) neither Paul nor the rest of the New Testament uses *ekklēsia* in this collective way. Also the notion of a unified provincial or national church is foreign to New Testament teaching. An *ekklēsia* was a meeting or an assembly. This primary sense of 'gathering' comes out clearly in 1 Corinthians 11-14 where expressions turn up such as 'when you assemble in church' (11:18) and 'to speak in church' (14:35; cf. vv. 4, 5, 12, 19, 28).

In one or two New Testament instances *ekklēsia* is found as an extension of the literal, descriptive use of 'an assembly' to deisgnate the persons who compose that gathering whether they are assembled or not. This is a natural extension or linguistic development of group words (note our use of the word 'team') and may explain references such as Acts 8:3; 9:31[7]; 20:17. However, two significant observations need to be made: first, the primary use of the word *ekklēsia* as 'gathering', 'assembly' predominates overwhelmingly in the New Testament — and indeed through the Apostolic Fathers to the Apologists. Secondly, no theological constructs are made on the basis of these very few *extended* uses.

It is of particular significance that at the beginning of the two Corinthians letters (1 Cor. 1:1; 2 Cor. 1:1; cf. 1 Cor. 10:32; 11:22; Rom. 16:16) the church is described as belonging to the one who brought it into existence, that is, God, or the one through whom this has taken place, namely, Christ. Such an *ekklēsia* was not simply a human association or a religious club, but a divinely created entity.[8] Just as for Israel of old, the gatherings referred to by our term were in order to hear the word of God and to worship. (For additional examples of this usage[9] in Paul as well as elsewhere in the New Testament see BAG, 240-241).

b. In a second group of references *ekklēsia* is again used as a descriptive term — as distinct from a metaphor — of an identifiable object, this time of a gathering that met in a particular home, a '*house-church*'. On occasion a whole congregation in one city might be small enough to meet in the home of one of its members, and it must be remembered that it was not until about the middle of the third century that early Christianity owned property for purposes of worship. In other places house-churches appear to have been smaller circles of fellowship within the larger group. In addition to Nympha's house in Laodicea (Col. 4:15) we know that in Colossae Philemon's house was used as a meeting place (Phm. 2). At Philippi Lydia's home seems to have been used in this way (Acts 16:15, 40), while at Corinth Gaius is described as 'host . . . to the whole church' (Rom. 16:23; the qualification 'whole' would be unnecessary if the Christians at Corinth only met as a single group, and implies that smaller groups also existed in the city; cf. 1 Cor. 14:23; note also 1 Cor. 16:19 and Rom. 16:5).[10]

c. Of particular significance for our study of the church as a heavenly and eschatological entity are those instances in the New Testament where *ekklēsia* has a *wider reference than either a local congregation or a house-church*. We begin with Col. 1:18 where it is stated that Christ is 'the head of the body, that is, the church'. At verse 24 a similar expression employed in the context of Paul's sufferings ('on behalf of his body, which is the church'). Most commentators interpret these references in Colossians (and the similar instances in Ephesians: 1:22; 3:10, 21; 5:23f., 27, 29, 32) of 'the church universal, to which all believers belong'[11] and which is scattered throughout the world. But there are two serious criticisms that may be levelled against this view: first, the term *ekklēsia* can no longer have its usual meaning of 'gathering' or 'assembly', since it is difficult to envisage how the world-wide church could assemble, and so the word must be translated in some other way to denote an organization or society. Secondly, the context of Col. 1:15–20 which is moving on a heavenly plane suggests it is not an earthly phenomenon that is being spoken of in v. 18, but a supernatural and heavenly one. This is not to suggest that believers have no relationships with one another if they do not gather together in church. As members of the body of Christ or of God's people they are not only related to Christ himself but also to one another even when separated by time and distance. But the point being made here is that *ekklēsia* is not the term used in the New Testament of those wider, universal links.

Earlier in the letter it had been mentioned that the readers have been fitted for a share in the inheritance of the saints in the kingdom of light, and have been transferred from a tyranny of darkness to a kingdom in which God's beloved Son holds sway (Col. 1:12–14). On the one hand, the Colossians are obviously members of an earthly realm (note the exhortations of 3:4–4:6 which are examined below) and the apostle looks forward to their being presented as 'holy, irreproachable and blameless' before God on the last day (1:22). On the other hand, they are described as presently existing in a heavenly realm. Since they have been raised with Christ they are to seek the things that are above where Christ is, seated at God's right hand (3:1). Because they live with Christ in this heavenly dimension (note that Christ who is their life is already in heaven, vv. 1, 3) they are assured that when he appears they also will appear with him in glory (v. 4).

Later references in Ephesians are thought to point in this same direction of a heavenly gathering: it is expressly mentioned that God 'made us alive with Christ . . . raised us up with him and seated us in the heavenly realms in Christ Jesus' (2:5, 6). The same readers of this circular letter have been 'blessed . . . in the heavenly realms with every spiritual blessing in Christ' (1:3). Again reference is made to Christ's headship over the 'church' (*ekklēsia*) which is his body (1:22, 23; see below with reference to 'body'). If the term *ekklēsia* is to be understood here as 'church' or a gathering taking place in heaven then this would mean that Christians participate in it as they go about their ordinary daily tasks. They are already gathered around Christ and this is another way of saying that they now enjoy fellowship with him. Further references in Ephesians (3:10, 21; 5:23, 25, 27, 29, 32),[12] though usually taken by commentators to refer to 'the church universal', could also be understood as designating that heavenly gathering around Christ.[13].

A passage of major importance in which *ekklēsia* appears

with eschatological and heavenly associations is Hebrews
12:22–24. Because of the cluster of significant ideas and the
context in which they appear it is necessary to look at it in
some detail. The unusual expression 'church of the firstborn'
(*ekklēsia prōotokōn*) appear at v. 23 within the paragraph:

> But you have come (*proselēlythate*) to Mount Zion, to the
> heavenly Jerusalem, the city of the living God. You have
> come to thousands upon thousands of angels of joyful
> assembly, to *the church of the firstborn*, whose names are
> written in heaven. You have come to God, the judge of all
> men, to the spirits of righteous men made perfect, to Jesus
> the mediator of a new convenant, and to the sprinkled blood
> that speaks a better word than the blood of Abel (12:22–24;
> NIV, our italics).

The writer to the Hebrews here contrasts the situation of
the Israelites, who assembled at Mt. Sinai to meet God (vv.
18–21), with that of Christians who have gathered together
to meet him at the heavenly Jerusalem (vv. 22–24). The
descriptive language of the latter is patterned to some extent
on that of the gathering on Mt. Sinai with its references to
angels, assembled participants, the God who presides, the
presence of mediator,[14] and so on. The picture presented is
that of 'the final encounter between God and his people'.[15]
The verb to 'come' (*proserchesthai*) at v. 22 is to be understood in terms of the journey motif, a prominent theme in
the letter: the people of God are a pilgrim people who are
treading the 'highways to Zion', and the goal of their whole
pilgrimage is the heavenly Jerusalem. Yet behind the writer's
use of this verb *proserchesthai* lies the personal encounter
with God through Christ,[16] and the perfect tense 'you have
come' (*proselēlythate*) indicates that 'Christians in their conversion have already, in some sense, reached their heavenly
destination'.[17] They already enjoy by faith the privileges of
that city which is to come (13:14).

The inhabitants of this heavenly Jerusalem to which the
Hebrew Christians of this letter have come, are spoken of
as:

(i) 'innumerable angels in festal gathering' (RSV) — a

reference to the myriads of angels who are God's servants (cf. Heb. 1:14).

(ii) 'the assembly (*ekklēsia*) of the firstborn who are enrolled in heaven'. This clause designates, neither the elect angels, since the notion of enrolment in a heavenly book is usually associated with human beings (cf. Lk. 10:20; Rev. 21:27),[18] nor Old Testament saints (as Calvin and others argued), for according to Heb. 11:40 they are not yet perfected, nor Christians here on earth,[19] because it is a heavenly scene that is presented in ch. 12:22ff. with God present in the midst as judge. This congregation is earthly only with regard to the origin of its participants. Rather, the expression denotes the whole communion of the saints including those 'militant here on earth'. Any view which limits or restricts the privileges of the firstborn to some special group fails to recognize that 'the Firstborn' and 'firstborn' belong closely together (cf. Rom. 8:29). As Bruce correctly observes: 'All the people of Christ are the 'firstborn' children of God, through their union with Him who is The Firstborn par excellence'.[20] Further, into this community believers have come — not simply into its presence as they have come into the presence of myriads of angels, but into its membership.[21]

(iii) 'the spirits of just men made perfect'. Although there is a variety of interpretations as to the meaning of this phrase, in our judgement the most satisfactory explanation is that which refers it to 'the saints of all ages as those who have been perfected by the work of Christ.'[22] The expression designates not simply OT saints or believers of pre-Christian days (as many argue), but points to the same group of people as 'the assembly of the firstborn who are enrolled in heaven', though looked at from a different angle. 'The spirits of just men made perfect' fulfils the words of Heb. 11:40 with the result that OT saints and Christians 'together enjoy the consummation of their hopes'.[23] The intervening phrase, 'a judge who is God of all' (RSV), suggests that in some sense this heavenly assembly is met for scrutiny or judgement. But from the immediate context, viz. the use of *panēgyrei* ('in joyful assembly', v. 22), the reference to Jesus as the mediator of a new convenant and his shed blood, as well as wider considerations within the letter itself (e.g. 10:14, which speaks of all who have been perfected by the sacrifice of Christ), it is clear that the results of that judgement for the assembled multitude are positive. 'The verdict to be pronounced on those assembled can be nothing else than complete divine favour and acceptance'.[24]

To sum up: Heb. 12:23 contains a remarkable reference to *ekklēsia* within the unusual expression, 'the assembly of the first-born' (*ekklēsia prōtotokōn*). Verses 22–24 paint the picture of the ultimate, eschatological encounter with God (cf. Rev. 4, 5). He, as the judge of all, and Jesus, the mediator of a new convenant, are at the centre of that vast assembly, comprising myriads of angels and believers of all ages, i.e. those perfected by the work of Christ, in other words, the whole company of heaven. Clearly this 'gathering' is both *heavenly and eschatological*. Yet Christians, in their conversion, have already come[25] to that heavenly assembly. In one sense, the heavenly city is still the goal of the Christian's pilgrimage (13:14; cf. 4:1–11). In another sense, they have already reached Mt. Zion, the heavenly Jerusalem, the city of the Living God (13:22). The letter to the Hebrews reflects the 'already — not yet' tension found elsewhere in the New Testament, and this points to the fact that Christians live in the overlap of the two ages. The reference to 'the *assembly* of the first-born' is found in a context that is both heavenly and eschatological but where the 'already' pole of that tension is strongly accented.

The New Testament does not discuss the relationship between the local church and the heavenly gathering. The link is nowhere specifically spelled out. Certainly the former is neither a *part* of the church of God nor *a* church of God, as the openings of several of Paul's letters make plain: so at I Cor. 1:2 the apostle writes to '*the church* of God which is at Corinth'. Perhaps it is best to suggest that the local congregations or house-groups are earthly manifestations of that heavenly assembly gathered around God and Christ.

Men and women are called into membership of this one church of Christ, the heavenly assembly, through the preaching of the gospel. Because of one's membership of the heavenly assembly gathered around Christ, Christians ought to assemble in local gatherings here on earth. Apparently this responsibility was not immediately obvious to some of the early Christians since they still needed to be exhorted not to forsake 'the assembling of themselves together' (Heb. 10:25)

C. SOME IMAGES OF THE CHURCH

We turn now to a study of several images or pictures employed of God's people in Christ.[26] Because of the large number of such metaphors used we will necessarily be highly selective. The basis of the choices made may seem rather arbitrary, though we will aim to isolate those particular images which are almost universally regarded as highly significant (e.g. the *body* metaphor in Paul), or have important OT antecedents and occur with relative frequency (e.g. the *temple* motif, which has important OT associations and which occurs a number of times among several New Testament writers). Some cross references — for example to the image of *the vine* — have been made where it is considered appropriate.

Further, it will not be possible, due to limitations of space, to examine every reference. In the treatment of these images dealing with the people of God two separate, though related, questions have been asked: (i) In the immediate context, who or what is denoted by the picture? That is, what is the referent of the metaphor? And (ii) what point is being conveyed or taught through the image? What does it connote?

1. The Temple

The figure of *the temple* is used metaphorically in the New Testament to denote God's people. This point was recognized in *Lumen Gentium*, the dogmatic constitution of the second Vatican Council and one of its principal documents when, in seeking to find a concise enumeration of important biblical ideas that express the entity of the Christian church, it stated that the church is the 'People of God, the Body of Christ, and the Temple of the Holy Ghost'.[27]

It is the apostle Paul, in particular, who develops this image of the church as the community of the redeemed which, through the sanctifying activity of the Holy Spirit, is constituted as the dwelling place of God:[28] this idea appears in 1 Cor. 3:16f.; 2 Cor. 6:16–18; and Eph. 2:20–22 (cf. 1 Cor. 6:19); outside of Paul the notion appears at Rev. 21:22 (on 1 Peter 2:4ff. see below).

Behind the Pauline teaching of the temple as representing God's people lie the attitude and teaching of Jesus regarding the temple at Jerusalem. While recognizing, on the one hand, that it was God's house (Mt. 12:4; cf. Jn. 2:16), having been sanctified by the one who dwelt in it (Mt. 23:17, 21), Jesus saw that it had become 'a cover for the spiritual barrenness of Israel'[29] (Mk. 11:12–26). Jesus himself was greater than the temple (Mt. 12:6). In a messianic action Jesus cleansed the temple (Mk. 11:15ff.); this led to greater opposition by the religious authorities and Jesus finally announced that by his death the temple would be destroyed while another was put in its place by his resurrection (Mk. 14:58; Jn. 2:19–21). That new temple was to be the eschatological congregation of Jesus the Messiah (Mt. 18:20; cf. Jn. 14:23).

a. 1 Cor. 3:16f.

In this first passage the apostle uses three figures of speech — a building (*oikodomē*), a field under cultivation (*geōrgion*) and the temple of God (*naos theou*) — to combat party strife in the church at Corinth (1:10ff.; 3:5ff.). Here *naos theou* specifically denotes the local congregation. That it implies 'the church universal' (as McKelvey and Fung assert)[30] is by no means certain and, as we shall seek to show, it is better to think in terms of a relationship between a particular congregation and a heavenly counterpart.

The specific teaching that is brought out by means of this image of the temple[31] is as follows: first, the congregation at Corinth is the temple of God because God's Spirit dwells in its midst (v. 16).[32] In the OT the temple was the dwelling-place of God. OT eschatology repeatedly linked together the new temple and the presence of God (e.g. Ezk. 43:1ff.);

without God's presence there could be no temple. But Paul's understanding of the divine tabernacling upon earth represents an advance over the OT teaching which says nothing about the Spirit of God indwelling the temple. Certainly the Spirit is spoken of as dwelling in Israel (Ps. 51:11; cf. Is. 63:9) while in some of the later prophecies of the restoration concerning Israel the outpouring of God's Spirit is the token of his presence with his people (Is. 32:15; 44:3; Ezk. 37:14; 29:29, etc.; Joel 2:28ff.). Here, however, the apostle states that the Spirit of God — and the gift of the Spirit is contingent upon the work of Christ — indwells the temple, indeed makes it the very temple of God by his presence.

Secondly, the congregation at Corinth is itself the dwelling-place of God. His tabernacling on earth is not apart from his people; rather, it is an indwelling within them (note v. 16, 'the Spirit of God dwells *in you*; v. 17, 'the temple of God . . . you are').

Thirdly, Paul stresses the unity and holiness of God's temple. At verse 17 the collective plural 'you' (*hymeis*) is employed as the apostle states: 'you Corinthians — all of you — together constitute God's dwelling place' (contrast 1 Cor. 6:19).[33] McKelvey aptly comments: 'Over against the splinter groups in the church at Corinth Paul sets the picture of the church as God's temple . . . [He] does not dwell in a multiplicity of temples. He is one, and there can be only one shrine which he can inhabit'.[34] The congregation is the temple of God and as such is holy; to defile it by internal schism, divisions or party spirit is to destroy it, and any attempt to do this will incur divine judgement.[35]

b. 2 Cor. 6:16-18

This text contains one of the clearest statements in Paul's letters of the idea of believers as God's temple. After a series of five antitheses (vv. 14–16) intended to warn the Corinthian Christians against compromise with heathen society, the apostle asserts: 'For *we* (*hymeis*) are the temple of the living God'. The very emphatic 'we' clearly has its primary reference to the members of the congregation at Corinth and 'is probably intended to impress upon the readers their unique status'.[36] At ths same time using the first person plural (which is the better attested reading)[37] Paul probably includes himself, and may even have intended to designate all Christians generally.

The OT quotation of Lv. 26:12 and Ezk. 37:27 which follows shows that god's people is the new temple in fulfilment of OT prophecy (cf. Is. 60:4–7; 56:6–8; 66:18–21). McKelvey[38] points out that the addition of *enoikēsō* ('live in') — a verb never used of God in the Septuagint — to the citation of Lv. 26:12 shows that for Paul God's dwelling in his people goes beyond being a fulfilment of a mere 'presence with or among' but is now an actual 'dwelling-in' them. He dwells in them, and *they* are his temple.[39] Although it is not explicitly stated that this temple is *holy*, it is clearly implied in the admonition which follows (v. 17, quoting Is. 52:11; cf. 7:1) for the Corinthians are exhorted to separate from all that is unclean.

c. Eph. 2:20–22

This third major temple reference in Paul's letters is of considerable importance to our examination of the heavenly and eschatological dimension for here, in a passage where the apostle[40] reminds the Gentile converts that through Christ's death they have been made heirs of God's promises, the church is set forth as the heavenly temple.

Lincoln has recently argued that in verses 14–18, where it is stated that the barrier between Jew and Gentile has been removed through Christ's death and one new man has been created, there is the further point being made that Christ is 'the bringer of cosmic peace, the reconciler of heaven and earth as the two parts of the divided universe'.[41] The image of the temple with which the paragraph culminates is conceived on a heavenly plane. In the preceding verses Gentiles were viewed in relation to Israel and her covenants: they were excluded from citizenship in the former and they were foreigners regarding the latter; and this state of affairs was indicative of a separation from God. They were thus in a hopeless situation. Now in verse 19 (note the emphatic, logical connection, *ara oun*, 'so then') those previously without hope are regarded from the standpoint of the heavenly realm which they have entered by becoming 'fellow-citizens of the angels'.[42]

In vv. 20–22 the temple is the dominant metaphor. According to OT prophecy the temple at Jerusalem was to be that place where all nations at the end time would come to worship and pray (Is. 56:4f.). The temple imagery here, as many commentators have recognized, should thus be understood in fulfilment of these promises. 'Through Christ Gentiles have been brought near, given access' and along with Jews have become the new temple, that place where 'God supremely manifests his presence (cf. verse 22)'.[43]

Several didactic points are made by the apostle as he conjoins the temple (*naos*) and building (*oikodomē*) images: first, the foundation is that of the apostles and prophets (v. 20a) — an assertion that Gentile converts are built on apostolic tradition, 'the bed rock of historic Christianity'.[44] Secondly, Christ's important place in the temple is that of 'cornerstone' (*akrogōniaios*) — a term which has been taken traditionally as the stone at the foot of the building, set in the corner to determine the line of the walls and so of the building as a whole.[45] On the other hand, Jeremias has argued on a number of occasions that here *akrogōniaios* denotes the final stone of the building, probably set over the gate, holding the building together.[46]

Final certainty as to the precise stone being described may not be possible but Lincoln[47] has made several valuable points in his support of Jeremias' theory regarding the *Abschlussstein*, the top or final stone which holds together the building. (i) The temple in Eph. 2 has a heavenly dimension (note the OT and Jewish antecedents to which he refers). In the light of Christ's exalted position, already mentioned in Ephesians, in which he is seated in the heavenly realms, far above all rule and authority (1:19ff.), the idea of Christ as the topstone seems appropriate. (ii) In rabbinic thought, commenting on Gen. 28:17 (cf. Yoma 54b; Gn.R. 4:2; 68:12 on Gn. 28:12, etc.), 'the stone was believed actually to belong to the heavenly world and thus to be the place of the presence of God and of the inhabitants of heaven'.[48] These ideas for the topstone, Lincoln argues, are appropriate to the role of the exalted Christ in Ephesians. On this view (*akrogōniaios*) draws attention to the primary significance of Jesus Christ in the structure of the temple which he dominates (note in v. 21 it is 'in the Lord').

The two expressions in vv. 21 and 22, 'a holy temple in the Lord' and 'a dwelling place of God in the Spirit', are parallel descriptions of the same thing.[49] 'Temple' and 'cornerstone' are synonymous. The latter term (*Katoikētē-rion*) was significantly used in the LXX of God's dwelling in the temple at Jerusalem (1 Ki. 8:13) and of his heavenly dwelling-place (1 Ki. 8:39, 43, 49). Here at Eph. 2 the temple is God's heavenly abode, the place of his dwelling. Yet that temple is his people in whom he lives by his Spirit. Believers on earth, recipients of this circular letter, are linked with the heavenly realm in and through the Spirit of the risen Lord.

Finally, by means of what McKelvey calls an 'inter-penetration of images',[50] the metaphor of the body is combined with that of the building to draw attention to the element of growth (vv. 21a and 22). Viewed as the temple the church is a dwelling inhabited by God; but from the point of its being a building it is still under construction.[51]

d. The Book of the Revelation

The image of the temple occupies an important place in the Book of the Revelation and in the confines of this paper it is possible to summarize the only salient points that bear on our theme.[52] Of special significance are the words of ch. 21:22 which describe what is not only heavenly but also eschatological and final, in other words having to do with the consummation of all things. The Seer of the Apocalypse writes: 'I saw no temple (*naos*) in the city, for its temple is the Lord God the Almighty and the Lamb'. The writer does not mean that the new Jerusalem has no temple, or that the whole city was a temple. Rather, 'the temple of the new Jerusalem is God himself, who is directly and fully accessible to his people through his Son the Lamb'.[53] This is no temporary or partial experience of the presence of God.

Instead, it denotes that perfected presence, bound up with the great dénouement for which the readers of this book have been prepared.

Towards the end of the first two great cycles of visions (1:9–11:19; 12:1–22:5) the writer dramatically announces that God's temple in heaven is opened and its contents, including the ark of the convenant, are there for all to see (11:19). This vision of the heavenly sanctuary, strategically placed at the conclusion of the first cycle, points forward directly to the consummation of all things. At ch. 21:3 the divine dwelling is said to be none other than God himself; and finally, John simply asserts that the temple is the Lord God Almighty and the Lamb. Every barrier separating man from God is removed so that ultimately 'His servants . . . shall see his face' (22:34). So the temple image is not simply 'the symbol of the life of the faithful in the world to come'.[54] it is all this and more, for it includes both *reign* and realm. 'The presentation of the temple scenario in the Book of the Revelation is a place in which universal worship is offered and thus as a symbol of unity under divine kingship'.[55]

Finally, although several scholars have argued strongly that *oikos* denotes the people of God as the new temple at 1 Peter 2:4ff., the matter is not clear, and it has been claimed with considerable justification that the reference is to God's house(hold). Because of the uncertainty we have not included it in our study.[56]

In sum, then, the temple imagery is applied to: (i) a local congregation at Corinth; (ii) the individual believer (1 Cor. 6:19); and (iii) Christians generally, whether Jews or Gentiles, who have become God's dwelling place by his Spirit. The specific teaching on the temple concerns God's indwelling presence and the unity and holiness of God's people, his temple. The heavenly dimension of the temple imagery comes to the fore in Ephesians, particularly in relation to Christ's exalted position for he is seated in that heavenly realm. Believers who are seated with him nevertheless dwell on earth and are linked with the heavenly realm in and through the Spirit of the risen Lord. Finally, in the book of the Revelation the temple describes what is heavenly as well as eschatological and final. It is bound up with the consummation of all things.

2. The Body of Christ

The second important image used to describe Christian believers in their relationships is that of 'the body of Christ' — regarded by most scholars not simply as one metaphor out of the hundred or so, but rather as a dominant concept, at least in Paul. Interestingly, in the survey taken a few years ago among Christian university students in Australia 'body' was almost unanimously the most popular term used to describe believers in their relationships with one another.

There is no consensus among New Testament scholars as to the source of Paul's treatment of the church as the body of Christ. The number of possible suggestions has been considerable: contemporary political thought (E. A. Judge), Stoicism (W. L. Knox, among others), Gnosticism (H. Schlier, E. Käsemann, R. Bultmann), rabbinic speculation on the body of Adam (W. D. Davies), the Christian eucharist (A. E. J. Rawlinson), and the OT concept of corporate personality (A. R. Johnson, E. Best).[57] Perhaps it is not particularly helpful to try to determine the source.[58] It might have come to him independently, anyway! Of greater significance for us is Paul's usage — his intentions in employing this metaphor and the meanings he sought to bring out by it. With most protestant interpreters we consider that the body concept is to be understood metaphorically, not literally and biologically, or mystically.

As with other images it is necessary to determine: (i) What is the entity being described? and (ii) What points are being conveyed or taught by the metaphor? Of particular significance for our study is whether the term 'body', when used of the people of God, has anything to do with a heavenly or eschatological dimension.

a. Earlier Letters: 1 Corinthians and Romans

The expression 'body of Christ' (*sōma tou Christou*) first turns up at 1 Cor. 10:16–17 with particular reference to the Lord's Supper. Participation in that Supper means partici-

pation in the body and blood of Christ, i.e. sharing in the
benefits of his death and of being in fellowship with him.[59]
Those who participate in Christ are one body — by implication the body of Christ — just as there is one loaf. Here,
then, in a text that deals with the Lord's Supper, the physical
body of Christ and the benefits flowing from his death are
brought into a close relationship with the church as his
body.[60] It is the congregation at Corinth which is so
described and, while the element of diversity is recognized,
the particular emphasis of the passage falls upon the unity
of the church.

At 1 Cor. 12:12–27, where the apostle is concerned to
impress on the Corinthian Christians that they have mutual
duties and common interests which they must not neglect, he
asserts, 'You are the body of Christ and severally members of
it' (v. 27). Within the body which is one, there is true
diversity — a multiplicity of function which is necessary to
its being a real body (vv. 17–20). Each member with his
particular function is necessary to the other member for the
good of the body as a whole (vv. 17–21). The Spirit's activity
is specifically mentioned: it is through baptism in or by the
Spirit (*en heni pneumati* v. 13) that members are added to
the body of Christ. The Spirit then refreshes them just as
he graciously gives them gifts for upbuilding (cf. 12:11).

The explicit reference to 'you' (*hymeis*) at the conclusion
of the paragraph (v. 27) makes it plain that this metaphor
of 'the body of Christ' is predicated of the local congregation
at Corinth. This church is neither a *part* of the body of
Christ nor '*a* body of Christ'. Such a description is similar
to that in the opening words of the letter where the congregation is called 'the church (*ekklēsia*) of God which is at
Corinth' (1:2) — it is neither a *part* of the church of God
nor *a* church of God in Corinth. Several commentators have
sought to get round this dilemma by asserting, for example,
that although the 'you' in verse 27 can only refer to the
Corinthian community, it is clear from vv. 13 and 28 that
Paul's perspective includes the whole Church, all the baptized in Christ.[61] But this does not deal with the tension at
all; a good case can be made out for understanding the
church in verse 28 as the congregation at Corinth rather

than some universal church comprising all Christians, while the statement of verse 13 about 'we' being baptized into one body suggests that the image of the body of Christ can be used of Christians generally (or at least a wider group than the believers at Corinth). We thus have two entities being referred to by the one expression — the local congregation at Corinth, which is specifically in mind at v. 27, and a wider group including Paul and possibly others (the 'we' of v. 13). When the distinction between these two is blurred the relationship between them is not satisfactorily explained. In our judgement it seems best to recognize that the phrase 'the body of Christ' can be used comprehensively of all who are united and also of a particular manifestation of that body, in this case a local congregation. This suggestion fits exactly with our interpretation of *ekklēsia* whereby the term can describe a local manifestation (in either a specific congregation or a house church) and a heavenly entity. The same applies, as we have seen, with reference to the temple motif.

Turning to the letter to the Romans, we note, somewhat suprisingly, that it is not addressed to the church (*ekklēsia*) in that city but 'to all who are in Rome'. This has suggested to a number of New Testament scholars that the Christian addressees might have been scattered throughout this capital city rather than being members of one congregation. The body metaphor (at Rom. 12:4, 5), if the above-mentioned suggestion is correct, would then have reference to the believers generally in their relationships with one another, rather than describing them as a single congregation.

At Rom. 12:4f. there is a slight change in terminology from 'the body of Christ' to 'one body in Christ'. However, the same reality is in view.[62] As in 1 Cor. 12 the twin themes of unity and diversity are handled. The notion of the body draws out attention primarily to the union of believers with Christ and then to their relationship with one another.

It is important to observe that in these earlier letters of Paul there is no spelling out of the precise relationship between the church as Christ's body and Christ himself. The union of believers with Christ, and their inter-relationships with one another, are certainly discussed; but Christ's position in relation to the church as his body is left unde-fined.[63] The 'head' of the body has no special position or honour: 'it is counted as an ordinary member'[64] (cf. 1 Cor. 12:21).

b. Later Letters: Colossians and Ephesians

In these two letters there is an advance in the line of thought — described by Best as 'a natural and legitimate development'[65] — involving the setting forth of the relation-ship which the church, as the body of Christ, bears to Christ as head of the body. Here the head is given a place of special pre-eminence which it did not have in the earlier letters. Perhaps as Bruce has suggested the 'advance from the langu-age of simile in 1 Corinthians and Romans to the real and interpersonal involvement expressed in the language of Colossians and Ephesians may have been stimulated by Paul's consideration of the issues involved in the Colossian heresy',[66] but whatever the precise reason, it is clear that the apostle who had repeatedly spoken of the church as the body of Christ *now* draws attention to his headship over the church in terms of an organic relationship in which he exercises control over his people as the head of a body exercises over its various parts. The living relationship between the members is kept in view (though it does not have the same emphasis as in the earlier epistles), while the dependence of the members on Christ for life and power,[67] as well as his supremacy, is reiterated.

At Col. 1:18, a passage we have examined in relation to *ekklēsia* Paul passes from a cosmological perspective to a soteriological one and affirms that Christ is the head of the body (*sōma*), that is the church. That headship, pointing to an organic and living relationship with his people, denotes his control over them and their total dependence on him for life and power. It is the risen Christ who is this head; as the beginning and firstborn in resurrection he is the founder of a new humanity.

Most commentators recognize that here and in v. 24 (where we find the enigmatic detail that Paul's sufferings are 'on behalf of his [Christ's] body, which is the church') the references are broader than to either the local congregation at Colossae or any house-church in that town. Usually it is considered that 'the universal church', scattered throughout the world, is in view. However, we have suggested above that the apostle has a heavenly entity in mind. The body of Christ is a reality which partakes of or participates in the life of heaven, even though in the next breath one may say it is truly present here on earth.

A new element of *growth* is brought out by the body image at Col. 2:19; in a polemical context Paul warns the false teachers[68] at Colossae that they are in danger of rejecting Christ as their head, the one who is the source of continuous life and nourishment by which his body lives, and the source of unity through which it becomes an organic whole.

The teaching on the church as the body of Christ is more fully developed (or at least the implications are more explicitly drawn out) in *Ephesians* than in Paul's earlier letters. Furthermore, this didactic material is of considerable significance to the subject of our paper because it is set forth in relation to the heavenly dimension, a motif that is so important in this letter. The church is first designated as the body of Christ at 1:22–23 in a context where Christ is said to have been raised from the dead, made to sit at the Father's right hand (an expresion that points to his position of supreme favour and honour, and thus his sovereignty) in the heavenly realm. Lincoln remarks: 'The fact that Christ has been exalted to heaven, where he now is (cf. 6:9), is crucial for an understanding of Paul's perspective on heaven in this letter, for it is what has happened to Christ that is determinative for the believer and for the church in their relationship to the heavenly realm'.[69]

Christ's rule extends over both this present evil age and the age to come (1:21). He is supreme over the whole universe (*panta*, v. 22) — heaven and earth, angels and people as well. Because of his position of supremacy in the heavenly realm Christ fills the universe, that is, he fills all things 'in terms of his sovereign rule as he directs them to their divinely appointed goal'[70] (cf. 1:10; 4:10). Christ as the cosmic Lord, Paul then adds, has been given by the Father to the church. In other words, Christ's supremacy over all things is for or on behalf of the church, described as his body (*hētis estin to sōma autou* v. 23). Such a statement shows that the church as Christ's body has a highly significant role in the purposes of God for the cosmos.

Lincoln further observes that 'in Ephesians the focus on the risen and exalted Christ colours the reference to his body and paves the way for the remarkable declaration of the glory of this body, it is his fulness'.[71] At Col. 1:19; 2:9, 10 it is stated that in Christ the fulness of God dwells, and that believers have come to fulness of life in him. Here at Eph. 1:23 the church as his body is called his fulness. The Christ spoken of here is the heavenly Lord whom God has exalted and with whom the church enjoys the benefits of relationship. Two questions immediately arise: first, who are members of this body of Christ? The answer can only be: all believers. To restrict it to some 'universal church' and thus exclude those who have already died in Christ is an unnecessary and unwarranted limitation. Secondly, where is the body of Christ? Clearly where Christ himself is, in heaven. We have already seen that Christ who fills his body with his fulness is the heavenly Lord. Of believers it is said that they have not only been blessed by the Father 'in the heavenly realms with every spiritual blessing in Christ' (1:3), but also that God has already raised them with Christ and seated them with him in that same heavenly realm (2:6). He is seated at the right hand of the Father in heaven. They, as members of his body, are with him in heaven; thus his body is in this heavenly realm too.

This is not to suggest, however, that the church as the body of Christ has no earthly dimension. On the contrary, throughout Ephesians it is clear that believers, both individually and corporately, have responsibilities to Christ as Lord in a whole range of earthly spheres: in marriage and the home, to fellow Christians and to outsiders. If they are truly heavenly-minded they will be of the maximum earthly use! And some of these responsibilities will be examined below.

A particularly important motif in Ephesians is the reconciliation of Jew and Gentile to God 'in one body' (*en heni sōmati*, 2:16) through the cross. In a passage which shows how Gentiles have been made heirs of God's promises (2:11–

22), the apostle focusses attention upon Christ's peace-making work upon the cross. God's purpose was to create out of the two great divisions of mankind 'a single new humanity' in Christ (2:15 NEB). This has been effected by reconciling Jew and Gentile to God in the body of Christ (cf. 3:3–6): the expression 'one body' refers, not to the physical body of Christ on the cross (spoken of as 'his flesh' in v. 15), but to the church of which Jewish and Gentile believers are alike members,[72] and it is equivalent to 'the one new man' of v. 15.

At chapter 4, in a lengthy passage which speaks of unity in diversity within the body of Christ, the apostle, concerned to keep the unity of the Spirit, speaks of one body (*hen sōma*) and one Spirit (v. 4). The unity and growth of the body are particularly in view in verses 11–16. That growth (*auxēsis*, v. 16) or upbuilding (*oikodomē*, v. 12) is said to derive from Christ (*ex hou*, v. 16) and leads to Christ (*eis auton*, v. 15), Fung's comment is worth quoting in full:

> . . . growth out of infanthood into maturity as it takes on the character of its Head (*eis auton*) takes place as (a) the Body is rightly related to its Head (*ex hou*) holding fast to him (cf. Col. 2:19) and receiving nourishment from him (cf. 1:23), and (b) as its members are rightly related to one another, each making its own contribution, according to the measure of its gift and function, to the upbuilding of the whole in love.[73]

In one sense the body of Christ is already complete: it is a true body, not simply part of one. In another sense that body is said to grow to perfection, a process that will be completed only on the final day. The body metaphor reflects the 'already — not yet' tension of the two ages. It is both complete and yet it grows. It is a heavenly entity and yet it is an earthly reality. And it is both present and future with a consummation occurring at the parousia.

Several statements by way of conclusion need to be made.

(1) The metaphor of the body of Christ, employed by Paul to describe the church, is a highly significant one,

being applied to a number of entities and with a range of connotations.

(2) There is no consensus among New Testament scholars as to the origins of this usage (perhaps it came to Paul independently), nor to the precise relationship between the physical body of Christ which was crucified on the cross and the metaphorical body of Christ, that is, the church. A number of passages examined (1 Cor. 10:16f.; 12; Eph. 2:15f.) shows that there is a very close relationship between the two though not an identity. Those who participate in the body and blood of Christ, in other words share in the benefits of his death, are members of that one body.

(3) The expression 'the body of Christ' is applied by Paul in his earlier letters to a local congregation (at Corinth, which is not thought of as a *part* of the body of Christ or *a* body of Christ), to *Christians* (at Rome) *in their relationships* with one another — Christians who were not necessarily members of the same congregation (Rom. 12:4, 5) — and a wider group, possibly including *all Christians* (1 Cor. 12:13), that is, all who have been united to the Lord Jesus Christ. In Colossians and Ephesians the 'body' image is used to denote *a heavenly entity*, that is, all Christians united to the Lord Jesus Christ. He is their life and is seated in heaven at God's right hand while believers themselves have not only been raised with Christ, but also have been made to sit with him in the heavenly places. Neither Paul nor the other New Testament writers spell out the relationship of this heavenly entity to the local congregations or other congregations or other earthly realities, but perhaps it is not inappropriate to suggest (as we noted with reference to 'church' and 'temple') that the local congregations or other groups are earthly manifestations of the heavenly body of Christ.

(4) It is through the Spirit's agency that members are united to the body of Christ. The Spirit refreshes them and graciously gives his gifts for the upbuilding of the body.

(5) The body is a living organic unity in which there is true diversity. Individual members with their multiplicity of functions are each necessary to the other and to the growth of the body as a whole. The unity is also spoken of as a unity between diverse races of the world (Eph. 2:16ff.).

(6) In the earlier letters, Romans and 1 Corinthians, there is no precise spelling out of the relationship between the church as Christ's body and Christ himself. But in Colossians and Ephesians there is an advance in the line of thought from that of a simile to a real and interpersonal involvement when Paul speaks of Christ as the head of the body. He is in an organic, living relationship with his people, being (a) the source of life and power to them, and (b) the one who is supreme over them, exercising loving control and headship.

(7) The notion that the church as the body of Christ occupies a highly significant role in the purposes of God is brought out particularly in Eph. 1:23 where it is asserted that Christ's rule over all things is for or on behalf of the church.

(8) The element of the body's growth is made plain in Colossians and even more so in Ephesians. Its upbuilding is mentioned in the context of unity in diversity; such a growth derives from Christ and leads to Christ as members are rightly related to him, to the head, and to one another.

(9) The church as the body of Christ is described as Christ's fulness (Eph. 1:23). In one sense it is complete, for it is already a body just as there is already a Lord (4:4–6). On the other hand, it grows and will be completed on the final day. The body thus partakes of the tension regularly seen in the New Testament between 'the already' and 'the not yet', between what it is and what it will be. The body is a present reality and yet it is an eschatological (which means future) entity. It partakes of the life of heaven where Christ is; and yet his body is also manifested on earth.

(10) A significant point to observe is that the metaphor of the body of Christ describes the relationships and responsibilities of the members *to Christ* and *to one another*. The image as such does not deal with relationships with the world. This is not to deny that Christians have responsibilities and duties to those outside of Christ. A member of the body who has the gift of evangelism will function as an evangelist in relation to outsiders. As he exercises this gift so the body will grow. But he is described as a member in

relation to Christ and to fellow-members of the body, not with reference to the world.

Thus the body image looks inwards and upwards but not outwards. To speak of the church as the body of Christ which is the extension of his incarnation in the world today, as is done in certain ecclesiastical, missionary and ecumenical circles, certainly exceeds the limits of Paul's teaching and fails, as Bruce points out, to take sufficient account of the contrast between Jesus' sinlessness and the church's sinfulness.[74]

3. The Bride of Christ

The picture of God's people as the bride of Christ[75] is one which is closely related to the metaphor of the body. However, at some points the two pictures are distinct and thus it is appropriate to examine the image of *the bride* separately.

The background to this metaphor of the people of God is clearly the OT where the prophets speak of Yahweh and Israel in terms of the marriage relationship (Ho. 1–3; Is. 54:5–6; 62:4–5; Je. 2:2; 3:20; Ezk. 16.)[76] At Is. 62:4–5, in particular, God expresses his joy over his people, Israel, for she is his bride. In the New Testament the church is the bride of Christ (2 Cor. 11:2; Eph. 5:25–27, 31f.; cf. Rev. 19:7; 21:2; 22:17). 'According to this picture the Lord Jesus is the divine Bridegroom and seeks His bride in love and enters into covenant relations with her'.[77]

The image of the bride and bridegroom first clearly emerges in Paul at 2 Cor. 11:2 where he states, with reference to the congregation at Corinth: 'I am jealous for you with a godly jealousy. I promised you to one husband, to Christ, so that I might present you as a pure virgin to him'. The betrothal (*hērmosamēn*, 'I promised') took place when the Corinthians were converted and the congregation was founded, while the marriage or presentation of the church to Christ will occur at the parousia (cf. Eph . 5:27).

It is in Eph. 5:22–33 that this nuptial metaphor is taken up and developed fully. Paul's primary aim is to give specific teaching about marriage, and in so doing 'bases his exhortations on the relationship of the heavenly bridegroom to his bride, the Church'.[78] There is an interplay between the earthly and the heavenly throughout the passage in which Paul argues from the heavenly marriage to human marriage, rather than the reverse. The marriage between the heavenly bridegroom and the church is the prototype and standard of instructions in human marriage.

Fung[79] has helpfully drawn attention to four features of this image of the church as the bride of Christ: first, the church sustains a two-fold relation to Christ — on the one hand, as a bride the church is distinct form Christ (v. 31); on the other hand, as a wife she is united to him as 'one flesh' (v. 31). Second, Christ's actions on behalf of the church demonstrate his great love, for having given himself up for her (v. 25) he continues to nourish and cherish her (v. 29); the church's duty of Christ is to be subject to him. Third, by means of language of presentation (v. 27), the eschatological note is clearly struck: the consummation of the union awaits the time when the church will be totally glorious. At 2 Cor. 11:2 Paul describes this goal of glorification for the local congregation. Here, Christ will achieve this for his bride, that is, all Christians as members of his body. Finally, as has been noted, the image of the bride has been linked with that of the body.

We thus again observe in Paul's use of an image for the church that there is an alternation between the present and future aspects. The mystery of the marriage union is applied to the presently existing relationship between Christ and the church (v. 32), while the future element in v. 27 (matched by its equivalents in Rev. 19:7ff.; 21:2,9) indicates that the 'already — not yet' tension is ever present.

In addition, the heavenly perspective to that relationship between Christ and his church gives importance to ordinary, daily activities.

D. SOME IMPLICATIONS

Our study has shown that the term *ekklēsia* and the images of temple, body and bride when used of the people of

God describe a number of related entities, such as a local congregation and a heavenly assembly, or Christians in a particular city as well as all who are united to Jesus Christ. We have observed, on the one hand, that the earthly entity is best regarded as a manifestation of the heavenly reality, for example a heavenly gathering around Christ, a heavenly temple, or the body of Christ in heaven. The New Testament, however, does not precisely designate the relationship between the two as a 'manifestation', although it certainly rules out the possibility of the earthly entity as a 'part' of some universal or heavenly reality.

In addition, we have noted that each of the images partakes of the tension regularly seen in the New Testament between the present and the future, the 'already' and the 'not yet'. So, for example, believers are described as God's temple in whom he, by his Spirit, already dwells. OT promises find their fulfilment in his people, the temple. But when the motif of the temple is conjoined with that of the body the element of growth is emphasized. Furthermore, in the Book of the Revelation the metaphor of the temple describes that which is final, for it points forward to the perfected presence of God and the consummation of all things.

What then are the responsibilities which the New Testament sets before the *people of God* who live in the overlap of the ages, between the first and second comings of Christ, and who already partake of the life of heaven while still dwelling on earth? For a comprehensive answer to this question it would be necessary to study each of the relevant passages we have noted (and a good many more besides!) and then synthesize the conclusions. However, instead of this we shall examine *one* passage which presupposes believers' incorporation into Christ, focusses attention on the heavenly realm while recognizing earthly responsibilities, partakes of the 'already — not yet' tension and sets forth a series of wide-ranging admonitions. I refer to Col. 3:1–4:6.[80]

At Col. 3:1–4, in a short pivotal paragraph, Paul exhorts the Colossians to pursue those things that belong to the heavenly realm where Christ reigns. The grounds for the admonition are two-fold: first, the Colossians died to that old order with its elemental spirits (2:20), its ascetic and enslaving regulations, visionary experiences and useless will-worship. Second, as those who have already been raised with Christ they now participate in his resurrection life. So their lives are to be different. Their interests are to be centred on Christ; their minds, aims, ambitions, in fact their whole outlook, are to be centred on that heavenly realm where he reigns and where their lives truly belong. The continuous ongoing effort required for such a cast of mind does not come automatically. That realm is to be sought diligently, and it is where Christ is, seated as king in the place of honour.

For the moment their heavenly life remains hidden, secure with Christ in God (3:3). Their new life as Christians in Christ is not visible to others and, in some measure, is hidden from themselves. It will only be fully manifest when Christ, who embodies that life, appears at his parousia (v. 4). Indeed the day of the revelation of the *Son* of God will be the day of the revelation of the *sons* of God. That manifestation will take place 'in glory' for it will involve the sharing of Christ's likeness and the receiving of the glorious resurrection body.

The exhortations to 'seek the things above' (v. 1) and to 'set the mind on the things above' (v. 2) find concrete expression and application in the following imperatives. Four distinctive catchwords of early Christian catechesis are found at the head of their respective paragraphs: 'put to death' (3:5–11; also 'put off', v. 8), 'put on' (2:12–f17), 'be subject' (3:18–4:1) and 'watch and pray' (4:2–6). Being heavenly-minded does not mean living in the clouds!

In the first of these paragraphs the apostle exhorts those who died with Christ (2:20; 3:3) to put to death whatever belongs to their earthly nature (v. 5). Using two catalogues of vices (vv. 5,8) similar to those found among pagan moralists and in the anti-pagan polemic and Jewish propagandists, Paul first describes five sins which must be rejected utterly by these believers of the Lycus valley; he moves from the outward manifestations of sin ('sexual immorality') to the inward cravings of the heart' ('ruthless greed'). Then the apostle exhorts them to discard their old repulsive habits of improper speech like a set of worn-out clothes (v. 8).

The Colossian Christians have put on the new man which is being renewed in the Creator's image (v. 10). Within this new humanity in Christ there is no inferiority of one class to another; men and women of completely diverse origins are gathered together in unity in Christ, sharing a common allegiance to their Lord. Christ is all that matters; he permeates and indwells all members of his body, regardless of race, class or background.

As those who have been raised with Christ the believers at Colossae are addressed by means of privileged titles — in fact, the very terms used of Christ himself: they are 'the elect of God', 'holy' and 'beloved' (3:12). Consequently they are exhorted to don as garments the graces of Christ himself: 'heartfelt compassion, kindness, lowliness, gentleness and longsuffering'. Each of these articles of clothing indicates how they should behave as God's elect in their dealings with others, particularly fellow-believers.

For those who live in the overlap of the ages Christ himself, who is the Lord of peace, is to be present and ruling in the midst (3:15). With an exhortation that is universal in its scope, covering every aspect of life (v. 17), the apostle makes it plain that every activity is to be performed in obedience to the Lord Jesus and acccompanied by the giving of thanks to God through him.

To those who have already been raised with Christ and who are urged to seek the things above, the household rules (3:18–4:1) indicate how that life which is submitted to the lordship of Jesus Christ is to be concretely expressed. No area of personal existence stands outside his control; and so the life ruled from above where Christ is reigning turns out to be a life in marriage, parenthood and everyday work.

Finally, in the concluding section of his catechetical material (4:2–6) the apostle admonishes those who live in the tension between the 'already' and the 'not yet' to persist in prayer as they look forward in anticipation of Christ's return, his glorious manifestation (3:4). While they live in the overlap of the ages they are to behave wisely toward non-Christians. This will involve them being tactful yet bold in their Christian witness as they make the most of every available opportunity. Their time is limited for the day of the Lord Jesus draws near.

Suprisingly in neither Colossians 3:1–4:6 nor elsewhere in the New Testament where the theme of our paper is touched upon is there anything directly stated about behaviour within 'a revolutionary setting'. There are no direct instructions in this sort of context, and any specific life-style which might appear appropriate in such a setting would need to be consistent with the above-mentioned admonitions.

3

Worship in the New Testament Church

RUSSELL P. SHEDD

INTRODUCTION

Christianity is by its very nature bi-polar. These two poles are faith's content, grounded in its revealed message; and practical worship, through which the believer and God maintain fellowship. They are not strengthened by repelling or ignoring each other but are vitalized by mutual support. A. W. Tozer's appraisal of worship as evangelical Christianity's 'missing jewel'[1] reflects the unhealthy dichotomy between the truth proclaimed and the vitality of worship today. We may take exception to the observation, 'Everywhere believers are losing interest in merely going through the motions at church',[2] for millions of Protestants, Catholics and Orthodox Christians appear quite content to participate in hollow, rigid forms with only a vague awareness of the biblical conception of worship in Spirit and truth.

Christians are generally unconscious that their worship reflects the practical theology of their community. The Puritan stamp on the dictum that 'the chief end of man is to glorify God and to enjoy him forever' is unmistakable.

The Westminster divines, with keen spiritual insight, focused the significance of man's whole existence on glorifying God and delighting in his fellowship, because that was simply the practical outcome of their beliefs.[3] Man-centered worship tends increasingly to deny the heart reality we confess. On the one hand, law threatens to displace grace as the foundational motive for adoring God. Both habit and the pursuit of spiritual peace must be suspect when we search for a biblical rationale for worshipping God.[4] In sum, liturgy is theology acted out,[5] our human response to God and his favour. But the forms persist while the content evaporates or shifts its centre from God to man. When liberalism denies the reality of a God 'who is there', it cannot avoid transmuting religious verities into myths. The result is seen everywhere in the secularization of the 'post-Christian man come of age'. When liberation theology seeks to contextualize worship in a programme of sociopolitical action conscience-raising becomes identified with God-awareness in the process of history.

Evangelicals tend to divorce the biblically–founded centrality of Christ's lordship from practical daily living, so that worship becomes, in effect, compartmentalized into hour-long capsules, and this despite their protestations that it is important to 'call on the name of the Lord together'. But the New Testament projects a vision of worship that infuses all of life with the presence and glory of God. The objective of this study is to show, through an examination of the conceptions of time, the temple, sacrifice and priesthood, how the New Testament has recast Old Testament forms of worship without annulling the importance of the meeting of the church.

FORM AND FREEDOM

From its inception, worship has been beset by two perils: 1) a formalism that deifies the external modes of liturgy while mortifying any vital relationship with God; 2) a spontaneity which because of disarray and confusion fails to stimulate any serious encounter with the God who searches for true

worshippers (Jn. 4:23).[6] The church of Corinth was free
and spontaneous to a fault. Liberty reigned in full, which
spawned confusion (cf. 1 Cor. 14:40). By cherishing freedom
the church lost sight of sanctification and community.

The risen Jesus condemned the church of Ephesus for
the loss of its first love (Rev. 2:4). This well-worn phrase
suggests that freedom had been eclipsed by formality. Of
Thyatira, Christ says, 'I know your deeds, and your love
and faith and service and perseverance . . . (2:19 NASB);
nevertheless we are also told that 'Jezebel' was continuing
to seduce the Lord's servants. Christ's incisive word is that
through judgment he will make all churches know that he
tries minds and hearts (v. 23). Neither correct form nor
freedom of expression should bear ultimate significance in
worship. Heart love and an obedient personal relationship
to God must be kept paramount. A. P. Gibbs defines worship
as 'the occupation of the heart, not with its needs, or even
with its blessings, but with God himself'.[7]

Jesus' condemnation of his contemporaries' religious practice and his own break with tradition supports this view.
Quoting Isaiah, he said, 'This people honours me with their
lips, but their heart is far from me. But in vain do they
worship me . . .' (Mk. 7:6f. NASB). For many Jews of Jesus'
day, both prayer and Scripture reading were most acceptable
to God when spoken in Hebrew. For Jesus the language was
not important — he spoke and prayed in Aramaic and
(possibly) Greek. The heart attitude was all-important.

Man's inauthenticity, as Bultmann has contended, consists primarily in his religion which too often is a veiled
form of rebellion against God. Jesus' negative evaluation of
Jewish traditional religion explains in part the radical break
which sundered the New Testament church from its Jewish
antecedents. While a dissimilar form of worship emerges
in the New Testament because of the Christian understanding of time, the temple, sacrifice and the priesthood, there
is no break with the Old Testament ideal of true worship.
Men such as Abel, Enoch, Noah, Abraham, Moses and
David were men of faith (Heb. 11); they responded with
worship in accord with God's standards. A person is not
free to worship as he or she wishes, but only in 'truth', that

is, according to God's commands. External expressions of adoration grew naturally out of a genuine relationship with God. Concluding from his analysis of Isaiah 6 that 'right worship is the proper acknowledgement of divine headship over nation and over the world',[8] W. J. Dumbrell accurately and succinctly summarizes the Old Testament ideal.

WORSHIP AND TIME

Worship, when expressed in ritual, demands time. Under the old covenant God made provision for daily, weekly, yearly and even (through the Jubilee year) generational time periods for fulfilling Israel's cultic obligations. The daily sacrifice (Num. 28:1–8), the Sabbath or seven day rest, the first days of the month and the five annual pre-exilic feasts were divinely ordained. 'Appointed times' (Num. 29:39)[9] were deemed central to the expression of the adoration of God in Israel, because past events in which God acted must never be forgotten.[10]

The Sabbath, the weekly day of rest and worship, is a prime example of consecrated time. While some pronounce the Sabbath a 'unique creation of the Hebrew religious genius and one of the most valuable Hebrew contributions to the civilization of mankind',[11] the Bible simply attributes the sanctity of the seventh day to God's law. It is grounded in God's rest after creation (Gen. 1:1–2:3). The fourth commandment enjoins its strict observance. It was both blessed and hallowed by God (Exod. 20:11). Being an integral part of the covenant, Israel accepted Sabbath observance as a required sign of national allegiance to God (Exod. 31:13; cf. Ne. 9:14). In sum, this weekly feast was instituted to remind man of his responsibility to worship God at 'stated times and places'[12] as well as to provide needed bodily rest.[13]

Despite the cessation of all manual labour, the priests continued their service (Lev. 24:8; Num. 28:9, 10; Matt. 12:5). Circumcision was performed (Lev. 12:3). The Sabbath, although only a weekly observance, was included in 'the appointed feasts of the Lord' (Lev. 23:1–3), 'a holy convocation', not to be profaned. Whether visiting a prophet

(2 Ki. 4:23) or participating in the temple worship (cf. 1 Chr. 9:32; 23:31; 2 Chr. 2:4; 8:13), the Hebrews who were engaged in such employment thought of it as naturally coinciding with the Sabbath's holiness. Isaiah challenged his readers to turn from their own pleasures and 'delight in the Lord' (58:13f.). Many other passages could be cited to show what significance the day was meant to have for the Israelite (such as Ps. 92).[14]

During and following the Exile, the prominence of the Sabbath increased. The rise of the synagogue further added to the centrality of worship on the Sabbath (cf. Lk. 4:16).[15] The sanctity of the Sabbath is reflected by attitudes such as the writer of Jubilees (50:13) expresses. He calls for the death penalty to punish Sabbath breaking. The Mishnah is more lenient, prescribing only a sin offering (Sanh. 7:8).

The critical importance of the Sabbath illustrates the prominence that other divinely appointed times had for the religious Israelite. Extreme caution was exercised in marking the beginning of the Passover. It was considered highly improper to celebrate one of the Lord's feasts on any day other than that prescribed by the divine instructions.[16] Any proper observance of the other holy convocations or feasts necessarily included strict adherence to the divinely scheduled times and seasons.[17]

For Christians, in the new covenant relationship with God, time is fundamentally important because of the salvation that God has wrought in history.[18] That major moment has brought to man history's meaning. The true people of God look forward because they believe in the 'blessed hope' of the return of Christ in time and a physical resurrection of the body at the terminus of history. For this reason it is all the more suprising that worship by the Spirit, under the aegis of the new age, breaks so decisively with the conception of 'appointed times' for worship prescribed under the old age.

Jesus repeatedly expressed his opposition to all that was legalistic in the contemporary Jewish manner of keeping the Sabbath (cf. Matt. 12:1–4; Mk. 3:1–5; Lk. 13: 10–17; 14:1–6; Jn. 5:1–18; 9:1–41). From celebration of God's goodness expressed in creation, the contemporary Jewish attitude sometimes transformed it into a test of loyalty to God as well as a meritorious work. Jesus reminded his critics that the Sabbath was made for man (Mk. 2:27),[19] but he also proclaimed himself to be the Lord of the Sabbath. His father did not cease his activity on the Sabbath (Jn. 5:17); therefore, neither would the Son (vv. 17f). By this claim the Lord pointed to the covenant reality in which God would always abide with his people. Old Testament laws governing Sabbath observances reach their fulfilment in the Christian Sabbath rest (Heb. 4:1, 3, 7-11), incorporating all time.

As soon as the new creation (2 Cor. 5:17) was inaugurated,[20] the first Christians adopted a distinct view of time and worship.[21] Time apparently became universalized or desacralized. But in fact, in keeping with the lordship of the exalted Christ, the Christian world-view sanctified *all time*. No doubt the Jewish Church continued to observe sabbaths and to celebrate the Jewish festivals,[22] but for the most perceptive the motivation no longer lay in a divine obligation, and the festivals were regarded merely as a cultural phenomenon. The weekly synagogue meetings offered evangelists a golden opportunity to proclaim Jesus as the Saviour Messiah (Acts 9:20; 13:14; 14:1; 17:1, 2, 10; 18:4); but in all likelihood Christian Jews such as Paul counted their participation in the synagogue worship or in a festival such as Pentecost (Acts 20:16) as no more than 'being all things to all men' (1 Cor. 9:20). As for the Gentile church, the Sabbath was considered as an inseparable part of the Jewish yoke to be shed along with the bondage to the whole ritual law (cf. Gal. 5:1; Col. 2:14). If the young churches were to consider 'days, months and seasons and years' (Gal. 4:10) essential to the worship of God, they would fall back into the slavery of the weak or beggarly elements or to the 'spirits' (*stoicheia*) which had formerly shackled them (Gal. 4:9).[23]

We may be quite sure that this bold shattering of the former consecration of special times originated in Jesus' own teaching and practice. He offered the only authentic 'rest' to all who, burdened by sin and guilt, would accept his yoke (Matt. 11:28-30).[24] The inspired author of Hebrews urges his readers to take full advantage of God's rest. No longer a literal day of the week, the rest has been transposed into the salvation heritage that faithful believers in Christ both share and await (4:1–11).[25] One may look in vain for any hint to support a belief that there remained required hours for worshipping God. True, Hebrews does emphasize the need for diligence to enter God's sabbath-rest (v. 11), but 'sacred times' have no part in the book's extended discussion of the new covenant worship. The writer was properly concerned that some Christians failed to meet regularly with the Christian community to worship (10:24, 25). They were bound to lose crucial spiritual benefits. However, neither specified days nor the frequency of the meetings of the church comes within his purview unless we are to see in Hebrews 3:13 an indication of a daily meeting. 'The gospel rest to which the Sabbath had always pointed' had dawned.[26]

From Acts it can be concluded that the members of the Jerusalem congregation met daily (2:46; 5:42. Lk. 24:53 has 'continually').[27] But we assume that no one was under divine obligation to attend all the gatherings. Rather, sufficient motivation to attend regularly some worship gathering, whether in the temple or in private homes, arose from the internal compulsion of the new found joy in worshipping the Lord.[28]

By the middle of the second century Justin had identified Christian living as a perpetual Sabbath which consists in abstaining from sin, not work.[29] Irenaeus understood the Sabbath to be a symbol of God's kingdom, still future, in which those who have served God 'shall in a state of rest, partake of God's table'.[30] Tertullian declared, 'We have nothing to do with Jewish festivals'.[31] Origen said of the perfect Christian, 'All his days are the Lord's and he is always keeping the Lord's day', even while he recognized that the majority were unable to keep every day as a festival.[32]

The New Testament writers (as well as the early Fathers) perceived that the new age requires that we see all of time as God's gift, suitable to any and all sacred activity. This may be the meaning underlying Jesus' prophetic pronouncement at Jacob's Well, 'An hour is coming, and now is when the true worshippers shall worship the Father in Spirit and truth' (Jn. 4:23).[33] For all who through faith and obedience abide in Christ as the true Vine (Jn. 15:1–11), 'holy' hours, days, or weeks become contradictory. The Spirit communicates the abiding presence of God in and with his people, both *in* and *out of* any sacred time reference. Paul exhorts the churches of Asia to buy up the opportunities, that is, time, because the days are evil (Eph. 5:15; Col. 4:5). Timothy must preach the word and stay at his post when it is convenient and when it is not (2 Tim. 4:2). These passages do not reflect any division between sacred and secular time, but the conflict between the Christian age and the world which is passing away (1 Cor. 7:31). The 'world' is equivalent to the 'present evil age'.[34]

Too frequently, down through history, set times of ecclesiastical forms would usurp the spirit of urgency which the 'last days' inculcated in the first generation of Christians. When the fire of the Spirit burns low, the external compulsion to sacralize the form intensifies.[35]

According to Paul's formula for the institution of the Last Supper, the phrase 'as often as you drink' is repeated twice (1 Cor. 11:25f.). Instead of establishing a schedule for the most important regular Christian celebration, Jesus and Paul left the decision concerning the frequency of the church's meeting up to its participants. As in the case of taking bodily nourishment, Christians could unite to observe the supper as often as they wished. Spiritual hunger would compel them to 'eat of Christ's flesh and drink his blood', symbolized in the bread and the wine (cf. Jn. 6:53–63). Jesus taught that partaking of such spiritual nourishment is vital to Christians who are abiding in Christ (v. 56). To less high-minded seekers for Jesus' provision of natural bread, he said, 'Work for the food that endures to eternal life, which the Son of Man shall give to you . . .' (6:27).[36] Later in the dialogue the Jews requested, 'Lord, evermore give us this bread' (v. 34). Following Jesus' death and resurrection, this bread would be provided 'evermore'; but not as the crowd understood the term — rather though Jesus' death as the 'bread of Life' (v. 35).[37] Within the same constellation of ideas, Jesus announced that those who 'hunger and thirst after righteousness will be filled' (Matt. 5:6). Similarly, in the model prayer that Jesus gave his disciples, the central petition calls for 'daily bread' or the 'bread of tomorrow' (*epiousios*), which they should eat regularly (or perhaps 'daily') (Matt. 6:11; Lk. 11:3). It seems likely that Jesus was referring to the same 'bread' for which the Jews were to work, which was Christ himself.[38]

It is mortally dangerous for believers to eat and drink of Christ in a formal, material way, as the redeemed people of God did in the wilderness, yet fail to profit from assimilating his holy life into themselves (1 Cor. 10:3–12). Paul incisively dissociates himself from any belief in magical properties in the Supper. The form is of no essential value in and of itself, if the deeper meaning is not transposed into practical holy living, all of which pertains to the outcome of true worship.

Just as Sunday came to symbolize the new beginning, a weekly Easter celebration,[39] so it was natural for the early church to adopt that day for public worship (Acts 20:7; 1 Cor. 16:2; Rev. 1:10).[40] Only the wealthy and the free would be able to relinquish their activities; slaves would have to secure permission to abandon their regular duties. Night hours therefore offered the most practical opportunity for the diverse social classes to meet together (Acts 20:7).[41] In that case the meeting would begin on Saturday night and continue until its close, often at dawn on Sunday morning (cf. Acts 20:11).[42]

The gathering of the community on the Lord's day gave eloquent witness to the reality of the new age.[43] Such meetings were regarded as a foretaste of the unending glory to be enjoyed in heaven. The breaking of bread each week (or whenever the church met)[44] symbolized God's unstinting giving of the true manna, his Son. The climactic 'Maranatha' invocation, proclaimed by the participants, drew attention to the presence of the risen Christ, joining the worshipping community according to his promise (Matt. 18:20). Thus the same Lord who had promised never to leave his disciples (Matt. 28:20), until the age's end, made his conscious presence felt among his people. When Christians came together in Christ's name, individuals indwelt by the Holy Spirit might gain a unique awareness of God's presence.[45]

To contend that this manifestation of God's presence held little significance for New Testament Christians would surely be false. The worship gathering provided the opportunity for expressions of joyful praise, doctrinal and ethical instruction and a vital sense of God's nearness.

John was in the Spirit on the 'Lord's Day' (Rev. 1:10), which suggests that it was a day that had special significance for worship, especially when we note the prominence of worship throughout the book of Revelation.[46] Apparently the church in Corinth also met regularly on Sunday (cf. 1 Cor. 16:2). Although no order was given either by Jesus or by the apostles, the first day became the common day of worship. Thus the traditional 'sanctity' of the first day of the week was born in the church.

The Old Testament stipulated specified times and ways of worship in Israel's feasts. The Passover and Feast of Unleaved Bread required meticulous attention to detail regarding time and ritual. But Paul's conception of the church's archetypal Passover has now been fulfilled in Christ: 'our passover Lamb has been killed, so let us celebrate the feast not with the old leaven, neither with malice [evil disposition] and wickedness [active practice] but with the unleavened bread [plural, suggesting the cakes eaten during the feast] of sincerity and truth' (1 Cor. 5:7f.).[47] The Jewish scheduled prayers have been recast into the Christian's concept of unceasing prayer (cf. Rom. 1:9; 1 Thess. 5:17; 2 Tim. 1:3). Such praying as believers offer up would be intermittent, like coughing, but the significance of scheduled hours for prayer was diminished, if not obliterated.

Again, just as the Sabbath became the Christian's spiritual rest, so the Passover was transposed from an annual festival celebrating the emancipation of Israel from slavery in Egypt, to a continual Christian celebrating (note the present tense cited above) of the significance of the cross in delivering believers from the power of sin. The feast of the former age has its new and only valid continuing significance in the day-to-day life of Christians. The specified time of the old ritual has been universalized, for it is important to avoid sin every day of the year.

Consider also the Feast of Tabernacles in the new conception of Jesus. No longer a remembering of the wilderness wandering, it now points to the unceasing flood of 'living water' which would flow from our Lord's own pierced body.[48] The meaning of the Jewish form was transposed by Jesus and offered to his followers as the permanent giving of the Spirit. All who come to Jesus in faith, and drink, will participate in the blessing to which the Jewish celebration pointed (Jn. 7:37–39). Jesus also assured the woman of Samaria that the water he would give to any who thirst and drink would then become a spring, continually overflowing with the life of the new age (a reference to the Spirit, Jn. 4:14). The freedom effected by the abiding Holy Spirit (cf. 2 Cor. 3:17) shatters the form, yet it gives visible expression to the new spiritual reality of the union of the Master with the followers.

But nothing that we have said above in any way contradicts the truth that 'human beings need to stop their involvement in physical/material pursuits and devote significant periods of time to the Lord in a regular, recurring cycle.'[49] Nevertheless, the New Testament outlook is that the physical and material world must be approached from a spiritual standpoint.

THE TEMPLE

In ancient Israel's worship, sacred *space* was comparable in importance to divinely appointed *times*. God chose special locations to reveal himself throughout Old Testament history (cf. Gen. 28:18; Exod. 3:1). Especially, after the Exodus and the institution of the law, the raising of the tabernacle meant the localizing of the glory of God in the Holy Place. God prohibited Israel from erecting sacrificial altars in any place other than where his name resided (Deut. 12:5; 11; 15:20; 16:2; 17:8). In the inaccessible recesses of the Holy of Holies, that awesome holy room in the tabernacle and temple where God 'dwelt', rested the mercy-seat and the ark that held the tables of his law. There blood of atonement for the sins of the nation was sprinkled in the most solemn of all annual rites of worship (Lev. 16). 'Worship is the protocol by which one may enter the divine presence.'[50]

The Holy of Holies represented Mt. Sinai, where God

met Moses, gave him his word and manifested the divine glory.[51] Thus the tabernacle and later the temple became historical extensions of the original meeting of God with Moses on Sinai, the archetypal model of worship for God's elect people. Toward God's dwelling place prayers ought to be made (2 Chr. 6:20, 40; 7:15). There sacrifices would meet with his pleasure, but not elsewhere (Deut. 16:2). There the consecrated first-born of the flock and a tithe of the land's produce were to be eaten (Deut. 12:18; 15:2).

In the New Testament, Jesus showed high regard for the temple. He purified it to enhance its holiness (cf Mk. 11:15–18; Matt. 23:16–22) and to render it a credible house of prayer for all nations.[52] Yet despite the identification of the temple with 'the Father's house' (Jn. 2:16), it was nevertheless doomed.[53] Jesus declared that a temple 'not made with hands' was destined to replace the awesome majesty of the Herodian architecture (Mk. 14:58; Matt. 26:61). The end of the temple would occur in connection with his death (through the rent veil) and the Roman invasion (Mk. 15:38 par; 13:2 par). The resurrection of Jesus' body from the grave would then create a temple of a different order to replace it (Jn. 2:19–21) — a conception comprehensible to the disciples only after the resurrection (v. 22), and only with the aid of the Paraclete (cf. Jn. 16:13ff.).

Further aspects of Jesus' pronouncement are to be found in his conversation with the woman of Sychar. The holy places such as Gerazim and Jerusalem would no more demand the gathering of true worshippers. Both Jews and Samaritans would no longer gain access to God via ceremonies performed in the sacred precincts of their traditional worship. The divine presence would be found uniquely in Christ[54] and by extension in his community. This new truth was reiterated by Stephen and provoked a violent reaction on the part of the Jews (Acts 6:14–7:50).[55] Clearly we are meant to understand that Jesus' resurrection life and the coming of the Spirit would annul 'holy' geographical distinctions. The shekinah glory, formerly localized in the temple, would then abide exclusively in the Son (Jn. 1:14) and be shared with all who abide in him (Jn. 17:22).

All believers united to him through faith form, with and

in the risen Christ, the Father's house. Jesus, being both the way to the Father and also the believer's destiny, provides in himself the 'dwelling places' (*monai* Jn. 14:2, 'rooms' such as travellers use) for believing pilgrims. Traditionally, the Father's house has been understood to be the believer's celestial home. However, John's 'realized eschatology' allows for this same temple to exist undivided on earth as well as in heaven. Jesus is both the resurrection and the life so that 'everyone who lives and believes in him will never die' (11:26). Believers are all occupants of the 'rooms' in the safety of the Father's house. There is only one temple which unites all of God's people into a single corporate unity.[56] A 'dwelling place' must be closely linked to the 'abiding' (*menein*) of the disciple-branches, as the root term 'abide' indicates (Jn. 15:4–7). To those who love and keep Jesus' word, he gives the assurance of the love of both Father and Son, as all three come (through the Spirit) to make in believers their trinitarian abode (*monē*, 14:23). The link between the eschatological temple and the raised body of Jesus is completed, then, in the formation of the temple composed of gathered believers. Local churches may be regarded as 'rooms' in the world-wide House of God. Through Jesus believers know the Father (Jn. 14:10). To pray in Jesus' name assures the petitioner that he will receive an answer (v. 12). Jesus will intercede on their behalf, in response to which God will send another (*allos*, 'one of the same sort') Helper (*paraklētos*, 'advocate', 'encourager') who will dwell in them. Thus, rather than existing as scattered orphans, the disciples will be formed into a family (14:16–18). It is precisely the Spirit, the paraclete, who makes possible a representation of the life of Jesus in the church which bears his image (Col. 3:10).

The New Testament consistently presents the essential unity of the church with Jesus Christ, actualized through the presence of the Spirit, just as the Shekinah glory filled the temple (1 Ki. 8:10f.; 2 Chr. 7:1f).[57] Only those born of the Spirit may see the Kingdom of God (Jn. 3:3,5). Jesus has received the Spirit without measure (3:34) and it is he whom the Father has appointed to baptize in or with the Spirit (1:33; cf. Mk. 1:8 pars.). True worship, then, must be offered to the Father in response to the Spirit and controlled by the truth (Jn. 4:23). Paul reinforces this outlook in Philippians: 'We are the circumcision, who worship in[58] the Spirit of God and glory in Christ Jesus . . .' (3:3 NASB). There can be no acceptable worship apart from the Spirit.

It would be erroneous to conclude, from this reinterpretation of the temple, that God manifests himself only to *individuals* in whom his Spirit abides. Rather, we are invited in the New Testament to recognize the crucial importance of the meeting of the Lord's people to hear the Word, to praise his majestic glory through song, to pray, to confess sins, and to celebrate the ordinances (or sacraments). It is at such times as these that the peculiar nature of God's presence amongst his children is experienced. Such corporate worship anticipates the joyful unity of the heavenly assembly of the church (cf. Heb. 12:22–24 as well as Rev. 4–22 *passim*). In the gathering for worship the reality of the 'temple' is to be manifested as the dwelling place of God, though it be made up of 'living stones' rather than wood, stone and mortar.

Paul challenged the Corinthians on the grounds that their factions negated the unity and sanctity of God's temple (3:16), and therefore impeded their worship. 'The temple of God is holy and that is what you are' (v. 17). Christ is both its foundation (v. 11) and corner stone (Eph. 2:20). He provides its frame and its structure. The eschatological community is being built into a holy temple (*naos*, 'shrine') in the Lord, a single, dynamically growing building, in which God dwells in the Spirit (Eph. 2:21f.),[59] because the members meet together to edify one another mutually and in it be edified (1 Cor. 14:26). Paul can therefore identify the church as those 'that in every place call upon the name of Jesus Christ our Lord' (1 Cor. 1:2), presumably in the assemblies of the 'saints'. We must not see any disjunction between the universal temple and each local congregation that composes it, also called a 'temple', or of the individual believer.[60] In this way, the ancient promise made to Israel has been fulfilled. 'I will walk among you and be your God and you shall be my people' (Lev. 26:11f.; Zech. 2:11; cf. Ps. 47:9).

Both the proclamation of Jesus as Lord (2 Cor. 4:5) and

the edifying of believers through community worship (cf. 1
Cor. 14:25f.), suggest that the temple of the new age was
conceived as a concrete, visible reality being 'constructed'
in its worship gatherings.[61] The Corinthians are really God's
building (1 Cor. 3:9), and so each 'builder' must be careful
how he builds (v. 10). Participants in the Corinthian services
were expected to contribute 'a psalm [a hymn, possibly
composed by the worshipper], a teaching, a revelation, a
tongue or an interpretation' (1 Cor. 14:26). But such participation may be an influence for good or evil depending on
the intentions and content of the contributing leaders and
their messages. Combustible materials, rather than 'gold,
silver, precious stones', were being used to build God's
temple (cf. 3:12). Irreparable loss will accrue to the 'builder'
who unwisely 'builds' without regard to the nature of the
'building of God'. Thus Paul condemns the use of the
meetings to promote carnal, factional interests at the expense
of sacred unity. Supremacy is Christ's alone (1 Cor. 1:10–
13). Similarly Paul chides the church in Corinth for gathering, 'not for the better, but for the worse' (1 Cor. 11:17 AV).
The purpose of the worship meeting can be served only by
expressions of sacrificial love of one another. Thus God will
be exalted in the midst of his people. Thus the world will
acknowledge the disciples as Christ's own (Jn. 13:35).

Along the same lines, Paul objects to the Corinthians'
immorality, drawing on the implications of the sanctity of
the temple. 'Do you not know that your [*plural*] body
[*singular*] is a temple of the Holy Spirit who is in [*or 'among'*]
you, whom you have from God and you are not your own?'
(6:19). To each Christian he assigns the responsibility of
maintaining the holiness of the entire body-temple. Because
it belongs to Christ, prostitution cuts (*aras*, 'taking')[62] the
erring member from Christ (v. 15), inasmuch as he has
become 'one body with a harlot'. Such a union is thereby
contrasted with the 'one spirit' (i.e. spiritual body) formed
by joining or marrying the Lord (v. 16).[63] Paul's use of the
temple theme in 1 Corinthians was made to convey both its
holiness and unity in love (cf. ch. 13).[64] But we must not
misunderstand what Paul writes. He does not mean that the
Church is 'Christ continued, the Incarnation continued . . .

In being the Body of Christ the Church meets her Lord; she does not prolong Him but she expresses Him here and now. She does not replace him, but makes him visible, demonstrates him without being confounded with him'.[65]

Peter presents a temple theology in his First Letter in agreement with that of both Jesus and Paul. For Peter, Christ is the living stone chosen by God. Formed out of that original foundation, regenerated believers by coming to him are 'built up as a spiritual house' (2:4f). The verbs, 'coming' and 'being built up' (pres. tenses) signify the meeting of believers[66] to worship God through the risen Christ. The temple is being formed by the numerical growth and the vital union that the individual worshippers (called 'living stones') experience with Christ and with each other.

The object of the temple's erection is to become a 'holy priesthood, to offer up spiritual sacrifices acceptable to God through Jesus Christ' (v. 5 NASB). Temple and priesthood are closely integrated figures. The first expresses the unity of the church, the second refers to its ministry. The nature of the offerings that the new age priesthood offer is supposed to correspond closely to the sacrificial Servant's obedience offered during Jesus' earthly life. The copy book (*hypogrammon*) Jesus left must be followed by walking in his footsteps (2:21).

SACRIFICE IN THE CHURCH

Because man is a sinner, he needs a propitiating sacrifice to remove any separating offense so that he can have fellowship with God. As 'Moses . . . stood in the breach before him, to turn away his wrath from destroying them' (Ps. 106:23), so priest and sinner under the aegis of the old covenant united in offering a sacrificial victim to propitiate God.[67] By following the divine orders sinners enjoyed the blessedness of sins covered (Ps. 32:1) or blotted out (Isa. 43:25; Ps. 51:1, 9). There is, nevertheless, a basic truth to be remembered. 'God is not acted upon by means of priestly sacrifice . . . It is actually God himself who performs the act of forgiveness and atonement, but the priestly cultus is designed to answer to his act and bear witness to his cleansing of the sinner.'[68]

Four distinct types of sacrifice were prescribed.

1) The burnt offering (from the Septuagint), literally 'that which ascends' (Lev. 1; 6:8–13). It produced a 'savour of satisfaction' so that from the altar in the court of God's house a perpetual fire and the twice-daily sacrifice might symbolize man's response to the promise, 'there will I meet with the people of Israel' (Exod. 29:38–43).[69] Only the best animal, an unblemished male, could be offered, which suggests utter devotion. The laying on of the hands portrayed complete identification.[70]

2) The cereal offering (Lev. 2; 6:14–18), literally a 'gift'. Offered along with the burnt offering and the peace offering, it required 'the salt of the convenant with your God' (2:13). The 'memorial portion' offered by fire and with frankincense to the Lord was to bring the convenant to God's remembrance. The symbolism suggested that God was the honoured guest.[71]

3) The peace offering (Lev. 3 and 7:11–34). Following a preparatory ritual identical to that which introduced the burnt offering, the offerer ate the sacrifice with rejoicing before the Lord. The resulting feast was not allowed to last more than a day (7:15f.) to make sure that a number of friends be included. It expressed the wholeness and well-being denoted by the *shalom* of God, shared with priests and colleagues.[72]

4) The sin and guilt offerings (Lev. 4:1–6:7; 6:24–7:10). Distinct from the three former offerings, which were voluntary, the latter were required when a sinner broke God's law and severed the relationship. Neither the congregation nor the High Priest were sinless; hence they needed blood to be sprinkled before the veil and applied to the two altars.[73] Once a year expiating blood had to be taken within the veil. The object of this sacrifice was to restore fellowship and gain access shown by the priest's admittance into the presence of God.[74] The ceremony of the Day of Atonement, when the sins of the nation were transferred to the two goats, depicted the removal of the guilt and the dependence upon God to forgive the people's sins (Lev. 16).[75]

Whether the basic idea of sacrifice in the Old Testament is that of a gift or of communion with God is a disputed question.[76] Doubtless we need to allow for both conceptions. The sacrificial focus of the New Testament falls essentially on Jesus. As God's High Priest (Heb. 2:17; 4:14ff.; 5:5–10; 7:1–8:6) and the Lamb which takes away the sin of the world (Jn. 1:29, 36),[77] all other sacrifice pales into insignificance. R. A. Ward puts it well:

> His sacrifice was rational voluntary and loving in contrast to that of the dumb beasts of animal sacrifice. The sacrifices were offered . . . at best with the animal's acquiescence (Isa. 53:7), he for the joy that was set before him endured the cross (Heb. 12:2). By that act eternal judgment was averted, eternal redemption secured, and eternal inheritance promised and an eternal bond between God and man established, the eternal covenant (Heb. 6:2; 9:12, 14f; 13:20). His work was absolute and final. Nothing more needs to be done. The means of such a sacrifice was essentially not his body (though his body suffered), as with the sacrificial animals, but his spirit.[78]

From the Christian point of view all animal sacrifice contrasts with the atoning death of Christ as shadow opposes reality (Heb. 10:1f.).[79] Only through the perfect offering of the Suffering Servant, God's Son, has any sinner full and free access to God's presence (Rom. 5:1; Heb. 10:19). In Jesus' self-offering, loving obedience became actualized, confirming what the Psalmist declared centuries before: God desires not animal sacrifice but obedience (Heb. 10:5–7; Ps. 40:6–8).[80] One looks in vain for any reference to sacrifice acceptable to God in the New Testament which is not vitally connected to this Christological tap-root. Jesus Christ is at once the fulfilment of the burnt offering, since he 'gave himself up for us, an offering and a sacrifice to God as a fragrant aroma' (Eph. 5:2) and is uniquely man's only sin offering (cf. 'the sprinkled blood', Heb. 12:24).[81] He has become 'our peace' (Eph. 2:14–18) as well as God's 'indescribable gift' (2 Cor. 9:15).

It may not be possible to find a direct line of fulfilment between all of the distinct Mosaic sacrifices and specific aspects of the significance of Christ's death.[82] It is sufficient to recognize that in the historic act of God in Christ, man who is God's enemy is offered reconciliation and access to him (2 Cor. 5:21; Rom. 8:3; 5:6–11).[83] United to the Son through participation in his archetypal sacrifice, sinners become 'holy ones'. God may without shame dwell in the midst of his purified people (1 Pet. 2:9).

For our purposes it is important to proceed to the other New Testament references where new covenant worship is offered to God through sacrifices by the redeemed without any design to propitiate God or expiate sin. In the light of the infinite quality of his grace, the sole obligation incumbent on believers must be gratitude issuing in praise and good deeds (Eph. 2:8–10).

Jesus invited everyone who wished to become his disciple to practise self-denial, take up his cross and follow Jesus (Mk. 8:34 par.). Paul seems to present the baptismal death of believers with Christ, and their rising up to 'newness of life', as his counterpart to Jesus' conditions for discipleship (cf. Matt. 28:19). Paul's claim, 'I have been crucified with Christ' (Gal. 2:20), which applies to all genuine Christians (Gal. 5:24), corroborates this understanding. The church, by baptism with Christ (cf. Mk. 10:38f.; Rom. 6:2–6; Col. 2:12), having been grafted into Christ by uniting in his corporate death and resurrection, assumes like him, the form of a servant (Phil. 2:7; cf. Jn. 13:10–16, where baptism and servanthood are united). For Paul this meant that the *imitatio Christi* implied his bearing 'in his body the dying of the Lord Jesus, that the life of Jesus might be made manifest in his mortal flesh' (2 Cor. 4:10f.). For this reason Paul's life took on the form of a sacrifice (*thusia*) and service (*leitourgia*, 'priestly worship') in union with the faith of the Philippians (Phil. 2:17).[84] A martyr's death should not be thought tragic, but rather a joyful act of worship in communion with the Christians for whom his death is an act of service.

Similarly the apostle rejoices in his sufferings for the sake of the Colossians, filling up what is lacking in the sufferings of Christ for the sake of his body, the church (1:24). Paul's sacrifice was not expiatory. Nevertheless, afflictions endured for Christ and to further his cause are acceptable Christian sacrifices.[85] Says L. Goppelt, 'The typological significance of Paul's service as a sacrifice becomes very clear when one remembers that Paul views both the beginning and the completion of this service as a dying with Christ' (Rom. 6:3–5 etc.; Phil. 3:10).[86]

For Paul baptism means, at the deepest level, a need for the candidate to consider himself 'dead indeed to sin but alive unto God' (Rom. 6:11). This expression is explained in succeeding verses: believers decline to offer bodily members as instruments of sin, but willingly present themselves to God as alive from the dead, and their members as instruments of righteousness (Rom. 6:13). Paul employs the same pregnant verb 'present' in Romans 12:1,[87] explicitly calling the Christian's body (i.e. 'their very selves' NEB) a sacrifice. Such an offering, consecrated once and for all,[88] means that the believer is offering a genuine or spiritual worship.[89] It must be a holy offering for God to accept it, having been offered through the 'mercies of God', available to Gentiles by faith in Jesus Christ. In the preceding paragraphs, the apostle has revealed God's unexpected mercy in grafting into the cultivated olive tree the Gentile church in place of the broken branches of Israel (11:22, 30–33). As with the acceptable old covenant sacrifices which met all of the conditions, this sacrifice pleases God because it coincides with his purpose in raising up a new man in Christ whose corporate life is maintained by the Holy Spirit and whose goal is to be presented to him 'holy, blameless and beyond reproach' (Col. 1:22).

It would be a mistake to conclude that Paul is primarily thinking of individual devotion. Romans 11 compares the salvation of the Gentiles to wild branches being grafted into a cultivated olive tree, but not as a forest of olive saplings. As lives are consecrated to God and minds are transformed to grasp God's will in its full goodness and perfection (Rom. 12:1f.), the result is a humble recognition of the nature of the one body in Christ (v.4).[90] Body and mind are not sacrificed on an altar in an old covenant fashion, but incorporated into active service within the body of Christ, the church. The charisms distributed by the Spirit are a clear sign of

God's approval of the living sacrifices which were offered to him.

As the gifts are exercised the body is actualized in the resulting worship (Rom. 12:6–8), as Paul's selection of gifts shows. The prophet makes God's voice to be heard and his will known (v. 6). The servant serves the brotherhood sacrificially, impelled by Christ's love (v. 7). The gifted teacher informs and clarifies the hearts of the uninstructed so that they too may be presented perfect in Christ (v. 7; Rom. 15:16; Col. 1:28). The exhorter[91] will offer individuals his loving encouragement (v. 8). The giver will delight in sharing material benefits with the needy (cf. Acts 2:42ff.). The leader will diligently take responsibility in leading and organizing the church and its activities to achieve its goals, and fulfil its mission. The compassionate will serve the body by alleviating suffering and extending sympathy (v. 8).

It is highly significant that all of this 'body action' (cf. 12:4) is included in Paul's conception of spiritual worship. Parts of the ritual worship expressed through prophecy, teaching and exhortation in the regular meetings of the church are integrated with service, expressed through leading and merciful deeds carried on in and outside the congregational meetings. As we have seen in discussing the concept of *time*, worship was considered by the New Testament writers as both ecclesial and extra-ecclesial in nature.

Other examples of the new meaning of sacrifice can be seen in Paul's 'priestly duty of proclaiming the gospel' (*hierourgein to euanggelion*). 'His service is priestly because he is in charge of a sanctuary (the gospel), but especially because his goal and achievement is the presentation of the Gentiles as a sacrifice sanctified by the Spirit and, therefore, acceptable to God (Rom. 15:16b).'[93]

We encounter similar sacrificial overtones in Paul's deeply committed pastoral service described in his last message to the Ephesian elders (Acts 20:17–35). Since the church was purchased with Christ's blood (v. 18), Paul did not hold his own life as dear to himself (v. 24). With humble dedication and tears (in imitation of his Master) he fulfilled his ministry in public proclamation and from house to house (v. 20, in the meetings). Now that his work in Ephesus has been completed, he is free from all blood guilt (v. 26). He can freely commend these leaders to God (v. 32). This entire passage confirms the conclusion that the central purpose of the meetings of the house congregations was to receive the perfecting influence of Paul and all the pastors who shepherd the flock, keeping the goal in mind of presenting the church to God without blemish.

Precisely this same purpose is brought out in the context of the love husbands should offer their wives. Christ gave himself up for his bride so that he might sanctify her (the church), 'having cleansed her by the washing of water with the word, that he might present to himself the church in all her glory, having no spot or wrinkle, or any such thing; but that she should be holy and blameless' (Eph. 5:25–27).[94] We should, then, see Paul's own life as a sacrifice, even as his ministry prepares the church to be offered in perfection as an acceptable response to Christ's own self-giving in death.

Because the presence of the new age dominates Paul's thinking, he does not hesitate to identify the financial contribution the Philippians sent him as 'an acceptable sacrifice, well pleasing to God' (4:18). He saw it as a kind of counterpart to the burnt offering described in Leviticus, for it too produced a 'fragrant aroma'. Material offerings may be considered true sacrifices if they are given by those who 'give themselves first to the Lord' (2 Cor. 8:5). Not that money is a valid substitute for life, but it may be a genuine expression of life when offered out of extreme poverty (2 Cor. 8:2, 'beyond their ability'). The widow Jesus extolled gave but two leptas, yet in them offered her whole life (Mk. 12:44). Such sacrificial sharing pertains to the priestly ministry (*leitourgia*) of the Philippians (2:30; cf. Rom. 15:27).

In a similar way the author of Hebrews portrays Christian worship as 'doing good and sharing' (13:16). The entire paragraph (10–17) is best understood in the context of the meeting of the church where the Christian 'altar' refers to the Lord's table. As the church gathered in memorial celebration to enact the remembrance of Christ's unique sacrifice (9:12), gratitude would prompt its members to share their material blessings with needy brothers.[95] As participation at the Lord's table is barred to those that serve the tabernacle (v. 10), the church's primary concern should be for the members of God's family. In similar fashion the first church in Jerusalem included 'sharing' (*koinōnia*)[96] in company with the teaching, the Supper and prayer (Acts 2:42).

In Hebrews, too, the worship offered in praise and gratitude expressed during the meetings of the church belongs to the category of sacrifice. 'Let us offer through him [Jesus] a sacrifice of praise to God continually. This is the fruit of the lips which confess his name' (13:15).[97] Here a genuine Old Testament theme surfaces in the church. Praise and thanksgiving are acceptable substitutes for material offerings on occasion (cf. 2 Chr. 29:31; Ps. 50:14, 23; 69:30f.; Hos. 14:2). A rabbinic tradition foresaw the end of all Mosaic sacrifices except the thank-offering.[98] But the church's post-crucifixion praise can be sacrificed only through Jesus. In vital union with Christ, who is the high priest of the new order, all Christians may offer vocal adoration through proclamation and song.[99] 'Since we receive a kingdom which cannot be shaken, let us show gratitude, by which we may offer to God an acceptable service with reverence and awe' (Heb. 12:28 NASB).[100]

According to the Old Testament, worthy subjects for praise were God's mighty acts (1 Chr. 29:12f.; Ps. 105:1–6) and goodness (Ps. 118:1–4), as well as salvation from disaster (Ps. 107:1, 8, 15, 21, 31) and conquest of enemies (Ps. 9:1, 2). The church of the firstborn should envision all reality from the spiritual viewpoint, elevating the reasons for thankful praise from earthly to heavenly motives. An illustration in Acts 4:21ff. introduces the multitude that glorifies God for his intervention on behalf of the followers of Jesus. Gratefully believers acknowledge that the Creator of the heavens and the earth has predetermined all that has happened to God's Anointed. In place of national liberation the omnipotent God has vanquished spiritual oppressors. The physical suffering endured by the persecuted community is of little concern in comparison with the divine purpose.

Peter too, refers to offerings in the church, but does not specify what the 'spiritual sacrifices' are that the holy Christian priesthood should bring. L. Goppelt is surely right: 'they are not physical acts that are carried out in obedience to the letter, but Spirit-inspired surrender to all kinds of service.'[101] In both Ephesians and Colossians Paul appeals to his readers to 'be filled with the Spirit' and indwelt by the 'word' (5:18 and 3:16). The expressions of worship in the meetings of the house churches should be punctuated with 'psalms, hymns and spiritual songs, singing and making melody with your heart to the Lord; always giving thanks for all things in the name of our Lord Jesus Christ to God' (Eph. 5:19f.). Despite the enthusiasm such meetings must have displayed, Paul sees no cleavage between the adoration of the community at worship and the ordinary daily activities. For he goes on to say that everything that Christians do or say should be offered as worship, as long as it is performed in the name of the Lord Jesus and accompanied with thanksgiving offered through him (Col. 3:17; 1 Cor. 10:31).

Against the Gnostic teaching that the material realm is evil, the apostle Paul argues that everything is good provided it is received with gratitude and sanctified by means of the word of God and prayer (1 Tim. 4:4f.).[102] In distinction to the occasional cultic celebration of ancient Israel the church in Christ is to rejoice always, pray without ceasing and give thanks in everything (1 Thess. 5:16–18).[103]

Among the traditional lists of admonitions to wives, husbands, children, parents and slaves, a remarkable illustration can be found of what Paul meant by the sacrifice of the whole of life to God. Christians in bondage are urged not to offer 'eyeservice' to please their masters. On the contrary they must consider themselves as slaves of Christ, serving him 'with sincerity of heart, fearing the Lord' (Col. 3:22; cf. Eph. 6:5–7). This language borders on the cultic. All Christians are encouraged to sing in their hearts to God (Eph. 5:19; Col. 3:16). Slaves are to work heartily, as if they were offering their service as a sacrifice to the Lord (rather than begrudging their unpaid labour).

Though these sacrifices of body, praise and good deeds may seem remarkably mundane, they are well-pleasing to God. Extraordinary acts of piety through self-affliction or ascetic abstinence, are not encouraged (Col. 2:16–23). What counts is love for God and neighbour. Without such genuine love, self-immolation is quite worthless (1 Cor. 13:3).

THE PRIESTHOOD OF BELIEVERS

Under the old covenant the priesthood united with temple, sacrifices and feasts to form an essential part of the ritual established by God, by means of which his people might worship him. The priests were living bridges between the uniquely holy God and sinful man. The meaning of the term 'priest' (*kohēn* in Heb.) is 'truth-sayer', showing the intimate connection of his role with prophecy.[104] Once God had committed to Israel the oracles of God (Rom. 3:2), the nation was consecrated as a 'kingdom of priests' (Exod. 19:6). The mission of the nation consisted in making God's name and will known throughout the nations.[105]

To celebrate the gracious intervention of God in the conquest of the Egyptians in the Exodus and the preservation of the Israelite first-born sons, each father presided as a priest over a redramatized Exodus in the annual Passover feast (Ex. 12). Indeed, Israel as a whole was God's firstborn (Ex. 4:22) and commissioned as his 'royal priests' (Ex. 19:6).[106] For practical reasons, the firstborn sons of every family were set aside in favour of the institutional levitical priesthood, founded on the principle of representation (Num. 3:12f.; 8:19f.).[107] Those priests were consecrated (Ex. 29:9f.), distinguished by wearing the prescribed priestly garments following ablution, and then anointed and sanctified by an offering partially consumed by them (Lev. 7:12f.).[108] The high priest alone was the Anointed One (*christos*, Lev. 4:13f.; 6:12f.) although his sons were also sprinkled with oil. The result was a hierarchy composed of high priest, priests and Levites separated from the rest of the nation. Only on pain of death would any non-priests venture into the holy place (Num. 3:10). Instead of a geographic inheritance, the priests were entitled to 'inherit' the Lord (v. 13). Both their labour and sustenance were to arise uniquely from their continual worship of God.

Now that the new age has dawned, the author of Hebrews

demonstrates, Jesus Christ draws all of the strands of the Israelite priesthood into his singular role as God's representative to and from man. He fulfils perfectly the human and divine mediatorial conditions to the eternal advantage of the elect (Heb. 5:1–10; 7:1–28). The grounds for this understanding are discoverable in the high priestly prayer of Jesus (Jn. 17).[109] For the sake of his followers, he consecrated himself (v. 17) — which included the idea of sacrifice[110] — so 'that they might be sanctified in the truth' (v. 19). Furthermore, he prays that they may be 'perfected [i.e. consecrated] in one' (v. 23).[111] Thus through his own self-offering, Jesus incorporated the new convenant people into a genuine priesthood which has as its source and ground his own role as priest.

Returning to Hebrews, it is evident that the high priesthood of Christ is the author's comprehensive means of describing his mediatorial significance.[112] Because he died once to take away sins, his present preeminent ministry is given over to expressing sympathy (2:17f; 4:14f.) and to intercession (7:25; Rom. 8:34).[113] In this way his earthly ministry continues in the heavens, for Jesus was known for his compassion and intercession both for his beloved followers and also for his tormentors (Jn. 16:26; 17:20f.; Lk. 22:32; 23:34).

Clearly, then, the extension of the privilege of priesthood to all believers [144] has for its source and model the One who unites them with himself in his own new covenant priesthood. 'He who sanctifies and those who are sanctified are all of one' (Heb. 2:11), 'for he had to be made like his brethren in all things' (2:17). Because Christians are part of the 'church of the firstborn who are enrolled in heaven', they are invited to enter the holy place (Heb. 12:23; 10:19–22).[115] That access into the Holy of Holies is restricted to those who have been incorporated into the 'house of God' over which he rules (Heb. 3:6; 10:19, 21). Goppelt thinks that the confession of the community (3:1; 4:14) must have included statements about the high priesthood (10:19ff., esp. 23) of Jesus (3:1).[116] Just such a confession concerning his name, i.e. who he is, was included in the sacrifices of praise that the worshipping community offered to the Lord (13:15).

By her union with Christ the church has become a 'kingdom' and its membership 'priests' (Rev. 1:6; 5:10; cf. 20:6; 1 Pet. 2:9). Elect from humanity as a whole, the new Israel has the responsibility of carrying out the original mission of Israel which is to proclaim the 'excellencies of him who called you out of darkness into his marvelous light' (1 Pet. 2:9).[117] In the role of God's royal priesthood, the church has the joyous responsibility of challenging the whole human race to recognize the virtues of the world's Saviour (cf. Jn. 4:42).[118] In accord with her High Priest's mission, the church must give priority to bridging the gap between the world and the Creator. This royal priesthood witnesses to her Lord's unique mediatorship by being sent into the world as he was (Jn. 17:18; 20:21; Acts 1:8; 1 Cor. 5:18–21). The Son came to expound the Father to the world (Jn. 1:18), and the church was commissioned to carry on that task until the age's end (Matt. 28:18–20). Therefore all that the church does to fulfil its mission can be rightly considered worship. Paul implies as much in Ephesians (4:12) by focusing the purpose of the church's leadership on the preparation of the saints to serve (Eph. 4:12). Jesus identified his own mission as that of the Suffering Servant, for he came 'not to be served but to serve and to give his life a ransom for many' (Mk. 10:45).

In the light of Jesus' infinite priestly compassion, it ought to be clear that any worship which isolates the church from the heart-breaking needs of the world, both spiritual and material, is unbiblical. Any such insulation denies the church's priestly calling. Through practical deeds of love the church fulfils its divine challenge to witness to the character of her own High Priest (Acts 1:8; 10:38; Eph. 2:10).

Similarly the Lord's Supper, as the supreme expression of New Testament worship,[119] expresses dramatically the union between the community as a priesthood and the incomparable gift of God's priest-victim, who bore the sins of the world in himself (1 Pet. 1:18f.; 2:24). By eating and drinking at the risen Lord's table, the church also looks forward to his triumphant reign, while proclaiming in the present his vicarious death until he returns (1 Cor. 11:26). Such a worship form should make the cross dramatically

contemporaneous and lead the church to renewed compassion for a world which is largely oblivious of God's free
salvation. The dramatic form of the worship offered in the
Supper should motivate Christians to announce vocally the
good news about his sacrifice and rule (2 Cor. 4:5f.), just as
they portray in daily actions the reality of the crucified life
(Gal. 2:20). Thus the significance of the Supper ought to
reinforce the priestly obligation of continually worshiping
God through service always and everywhere.

The church has also been consecrated to minister on
behalf of men through intercession. As incense, the prayers
of the Lord's priests ascend before his throne (Rev. 8:3, 5;
cf. Ps. 41:2). When the church takes the obligation to pray
for all men seriously (1 Tim. 2:1–4),[120] she participates in
the heavenly intercession of her High Priest (Heb. 7:25). As
believers pray in his name and secure his endorsement
(Jn. 14:12f.), the benefits offered through his propitiation
overflow the bounds of the elect to embrace the whole world
(1 Jn. 2:2),[121] for 'he is not willing that any should perish'
(2 Pet. 3:9). The prayers of the saints should reflect this
divine concern. From all tribes, tongues, peoples and nations
he has purchased people with his blood (Rev. 5:9). Thus it
is the church's priestly duty to pray that those who have
been bought might know it and thereby be added to the
worldwide band (cf. Matt. 9:38; Lk. 10:2).[122]

The priesthood of the church means, furthermore, that
all believers have a mutual priestly ministry to one another
within the living temple founded on Christ. This responsibility is implied in the nature of the church as the recipient
of her exalted Lord's gifts (Eph. 4:11f.; 1 Cor. 12:4–11;
Rom. 12:6–8), and it does not support the almost universal
cleavage between what are called 'clergy' and 'laity'.[123] Paul's
ministry (*leitourgia*) had for its goal the perfecting of the
Gentile churches through his priestly ministry of announcing the gospel (Rom. 15:16); but Epaphroditus was also a
'priestly minister' (*leitourgos*, Phil. 2:25), although his service
for Paul was primarily transporting the Philippians' gift.
Similarly, the whole church of Philippi performed priestly
service (*leitourgia*) in sending Paul aid (Phil. 2:30). Nor does

Paul hesitate to call the collection for the poor Christians of Jerusalem 'priestly service' (*leitourgia*, 2 Cor. 9:12).

A wide range of mutual ministries is urged on the churches. Timothy has earned the privilege of ministering to the Philippians because of his kindred spirit with Paul. He is a proven servant who has a genuine concern for the church's welfare (Phil. 2:20), possessing qualities that need to characterize all the priesthood. Thus, Christians are to pray for their fellows (Eph. 6:18), even when they have fallen into sin (1 Jn. 5:16, apostates excepted), thereby sharing in Christ's celestial intercession. Therefore Paul prays for the churches (Eph. 1:16; 3:14ff.; Phil. 1:9; Col. 1:9; 1 Thess. 1:2; etc.) and asks them to pray for him (Eph. 6:19; Phil. 1:19). The repeated expressions of mutual aid within the fellowship of the church belong to this same category of priestly ministry. Some thirty-five examples of mutual responsibility within the church, indicated by the phrase 'one another' accumulate on the pages of the New Testament.

Although the term 'priest' (singular) is not applied to an individual believer in the New Testament (nor is the word 'king'), for it belongs uniquely to Christ, nevertheless the ministry of the word, encouragement, intercession and sharing is 'priestly service' or worship. This basic outlook suggests reasons why Paul's description of the worship service leads naturally to mutal subordination (Eph. 5:20) and obedience, for it is Christ himself who is at work ministering as governing High Priest in and through his body and temple. D. G. Peterson reminds us:

> The use of such expressions as 'going to worship' obscures the NT emphasis on meeting together to encourage one another. Even when we are singing hymns and 'making melody to the Lord', Paul tells us that we are to be 'addressing one another' (Eph. 5:19f., Col. 3:16). The exercise of gifts both inside and outside the congregational meeting is to be an expression of that grateful obedience which is 'your spiritual worship' (Rom. 12:1–8).[124]

CONCLUSION

Eternity invaded time when the Son of God became flesh, died and rose from the dead. Those who believe on him and die and rise with him in baptismal union (Rom. 6:2–6; Col. 1:12), share with him the life of the 'age to come', mediated through the Spirit. All experiences lived out in the new creation and worthy of its Lord, should therefore be considered as 'worship'.[125] The total transposition from 'death in sin' to 'life in God' (Col. 3:3) is even more radical than the metamorphosis of a worm into a butterfly (cf. Rom. 12:2). The veil has been removed in the new covenant reality so 'we all reflect as in a mirror the splendour of the Lord: thus we are transfigured into his likeness, from splendour to splendour; such is the influence of the Lord who is Spirit' (2 Cor. 3:18 NEB).

All time is to be lived out in joyful service. Every obedient action pertains inseparably to the realm of adoration (1 Cor. 10:31; Col. 3:17), hence to attribute a legalistic 'holiness' to certain days, seasons or festivals means in effect to annihilate the very essence of the 'completion' to which we have been brought in Christ (Col. 2:10–23; Gal. 4:9). The optional selection of days, hours or periods to pray (cf. 1 Cor. 7:5), or observe any religious rite, must never cloud this outlook if one is to avoid slipping back into the captivity of the elemental spirits (*stoicheia*, 'elements [spirits?] of the universe', Col. 2:8; Gal. 4:9 NEB).[126] The former obligation of the law has succumbed to the impulse of the 'law of the Spirit of life in Christ' (Rom. 8:2).

It is more important for the redeemed continually to rejoice in the Lord (Phil. 3:1; 4:4; 1 Pet. 1:6, 8) than it is for the angelic hosts to praise him unceasingly (Rev. 4:8). All who are sealed by the Spirit (Eph. 1:13; 2 Cor. 1:22; Rev. 7:3ff.) have a far more compelling reason to exult in the worthiness of the Lamb and in him who sits on the throne than do the celestial beings. Therefore the New Testament writers evince no embarrassment in urging their readers to 'offer up *continually* a sacrifice of praise' (Heb. 13:15; cf. Eph. 5:20).

But what of the Christians' sins, the deep-seated root of

unextracted unrighteousness? How does the New Testament face the anomaly of the saints' transgressions? Paul states that any Christian's thought, word or deed practised in unbelief is sinful (Rom. 14:23). That means he has ceased to worship. The good conscience which is incumbent upon believers (1 Pet. 3:16) must be restored through confession and trust in the complete cleansing from all sin that Christ faithfully effects (1 Jn. 1:9) so that the interruption in the flow of worship be terminated immediately. Similarly, allowing time to pass unused (i.e. 'unredeemed') means that we concede it to the old age which is fatally evil (Eph. 5:16; Col. 4:5).

What better summary of the new age conception of time and worship can be found than that which Brother Lawrence shared with a sympathetic ear more than three centuries ago?

> He said that our sanctification did not depend upon changing our works, but in doing for God's sake, which we commonly do for our own . . . That the most excellent method he had found of going to God was that of doing our common business without any view of pleasing men, and (as far as we are capable) purely for the love of God. . . . The time of business does not with me differ from the time of prayer; and the noise and clutter of my kitchen, while several persons are at the same time calling for different things, I possess God in as great tranquillity as if I were upon my knees at the Blessed Sacrament.[127]

The New Testament conception of the temple has various implications which we should note.

1) The identification of Christ with his people in the temple should remind us that worship is what we do together, whether we are geographically in the same place or not (cf. 1 Cor. 5:4). Apart from him there is no true worship; and so gathering in his name 'means' that the fellowship is united in accordance with his teaching (Matt. 28:20), to glorify the Father through him (1 Pet. 4:11). When Christians meet as a fellowship in Christ, the presence of the risen Lord is assured. Visible expression of the church's union

with Christ is not optional. It belongs, along with baptism and the Supper, to the essence of the church's audible confession and visible worship.

2) The unity of the church is fundamental to its nature as God's holy temple. Therefore profaning the community through schism or rivalry calls down an anathema on any perpetrator of disunity (1 Cor. 3:17). Christ's Holy Spirit designs to inhabit the temple, and so effects and certifies its holiness (1 Cor. 3:17; Eph. 2:21), thereby making inter-Christian relationships sacred also.[128] Thus one's real union with a God who is 'our Father'[129] and with our spiritual brothers, belongs to the vital nature of worship. There can be no private acts in the temple of the living God even though individuals, congregations and denominations may be widely separated by space, belief and practice.[130]

3) The composition of the temple is unrestricted to any race, age, or gender. All men and women who have received the Son are incorporated into this eschatological house of God. This biblical figure reflects the basic continuity of salvation history. God's original purpose in electing a people for his own possession (Exod. 19:5; 1 Pet. 2:9) has been fulfilled in his choosing to dwell in their midst. In fact, God is omnipresent and affirms that all the earth is his (Exod. 19:5); and hence the transformation of the material temple of Palestine into one built 'without hands' out of men of all lands, means the original goal of universality is thereby attained.[131]

4) The temple is still under construction. 'It must always be accepted for what it is in its incomplete state.[132] All that adds to its perfection ought to be considered worthy of inclusion in its liturgy. All that detracts from it should be eliminated.

5) Each local congregation should be effective in convincing people of the reality of God's dwelling on earth in and among his people. The life of the church, in all of its myriad activities and attitudes, ought to reflect the divine perfection. It should present a vision such as Isaiah saw in the temple (6:3-5) and create a penetrating awareness of guilt that produces the repentant cry 'Woe is me'.[133] A fellowship

which is truly spiritually therapeutic should also attract those that suffer the pain of guilt.

6) New Testament worship must be more than a mere network of diverse people who meet occasionally, and create instead true groups of individuals who mutually influence each other's identity, behaviour and values for life.

Christian sacrifice and the universal priesthood of the church, viewed through the prism of the New Testament's authors, become integral aspects of our definition of worship. 'The whole of life is related to and situated within the missionary movement of God to men'.[134] Like a flowing spring, a continuously renewed fellowship with him who sacrificed himself unreservedly for the church ought to motivate all who worship to bring God's saving solution to the world's desperate need.

Conceived thus, worship in the church becomes, as H. Berkhof has described it:

> an antiphonal event in which, to the one side, God comes to us in such elements as proclamation of grace, command, Scripture reading, preaching, meal, and benediction; and in which to the other side we come before God with out confession of sin, litany of praise, profesion of faith, prayers and intercessions, gifts for his work in the church and in the world, and hymns of humiliation and adoration, of praise and petition.[135]

But such familiar exercises in worship are not worthy of him who lived his *whole* life for us unless the members voluntarily choose to respond attitudinally in a manner that moves them joyfully to offer *all* of their actions and service on the altar of sacrifice. The average congregation, with its facile, traditional approach to worship, sees a duty to perform in the acting out of the liturgy as though that were the sum of the *leitourgia* (priestly service) the new Testament priesthood is invited to bring to God. Once the hour of service has ended, the Christian feels free to sink back into the neutral ('secular') routine of daily living in the world. I have no desire to denigrate the significance of repeated worship services, but the New Testament surely challenges us all to recapture the totality of its conception of worship. All thoughts, words and deeds should be performed as worship because the Lamb is 'worthy to receive power and wealth and wisdom and strength and honour and glory and blessing' (Rev. 5:12). The sevenfold offering, which the inumerable angelic hosts proclaim the slain Lamb is worthy to receive, can be given in reality only by the redeemed on earth. For his honour, glory and blessing, we speak, write, work, play, eat and sleep, for he is worthy of all of the life power that pulsates within us.

The public gatherings of the church ought to have this objective in constant view. Her members should be stimulated, even as they participate in the liturgy, to practise actions of love and good deeds (Heb. 10:24). Together or scattered, the church should be a glorifying community. Only such two-faceted worship is worthy of him who gave himself for the church with the intention of securing her perfection (Eph. 5:27). For we are not our own, but have been bought with a price (1 Cor. 6:20), meaning that Christians have as much free time as slaves! 'Therefore whether you eat or drink or whatever you do, do everything for the glory of God' (1 Cor. 10:31).

4

Ministry in the New Testament

RONALD Y. K. FUNG

It is fitting that the subject of this chapter should appear in a volume that is intended to be a 'biblical and practical theology of the church'.[1] For the ministry has meaning only in the light of the church, so that, whilst the latter subject can be studied on its own, without reference to the ministry, the former subject (the ministry) can be properly treated only with reference to the church. The prsent paper does not aspire to provide a systematic survey of all the relevant NT passages but concentrates attention on three inter-related aspects of our subject: (1) the matter of giftedness, which entails a discussion of spiritual gifts; (2) the question of style, or, to be more specific, the question whether ministry is to be conceived in terms of office or function; and (3) the problem of the place of women in the ministry of the church. All these are issues — even divisive issues, though in different degrees — confronting the worldwide church today. In the nature of the case, our study will be based primarily on the Pauline writings (including the Pastoral Epistles, the authenticity of which is here assumed); this more limited approach may be justified by the consideration that, as compared with the wealth of factual information and developed teaching in the Pauline corpus, the contributions of the other NT books to our subject are slight and can be briefly summarized.[2] We should also like to observe at the outset that in this paper the three subtopics will not be receiving equal treatment in terms of the space devoted to each. This is because in our discussion of the first two we are able to refer, where elaboration might be desired, to previous studies which are readily accessible,[3] whereas the section on women's ministry represents a fresh attempt on our part to wrestle with what is admittedly a most difficult and sensitive issue.[4]

I SPIRITUAL GIFTS

Although there is a sense in which one could speak of 'spiritual gifts' in the Gospels and Acts and even in the Old Testament,[5] yet strictly speaking it is more correct to say that ' "charisma" is a concept which we owe almost entirely to Paul'.[6] Certainly the seventeen occurrences of the word *charisma* in the New Testament are all to be found in the Pauline corpus, with the sole exception of 1 Peter 4:10. Its close connection with *charis* (cf. 1 Cor. 1:4, 7; Rom. 12:6) shows that a charisma is a grace-gift, i.e. a free gift which has its source in and is an expression of God's grace to his people, both individually and as a body; while the close connection between the gifts and the Holy Spirit is explicitly stated in 1 Corinthians 12:11 (the charismata are endowments of the Spirit), indirectly affirmed in the unique expression *charisma pneumatikon* in Romans 1:11, and clearly reflected in the familiar rendering of *charisma* as 'spiritual gift'. The word is used in the New Testament in a variety of meanings, but here we are concerned only with its more specialized sense of an endowment or equipment bestowed on the believer by the Holy Spirit for Christian service.[7]

Putting the four lists of spiritual gifts mentioned by Paul in parallel columns yields the following synoptic view (the numbering is based on the second list):

(A) 1 Cor. 12:8–10	(B) 1 Cor. 12:28–30	(C) Rom. 12:6–8	(D) Eph. 4:11
3b *logos sophias*	1 *apostoloi*	2 *prophēteia*	1 *apostoloi*
3c *logos gnōseōs*	2 *prophētai*	12 *diakonia*	2 *prophētai*
10 *pistis*	3a *didaskaloi*	3a *ho didaskōn*	17 *euangelistai*
5 *charismata*	4 *dynameis*	13 *ho*	3a [7b]
iamatōn	5 *charismata*	*parakalōn*	*poimenes kai*
4 *energēmata*	*iamatōn*	14 *ho*	*didaskaloi*[8]
dynamēn	6 *antilēmpseis*	*metadidous*	
2 *prophēteia*	7 *akybernēseis*	15 *ho*	
11 *diakriseis*	8 *genē glōssōn*	*proistamenos*	
pneumatōn	9 *hoi*	16 *ho eleōn*	
8 *genē glōssōn*	*diermēneuousin*		
9 *hermēneia*			
glōssōn			

There seems to be no conscious attempt in these lists at systematic classification; they are manifestly incomplete, being selective and illustrative rather than exhaustive,[9] and probably no effort to force the various gifts into a neat scheme will prove completely satisfactory.[10] Nevertheless, the following grouping, whose twofold division is suggested by Acts 6:2, 4 and 1 Peter 4:11, may serve as a workable classification:

ENDOWMENTS FOR MINISTRY IN WORD

A. *Gifts of evangelic proclamation*
   1. Apostles (1)
   2. Evangelists (17)

B. *Gifts of inspired utterance*
   1. Prophets (2)
   2. Ability to distinguish between spirits (11)
   3. Various kinds of tongues (8)
   4. Interpretation of tongues (9)

EQUIPMENTS FOR MINISTRY IN DEED

D. *Gifts of supernatural power*
   1. Miracles (4)
   2. Gifts of healing (5)
   3. Faith (10)[13]

E. *Gifts of administrative leadership*
   1. Administrators (7a)
   2. Pastors (7b)[14]

C. *Gifts of didactic speech*   F. *Gifts of practical assistance*
1. *Teachers (3a)/Pastors*   1. *Helpers (6)*
        (7b)[11]   2. *Service (12)*
2. *Utterance of wisdom (3b)*   3. *Sharing (14)*
3. *Utterance of knowledge*   4. *Caring (15)*[15]
        (3c)[12]   5. *Showing mercy (16)*
4. *Exhortation (13)*

A study of the individual charismata will reveal that some of the categories overlap in the sense that certain gifts placed in different categories may overlap or be closely associated. We may note the following examples: (1) If Paul was to any degree representative of the apostles as a group here, they probably each possessed a rich variety of gifts, if not indeed all the charismata listed by him.[16] More particularly, (2) the apostles are closely associated with the prophets in Ephesians 2:20 (both together constituting the foundation of the church) and 3:5 (both together being recipients of the mystery of Christ).[17] (3) The apostles were undoubtedly also teachers: Paul, for instance, describes himself in the same breath as 'an apostle and a teacher' (2 Tim. 1:11); the same combination occurs in 1 Timothy 2:7, where the parenthetical assertion of veracity makes it even more apparent that *didaskalos* is epexegetic of *apostolos* (or *kēryx kai apostolos*). (4) The gift of prophecy, in turn, overlaps with certain gifts of didactic speech. In 1 Corinthians 13:2a, the possession of prophetic powers is closely associated with knowing 'all mysteries and all knowledge', so that prophecy either corresponds to knowing all mysteries and all knowledge, or it involves (as its content) mysteries and knowledge — in either case forging a link with the gift of *logos gnōseōs*.[18] Again, both 1 Corinthians 14:3 and Acts 15:32 show that the prophetic activity involves an element of exhortation. Thus, apart from the general consideration that the apostles probably possessed gifts which span all the categories, we have noted more specifically an overlap between A 1 and B 1, A 1 and C 1, B 1 and C 3, and B 1 and C 4; and it is noticeable that the overlap occurs not so much in the area of the deed-charismata as in that of the word-charismata.

Passing by any detailed consideration of the individual charismata we proceed to some observations on the spiritual gifts as a whole. First, a few general facts and principles may be mentioned. (1) The charismata have their origin in the work of the triune God, being attributed equally to the Father (1 Cor. 12:6) and the Son (Eph. 4:7, 8–10) as their source, and to the Holy Spirit (1 Cor. 12:11, 8f., 4) as the channel through which they proceed from the Father and the Son. (2) Their distribution is traced to the will of the triune God (Father, 1 Cor. 12:28; Son, Eph. 4:7; Spirit, 1 Cor. 12:11); given in rich variety and covering every individual believer (1 Cor. 12:7, 11; Rom. 12:3f.; Eph. 4:7), though not bestowed indiscriminately (1 Cor. 12:8–10, 29f.; Rom. 12:6) or so as to exclude the possibility of a recipient having more than one gift (cf. 1 Cor. 14:13), the charismata make for a variegated functional diversity (cf. 1 Pet. 4:10, *poikilēs charitos*) within the organic unity of the Body of Christ. (3) The charismata are given for the supreme purpose of the *oikodomē* of the church (1 Cor. 12:7; 14:1, 3, 4–6, 12, 17, 19, 26; Eph. 4:12). (4) They are to be employed in love (1 Cor. 12:31; 14:1), in the way of service (1 Cor. 12:5), and in obedience to the lordship of Christ (1 Cor. 12:3; cf. Jn. 16:14).[19]

Secondly, it is noticeable that each of the three lists — treating, for the present purpose, (A) and (B), which come from the same chapter, as one list — together with its context seems to highlight some particular truth about the charismata. (1) In 1 Corinthians 12, all the six categories of gifts in our classification are represented: A 1, B 1–4, C 1–3, D 1–3, E 1, F 1. Thus, non-spectacular gifts such as those of 'administrators' and 'helpers' take their place as charismata apportioned by the Spirit (note the fourfold emphasis in 1 Cor. 12:8f. given by the repeated mention of the Spirit) alongside gifts of unique commission ('apostles') and direct inspiration ('prophets'), as well as more spectacular gifts such as 'miracles', 'healing' and 'tongues'; they are, moreover, deliberately ranked above the gift of glossolalia so highly valued by the Corinthian enthusiasts.[20] And in the context, the metaphor of the Body makes plain that the diversity of gifts and functions is always present (vv. 14–16) and necessary, not only for the Body as a whole (vv. 17–20) but for the mutual benefit of the members themselves (v. 21); and that the humbler and weaker members of the church (those possessed of fewer and less flamboyant gifts) should not be treated with contempt but with special honour (vv. 22–24). These facts plainly show not only that there are no 'non-charismatic' Christians over against 'charismatic' ones, since all are endowed with charismata,[21] but also that the distinction between 'charismatic' and 'non-charismatic' gifts is falsely drawn, since all gifts, whether spectacular or non-spectacular, are equally endowments of the Spirit and therefore 'charismatic' in the proper sense of the word.

(2) The more spectacular gifts do not find expression in Romans 12 or Ephesians 4 (except in so far as some of them are included in the gifts of apostleship and prophecy). In the Romans passage, particular stress is laid on the fact (implied also in 1 Cor. 12:8–10, 29f.) that believers have received gifts that do differ from one case to another (*charismata diaphora*, v. 6), and that each believer should, in a sober estimate and humble acceptance of his own gifts (v. 3), exercise them faithfully within the limits set by them. This last thought is already implicit in verse 3c: *hōs ho theos enerisen metron pisteōs*;[22] it comes to lucid expression in the parallel constructions of verses 7–8a:

> *eite diakonian, en tē diakonia eite ho didaskōn, en tē didaskalia*
> *eite ho parakalōn, en tē paraklēsei*

The point we wish to make here can hardly be made in a better way than has been made by C. E. B. Cranfield in his comment on the meaning of *en tē diakonia*:[23]

> those who have received this particular gift, the spiritual capacity for practical service, are to give themselves wholeheartedly to the fulfilment of the tasks to which their particular endowment is also their divine vocation.[24] They are to use the spiritual gift they have received to the full, and they are to use it for the purpose for which it was given [a warning against the temptation to undertake services for which one is not divinely equipped would seem to be implicit].

'This explanation of *en tē diakonia*', it is appropriately

added, 'applies equally *mutatis mutandis* to *en tē didaskalia* and *en tē paraklēsei*.'[25]

These two principles — the truly 'charismatic' nature of all spiritual gifts and the wholehearted and single-minded exercise of one's gifts within the limits set by them — to which 1 Corinthians 12 and Romans 12 respectively seem to give particular emphasis also find expression in 1 Peter 4:10f. Verse 10 speaks of *charisma* as a manifestation of God's manifold grace, and verse 11 proceeds to give two examples of specific activities within the Christian community; if in the first example given *lalein* refers to 'routine functions like teaching and preaching' (cf. Acts 10:44; 2 Cor. 2:17, where the verb has this connotation), this clearly implies that gifts like teaching, preaching and practical service (which constitutes the second example), 'though lacking the outward tokens of Spirit-possession, should be regarded . . . as in the true sense charismatic'.[26] As for the other principle, not only is it expressed in the correspondence between *hekastos kathōs elaben charisma* and *auto diakonountes* (cf. RV, 'ministering it'; AV, 'minister the same'), it is surely also implied in the designation *kaloi oikonomoi*: for since it is required of stewards that they 'prove faithful' (1 Cor. 4:2, NIV), so 'good stewards' in our context are those who use their gifts in a responsible manner, 'faithfully administering God's grace in its various forms' (NIV) — and not dabbling with ministries for which they are not equipped.

(3) As compared with 1 Corinthians 12 and Romans 12, the list of charismata in Ephesians 4:11 is unique in that it consists exclusively of men — specially-endowed men given to the church by the Lord of the church — and also in that all the men listed are 'persons who fulfil their service by speaking: they are "Ministers of the Word"'.[27] But of greater importance for our present purpose is the observation that, more clearly than in the other passages, here the charismata are closely intertwined with the *goal* of the church (vv. 12c, 13) as the divinely-given *means* by which that goal is to be reached: the men of charismata constitute what may be called a 'special ministry' which is given for the immediate purpose of equipping 'God's people for work in his service,

to the building up of the Body of Christ' (v. 12, NEB). The meaning (as we understand the Greek *pros . . . eis . . . eis*) is that the ministers are instituted by Christ to equip the other members of the believing community to exercise their gifts (v. 7, cf. v. 16) in Christian service, to the end that, by means of *both* the 'special ministry' of apostles, prophets, etc., *and* (what for convenience may be termed) the 'common service' of believers, who are all endowed with gifts from the ascended Lord of the church (v. 7), the Body of Christ may be built up (vv. 12b, 16; cf. v. 13b).[28] The special ministry, therefore, is largely pioneering in nature: it leads the way in service to the church, and equips the church for analogous service to itself (and to the world).[29] It thus has a special place in the Lord's purpose for the church, for the fulfilment of which, however, the common service of the believing community itself is also indispensable.[30]

Thirdly, we must try to answer two or three questions that are raised by the Pauline presentation of charismata. (1) Are the charismata 'possessions' in the sense of aptitudes or abilities, or are they simply the activities of service themselves? It has been emphatically asserted that 'charisma is always an event, the gracious activity (*energēma*) of God through a man' which manifests God's grace and power 'in a particular instance and only for that instance.'[31] This claim would seem, however, to be exaggerated, if only because Paul can speak of believers 'having' (*echontes*, Rom. 12:6) differing gifts and can exhort them to use or exercise them in the service of the community (cf. 1 Pet. 4:10).[32] It is certainly true that in cases where the exercise of the gift seems to depend upon the Spirit's immediate inspiration (e.g. prophecy), the 'charisma is not something an individual can put in cold store, as it were';[33] but other gifts (e.g. those of administrative leadership and practical assistance) may as certainly be understood as abilities possessed by individuals.[34] In view of this mixture and the fact that Paul himself gives no definitions in his lists, 'it is likely that he did not make a clear distinction between them [sc. activity and possession]'.[35]

(2) A closely related question is the relation of charisma to natural talent; here again no explicit answer is available

from Paul himself. We may agree that 'charisma is not to be confused with human talent and natural ability' as such;[36] at the same time, it seems reasonable to assume that, particularly in the case of the non-spectacular gifts, the charisma may be built upon an already present or latent natural quality.[37] To be more precise, while such functions as prophecy, miracles, healings and tongues are immediate endowments of the Spirit probably unrelated to any inherent quality in the individual, the gifts of administrative leadership and practical assistance may well be the result of the heightening or intensification by the Holy Spirit of natural qualities that are dedicated to the service of the Lord.[38] We therefore concur with the dictum that 'the direction of Paul's teaching is fairly expressed as follows: any capacity of the believer, including aptitudes present before conversion, brought under the controlling power of God's grace and functioning in his service is a spiritual gift'.[39] This is one aspect of the larger question of the relation between the divine and human factors in the matter of charismata; two other aspects may be mentioned in this connection. (a) Spiritual gifts may be earnestly desired (1 Cor. 14:1; cf. 14:39; 12:31), subject to the disposition of the sovereign Spirit (1 Cor. 12:11). (b) A charisma, even though it is divinely bestowed, does not operate automatically; it can fall into desuetude through neglect (1 Tim. 4:14; cf. Mt. 25:29) and must be kept ablaze through diligent use and constant revitalization (2 Tim. 1:6).[40]

(3) Do the various charismata denote functions or offices?[41] Looking at the four lists again, we may note that list (A) is composed entirely of gifts and not persons, list (B) consists of a personal triad followed by non-personal gifts, list (C) comprises two gifts followed by five persons, while list (D) is made up entirely of persons.[42] Some scholars take the view that in enumerating the charismata Paul 'refers partly to designations of office and partly to functions';[43] Ephesians 4:11, in particular, is thought to refer to office-holders in the church, or at least as containing a double reference — to offices as well as gifts.[44] However, the terminology used in connection with charismata in 1 Corinthians 12:4–6 (diakoniai, acts of service; energēmata, activities), the corre-

spondence between 1 Corinthians 12:28 and verse 18 (*etheto ho theos* the various gifts in the church just as *ho theos etheto ta melē . . . en tō sōmati*, with differing functions), the explicit reference to variety of functions preceding the Romans list (*praxin*, Rom. 12:4), and the immediately following context of Ephesians 4:11 with its emphasis on harmonious functioning among the members of the Body of Christ (vv. 12f., 16) — all these factors strongly favour the conclusion that the charismata refer only to functions appropriate to the gifts, and not to offices.[45] This need not, however, be taken to mean that charisma is to be defined solely in terms of function or activity; rather may it be said that 'the gifts are given for the fulfilment of different functions.[46] Nor does it follow from the conclusion just mentioned that charisma and office are mutually exclusive; the fact is that Paul's teaching on charismata was not designed to answer questions about the organizational aspect of the ministry,[47] and the whole question of the relation between office and function has to be dealt with as a separate issue in greater detail. And that brings us directly to the next section.

II FUNCTION OR OFFICE

A succession of scholars has seen the relation between spiritual gifts and ecclesiastical office, charisma and church order, basically in terms of separation, tension or even opposition.[48] E. Käsemann, in particular, has raised the question of the relationship between the two in a radical form: he sees an irreconcilable conflict between spiritual gifts and all organization of the ministry — except such as results automatically from a free exercise of the charismata.[49] We must ask on the basis of the NT evidence whether such positions can be sustained and, if not, what the true relation is between function and charisma on the one hand, and office and order on the other.[50]

A. The New Testament Evidence

Jesus and His Disciples.[51]

Jesus does not seem to have appointed any of his disciples to any permanent posts; there is no hierarchy among them and even less in evidence is any distinction between priests and laity in the community of Jesus. Yet the very fact that he constituted twelve apostles may indicate that even the early followers of Jesus were not a mere haphazard band, while the picture of the retinue of Jesus during his ministry as one of a series of concentric circles of people provides some evidence of 'degrees of intimacy and of responsible sharing in the work of the Ministry' even at this early stage.

The Primitive Church in Jerusalem.[52]

Leadership of the Jerusalem church was originally in the hands of the twelve apostles, with Peter assuming the role of *primus inter pares*. By the time, however, of the Jerusalem conference, if not earlier (cf. Gal. 2:9), James — the brother of the Lord — had emerged as the undisputed leader in the church (Acts 15:13–21), a position which he maintained up to the time of Paul's fateful visit to Jerusalem (Acts 21:18) and beyond. Closely associated with the apostles throughout the period covered by Acts were the Christian elders; these probably arose by analogy with the elders of Judaism, who had a manifestly official status, and this close connection suggests that the term is to be regarded as an official title and not merely indicative of function.

With the appointment of the seven to assist the apostles (Acts 6:1–6) — the number seven may rest on analogy with the Jewish synagogue, thus again suggesting the official character of this group, even though there is a general consensus of opinion that their appointment does not represent the origin of the diaconate — a highly significant moment had been reached in the development of the ministry in the early church. It is significant as 'a typical example of how the Church may be guided by the Holy Spirit in the formation of new institutions', in this case 'the creation of a new office with appropriate functions' to which suitable persons were elected. It is also significant 'as the first example of that delegation of administrative and social responsibilities to those of appropriate character and gifts, which was to become typical of the Gentile churches, and the recognition of such duties as part of the ministry of Christ'. Its highest significance, for our immediate purposes, lies in its being an illustration of the perfect manner in which charisma, office (order) and function (ministry) are inter-related: seven men of appropriate *gifts* (v. 3) are appointed to their *office* (of almoner) (vv. 3b, 6) for the *ministry* (v. 2, *diakonein*) of serving tables. The priority manifestly rests with the charismatic qualifications of the men, and this provides a warrant for assuming that the apostolic church chose its 'ministers' (using the term *diakonos* in a broad sense) consistently 'from among those persons in whom the Spirit's gifts were most evident'.[53]

There were also prophets in the Jerusalem church, but they do not appear to have played any part in its administration.

The Pauline Communities.[54]

That there was some kind of public or specialized ministry in some of the Pauline churches is attested by a number of scriptures: e.g. Galatians 6:6, where the reference to *tō katē-chounti* suggests the existence of a class of teachers fully supported by the congregation; 1 Thessalonians 5:12f., where the notion of a leadership *vis-à-vis* the rank and file of church members is obvious, and the ground given for the high esteem to be shown towards the leaders (*dia to ergon autōn*) seems to suggest a definite, specialized ministry; Romans 16:1, where the term *diakonos* is probably a desig-nation of office, thus making Phoebe a deacon (or some other sort of 'minister') of the church at Cenchreae; Colossians 4:17, with its reference to the *diakonia* which Archippus is to be solemnly charged to execute fully — probably some recognized, official ministry in the church at Colossae; and Colossians 1:7 (cf. 4:12), in which Epaphras appears as an evangelist of the Lycus Valley and Paul's authorized representative in Colossae.

Some of these churches probably had a rudimentary form of official organization: according to Acts 14:23, Paul and

Barnabas appointed elders as leaders in each of the Galatian churches they had founded, and it is not unreasonable to assume that Paul pursued the same method wherever necessary and possible. This assumption finds support in the fact that Acts 20:17–28 attests the presence of elders in the Ephesian church. In this passage, as in Titus 1:5, 7, *presbyteroi* and *episkopoi* appear as clearly synonymous (vv. 17, 28); this identification implies that there was in apostolic times a certain fluidity about the titles of church officials. On this showing, different titles may have been assumed by the same church leaders: 'elder' conjuring up the notion of office or status, 'overseer/bishop' bringing to the fore the idea of function, as does also the implied title of *poimenes* (Acts 20:28), which links up significantly with the *poimenes* of Ephesians 4:11 (even though the charismata listed there refer to functions and not offices). Of even greater significance is the fact that the appointment of these presbyter-bishops is directly attributed to the work of the Holy Spirit (*hymas to pneuma to hagion etheto episkopous*, v. 28), which probably means, in view of Paul's teaching on spiritual gifts in general and the particular correspondence between Acts 20:28 and Ephesians 4:11 (where the subject is spiritual gifts), that these men were marked out for their ministry by their possession of charismata. This again (as in the case of Acts 6:1–6) illustrates the perfect blending of charisma, office and function: the elders/presbyters (*office*) were endowed by the Holy Spirit with the appropriate *gifts* for the discharge of their work as overseers/bishops and pastors/shepherds (*function*); here again, the sovereignty of the Spirit — and hence the possession of charisma — takes pride of place.

The picture of the local ministry in Corinth, indeed, appears to be quite different: the church workers there (1 Cor. 16:15f.) owed no appointment to apostle or church but were self-appointed (*etaxan heautous*), and the rest of the letter bears out the conclusion that there were no church officers in Corinth. This, however, is probably an exception and should not be regarded as exemplifying a general pattern of the local church ministry; the various disorders, both on the individual and on the corporate level, reflected in 1 Corinthians show that Paul's lament in 3:1–4 was amply justified in regard to more matters than that of dissension within the church, and lend colour to the suggestion that Corinth was exceptionally without a clearly-defined body of elders because 'perhaps the qualities of leadership were slow in manifesting themselves in the Corinthian Church'.[55]

At Philippi there appears to have been a comparatively more advanced system with its *twofold* division of overseers and deacons (Phil. 1:1); here the terms *episkopoi* and *diakonoi* are probably best taken as denoting church officials, though not in the highly developed ecclesiastical sense of a later age. The same categories of people appear as definite officers in the Pastoral Epistles where, indeed, the local ministry shows an even more advanced degree of organization — with apostolic delegates (Timothy, Titus) exercising supreme authority and transmitting the authentic gospel, with bishop-presbyters (Tit. 1:5, 7) engaged in preaching, pastoring, ruling and in their turn passing on the tradition, with deacons (both male and female, 1 Tim. 3:11) rendering service of a more practical and temporal sort, and with suitably qualified widows (1 Tim. 5:9–16) probably assisting the whole by providing ministries particularly adapted to the needs of women.[56] With regard to this picture of the ministry in the Pastorals, which in the view of Käsemann and others manifests tendencies of 'Early Catholicism' and is at odds with Paul's doctrine of charisma,[57] a number of observations may be offered by way of elaboration or emphasis.

(1) Timothy and Titus are apostolic delegates, not adumbrations or the first concrete examples of the monepiscopate in a line of 'apostolic succession': they were temporary delegates sent to deal with specific situations. It would appear that while they were Paul's fellow-labourers on a permanent basis, they were his personal delegates only on those occasions when they were thus commissioned with apostolic authority (as here and at 1 Cor. 4:17; 16:10; 2 Cor. 7:6; 8:6; 12:18).[58]

(2) As in Acts 20:17, 28, the terms 'elder' and 'overseer' seem to be used interchangeably in Titus 1:5, 7. The singular *ho episkopos* in both its occurrences (1 Tim. 3:2; Tit. 1:7) is almost certainly to be taken as generic, referring 'to the bishop as a type and not to the number of bishops in a given

place',[59] while the fact that never in these writings is there mention of 'bishop, presbyters and deacons' in one breath indicates that these terms 'cannot be interrelated along the lines of a three-tiered hierarchy'.[60] If, then, the terms 'bishop' and 'elder' are synonymous and there is clearly a plurality of elders, there is even in the Pastorals no indication of monepiscopal government, the origins of which belong to a later period of church history.

(1) Timothy and Titus are apostolic delegates, not adumbrations or the first concrete examples of the monepiscopate in a line of 'apostolic succession': they were temporary delegates sent to deal with specific situations. It would appear that while they were Paul's fellow-labourers on a permanent basis, they were his personal delegates only on those occasions when they were thus commissioned with apostolic authority (as here and at 1 Cor. 4:17; 16:10; 2 Cor. 7:6; 8:6; 12:18).[58]

(2) As in Acts 20:17, 28, the terms 'elder' and 'overseer' seem to be used interchangeably in Titus 1:5, 7. The singular *ho episkopos* in both its occurrences (1 Tim. 3:2, Tit. 1:7) is almost certainly to be taken as generic, referring 'to the bishop as a type and not to the number of bishops in a given place',[59] while the fact that never in these writings is there mention of 'bishop, presbyters and deacons' in one breath indicates that these terms 'cannot be interrelated along the lines of the three-tiered hierarchy'.[60] If, then the terms 'bishop' and 'elder' are synonymous and there is clearly a plurality of elders, there is even in the Pastorals no indication of monepiscopal government, the origins of which belong to a later period of church history.

(3) The meaning of Timothy's ordination (1 Tim. 4:14; 2 Tim. 1:6) is probably to be sought not in such passages as Acts 8:17; 9:17; 19:6, where the laying on of hands is accompanied by an impartation of the Spirit, apparently as a part of the conversion-initiation experience, but in the precedents of Acts 6:6 and 13:3f., where those receiving the imposition of hands were already Christians had received the Spirit. Interpreted in the light of the latter references, Timothy's ordination probably had the significance of a setting apart for the ministry, though in this particular

instance there also was the actual conferring of a charisma. As for the 'ordination' of elders indicated in 1 Timothy 5:22, there is no warrant for supposing that it is also accompanied by the impartation of charisma, Timothy's case being exceptional; its meaning may simply be the setting apart for service of those who have been duly tested and approved as possessing the necessary qualifications or appropriate gifts for their office. It follows that a firm exegetical basis is lacking for the assertion that in the Pastorals the primitive Christian view of every believer receiving the Spirit in his baptism has given place to the principle of ordination which means the bestowal of the Spirit and induction to an office which is 'now the real bearer of the Spirit', so that 'we can now speak inelegantly, but with absolute accuracy, of the Spirit as the ministerial Spirit'.[61]

(4) If Paul's charge to his understudy in 2 Timothy 2:2 seems to advocate 'a principle of tradition and legitimate succession', it is important to note its true meaning and significance. It should be observed that the apostle's concern in the verse is with succession of *doctrine, not* with succession of *office*. It is possible that some of the 'faithful men' of this verse would be the same as those envisaged as being set apart for the ministry in 1 Timothy 5:22, in which case it is significant that 'ordination' is not so much as mentioned in the present verse. This failure to mention a succession of office means that we are far from the doctrine of apostolic succession which began to find expression in Clement of Rome; while the emphasis on the succession *of sound doctrine* is in close accord with the importance which Paul attaches to the apostolic *paradosis*. Such an emphasis is consonant with the period of the Pastorals, which 'demanded not creativity but faithfulness to the message that had been received'.[62] The apostle must have realized that when the personal supervision was no longer available it would be essential to have a continuous succession of men who were faithful to the truth, to whom the apostolic message could be entrusted. Now that false teachers were already upon the scene, threatening to endanger the purity of the church's faith and morals (1 Tim. 1:3–7, 19f.; 4:1–5; 6:3–5; 2 Tim. 2:14, 16, 23; Tit. 1:10, 14; 3:9), urgency was added to

necessity to make such a 'principle of tradition and legitimate succession' indispensable for the safe perpetuation of the church. From this perspective, the structure of the ministry in the Pastorals can be traced directly to Paul and need not be taken[63] as an upstart innovation of the church of the Pastorals, as a development that found its theological justification only in a fabricated theory of tradition and legitimate succession.

(5) Throughout 1 & 2 Timothy the priority of the Holy Spirit is clearly evident. It was the Spirit who both inspired the prophecies which led to the choice and ordination of Timothy (1 Tim. 1:18) and dispensed to him the charisma needed for his task (1 Tim. 4:14; 2 Tim. 1:6); the Spirit is the one who will enable him — and all those who are to be transmitters of the gospel (2 Tim. 2:2) — to keep the tradition of sound doctrine (2 Tim. 1:14, *phylaxon dia pneumatos hagiou*). In the same way the Spirit is the giver of the charisma of teaching — the aptitude to teach (*didaktikon*) — which is required both of Timothy and of all other servants of the Lord (2 Tim. 2:24). Not least is it required of the presbyter-bishops of the local church (1 Tim. 3:2; Tit. 1:9) and the faithful transmitters of the apostolic message (2 Tim. 2:2). All this shows that the Spirit remains above the ministry as the Lord of charismata and the enabler for its faithful and fruitful discharge, and that neither in the matter of 'ordination' nor in the matter of 'legitimate succession' is there warrant for speaking of 'an *institutionally guaranteed* ecclesiastical office'.[64] The holding of an office is conditional upon the person's faithfulness to the truth and his possessing the gift to teach it to others, and in both respects the person is directly dependent upon the Holy Spirit. Notwithstanding the more developed ecclesiastical structure of the Pastorals, the Holy Spirit is far from being forgotton or imprisoned as 'the ministerial Spirit'; he is still upheld as the sovereign Spirit in his prophetic (1 Tim. 1:18; 4:14; 4:1) and enabling (2 Tim. 1:14) as well as regenerative (Tit. 3:5) power, and thus still recognized as the one on whom the ministry is vitally dependent.

(6) Furthermore, the inter-relation between office, gift and function is illustrated, for the third time (cf. Acts 6:1–

6; 20:17, 28), by their juxtaposition in a single passage (1 Tim. 3:1f.): the ministry of an overseer is at once an *office* to hold (*episkopē*) and a task or *function* to perform (*ergon*), for which equipment by the Spirit with the appropriate *gift* (v. 2, *didaktikon*) is a prerequisite.

The Community in Hebrews.[65]

In this epistle a distinct group of church leaders is given special mention and prominence (13:7, 17, 24), perhaps with the intention of strengthening their authority. The word used of these leaders (*hēgoumenoi*) is one which suggests authority rather than office, and obedience is urged not as due to an office as such, but to the pastoral ministry that the leaders are actually exercising, just as the ministry of teaching is based on spiritual maturity expressed in discernment (5:14). This, however, need not in itself preclude the existence of officials in the church, particularly in view of the fact that the author's apologetic aim to present the absolute superiority of the new order to the old has led to an intense concentration of ministry in the final and perfect high priest, Jesus Christ. In the light of the clear distinction between the leaders and the led (cf. 1 Thess. 5:12f.), the *hēgoumenoi* are probably best interpreted as representing 'a primitive form of church order' without exclusion of the possibility that they are the people elsewhere called bishops or presbyters.

The Church of the General Epistles.[66]

In the Epistles (as in the Gospel) of John and in the Epistle of Jude, there is no mention of special ministries, charismata or offices. But the teaching of 1 Peter 4:10f. shows very close affinities with the Pauline concept of charisma, as we have noted already in our discussion of spiritual gifts.[67] The variegated grace of God manifests itself in the many different charismata of the community, whose members have received each his own gift, and they are to employ their gifts in loving service (cf. v. 8) to one another as good stewards of that same grace. Verse 11 cites two examples of specialized tasks, which representatively divide the exercise of charismata into ministry of word and ministry of deed (cf. Acts 6:2). In common with Paul, the passage makes it abundantly clear that the gift bestowed by God constitutes a call to ministry (cf. Rom. 12:6–8) and that all ministry is grounded in, derived from, and supported by God's power (v. 11b).[68] The fact that the verb *lalein* is used elsewhere with the connotation of teaching and preaching (e.g. Acts 10:44; 2 Cor. 2:17; 4:13; Phil. 1:14) and the parallelism between *eitis lalei* and *eitis diakonei* have led some interpreters to see in verse 11 a reference to church officials;[69] if this is correct, we have here yet another illustration (besides Acts and the Pastorals) of the interweaving of gift, task and office.

In any event, an ordered ministry is clearly envisaged in 1 Peter 5:1–4, with a definite body of elders whose function is described in terms of 'pastoral oversight' (if *episkopountes* in v. 2 is original) and 'shepherding' God's flock committed to their charge (*poimanate to . . . poimnion*, v. 2; cf. Acts 20:28) and who are warned against the possible abuse of authority (v. 3). Alongside the 'charisma constitution' of 4:10f., then, is placed 'the constitutional office of the elders' here;[70] on the basis of the earlier passage, the elders may reasonably be regarded as having received the appropriate gifts for their office — thus confirming the evidence of, or at least providing firmer evidence than, 1 Peter 4:10f. that gift, function and office can and do blend together in perfect harmony.

In the Epistle of James we find mention of 'teachers' (3:1) and 'elders' (5:14f.). The former passage suggests that there was a recognized group of teachers comparable to those in other early Christian communities (cf. Acts 13:1; 1 Cor. 12:28f.) and that unworthy candidates were eagerly going after the office without taking its responsibilities seriously. In the latter passage, the elders of the church — office-bearers rather than just senior men of the congregation (note, *tous*) — are envisaged as praying over a sick member who is then miraculously cured in response to the prayer of faith (cf. v. 16b). This presupposes the early Christian experience of charismata and involves in particular the gifts of faith and of healing — or perhaps we should say the charisma of 'healing intercession'.[71] It is unnecessary, however, to suppose that each elder will have this particular gift by virtue of his office;[72] it seems preferable to take *tous presbyterous* as a generalizing plural, and to suppose that those who possessed the charismata in the largest measure would be included in the body of elders and the latter would, on notification of the case of sickness, consider whether it was a fit case for the exercise of the charisma of healing intercession and depute some of their number to pray for the sick person.[73] It is also noteworthy that this gift is not confined to the body of elders as their sole prerogative: verse 16 suggests that anyone with the gift of healing intercession could heal the sick by prayer.[74] Thus James 5:14f. not only provides a fifth instance of the harmony between gift, function and office which we have seen illustrated in the Acts, the Pastorals and 1 Peter; taken with verse 16 it also hints at another important principle, namely that while charismata can and do find expression in office, charisma cannot be subsumed under the rubric of ecclesiastical office. Further, the three verses together illustrate the distinction between the 'specialized ministry' (here the elders) and the 'common service' (whoever has the charisma) to which attention has already been drawn.[75]

The Church in Revelation.[76]

The book of Revelation makes no reference to any church officials: the elders who appear in the heavenly throne-room (e.g. 4:4; 5:5; 7:11; 11:16; 14:3; 19:4) are probably best understood as an exalted order of angelic beings; the apostles appear (21:14) as the foundation-stones of the New Jerusalem and so belonging to the founding era of the church. The references to prophets (10:7; 11:12, 18; 16:6; 18:20, 24; 22:6, 9) in themselves shed little light on church order in the Apocalypse, but since 'testimony' is expected of the church in general (12:17) and testimony to Jesus is supremely the hallmark of 'the spirit of prophecy' (19:10), in principle the whole church is understood as a community of prophets, even though some are specially called to seal their testimony and 'prophecy' with their blood (6:9; 12:11). Insofar as this may be accepted as a determining factor, we may concur that the church as presented in Revelation 'is guided spiritually and prophetically rather than according to fixed offices'.[77]

B. Concluding Observations[78]

On the basis of the evidence surveyed above, we may now draw the threads together in an attempt to answer the question which we set ourselves at the beginning of this section (II), which was: Is there any contradiction between charisma and church order, and what is the true relation between function, gift and office?

(1) The existence of some kind of specialized ministry, or more specifically of church officers, is attested for the primitive church in Jerusalem, for all the Pauline churches with the sole exception of Corinth, and for some of the churches in the General Epistles (1 Peter, James). If a different picture obtains in the Gospel and Epistles of John and Revelation, this suggests only that church organization was still fluid during the New Testament period, that 'there is no such thing as *the* New Testament Church order', and that different lines of development are discernible;[79] the existence of an organized and official ministry remains unaffected.

Further, it is possible, and perhaps even likely, that varying nomenclature used of church leaders refers basically to the same group, so that while 'functional' terms are sometimes employed to emphasize that aspect of the ministry, they point to the same 'functionaries' who are elsewhere described with a more official title; here we think especially of those who are referred to as *proistamenoi* (1 Thess. 5:12), *poimenes* (Eph. 4:11), *hēgoumenoi* (Heb. 13:17, 24), all of whom may well be identical with those designated elsewhere as elders and overseers. In any event, there is ample evidence which more than suffices to show that the early Christian communities were not amorphous associations run on haphazard lines; on the contrary, most if not all of them had at least a rudimentary, and some had a more advanced, form of church organization — although, on the other hand, there are no grounds for thinking that the monepiscopate is to be found within the pages of the New Testament.

That the ministry should have been organized to greater or lesser degree is not only consistent with Jewish influence upon the structure of the church; it is consistent also with the practical demands of expanding communities,[80] and with the simple fact that the local church, composed as it is of people 'who belong simultaneously to the natural and the supernatural order of life . . . [,] cannot be severed from the earthly conditions of existence'[81] — among which organization is essential and indispensable.

(2) There is no intrinsic incompatibility between spiritual gift and an organized ministry involving ecclesiastical office and official authority. The fact that Paul, though doubtless a 'charismatic' himself, possessed an official status and official authority as an apostle suggests that the doctrine of charismata is not in principle at odds with the idea of official authority. More specifically, there need be no conflict between Spirit of office; the latter 'is not unspiritual just as long as it remains obedient to the Spirit of Christ, and performs that service of the Gospel of Christ for which it was appointed'.[82] That there is no opposition in practice between spiritual gift and ecclesiastical office is clearly illustrated in at least two ways. First, time and again in the above survey (section A) it has clearly emerged that function, gift and office are perfectly fused into a united whole; not only in Acts (the appointment of the seven, 6:1–6; the Ephesian elders, 20:17, 28) and in Paul (the Pastorals), but also in 1 Peter (5:1–4; perhaps also 4:10f.) and in James (5:14f.), the three are seen as existing in perfect harmony. Second, several of the charismata mentioned by Paul significantly find their counterparts in the qualifications laid down for presbyter-bishops and deacons in the Pastorals, thus:

diakonia	(Rom. 12:7)	*diakoneitōsan*	(1 Tim. 3:10)
didaskalia	(Rom. 12:7)	*didaktikos*	(1 Tim. 3:2; cf. Tit. 1:9)
paraklēsis	(Rom. 12:8)	*parakatien*	(Tit. 1:9)

| *hoi poimenes* | (Eph. | *hoi proestōtes* | (1 Tim. 5:17; cf. |
| | 4:11) | | 3:4, 5, 12) |

Further, the gifts of *antilēmpsis* and *kybernēsis* mentioned in
1 Corinthians 12:28 (numbers [6] and [7a] in our list [B])
are most probably to be linked with 'deacons' and 'overseers'
respectively.[83] This alignment of gift with office indicates,
on the one hand, that gift can find expression in office and,
on the other hand, that office must not be severed from gift.
The true relationship between function, gift and office,
therefore, appears to be this: office and function are two
aspects of the person's ministry (i.e. in the case of someone
who holds office), for which he must have the appropriate
gifts.

All this goes to show that the antithesis which Käsemann
and others have set up (in the name of Paul) between
charisma and office is not substantiated by the New Testament evidence; rather is it 'highly questionable whether in
Paul's mind [or in Peter's, for that matter] the two things
were ever separated'.[84] What must never be lost sight of,
and can never be over-emphasized, is the priority of the
Spirit and his gifts in the mutual relations of function, gift
and office which we have repeatedly noticed (in discussing
the passages in Acts 6, 20; the Pastorals; 1 Pet. 4, 5; Jas. 5).
It is the charisma, not the office, that creates the ministry:
the office is but the channel through which the office-bearer
may exercise the given charisma for a particular function;
and the church's appointment to office (where such is
involved) is but a sign of recognizing a person's spiritual gifts
and response to God's will made known in the bestowing of
those gifts. In all of this, the Spirit stands sovereign — over
office, function and gift alike.

(3) The fusion of function, gift and office underlined
above does not mean however, that spiritual gifts cannot be
expressed independently of office. The truth is rather that
while office must be accompanied by charisma corresponding to the function of the office, charisma can be employed
in service either through office or apart from office — a
principle we saw hinted at in James 5:14–16.[85] As far as the
actual lists of charismata are concerned, a distinction may

be drawn between the more private gifts (sharing, caring, showing mercy: F 3–5 in our classification) to be exercised perhaps largely in a personal capacity and the more public ones (A 1, B 1, C 1, 4, E 1–2, F 1–2) designed to be used regularly and constantly within the community. It is significant that besides 'apostles' and 'prophets', all the other gifts just mentioned can be associated with overseers and deacons (administrators = pastors, helpers) and even definitely identified with their qualification or functions (teaching, exhortation, service, pastoring = administration); it thus appears that the more public gifts are intended for, and are actually exercised by, those who represent the public ministry of the church: apostles, prophets, teachers, presbyter-bishops and deacons. A further distinction should probably be made between 'gifts of permanent validity and value, and gifts of temporary and apostolic usage, now withdrawn'[86] — among which apostles and prophets may be classed.[87] These distinctions can be correlated with a third one: that between the 'specialized ministry' and the 'common service';[88] the specialized ministry comprised with more public gifts and hence the regular ministry of the church, which, with the passing away of the unique order of apostles and the distinctly miraculous order of prophets, became essentially identical with that of the presbyter-bishops and deacons. James 5:14f. stands as a salutary reminder that a supernatural charisma (such as that of healing intercession) is by no means incompatible with the official ministry of presbyter-bishops.

III THE MINISTRY OF WOMEN

We have seen in the previous section that no incompatibility exists between the (specifically Pauline) doctrine of charismata and the picture of the *outward form* of the ministry, so far as this is reflected in the New Testament writings. It will be useful now to recall that between the doctrine of charismata and the *inner nature* of the ministry as conceived by Paul there is perfect consistency and complete correspondence.[89] Two points in the relation may be worth repeating in the present context: (1) As the charismata have their origin in the work of the triune God and are distributed according to his will, so the ministry has its origin in God and is dependent on him. The (special) ministry, in fact, consists of men endowed with charismata who are given by the church's Lord; and inasmuch as the ministry and the charismata have the same ultimate goal in view (viz., the *oikodomē* of the church as the Body of Christ), it may reasonably be deduced that the charismata are the wherewithal, the tools, the means of the ministry. It is because there are men endowed with charismata that there is such a thing as the Christian ministry; it is by the endowment of charismata that its ministers are made sufficient. (2) As there is a multiplicity of charismata within the unity of the Body of Christ, so the same principle marks both the 'special ministry' and the 'common service': unity within the structure of the one Body and multiplicity in the variety of functions in its members. Because none is without gift, all may take part in ministry; hence the common service. But because the gifts are not distributed indiscriminately, there is not only differentiation of function from function within the common service, but also the distinction between that and the special ministry as well as within the special ministry itself.

That this intimate relation between charismata and ministry has an important bearing on the issue of women's ministry is made crystal clear by the following quotation:

> The principal task of the church in community is to edify its diverse membership. The medium through which this is to be accomplished is that of spiritual gifts. These are distributed variously thoughout the congregation, without respect to sex. There is not the slightest hint in the relevant Scriptures that those gifts which could equip for leadership positions (preaching, teaching, prophesying, etc.) will be restricted to men, while those equipping for other ministries (giving of money, practising hospitality, demonstrating love, etc.) will be bequeathed on women. . . . If gifts equipping for leadership positions are distributed by *God* to women, what higher authority does the Church have for denying the women their expression?[90]

This seems to be a potent argument in favour of the view that women should be free to participate in the complete range of Christian ministries to the full extent of their gifts. It might further be claimed that the doctrine of spiritual gifts assumes an even greater significance for women's ministry today than in Paul's day. The fact that women in general were not highly educated then was bound to have a limiting effect on the variety of their gifts and hence on their mode of ministry; however, with the far greater educational opportunities that are available to women in our century, and the vastly different cultural and societal situation of today (I am speaking primarily, but not exclusively, of western society), we may reasonably expect a broadening of the variety of women's gifts and hence the scope of their ministries.

In view, then, of the undistinguishing manner in which the Spirit is said to bestow gifts on men and women alike, and secondarily, of the altered cultural situation of modern times, we are much inclined to concur with the following statement:

> The variety and flexibility of ministry in the New Testament in the light of the needs of the situation and the gifts exercised in any given church would suggest that this is the pattern and precedent to be followed in thinking about ministry today. We should not ask whether there is a formal precedent but whether there is a gift of the Spirit and a need. With regard to the ministry of women we should not try to reproduce their rôle in the first-century milieu. We should rather ask what is their status in Christ, and what gifts and opportunities has the Spirit given to women in the church today.[91]

At the same time, however, it has to be remembered that, important as they are, the charismata do not constitute the only or all-determining factor in considering the role of women in the church, and that Paul's practice and his teaching with regard to women in ministry also need to be taken into account. The following pages, then, are devoted to an examination of this, and we will deal with Paul's attitude to women in ministry and four key passages of scripture bearing on our subject.[92]

A. Paul's Attitude to Women in Ministry

It is commonly agreed that Paul's general attitude to women, like his Master's, was in marked contrast to that of the rabbis. In his letters, a number of women are mentioned by name, not a few with obvious affection and respect. Of the twenty-eight persons named in Romans 16, seven or possibly eight are women. (i) Phoebe (vv. 1f.) — the only person named in the New Testament as a *diakonos* of a local church — was probably a deacon in the church of Cenchreae;[93] her further designation as a *prostatis* ('protectress, patroness, helper', BAG *s.v.*) of many, including Paul, may imply that she was a woman of means, but, particularly if taken with *diakonon*, could equally well suggest that the help rendered was material and administrative assistance given in her capacity as a deacon of the church.[94] (ii) That Priscilla and Aquila (v. 3) participated in the gospel ministry with Paul is shown by their designation as his *synergoi* (used in the singular of Timothy in 1 Thess. 3:2 and of Luke in Phm. 24) 'in Christ Jesus'.[95] Priscilla, in particular, appears to have had the gift of teaching (cf. Acts 18:26), although there is no evidence that she engaged in public teaching; the fact that her name precedes that of her husband in four of the six references to this couple is probably an indication that she played a more prominent part than he did in the life and ministry of the church — unless, in line with the custom of the secular society of the time, it is purely a reflection of her superior social status. The couple may have been founder-members of the Roman church, and probably, as host and hostess, played a leading role in the house churches with which their names are connected (1 Cor. 16:19; Rom. 16:5). (iii) In Romans 16:7, the correct reading appears to be not *Ioulian* (as in v. 15) but *Iounian*,[96] and the most natural reading of the phrase *episēmoi en tois apostolois* makes Andronicus and *Iounian* persons of note among 'the apostles'; but it is debated whether *Iounian* should be accented (with circumflex) as masculine (as in Nestle-Aland[26] and BFBS[2]) or (with acute) as feminine. If the feminine form is preferred, then Junia, likely the wife of

Andronicus,[97] is a female 'apostle' — though *apostolois* here probably does not have the technical sense of the word (as in Rom. 1:1), but rather the broader sense of commissioned representatives of the churches (as in 2 Cor. 8:23; Phil. 2:25). Even if one prefers the feminine form, then, it would be unwise to place too much weight on this text, particularly in view of the ambiguity giving rise to the feminine/masculine debate. (iv) Of the remaining five women in Romans 16, four share a common feature — their hard work in the Lord (vv. 6, 12). The verb *kopiaō* is elsewhere used by Paul of his own ministry (five times: 1 Cor. 15:10; Gal. 4:11; Phil. 2:16; Col. 1:29; 1 Tim. 4:10) and of the service of others in the church (three times: 1 Cor. 16:16; 1 Thess. 5:12; 1 Tim. 5:17);[98] particularly noteworthy is the construction in verse 6 (*ekopiasen eis hymas*), which closely parallels that of Galatians 4:11 (*kekopiaka eis hymas*). These considerations would seem to suggest that the 'labour' of these women for the church and for the Lord included, or at least may have included, the activities of preaching and teaching.

In Philippians 4:2f., two women, Euodia and Syntyche, are mentioned together with Clement and others as belonging to the company of Paul's fellow-workers (*synergoi*, as in Rom. 16:3); the reference to their having laboured (*synēthlē- san*) alongside the apostle in the gospel in most naturally understood of their participation in preaching the gospel.[99] The fact that Paul thus publicly in the letter appeals to them to iron out their differences reflects their prominent position in the church: it would appear that his repeated appeals for unity earlier in the letter (1:27–2:11) are to be understood against the possible background of their influential position which made their personal conflict or rivalry a threat to the unity and well-being of the community.

In addition to these examples of individual women distinguished by their participation in ministry, 1 Timothy 3:11 mentions certain women who are probably to be understood as women deacons.[100] That nothing is said about their family responsibilities or relationships may indicate that they were single or more elderly women who could devote themselves more whole-heartedly to serving the church.[101] Mention is also made of certain widows (1 Tim. 5:9–16, distinct from those mentioned in vv. 3–8) who were 'enrol-led' in an officially recognized list (vv. 9, 11), showing that there was at that time a definite order of widows;[102] it is not clear, however, whether they had any official duties or not.

The above survey shows that Paul acknowledged the service of a woman deacon in a local church, accepted several women as being among his fellow-workers, showed appreciation for the ministry of certain other women, and *perhaps* recognized another as an 'apostle' — albeit only in the broad sense of the word. We are thus warranted in saying that Paul allowed women an active part in the ministry of the church and the service of the gospel, and that some of them *may* have taken a leading role, including *possibly* participation in the work of preaching and teaching. Such a conclusion is in harmony with Paul's teaching concerning spiritual gifts, which are bestowed without regard to distinc-tions of sex. At the same time, it is worth noting that the evidence nowhere suggests that any woman was recognized as occupying a teaching office,[103] and this fact may be signifi-cant for an understanding of Paul's teaching on the role of women in church.

No 'Male and Female' (Gal. 3:28)

Paul affirms in Galatians 3:28 that in Christ Jesus 'there is no such thing as . . . male and female' (NEB). It has been said that 'this word from Paul gathers up the intention in creation and redemption into one phrase and gives it expression'; more specifically, the verse has been called the 'magna carta of Christian feminism.'[104] That this verse is one of the most important statements ever made by Paul is beyond question, but its precise significance for the issue of women's ministry remains a matter of debate and merits some discussion here.

It is noteworthy that the actual words used are not the customary ones for man and woman (*anēr*, *gynē*) but the more technical terms denoting male and female (*arsen kai thēlys*, cf. Gen. 1:27 LXX; Mk. 10:6), thus indicating that Paul has the relationship between the sexes (not specifically husband and wife) in view. On the basis of a comparison with the parallel structures in 1 Corinthians 12:12f. and Colossians 3:9–11, Galatians 3:28 has been judged to be 'almost certainly a fragment of an early baptismal formula.'[105] Certainly, the context clearly shows that the primary emphasis of the verse is on the idea of unity in Christ — all who have put on Christ through baptism into Christ form a corporate unity (*heis*, masculine: NEB 'one person', RV 'one man') — rather than an equality of the sexes;[106] if the notion of equality is also involved, it is only secondary and has regard to the sexes' relationship to Christ and membership in the community.

An impressive list of scholars have gone beyond this to draw out important implications of Paul's statement for women's ministry. Thus, it is maintained that the three antitheses which Paul lists in the verse, representing the 'three deepest divisions which split the society of the ancient world', are manifestly intended to be treated as parallel to one another; on the basis of this parallelism it is contended 'that all three of these pairs have the same potential for implementation in the life and structure of the church, and that we cannot dispose of the third by confining it to the realm *coram deo*'. Hence, if Gentiles as well as Jews may be entrusted with the responsibilities of spiritual leadership in the church, and slaves as well as freemen, by analogy women may be equally entrusted as men; viewed in this light, Galatians 3:28 is 'an affirmation which does not deny the distinction between the two sexes but abolishes any inequality between them in respect of religious roles'. If nevertheless the statement can be said to represent 'a Pauline dream . . . that was not completely realized in the Pauline communities', that is because, 'in its implementation, the New Testament church reflects, to a considerable extent, the prevailing attitudes and practices of the times'; Paul's fundamental principle is represented by the dream, not by its incomplete realization.[107]

In spite, however, of the attractiveness of this view (it is fully consonant with Paul's doctrine of charismata) and the weight of authority behind it, we are bound to ask whether it is squarely supported by the text itself. Besides the doubt cast upon it by the contextual consideration that Paul's statement is not concerned with the role relationships of men and women within the Body of Christ but rather with their common initiation/integration into it through faith and baptism, it may be questioned whether the parallelism between the male-female pair and the other two pairs has not been unduly pressed. It appears that the three categories differ in nature, and that accordingly the social implementations for them are not the same. Whereas slavery, as a social institution created by sinful men, can and should be abolished, and the Jew/Gentile distinction, which retains its validity as a purely ethnic reality, has been transcended through the reconciliation accomplished by Christ (Eph. 2:14–16), the male/female distinction, unlike the other two, has its roots in creation itself and continues to have significance in the realm of redemption. Thus 'each of these pairs must be understood in terms of itself, in the way that Scripture understands them'.[108] It would seem precarious, therefore, to appeal to Galatians 3:28 in support of any view of the role of women in church; for clearer light on Paul's conception of women's ministry (in so far as such is available) we must look to other scriptures.

C. Women to Cover Their Heads (1 Cor. 11:2–16)

This passage is the first of a series in which Paul deals with several disorders and abuses at worship which had arisen in the Corinthian church:[109] they concern the 'veiling' of women (11:2–16), the Lord's Supper (11:17–34) and spiritual gifts (12–14). The issue of head-coverings for women appears to have been occasioned by certain 'emancipated' women at Corinth who were asserting their equality with men which they understood to be implicit in the gospel (cf. Gal. 3:28) by praying and prophesying without any covering on their heads. Paul holds that they should have their heads covered, and adduces three arguments in support of his position. He appeals to the creation order (vv. 3–12), to the criterion of propriety and the indication of 'nature' (vv. 13–15), and to the custom of the churches (v. 16).

The first argument is doctrinal in nature: the introductory formula (*thelō de hymas eidenai*, v. 3a) indicates that Paul here 'wishes to emphasise an important point of doctrine,[110] which is stated in three parallel clauses:

pantos andros hē kephalē . . . . *ho Christos estin,*
kephalē de gynaikos . . . . . *ho anēr,*
kephalē de tou Christou . . . *ho theos.*

In this foundational statement, the second clause is generally taken in the sense 'the head of a woman is the man' (cf. KJV, RV, NEB, NASB, NIV), but the RSV rendering — 'the head of a woman is her husband' (cf. NEB mg.) — is attractive and has many supporters.[111] One or two considerations are indeed in favour of this understanding. (i) The close resemblance between 1 Corinthians 11:3b and Ephesians 5:23a (*anēr estin kephalē tēs gynaikos*), which in its context obviously means 'the husband is the head of the wife' (NIV), could suggest that the same essential fact of the headship of the husband over the wife may be in view here as well. (ii) The last statement in verse 7 (*hē gynē de doxa andros estin*) is supported in verses 8f. by reference to the creation account in Genesis 2:18–24, which describes how Adam acquired Eve as his partner and the two entered into a 'one flesh' husband-wife relationship, the latter emphasis being brought out particularly clearly in verses 23–25.[112] This could suggest that in appealing to the creation order here Paul is thinking not in general terms of the male-female relationship but rather specifically of the husband-wife relationship. Now it may reasonably be assumed that in the Corinthian church most women were in fact married (cf. 1 Cor. 14:35a),[113] and it may be readily admitted that Paul in this passage does have married women chiefly in view. But the presence of unmarried and widowed women in the church was probably well known to Paul (cf. 1 Cor. 7:34, 39); these should also be included within his purview. Moreover, it is not entirely clear that *anēr* in verse 7 refers to the husband specifically, and correspondingly that *gynē* refers to the wife; the parallelism between verse 12a (with its reference to woman's creation from man) and verse 12b suggests that the latter has general reference to man's pro-creation through woman (even though in each individual case this takes place or should take place, of course, in the context of the husband-wife relationship). In verse 3 itself, *anēr* in the emphatic *pantos andros* is surely to be understood of man in general; this creates a presumption in favour of taking *pas anēr* and *pasa gynē* in verses 4–5 in the sense of 'every man' and 'every woman' — unless it can be shown that a change of nuance in *anēr* has occurred between verse 3a and verse 3b, which is not obviously the case. It would seem best, then, to adhere to the more common understanding of verse 3b as announcing the general principle of the headship of man in relation to woman, a principle which finds its primary application and obvious illustration in the specific husband-wife relationship.[114]

Two facts are emphasized in verse 3: the fact of 'headship', and the distinction between the sexes — as Christ has God (the Father) as his head, so every man has Christ as his head and woman has man as her head. *Kephalē* is often taken to mean 'source' or 'origin', with or without involving as a collorary the idea of subordination on the part of the one who is derived; alternatively, the term may be understood as referring to a position of authority.[115] The latter view is here preferred for the following reasons: (i) An important recent lexical study has sufficiently demonstrated that the claim that *kephalē* could mean 'source' at the time of the New Testament 'has so far been supported by not one clear instance in all of Greek literature, and is therefore a claim without any real factual support'. On the other hand, the same study has conclusively shown, the meaning 'authority over' was a well-established and recognizable meaning in Greek literature at the time of the New Testament.[116] (ii) Even if the meaning 'source' were attested for *kephalē* taking the word in that sense in 1 Corinthians 11:3 would not yield 'a satisfactory set of parallels'.[117] (iii) Paul does not elsewhere describe God the Father as the origin of Christ, but does speak of Christ's subordination to the Father (1 Cor. 3:23; 15:28), making it probable that the reference in the third clause is to the fact of Christ's subordination (in his capacity as the Messiah or as the Son) to the Father.[118] (iv) Ephesians 5:22–24 teaches the subordination of the wife to her husband as her head, on the analogy that the church is to submit to

Christ its head; thus 'headship', as standing over against the idea of submission, acquires the sense of 'authority over'. Since the principle in the second clause of our verse has primary application to the marriage relationship, *kephalē* is likely to have the same connotation as in Ephesians 5, that is, 'head over'. (v) Kephalē in the first clause is best taken in a sense consistent with its meaning in the other two clauses. (vi) Kephalē is the almost exclusive translation in the Septuagint for Hebrew *rô'sh* and is used for the head or ruler of a society (as in e.g. Judg. 10:18);[119] its use in a similar sense in our passage would have come naturally to Paul.

The fundamental principle of man's headship over woman is in verses 4–6 applied to the matter of covering the head in worship. The precise nature of the 'head-covering' is a matter of debate, with the traditional understanding of its being some kind of 'veil' or shawl concealing the hair and upper part of the body being called into question by recent interpretations which see Paul's requirement for women in terms of long hair or a particular coiffure (cf. NIV mg.);[120] but since Paul's argument in the passage is not substantially affected by the precise nature of the head-covering,[121] we may for our present purpose follow the more common view. Paul rules that for a man, who is the image and glory of God (v. 7) and thus under subjection to no other creature, to pray or prophesy with his head *covered* would be to dishonour his head — by practically abdicating the dignity bestowed on him by his Creator, thus doing despite both to his physical head (which as the symbol of his dignity represents himself) and to his metaphorical head, who is Christ.[122] A woman, however, who prays or prophesies with her head *uncovered* dishonours her head — both her physical head (as vv. 5b–6 clearly shows)[123] and her metaphorical head, i.e. man: for to cast aside the symbol of her differentiation from man was tantamount to denying her relation to man as designed by the creation ordinance; more specifically, in the case of a married woman, her metaphorical head would be her husband, and to cast aside the symbol of her subordination to her husband was tantamount to denying his headship over her and thus dishonouring him.[124] In fact, according to Jewish custom, a woman who appeared with uncovered head could be regarded as holding her marriage oath in contempt and this would constitute a legitimate ground for divorce by her husband;[125] thus Paul's injunction here may have been motivated in part by his desire, in harmony with his own stated principle of not giving offence (1 Cor. 10:32), to guard the sanctity of Christian marriage from being slandered, through women not covering their heads in public worship, by Jews who may well have cast a critical glance at the activities of the church.[126] But Paul is chiefly concerned, it seems, to point out that the principle of the headship of man (and of the husband in the marriage relationship) as ordained by God in creation remains unaltered by Christian conversion, and that a woman should acknowledge this principle by covering her head while praying or prophesying, thereby also safeguarding Christian marriage from possible reproach.

What has been put negatively in verse 4 about the man is reiterated, explained and supported by means of a positive reason in verse 7a: man ought not to cover his head because he is created in the image of God and thus reflects his splendour.[127] Similarly, what was expressed negatively in verses 5f. about the woman is now put positively in verses 7b–10. The statement of verse 7b — woman is the glory of man[128] — is supported in verses 8f. (note *gar*) by reference to the second creation account (Gen. 2:18–23), from which Paul brings out two points: woman's derivation from man, and her being created for the benefit of the man. In the light of verse 3b, it would appear that Paul conceives of woman's derivation from man (and not the other way round) as giving rise to the principle of man's headship and woman's subordination; while his affirmation that woman was created *dia ton andra* recalled the word *ēzer* in the Hebrew text (LXX *boēthos*), which focuses on the help and support that Eve was to be to Adam. By designating woman as the glory of man, then, Paul would seem to be saying that woman is the source of honour and pride for man — *doxa* being taken in the subjective sense of 'that which gives glory to someone' — in that by her subordination to man she honours his position of headship and by her support and help brings him honour and blessing. (This understanding of vv. 7b–10 can be most fittingly applied to the specific husband-wife relationship, as simple substitution of the words 'woman' and 'man' by 'the wife' and 'the husband' will show.)[129]

Verse 10 restates the rule in a different form by saying that a woman ought to have *exousia* on her head, and further justifies it by reference to the angels. In the phrase *dia touto*, 'this' refers immediately to the statement of verse 7; but as the 'glory' spoken of in that verse is closely connected with the fact of 'headship' spoken of in verses 3–6, *touto* in the long run refers to the content of the entire preceding section (vv. 3–9) in which Paul expounds the difference between man and woman in terms of the creation ordinance.[130] It is tolerably certain that *exousia* here means 'a sign of authority' (NIV), but it is not entirely clear whether the authority concerned is (*a*) the authority to which the woman is subject or (*b*) the authority which the woman exercises.[131] In favour of the latter meaning is the fact that elsewhere in the epistle the word uniformly bears an active sense; over against this is the consideration that the use of *exousia* to mean 'sign of authority' here appears to be unique in the New Testament and hence the question whether the authority in this case is that of the woman herself or of someone else has to be determined from the context.[132] Now the preceding context lays emphasis on the fact that the man is the head of the woman and makes this headship the ground for the ruling that the woman should cover her head while praying or prophesying at worship; this contextual consideration would seem to favour meaning (*a*). Conceivably a mediating position is possible: the *exousia* might be the authority which the woman exercises by virtue of her relationship to the man as her head — thus a kind of 'delegated' authority.[133] At any rate, this much of Paul's meaning seems clear; by covering her physical head, thus acknowledging her subordination to her metaphorical head, a woman may pray and prophesy at public worship.[134] As for the supplementary reason (*dia tous angelous*) appended to verse 10, the meaning is unlikely to be that the angels might be tempted to have evil designs on women without a head-covering;[135] they are rather to be viewed, possibly, as guardians of the created order who will be offended at women who violate the order expressed in verse 3, or, more probably, as unseen visitants at Christian gatherings (cf. 1 Tim. 5:21; Ps. 137:1 LXX, *enantion angelōn psalō soi*) whose presence calls for decorum (cf. 1 Cor. 14:40) in the worshippers' demeanour[136] — including, on the part of women, the wearing of a head-covering while praying or prophesying.

The qualifying statement of verses 11-12 (which RSV, probably rightly, considers parenthetical) is not to be set over against the preceding argument as though the latter had merely the old order in view and verses 11f. alone describe the new order 'in the Lord';[137] for the concern of verse 3 is to state an important doctrinal truth and there it is laid down that the man is the head of the woman. Hence the word *plēn* (v. 11) is to be understood as introducing a restriction:[138] Paul apparently wishes to forestall any misunderstanding or abuse of the concept of man's headship and stresses that the male-female relationship is, nothwithstanding the headship principle, basically one of mutual dependence and indispensability: *en kyriō*, i.e. '*in the Lord's intention*, in the original creation and in its restoration,'[139] each is not independent of (*ou . . . chōris*) the other; just as the first woman was derived from (*ek*) man, so now each man is born of (*dia*) woman and all things are from God, on whom man and woman, together and alike, are dependent. This being the case, Paul implies, the woman should not disregard the headship of the man, nor should the man see himself as ruler of the woman and abuse his authority. That this statement has its bearing on the husband-wife relationship is obvious.[140]

Paul's second argument (vv. 13-15) is an appeal to the Corinthians' own inner sense of propriety (*prepon*, v. 13) which should be informed by the external guidance of nature (vv. 14f.):[141] since long hair has been permanently bestowed on them as a head-covering,[142] women should follow the indication thus given and cover their heads while praying or prophesying at public worship. The concluding appeal (v. 16) — which makes up Paul's third argument — points to the consistency between the custom of the churches and Paul's teaching: neither 'we' (says the apostle) nor the churches of God have such a practice — the reference being probably not to debating with the apostle or women praying with heads covered,[143] but to women not covering their heads while praying or prophesying (cf. v. 5). Such an appeal to the common practice of the churches to augment the authority of his own teaching was particularly fitting for the Corinthians, who in their self-conceit had a tendency to disregard the ways of other Christian communities (cf. 14:36).

If the above exegesis is sound, Paul's ruling that a woman should cover her head when praying or prophesying at public worship is grounded basically in the male-female relationships as intended in God's creation, wherein the man enjoys the status of 'head' over the woman. The other two reasons (the appeal to 'nature' and to the custom of the churches) are clearly subsidiary to, though supportive of, the main reason.[144] Whether the passage (especially v. 5) has in view certain women who possessed the gift of prophecy and exercised it regularly or the occasional phenomenon of some women acting under immediate inspiration,[145] it equally testifies to the fulfilment in the NT church of the OT prophecy concerning daughters as well as sons prophesying in the last days (Joel 2:28; Acts 2:17; cf. Acts 21:9). Paul recognizes the right of women to pray or prophesy at public worship, the only proviso being that they do not repudiate the foundational principle of the man's headship — by discarding the contemporary symbol of woman's differentiation from man (which was also a symbol of the wife's subordination to her husband), thereby also bringing Christian marriage into disrepute.[146] It should be stressed that Paul's discussion 'reflects primarily upon the situation of a married couple', though 'it also affects the generic situation of women in worship'.[147]

D. Women to Keep Silence in Church (1 Cor. 14:33b–36)[148]

That 'the women should keep silence in the assemblies of the church' represents a standard procedure in the Pauline communities; this is shown by verse 33b (cf. 7:17b; 16:1);[149] but the exact nature of this injunction is variously explained.

A preliminary problem is the meaning of verse 34b, which raises two related questions: What does *ho nomos* refer to? And what is the meaning of *hypotassesthōsan*? The frequently voiced opinion that the reference is to God's pronouncement on Eve in Genesis 3:16 ('your husband . . . will rule over you)[150] can hardly be correct: for that verdict was not strictly a curse inflicted upon the woman, but a predictive warning, and in no sense a command.[151] Other interpretations point to the model of male leadership in religious matters throughout the Old Testament, or to a rabbinic oral tradition in first-century Judaism according to which women should be silent in synagogue worship out of respect for the congregation.[152] All these views take *hypotassesthai* (correctly) in the sense of subordination. Yet another view renders the verb as 'control oneself' (supposedly by analogy with the use of the same verb in v. 32) and understands *ho nomos* of the legal efforts which were made to control ecstatic female behaviour in Graeco-Roman society.[153] Even in verse 32, however, *hypotassesthai* retains its basic meaning of 'submission', and elsewhere in Paul there is no instance of this verb being used in the sense of self-control, which is conveyed by a different word-group (*engkrateia*/*engkrateuomai*/*engkratēs*). It seems best, therefore, to retain a similar meaning for the word here and to render it as '[they] must be in submission' (NIV).

To whom this submission is due is a question intimately bound up with the interpretation of *ho nomos*. To take this as a reference to rabbinic oral tradition is to fall into the fallacy of adopting a meaning of the word which, to judge by his own usage, is unlikely for Paul.[154] Since in two other passages in Paul (Rom. 3:19; I Cor. 9:8) the same Greek phrase refers to the OT law, it most probably has a similar sense in the present verse (which bears a specially close similarity to I Cor. 9:8, *kai ho nomos . . . ou legei*). Its specific reference may be to (*a*) the entire corpus of OT laws concerning women, which were designed to teach the wife's submission to her husband, or to (*b*) the principle involved in the order of creation as reported in Genesis 1 and 2.[155] If view (*a*) is favoured by the mention of 'wives' in the context (v. 35), it is rendered less likely by the absolute use (i.e.

without a following dative) of *hypotassesthōsan* and its separation from *tous idious andras*, which is mentioned in specific connection only with 'asking' and not with 'showing submission'; view (*b*) is strongly supported by the fact that the principle of man's headship, which Paul seems to have derived from the second creation account, has already been clearly enunciated in 1 Corinthians 11:3b (cf. vv. 8f.), and therefore appears to be the intended meaning here.[156]

We may now turn to a discussion of various interpretations of verse 34a. (1) *This is an absolute statement prohibiting any form of speaking — including the asking of questions (v. 35) — on the part of women.*[157] It is difficult, however, to think that Paul would stipulate the necessary condition for women to pray and prophesy in church in 11:2–16, only to nullify his previous instruction now by a blanket prohibition against women speaking. (2) *The prohibition has reference to women's idle talk or chatter in the church service.*[158] But there is nothing in the context to support such a conjecture; elsewhere in the chapter the word *lalein* is used consistently of glossolalia or prophesying (vv. 2–6, 13, 18, 23, 27, 28f., 39) and never has the sense 'to chatter'. (3) *The* lalein *in question is self-willed speaking and Paul is preventing women from taking the initiative in speaking.*[159] The usage of *lalein* just noted, however, is against its having in verse 34b such a broad meaning which is unrelated to the exercise of charismatic gifts. (4) The view that *the prohibition is against women speaking (or clamouring to speak) in tongues or engaging in charismatic activities in an unacceptable manner*[160] accords well with the Corinthians' patent obsession with glossolalia (cf. vv. 6–12); but verse 35a is difficult to fit in with this view — what would women eager to speak in tongues desire to learn? — and it is doubtful that this enthusiasm was equally shared by 'all the churches of the saints', among which there must have been some that were less charismatically inclined than the Corinthian church, so as to require Paul's ruling here to be applicable to them as well.

Perhaps the most widely expressed opinion is (5) that *the reference is to women interrupting the service with their questions*, thus causing disorder and perhaps even chaos.[161]

In favour of this view is the explicit injunction that women should save their questions to put them to their husbands at home (v. 35): on the other hand, it is doubtful that the *lalein* of verse 34 can be thus confined to *eperōtan*; it would seem rather that verse 35a represents an application of a general principle to a particular matter.[162] The same considerations (both positive and negative) apply to (6) the view that *Paul here prohibits women interrupting the evaluation of prophetic messages by asking unnecessary questions.*[163] (7) Paul's prohibition is aimed at the Corinthian women who were 'putting in a bid for equality with their husbands . . . as *teachers of men in the congregation'*, 'speaking' in inspired language and laying claim to introduce fresh revelations that they were not willing to have assessed and corrected by the assembly and in accord with apostolic standards'.[164] The chief difficulty we find with this proposal has to do with its interpretation of *hypotassesthōsan* as 'let them be *under control'* and of *ho nomos* as a reference to Paul's own ruling. (8) *The prohibition is directed against the co-participation of wives with their husbands in the prophetic ministries of a Christian meeting*, which may involve her publicly testing her husband's message; understood thus, 1 Corinthians 14:3f. 'represents the application, in a particular cultural context, of an order of the present creation concerning the conduct of a wife *vis-à-vis* her husband'.[165] This otherwise attractive view faces the objection that, in spite of the reference to 'their own husbands', it is not certain that the passage has only wives in view.[166]

(9) *The prohibition is against women preaching or teaching in church*, for this would be a violation of the role relationship of the sexes as designed in God's creation.[167] This view has been criticized for wrongly choosing 1 Timothy 2:11–14 as the interpretative key and failing to consider the context;[168] the criticism is perhaps justified to the extent that the context is in favour of giving *lalein* a narrower meaning than the general sense of preaching and teaching. This leads to what appears to be the least unsatisfactory view, viz. (10) that *women are here forbidden to participate in the congregation's discussion and evaluation of prophetic utterances*; this interpretation has the merit of being most suited to the context and

strongly supported by the structure of the larger unit (14:26–36) as a whole.[169] Since questions 'could be used as a platform for expressing in a none-too-veiled form the very criticisms Paul forbids', verse 35a is added to anticipate this possible evasion of the directive in verse 34.[170] The implication of Paul's reminder to the Corinthian church in verse 36 is that the very phenomenon Paul's injunction was intended to prevent was actually happening in Corinth, which the church as a whole did not find objectionable; this doubtless had something to do with their self-conceited tendency (cf. 4:6; 5:2) to ignore other churches and go off on an independent course of their own. Hence the reminder, which serves as an appeal to follow the general practice of the churches of the saints.[171]

The relationship between 1 Corinthians 14:33b–36 and 11:2–16 merits further discussion, particularly in view of the observation that 'it seems strange that Paul would at one and the same time grant to women the function of prophecy [11:5] and yet deny to them the responsibility of evaluating what the prophets had said'.[172] We may reject out of hand, (1) the extreme view that both passages are interpolations,[173] which is unsubstantiated, and (2) the unsatisfactory dualistic approach which regards the apparent contradiction between the two passages as the result of a conflict in Paul's mind between his rabbinic training and the freedom which the gospel brought.[174] (3) That 1 Corinthians 11:5 may refer to a hypothetical case[175] is difficult to square with the considerable trouble to which Paul puts himself in order to give guidance on the issue. (4) It has been argued that while 1 Corinthians 14 expresses the rule, 1 Corinthians 11 represents a very exceptional phenomenon with might have been confined to Corinth and which, moreover, Paul may not necessarily have approved.[176] It is, however, commonly held (correctly) that in 1 Corinthians 11 Paul's disapproval rests only on women prophesying without a head-covering, not on their activity of prophesying as such; and even supposing that the phenomenon was confined to the Corinthian church, the fact that Paul lays down a rule to regulate it indicates that he allows women to prophesy under certain conditions, and not merely that he was aware of the phenomenon and disapproving of it.

(5) A distinction is sometimes made between the formal meeting, in which women are to keep silence, and the informal gathering, where women are permitted to pray and prophesy.[177] But not only is such a distinction difficult to substantiate from the New Testament generally, but the particular contexts provide positive evidence that both passages have assemblies of the whole community in view (11:18; 14:26), and the activity of prophecy is one which should take place in the assembly of the church to the edification of the entire congregation (14:3–19). (6) The distinction is seen to be between charismatically gifted women who have a right to bring a message (1 Cor. 11) and women who are present at worship as ordinary members of the congregation who are to be silent (1 Cor. 14).[178] But, as already mentioned, the context suggests that the silence enjoined is not a general prohibition but rather has specific reference to the participation of women in the evaluation of prophetic messages. (7) Another suggestion sees 1 Corinthians 11:5 as reflecting 'the procedures used within the prayer sessions of the pneumatics' and 1 Corinthians 14 as representing Paul's attitude 'toward the participation of wives in the worship service';[179] but quite apart from the doubtful restriction of 'the women' to 'wives', this view faces the difficulty that the general context of chapters 11–14 strongly suggests that in chapter 11 as well Paul has in view not some special session of a charismatic coterie, but the general worship service of the church.

(8) In view of the twofold conclusion we have accepted above — 1 Corinthians 14 has reference to the prohibition of women's participation in the public evaluation of prophecies, and ho nomos in verse 34b is an allusion to the principle of man's headship over woman which is entailed in the creation order — we may reasonably infer that for women to partake in the public evaluation of prophecies would be 'insubordinate' conduct involving a violation of the principle of man's headship over woman, which violation is not involved by women praying or prophesying (with their heads covered). Why the principle of headship/subordination is considered

to be violated by the one activity and not by the other two is not evident from the Corinthians passages themselves, and we shall return to this question after we have examined our final key passage (1 Tim. 2:11–15) in the next subsection. Meanwhile, we may observe that, if the above reasoning is correct, there is no contradiction between the two passages: 1 Corinthians 11 gives Paul's general instruction regarding women praying or prophesying under inspiration, while 1 Corinthians 14 represents a special restriction on the ministry of women, in that they are not to participate in the public evaluation of prophecies, since that would involve them in a violation of the principle of headship/subordination. It is noteworthy that in both passages the basic reason for Paul's injunction to women has to do with this foundational principle of the headship of man over woman, and correspondingly the subordination of woman to man.

E. Women Not to Teach or to Have Authority over Men (1 Tim. 2:11–15)[180]

In the verses preceding this passage, Paul gives Timothy instructions concerning public prayer (2:1–7) and then mentions in the same breath how men should pray (v. 8) and how women should adorn themselves (vv. 9f.). The word *hōsautōs* indicates that verses 9f. are a continuation of the preceding instructions about public prayer and therefore concerned with the question of women's dress and deportment at public worship.[181] Beginning with verse 11, Paul describes how women are to conduct themselves in church.

The positive statement of verse 11 clearly shows that the main concern here is with the matter of women's 'learning' or receiving instruction in the Christian faith.[182] In this matter, the correct attitude enjoined upon the women is described in the two prepositional phrases *en hēsychia* and *en pasē hypotagē*. Elsewhere in Pual the noun *hēsychia* (2 Thess. 3:12), like its cognate verb *hēsychazō* (1 Thess. 4:11) and adjective *hēsychios* (1 Tim. 2:2), does not denote primarily verbal silence but rather an attitude of quietness or a state of peaceableness; on the other hand, the word-group is used by Luke mostly in the sense of 'silence' or 'keeping quiet'.[183] In the present context, it seems best to regard the word as indicating the outward condition of silence resulting from an inward attitude or state of quietness. As for *hypotagē*, it carries the sense of 'submission' (NEB, NIV; cf. KJV, RV 'subjection') or 'submissiveness' (RSV, NASB) (cf. 2 Cor. 9:13; Gal. 2:5; 1 Tim. 3:4). Its immediate reference seems to be submission to the teacher[184] and his instruction, which is obviously assumed to be 'sound doctrine'[185], although, in view of verse 12, it is not impossible that submission to men is also present as a subsidiary thought.[186]

A restriction is imposed in the negative statement of verse 12. The teaching that is disallowed here obviously does not include the activity of older women teaching what is good (being *kalodidaskalous*), giving advice and encouragement (*sōphronizein*) to younger women (Tit. 2:3, 4), or instructing children in the faith (cf. 2 Tim. 1:5; 3:15); it most likely refers only to official and authoritative teaching in the assemblies of the church.[187] It is doubtful that *authentein* — a biblical *hapax legomenon* — carries the notion of 'usurping authority' (so KJV);[188] not infrequently it is taken to mean 'domineering over' (so NEB),[189] but lexical evidence is firmly in favour of giving the word the sense 'to have authority over' (RSV, NIV), a closely similar rendering being 'to exercise authority over' (NASB).[190] Some scholars take *andros* as the object of both *didaskein* and *authentein*, the sense being that in the life of the church of woman is not permitted to 'teach or have authority over' a man; and since teaching and having authority (equated with ruling) are among the chief functions of the *presbyteros* or *episkopos* (cf. 1 Tim. 3:2; 5:17) — the presbyter-bishop gives the congregation authoritative teaching which is enforced by means of church discipline — Paul is taken to mean that women are prohibited from serving in ruling and teaching offices or functions.[191] To this way of construing the grammatical function of *andros*, it has rightly been objected that it is 'too far removed from "to teach" to be understood as qualifying the meaning of that verb as well';[192] if Paul's intention had indeed been to say 'I do not permit a woman to teach men or to have authority over a man' he would probably have written either *didaskein andra . . . ouk epitrepō oude authentein andros* or, if that be considered a little clumsy, *didaskein andra . . . ouk epitrepō oude authentein* [sc. *andros*], to judge by similar constructions with *ouk . . . oude*.[193]

Nevertheless, it does seem necessary to regard verse 12 as containing two separate prohibitions: in church, a woman is not permitted to teach, nor is she to have/exercise authority over a man (note the punctuation of BFBS², UBS², KJV, RV, NEB, J. B. Phillips). This understanding is required by the use of *oude*, which in similar constructions elsewhere in Paul mostly envisages two separate provisions,[194] and it is further strengthened by the apparently chiastic structure of verses 11–12 (as noted in n. 186 above). Moreover, the flow of thought in verses 11–12 makes it appear that *oude authentein andros* has the character of a parenthetical addition, thus:

11 a woman is to learn in quietness with all submissiveness
12a she is not to teach
(12b nor is she to exercise authority over men)
12c but she is to be quiet

The sole concern of verse 11 is with women receiving instruction in church; their proper attitude in doing so is to be one of quiet submissiveness. Verse 12a mentions 'teaching' as the natural opposite of 'learning' ('teaching men' would not be as natural an opposite). The thought of verse 12b seems to be suggested by the mention of 'submissiveness' in verse 11, and/or possibly by the thought of 'teaching' which involves the exercise of (doctrinal) authority; but verse 12c returns to the thought of 'quietness' which, as verse 11 clearly shows, has to do with 'learning' over against 'teaching' (not over against 'exercising authority over a man'), the emphatic '*all*' thus pointing to a contrast between 12c and 12a (not between 12c and 12b). On this analysis, in other words, the positive statement about women 'learning' in verse 11 leads to the prohibition about women 'teaching' in verse 12a, which in turn leads to the reassertion about women being quiet in church in verse 12c, while the prohibition about women 'exercising authority' over men in verse 12b is thrown in as an additional thought in connection with the injunction that they should not teach in church.[195]

It has indeed been argued that both the preceding and the following context suggest that Paul has only one thing in view:

> Verse 11 calls for quiet and submissive learning. Verse 12 forbids teaching or exercising authority over men. The two are visibly parallel. Quiet learning inversely parallels (verbal) teaching and full submission inversely parallels exercising authority. Both verses have the same situation in mind, one in which women are not to teach authoritatively but are to learn quietly. The closing remark of verse 12 makes this clear by summing up both verses with a single short statement: 'she must be silent'.[196]

This appeal to the context might be strengthened by several instances in Paul where *oude* introduces the second element of what appears to be a synonymous parallelism (e.g. Rom. 2:28; 9:6f.; Phil. 2:16). But it is doubtful that 1 Timothy 2:12 can really be said to contain such a parallelism, and the force of this appeal to the context is blunted when *oude authentein andros* is taken (as suggested above) parenthetically as an additional prohibition.[197] We conclude, therefore, that not only formally but materially as well two separate prohibitions are in view, denying to women the function and office of an authoritative teacher in church, as well as any exercise of ecclesiastical authority over a man; the two prohibitions are related in that for women to assume the role of an authoritative teacher would constitute a form of 'wielding authority' over men.[198]

The words *gynē* and *andros* here are usually construed of the relationship between woman and man in general, but more than one scholar is of the opinion that *andros* should really be taken to mean 'husband'.[199] Grammatically, indeed, *andros* could be taken as an instance of the word being anarthrous 'when anaphora is ignored' and in fact meaning 'over *her* husband';[200] and the asyndeton between verse 10 and verse 11 could have the function of indicating 'transition from one subject to another' — or, in this context, from one aspect of the subject (vv. 9f.) to another (vv. 11f.) — in keeping with 'the less careful epistolary style' as compared with 'the more polished workmanship' of classical works, where 'new paragraphs or sections in didactic writings are in general joined to the preceding', so that the fact that *gynaikes* in verses 9f. refers to women does not in and of itself demand that *gynē* in verses 11f. has to be similarly understood.[201] Nevertheless, since the terms *anēr* and *gynē are* meant generally in verses 8–10 and nothing in the context indicates that a change in meaning has occurred, it is most natural to understand them in the same way in verses 11f. Moreover, in the context believers are being addressed as worshippers, and not as family members; 'indeed, the concluding injunction of silence could not apply to the Christian home and the whole verse must therefore relate to the community'.[202]

Two reasons are given in verses 13–14 in support of the ruling laid down in verse 11–12.[203] First, as in 1 Corinthians 11:8f., reference is made to the order in the creation of man and woman in order to point out the principle of primogeniture: by virtue of his temporal priority, the man became the head of the woman in what was essentially a relationship of mutual dependence and complementarity (cf. 1 Corinthians 11:11f.).[204] Since, in the terminology of 1 Corinthians 11:3, the head of a woman is the man, it would obviously be inappropriate for a woman to exercise ecclesiastical authority over a man; for a woman to assume the role or office of an authoritative teacher in church would similarly be a violation of the principle of headship/subordination. Second, the fact of Eve's deception in the Fall is mentioned (v. 14). Since 'the significance of Eve's deception as a reason for the prohibition [of v. 12] is not indicated here or elsewhere in the Scriptures',[206] certainty on this question is probably not to be expected. Some scholars hold that the point of verse 14 is women's unworthiness to be entrusted with the responsibility of teaching, in view of the facile susceptibility of Eve — considered as the archetypal woman — to the serpent's deception.[207] But if it were the case that women are more gullible and therefore less trustworthy, how can they be trusted to teach other women and children? And if Adam was not deceived into sinning but transgressed with his eyes open — thus actually incurring greater guilt than Eve[208] — then why are men more qualified to teach than women? It is to be observed, moreover, that in 2 Corinthians 11:3 the selfsame fact is used to warn the whole church (not just the women) against being deceived as Eve was. These considerations make it appear unlikely that Paul is thinking here of a tendency to be gullible as integral to the nature of woman as opposed to man.

Perhaps the clue to Paul's meaning is provided by the sharp contrast which is drawn between Adam and Eve on the point of deception: 'Adam was not deceived, but the woman was deceived and became a transgressor' (RSV).[209] This statement has been taken as providing an answer to the question 'Who was at fault at the Fall?'; the answer reads: the fault lay not with Eve, who transgressed because she was deceived; it lies with Adam, who was not deceived but transgressed with understanding and by choice. The inference to be drawn from this is that Adam had been given by God the position of headship and responsibility both in the home and in religious matters, and Paul's point in verse 14 is, it would seem, 'to suggest the need to restore the pre-fall situation in which the man bears responsibility for religious teaching'.[210] This interpretation harmonizes with Paul's clear teaching elsewhere that it was through Adam's transgression that sin entered the world (Rom. 5:12, 17); and it is supported by the principle of headship/subordination enunciated clearly in 1 Corinthians 11:3 and presupposed both in 1 Corinthians 14:34f. and in 1 Timothy 2:13. It would seem to have the further advantage of making verses 13–14 give *positive* rather than *negative* reasons for the restriction on women: women are not to teach (or have authority over men) in church, not because woman is inferior (Eve was created after Adam) or more gullible (Eve was deceived) and therefore less trustworthy, but because to *man* (cf. the emphasis in the original: *Adam gar . . . kai Adam ouk . . .*) belong the primogeniture (Adam was created first) and the appointive headship in religious instruction (Adam was not deceived — he *knew* what he was doing).

A slight adversative (*de*) introduces the conditional sentence of verse 15, the apodosis of which states: *sōthēsetai . . . dia tēs teknogonias*. Different meanings given to each of the three words (verb, preposition, noun) have resulted in a great variety of interpretations of this statement, several of which will be examined here. (1) *hē teknogonia* refers to that great child-bearing which gave birth to the Messiah, through (*dia*) which women's salvation (in a spiritual sense) is derived.[211] The term by itself, however, signifies child-bearing in general and the use of the preceding article here is probably generic, referring to the entire process of child-bearing and birth, and not to a particular birth.[212] (2) Paul seeks to apply the concept of Proverbs 14:23a ('All hard work brings a profit', NIV) to the female's vocation: her profit is that her attitude will be a healthy one or she will be a whole person in motherhood.[213] But this ingenious view is surely rendered suspect by the meaning it gives to *sōzein/sōzesthai*, which in Paul characteristically denotes salvation in a soteriological/eschatological sense.[214] (3) Women will be preserved through (*dia*) the process of childbirth.[215] This view faces the same objection as the previous one, and in addition yields what has been called 'an intolerably banal sense'.[216] (4) Although women still bear in the pain of childbirth the continuing mark of divine displeasure, yet they fully share in the offered salvation.[217] But surely the *dia* with genitive construction is most naturally to be taken in an instrumental sense, and whilst it may, when warranted by the context, acquire a sense approximating 'even though' (as in Rom. 2:27), this is not the case with our verse. (5) By way of her child-bearing, the Christian mother reaches her goal of being saved, i.e. 'by faith in God's covenant promise' she 'looks forward to all the joys of Christian motherhood unto the glory of God'.[218] (6) Child-bearing is woman's normal and natural duty; in the discharge of this duty she 'works out her own salvation'.[219] This and the previous interpretation share the common weakness that sense of *sō thēnai* is thus illegitimately reduced to that of satisfaction or endeavour in this life. (7) Women's path to salvation (in the eschatological sense) consists in accepting the role assigned her by God, that of Christian motherhood.[220] This view commends itself to us as doing the fullest justice to the Greek: *sōthēsetai* is taken in its characteristic Pauline sense, *dia*-cum-genitive has its most natural, instrumental force, *teknogonia* is used with its normal meaning.

In the protasis of verse 15b, the number of the verb changes from the singular to the plural (*meinōsin*) and raises the question of the identity of the subject. Some take it to be the subject of *sōthēsetai* (the woman) together with her husband;[221] but since in the preceding context Paul has used both the plural 'women' (vv. 9f.) and the singular 'woman' (v. 12), it is probable that here he is still referring to women (in the plural) without including their husbands.[222] Of the virtues in which Christian women are to abide, *sōphrosynē* — meaning 'a suitable restraint in every respect'[223] — is not a specifically Christian virtue; its being added to faith, love and holiness here is probably due to its relevance to the intent of the present passage: in church women are not to engage in public teaching or exercise authority over men, for to do so would be to fail to exercise the proper restraint and observe the decorum expected of them.[224]

Having set forth above what we believe to be a correct interpretation of 1 Timothy 2:11–15, we note briefly two other approaches to the passage. The first may be called a socio-cultural approach. It has been suggested that 'the distinction between prophecy [1 Cor. 11:5] and teaching [1 Tim. 2:12] can be paralleled in pagan authors who are obviously independent of Paul', and that in Paul 'permissible roles seem to have been established on the basis of cultural norms, not absolute theological considerations'; or, to take another example, the passage is interpreted solely in terms of the intellectual inferiority of women in the social and cultural context of Paul's day.[225] The other, related approach (sometimes combined with the first) may be described as historical, the basic theory being that Paul's teaching here is addressed to, and can be explained solely in terms of, the crisis constituted by heresy then invading the Ephesian church, in which crisis women were in one way or another especially involved.[226] Some evidence in the Pastoral Epistles is indeed amenable to such an approach. Thus, the churches of Ephesus and Crete were being confronted with a heresy which has been described as 'a Gnosticising form of Jewish Christianity',[227] an element of which was its ascetiscism.

Paul refers to 'hypocritical liars' who 'forbid marriage and inculcate abstinence from certain foods' (1 Tim. 4:2, NIV; 4:3, NEB); the asceticism in sex could be linked with an 'emancipationist' strain in their teaching.[228] At least in Ephesus, there were some very unstable women: Paul speaks on the one hand of some who had already turned to follow Satan (1 Tim. 5:15), and on the other of 'weak women . . . who will listen to anybody and can never arrive at a knowledge of the truth' (2 Tim. 3:6, 7, RSV) — easy prey of those 'who worm their way into homes and gain control over weak-willed women' (2 Tim. 3:6a, NIV). There also appears to be a very close affinity between 2 Timothy 3:13f. and 1 Timothy 2:14f.: there it is predicted that 'evil men and impostors will go from bad to worse, deceiving and being deceived [*planōntes kai planōmenoi*]', but Timothy is exhorted to 'continue in [*mene en*] what you have learned and become convinced of' (NIV); here, by implication, women are warned against being deceived, as Eve was (*exapathē theisa . . . gegonen*), and exhorted to continue in (*meinōsin en*) faith, love and holiness with propriety.[229] It is doubtful, however, that the sort of reconstruction of the background that has been suggested by proponents of the historical approach is really substantiated by clear evidence in the texts themselves.[230]

Against both the socio-cultural and the historical approach is the stubborn fact that Paul in 1 Timothy 2:13f. appeals, not to the current situation of the Ephesian church or to the socio-cultural context of the times, but to the creation order and the circumstances surrounding the Fall: this suggests that the right approach has to be scriptural-theological. That stubborn fact alone would seem to require that Paul's teaching in 1 Timothy 2:11–15 be understood as applicable to the situation of church worship in general and not restricted to the specific situation of the Ephesian church at the time. When this is strengthened by the general nature of the activities envisaged in the passage, by the general intention of the author in giving his instructions as indicated in 1 Timothy 3:14f., and by the clear enunciation of the principle of headship/subordination elsewhere in Paul (1 Cor. 11, cf. 14), the conclusion seems well supported that

While Paul's advice to Timothy is undoubtedly occasioned by specific circumstances in the first century Ephesian church, and is directed primarily to those circumstances, the 'situation' in which Paul's advice is applicable extends far beyond that occasion, embracing every Christian worship service in which men and women descended from Adam and Eve participate.[231]

F. Concluding Observations

We are in a position now to take up the question that was raised but left undiscussed at the end of sub-section D, viz.: Why is the principle of headship/subordination considered to be violated by women's participation in the public evaluation of prophecies but not by their engaging in prayer and prophesying?

It will be helpful first to substantiate our earlier statement that the teaching which is forbidden women in 1 Timothy 2:12 most likely refers only to official and authoritative teaching in the assemblies of the church. An examination of *didaskō/didaskalos* and related words as used in the Pastoral Epistles reveals the following facts. (1) The noun *didaskalia* frequently occurs in such expressions as 'sound doctrine' (1 Tim. 1:10; 2 Tim. 4:3; Tit. 2:1; 1:9; see n. 185 above), 'good doctrine' (1 Tim. 4:6), 'the teaching' (1 Tim. 6:1), 'godly teaching' (1 Tim. 6:3), 'the doctrine of God our Saviour' (Tit. 2:10), and — over against those — 'doctrines of demons' (1 Tim. 4:1). Scripture is said to be profitable, among other things, 'for teaching' (2 Tim. 3:16). In several instances the word is used to refer to the teaching of the apostle Paul (2 Tim. 3:10), of Timothy (1 Tim. 4:13, 16), of Titus (Tit. 2:1, 7), of elders (1 Tim. 5:17), and of the bishop/overseer (Tit. 1:9). (2) The word for 'teacher' (*didaskalos*) appears twice as a self-description of the apostle Paul (1 Tim. 2:7; 2 Tim. 1:11), and once in reference to teachers who (as the context makes plain) do not teach sound doctrine (2 Tim. 4:3). Reference is made to certain persons who desire to be teachers of the law (*nomodidaskaloi*) but are without proper understanding. Older women are to be bidden 'to teach what is good' (to be *kalodidaskaloi*, Tit. 2:3).

(3) The verb *didaskō*, whose meaning in 1 Timothy 2:12 is the object of the present inquiry, is used of the teaching of Timothy (1 Tim. 4:11; 6:2), of the activity of the faithful transmitters of the apostolic gospel (2 Tim. 2:2), and — over against those — of the teaching of false doctrine (Tit. 1:11, contrast v. 9). Twice, a compound verb is employed to convey the idea of teaching doctrine or giving instruction that is not in agreement with apostolic teaching (*heterodidaskaleō*, 1 Tim. 1:3; 6:3). (4) Another noun (*didachē*) once refers to the teaching activity of Timothy (2 Tim. 4:2) and once in reference to the bishop/overseer's activity who is to 'hold firmly to the trustworthy message as it has been taught' (Tit. 1:9, NIV; *katatēn didachēn*). (5) The adjective *didaktikos* is used of the aptitude to teach which is required both of the bishop/overseer (1 Tim. 3:2) and of 'the Lord's servant' (2 Tim. 2:24).

These data make it abundantly clear that the Pastoral Epistles the *didaskō* word-group is used predominantly if not exclusively with the nuance of public and official teaching in church or at least of doctrinal instruction. This emphasis comes through most forcefully in Paul's instructions to his personal delegate in 1 Timothy 4, especially in verses 11–16 (cf. vv. 1, 6): '*Command* and *teach* these things. . . . Till I come, attend to the *public* reading of scripture, to preaching, to *teaching* . . .' (vv. 11, 14, 16 RSV, emphasis added). By way of contrast, when Paul tells Titus to bid older women to be 'teachers of good things' (Tit. 2:3), the nuance of the word in context is distinctly non-official. We may therefore take it as well established that when Paul says, 'I do not permit a woman to teach', he means this kind of public and official teaching in church; his concern seems to be to prevent women from assuming a role or position involving doctrinal authority over men. It may be that what he has in view is specifically the *magisterium* of teaching in the church.[232]

Now, when this question of doctrinal authority is brought to bear on the apparent contradiction between Paul's prohibitions in 1 Timothy 2 and 1 Corinthians 14 and his tacit permission in 1 Corinthians 11, it appears that in his view the activities of praying and prophesying do not involve women in assuming a position of doctrinal authority over men and are therefore permitted, whereas teaching and the public evaluation of prophecies would involve women in assuming such a position and is for that reason forbidden. This understanding presupposes that there is an essential difference between prophecy and teaching:

> Whereas the prophet of the early Church was immediately inspired, the content of his message being a particular and direct revelation, the teacher based his teaching upon the Old Testament scriptures, the tradition of Jesus and the catechetical material current in the Christian community.[233]

It also assumes that the evaluation of prophecies is considered to partake more of the nature of teaching than of prophecy. If Paul did have the *magisterium* of teaching in view, his investing of doctrinal authority in the teacher rather than the prophet may perhaps be connected with the fact that prophecy, together with apostleship, would disappear from the scene in due course (see our earlier remark in the last paragraph of section II above).

It may be worth pointing out that, as we understand the matter, Paul's permission for women to prophesy is not due to his attaching to prophecy a lesser authority than teaching. For, as indicated by the use of *prōton, deuteron, triton* in 1 Corinthians 12:28 (which suggests a definite sequence of descending scale), Paul ranks prophets directly below apostles (also v. 29; Eph. 2:20; 3:5; 4:11; cf. Rev. 18:20) and above teachers and others (1 Cor. 12:29; Eph. 4:11; Rom. 12:6f.; cf. Acts 13:1). The preference thus given to prophecy over teaching and all other gifts of grace, the apostleship excepted (1 Cor. 14:1), would make it difficult to see why women may be allowed to pray and prophesy but not take part in the evaluation of prophecies or teach in the assemblies of the church, if his different rulings were dictated by considerations of relative authority.[234] Rather, the explanation seems to lie in the nature of prophecy as derived from immediate inspiration and of teaching as being more directly related to Scripture and tradition: the less directly 'pneumatic' character of teaching means that correspondingly greater 'personal' authority is involved in teaching than in prophesying;[235] and apparently Paul considers that the evaluation of prophecy similarly entails the exercise of such 'personal' authority, and that for women to exercise such authority would be a violation of the principle of woman's subordination to man.

We are also in a position now to answer the question posed in the introduction to section III above: whether Paul's teaching and practice in regard to women's ministry would confirm, contradict, or call for modification of the opinion that the issue of women's ministry today is to be decided solely on the basis of possession of spiritual gifts. Our discussion in the preceding sub-sections (A-E) leads us to the conclusion that that opinion stands in need of an important modification: in church, a woman is not permitted to assume the role or office of an authoritative teacher, and she is not allowed to exercise authority over men. The evidence regarding Paul's attitude to women in ministry will have to be understood in that light: at the conclusion to sub-section A we noted that the evidence nowhere suggests that any woman was recognized as occupying a teaching office, and we are now able to say that any teaching or preaching any of those women may have participated in would not have involved them in a position of doctrinal or ecclesiastical authority over men and hence in a violation of the principle of headship/subordination. This does not mean that there is any contradiction between Paul's teaching concerning the indiscriminate distribution of spiritual gifts to men and women alike, and the restrictions which Paul imposes on women's ministry by reason of woman's subordination to man; both are integral parts of Paul's teaching, and it would be just as unsatisfactory to restrict God's gracious distribution of gifts by appealing to the subordination passages as to evade the fairly plain insistence on the distinctions in roles by appealing to the undistinguishing manner in which God bestows his gifts on men and women alike.[236] What it does mean is that *gift* and *role* are to be distinguished: a woman who has received the gift of teaching (or leadership, or any other charisma) may exercise it to the fullest extent possible — in any role which does not involve her in a position of doctrinal or ecclesiastical authority over men.

C.I.B.W.—N

If our exegesis of the three classic passages (1 Cor. 11, 14; 1 Tim. 2) is not mistaken, then it has emerged repeatedly that the principle which underlies Paul's restrictions on women's ministry in church is the principle of headship and subordination in the male-female relationship as designed by God's creation. This principle holds in redemption, for redemption does not alter the created relationship of the sexes but rather restores it to its pristine state of unity, complementarity and harmony which had been designed by God but was perverted by sin and selfishness (Gen. 3:16). It is important to emphasize that the outworking of the headship principle is to be informed and governed by the model of Christ's relation to his church (Eph. 5:22f.) and other clear scriptural teaching which warns against an abuse of authority (e.g. 1 Pet. 5:3; Lk. 22:25–27). Worth emphasizing also is the fact that the principle of headship is expressly applied by Paul to the marriage relationship in the home and to women's ministry within the church; this suggests that there is a kind of analogy between the family and the church, as a recent ecclesiastical document explains:

> the church as such is not a secular institution but an extended example of family life, and . . . therefore its canons follow much more closely those of the family, especially as the church normally involves whole families in its life and worship in a way that other areas of life do not. It seems to us [sc. the study committee] that it is in this context that Paul was unwilling to put a woman in a 'ruling' position, lest this makes the maintenance of the biblical pattern of relationships, especially in marriage, difficult if not impossible.[237]

Similarly, another recent, full-scale study comes to the conclusion that

> The New Testament does not teach subordination of all women to all men . . . Women were subordinate to one man [husband or father], not to all men. . . . In short, rather than saying that the New Testament teaches the subordination of women, we should more accurately say this: The New Testament teaches the subordination in marriage and family of women to a man, the head of the family, and the pattern

of roles in the community which entrusts the government of the community to men and which thereby supports the pattern in the family.[238]

If the created relationship of the sexes is to be faithfully observed and applied to the issue of women's ministry today, then we are bound to say that any form of ministry which contravenes the principle of male headship and female subordination would be clearly unbiblical.[239] If the prohibition of 1 Timothy 2:12 does have the *magisterium* of teaching in view, it *may* be consonant with the biblical principle for women with preaching and teaching gifts to use them 'to the full in situations where male ministers are in charge and the woman's ministry of the Word is felt as supporting and supplementing their own preaching and teaching', although such an application of the principle is open to discussion.[240] It is also conceivable that exceptions to the biblical pattern may be found and permitted under special circumstances: the ministry of Deborah as one of the judges of Israel (Judg. 4:4) may be a case in point.[241] Deviations from the biblical principle due to cultural influences, though understandable, are perhaps more difficult to justify.[242] Finally, it has been urged that if there are genuinely biblical restrictions on women, whether in the home or in the church, then they are to be seen as given by God for the *good* of his people, and should in that context be believed and taught as something to be prized, not merely tolerated.[243]

IV CONCLUSION

It will have been apparent that of the three sub-topics discussed in this essay, the first provides the essential link with the other two and in that sense the unifying element of the entire discussion. As a concluding statement, we may say.
(1) that spiritual gifts, which presuppose the call of, and represent the equipment by, God and Christ through the Holy Spirit, constitute the most essential and indispensable component in Christian ministry;

(2) that where ecclesiastical office is involved, *office* and *function* are two aspects of ministry over both of which *charisma* takes precedence: but while office must be accompanied by charisma corresponding to the function of the office, charisma can be employed in service either through office or apart from office; and

(3) that inasmuch as spiritual gifts are bestowed without regard to distinctions of sex, women may take part in the ministry of the church to the full extent of their gifts — the only restriction being the necessity to avoid any office or function which would involve them in exercising doctrinal or ecclesiastical authority over men.

5

Church and Mission: Reflections on Contextualization and the Third Horizon

D. A. CARSON

A. INTRODUCTION

No work proposing to discuss some of the more disputed biblical themes relating to the church can afford to ignore the current ferment over the mission of the church. The field is vast and the disputed areas many; but this essay focuses on the interface between the new hermeneutic and contextualization. Before addressing such matters directly, however, it may be worth mentioning a couple of other matters that impinge deeply on the current discussion over mission, even if they cannot be probed here.

First, in the contemporary climate the notions of evangelism and mission are deeply offensive to some. Many Western theologians consider the idea of winning people to Christ a parochial vestige of past imperialism; and not a few 'third world' theologians agree. A recent volume by the Chaplain of the University of Kent,[1] for instance, argues against both exclusivism and inclusivism, and for the pluralism represented by Ernst Troeltsch, W. E. Hocking, Arnold

Toynbee, Paul Tillich and John Hick. Another recent volume records discussion on such points amongst participants
from a broad theological spectrum.[2] There is little agreement; but what becomes readily apparent is that the most
fundamental division of opinion has more to do with the
authority status of revelation than with mission theory itself.
Those who hold that God has revealed himself proposition-
ally in the Scriptures, and definitively in the person and
work of Jesus the Messiah, emphasize mission; those who
argue that the religion of the Bible has no authority or
revelatory status above the documents or traditions of other
religions tend to de-emphasize mission. Of course, there are
many mediating positions. It is common to stress the light
given to all men (a variation on the argument of Acts 17)
and affirm that Christianity preserves the highest revelation,
not the only revelation. In itself, the argument is innocuous
enough, and few thoughtful conservatives would wish to
disagree with it;[3] but it easily becomes the justification for
the dubious theory of the anonymous Christian — and, *pace*
Karl Rahner,[4] it is hard to see how that theory can fail to
vitiate at least the urgency of mission. Senior and Stuhlmueller have recently tried to ground Christian mission in the
sense of mission exemplified in the early church;[5] but despite
the many useful insights in their work, their mediating
position is rather more historical in its orientation than an
attempt to determine what is in any sense normative for the
church today. And much as conservatives may disagree with
his conclusions, S. G. Wilson is nevertheless right in his
analysis:

> . . . we must face squarely the central, obstinate fact of
> [Paul's] christological exclusivism. If we leave this untouched
> then we shall, like Barth, remain essentially faithful to Paul.
> For many, however, his exclusivism has to be abandoned
> and his absolutism relativized. And Paul, of course, does not
> stand alone. The rest of the New Testament and most forms
> of Christianity since share essentially the same view . . . We
> are engaged, therefore, in no mean undertaking but can at
> least take comfort in the thought that we are dealing with *the*
> central issue. For if the challenge of other religions affected

only the peripheral parts of Christian tradition . . . the problem could readily be resolved at least for those who are
already satisfied that they can be reinterpreted or jettisoned
without loss. We are dealing, however, with the heart of
Paul's gospel . . .[6]

It would take us beyond the scope of this paper to attempt
to justify, exegetically and epistemologically, the view that
biblical Christianity is a uniquely revealed and authoritative
non-negotiable; but even these brief remarks may help us to
see that behind the hermeneutical questions there sometimes
lurk even more fundamental questions about the authority
status of biblical Christianity.

Second, a large number of technical essays on the New
Testament have reached conclusions that put a substantial
distance between any commandment of Jesus and the actual
cross-cultural evangelistic practices of the early church. For
instance, both Best[7] and Scobie[8] argue that although Jesus
allowed Gentiles some participation in the blessings he
inaugurated and envisaged, he authorised no Gentile mission. The post-resurrection 'great commission' records cannot be treated as the commands of the *historical* Jesus
(especially in Scobie's thought); and the actual impetus to
evangelize Gentiles is thought to have originated with the
Hellenists who scattered from Jerusalem after the martyrdom of Stephen. There can be no fundamental objection to
the historical analysis of where such cross-cultural (or, better, cross-racial) evangelism was first practised; but slightly
different application of critical thought might happily conclude that the ultimate impetus goes back to Jesus himself —
and behind him to a host of Old Testament texts understood
in the light of the person and work of Christ. The narrower
focus of Best and Scobie and others tends to reduce the
urgency of such evangelism by making it in its origins almost
a sectarian enterprise.

Of course, it is true that there is no good evidence that
the church as a whole, after the resurrection and ascension,
promptly set out to obey the great commission.[9] Much of
their witness was the overflow of their life in the Spirit. But
this fact cannot reasonably be used against the relative

importance of the great commission; for even after Pentecost the church had to go through repeated struggles in order to come to grips with such matters as the relationship between the Mosaic covenant and the new one promised by Jeremiah and inaugurated by their Lord before his death, or the precise force the law of Moses was to have in this new eschatological situation — even though such matters had been dealt with, sometimes directly and sometimes in symbol-laden language and acts, by the Master himself in the days of his flesh. Both Acts and the epistles testify to the fact that, guided by the Spirit, the early church grew in its understanding of its message and task. This means that we dare not seek to limit our grasp of that message or task by focusing too narrowly on some early period where the church's understanding was still immature.

Numerous other questions spring to mind, but they cannot be addressed here. I need only mention that there are many useful books that attempt to give a theology of mission, a biblical foundation for the enterprise;[10] and in addition there are a few more recent works that deal sensitively and powerfully with the relationship between 'doing justice and preaching grace'.[11] One might also mention recent works analysing Paul's mission theology and practice,[12] a penetrating doctoral dissertation on Paul's self-understanding of his vocation,[13] another that sheds considerable light on one of the reasons why Paul was able to operate effectively in so many cultures — namely his careful training of and partnership with local co-workers,[14] an essay that explores the extent to which even Paul's theology finds its genesis in mission,[15] and, conversely, another essay that calls contemporary theology back to its central missiological task.[16] All of this is only to say that we are in a period of immense ferment over the subject of missions; and the complexity of the issues and the diversity of viewpoints loads even the narrow subject of communication to the third horizon with cumbersome and interrelated problems.

We may begin with some elementary observations on the new hermeneutic. Older hermeneutical models focused on the processes by which the interpreter, the 'subject', interpreted the text, the 'object'. The unwitting premise was very often the historical positivism of von Ranke. The 'new hermeneutic' posits a 'hermeneutical circle' between the interpreter and the text. When the interpreter in attempting to understand the text asks questions of the text, the questions themselves emerge out of the limitations that characterize the interpreter; and therefore the responses that the interpreter hears the text giving are skewed to fit his own grid. Inevitably, however, those responses in turn shape the interpreter, and make him marginally different from what he was before he approached the text. Therefore the next time the interpreter asks questions of the text, the questions emerge from a slightly different matrix than did the first set of questions; and therefore the new responses will be skewed to a slightly different grid. Thus not only is the interpreter interpreting the text, but the text is 'interpreting' the interpreter. And this interchange can go on and on, setting up a 'hermeneutical circle'. In this model, understanding does not depend in any important way on a grasp of the referents of words, but emerges out of the heart of language itself. Mere words kill; advocates of the new hermeneutic speak of 'language poisoning'. Authentic understanding takes place when a text so 'interprets' the interpreter that a flash of insight occurs, a kind of revelatory experience, a 'language-event' (*Sprachereignis*).

There is much to be learned from the new hermeneutic. We human beings cannot escape either our sinfulness or our finiteness; and both are guaranteed to make the matrix out of which our questions emerge different from the matrix of every other human being. There is a 'horizon of understanding' unique to each individual. Pushed too far, of course, the new hermeneutic must result in the unqualified subjectivity of all knowledge — even that of the more radical skeptics who try to convince us by their writings that they are right. How then may two individuals communicate? How may an interpreter discover 'the meaning' of a text, without succumbing to a theory that postulates unqualified polyvalence of meaning — a different meaning for each interpreter, and indeed for the same interpreter at each new approach to the text? The solution seems to be along the following lines.

Each knower must begin with thoughtful 'distanciation',
i.e. a careful distancing of himself and his own 'horizon of
understanding' from that of the text or of the other person,
in order to hear what the text or the other person is saying
with as little interference as possibile from the knower's
own mental baggage. By coming to understand the many
differences between one's horizon of understanding and the
horizon of understanding of the text or of the other person,
it becomes possible to make appropriate allowances. If the
knower then tries to put himself or herself into the other's
place as it were (or, to use the modern jargon, if the knower
attempts to fuse his horizon of understanding with that of
the text), there is less danger of major semantic distortion.
The hermeneutical circle becomes a hermeneutical spiral,
enabling the interpreter, the knower, to approach the meaning of the text asymptotically.[17]

We have thus been introduced to two 'horizons' — the
horizon of understanding of the knower or interpreter, and
the horizon of understanding of the text. Contemporary
discussion of mission, however, goes a step farther and deals
with the 'third horizon' — viz, the horizon of understanding
of the group or people being evangelized. The first horizon
is that of the biblical documents or, as some would have it,
of the first generation of Christian believers as that perspective is preserved in the New Testament. The second horizon
is ours — i.e. that of established Christians who seek to
understand the Scriptures. There are, of course, some major
hurdles to cross if we are to understand the Scriptures
aright — if we are going to fuse our own 'horizon of understanding' with that of the text so as to arrive at an accurate
understanding of that text. Similar hurdles also present
themselves when we try to cross from the second horizon
to the third: in short, when we try to evangelize and teach
the content of Scripture to another group or people. Indeed,
the greater the cultural gap between the evangelizing church
and the target people (or, otherwise put, between the second
and the third horizon), the greater the potential for massive
distortion of the message.

Two preliminary caveats should be entered at once. First,
the terminology just introduced already masks a considerable

oversimplification. It is rare to find a Christian who has been converted simply by reading the New Testament. More commonly there has been at least one intermediary and perhaps there have been many — other Christians who have presented Christ to him and borne witness to the truth of biblical Christianity in their own lives. Therefore the person whom we now label as belonging to the second horizon at one time belonged to the third — or even the fourth, fifth, sixth or *n*th. And even if someone becomes a believer simply by reading the Bible, without any human intermediary, in one sense there were intermediaries involved in the Bible translation that made the Scriptures available to him in his own language. I shall return briefly to this question at the end of this paper; but for the moment it is enough to note the complexities while nevertheless using the simplified terminology. Second, although there are many important parallels between, on the one hand, the move from the first to the second horizon, and, on the other, the move from the second to the third horizon, so far as the difficulties in communication are concerned, there is nevertheless one important distinction. In the former, the onus is on what we might call the receptor — i.e. on the person belonging to the second horizon; for it is that person who is trying to understand the Scriptures. But in passing from the second horizon to the third, the onus is on what we might call the donor — i.e. on the person who is trying to communicate the message. That person is still at the level of the second horizon.

If there are ambiguities surrounding the 'third horizon' terminology, they are nothing compared with the range of meaning ascribed to 'contextualization'. In this instance, however, definition stands at the very heart of the issue, since it is determined by the entire synthesis that is adopted. It seems wise therefore to approach 'contextualization' a little more inductively. I shall not attempt to sketch in what I understand by the term, and how it relates to the third horizon, until the closing pages of this paper. This much at least may be said: the term is very slippery. At one point it was indistinguishable from 'experimental theology';[18] but it soon came to serve as the term that commonly supersedes 'indigenization'. The latter was frequently summarized under the 'three selfs': an indigenous church is self-support- ing, self-governing and self-propagating. 'Contextualization' goes beyond this to include the notion that the church is doing its own theology in its own context. Broadly speaking there are two brands of contextualization. The first assigns control to the context; the operative term is praxis, which serves as a controlling grid to determine the meaning of Scripture. The second assigns the control to Scripture, but cherishes the 'contextualization' rubric because it reminds us the Bible must be thought about, translated into and preached in categories relevant to the particular cultural context.

The concerns of the new hermeneutic and of contextualiz- ation have thus begun to merge. Both are concerned with the difficulties inherent in passing content from one knower to another, or from a text to an interpreter. To put the matter another way, the theoretical and practical difficulties in moving from the first horizon to the second remain in place when moving from the second to the third. Indeed, as we have seen, a new difficulty is introduced. In the models we have used, when communication takes place form the first horizon to the second, the burden of responsibility rests with the second (i.e. the receptor); but when communication takes place from the second horizon to the third, the burden of responsibility *still* rests with the second — now the donor. That stands at the heart of missionary endeavour.

It is important to recognise how innovative these modern concerns for the third horizon really are. Fewer than twenty years ago, it was possible to publish a hefty volume on evangelism and mission and never mention the hermeneuti- cal difficulties involved in communicating the gospel to the third horizon.[19] But today a tremendous amount of energy in missiological circles is poured into problems connected with contextualization.

This phenomenon manifests itself in many ways. It is seen not only in endless journal articles, many of them more or less popular, that tell how some missionary or other overcame an unforeseen cultural or linguistic hurdle,[20] but in a long stream of major articles and books that tackle the question head-on.[21] Popular books relate how a proper understanding of a local culture make possible the effective communication of the gospel;[22] and more serious studies grapple with the relationships between Christianity and culture.[23] Technical works on cultural anthropology and its relation to mission abound; and the work of Wycliffe Bible Translators and the United Bible Societies continues to pour out a stream of technical monographs and books, some of which have become standard texts for new generations of seminary students.[24] Various theological syntheses are being produced in the 'third world';[25] and experts are applying insights from contextualization theory to related questions such as TEE (theological education by extension) programmes.[26] None of this means there is widespread agreement. Far from it: there is massive theological and methodological disarray in the area. The sole point to be made at the moment is that the subject is everywhere being discussed.

In order to keep the subject narrowly focused, the rest of this paper proceeds in dialogue with the influential article of Daniel von Allmen on the birth of theology.[27] Some essays capture a mood or put into words what many others have been struggling to articulate. When such essays are published, they immediately gain assent and wide recognition — not necessarily because they are cogent or their arguments unassailable, but because they burst onto the theological scene just at the time when they seem to confirm the opinions of many readers. Apparently, something like that has happened to von Allmen's important essay; and so it provides a suitable backdrop to the following reflections on the third horizon.

In what follows I shall first of all summarize von Allmen's arguments, and then proceed to a discussion of exegetical and methodological problems associated with his work. Finally, I shall try to assess von Allmen's judgment of the kind of contextualization that ought to take place as one attempts to evangelize people of the third horizon, and conclude with some slightly broader formulations.[28]

B. A SUMMARY OF VON ALLMEN'S ARTICLE

At the heart of von Allmen's thesis is his argument that the correct model of contextualization is already provided for us in the New Testament. It is this feature that makes his work so crucial. Von Allmen's essay was itself a response — indeed, a response to a response. The late Byang Kato had responded to the growing dangers he perceived in the work of such African theologians as Harry Sawyer and John Mbiti.[29] Emerging as the dominant evangelical voice in African theology before his untimely death,[30] Kato had detected in certain strands of African theology what he variously called 'Christo-paganism, syncretism or universalism' and in which he saw 'a real threat to the future evangelical church' of Africa.[31] Against this protest, von Allmen suggests Kato is too tied to Western theology. Von Allmen sets out 'not only to reaffirm that an African theology is *necessary*, but also to show how it is *possible* on the basis of a true fidelity to the New Testament'.[32] In other words, the force of von Allmen's criticism of Kato is that he is not biblical enough, and that Scripture itself authorises the kind of contextualization von Allmen advocates.

Von Allmen turns to the New Testament, and begins by assuming that the 'Judaic, that is Semitic, character of the Christian faith at its birth is beyond question'.[33] Within one generation, however, the church found its firmest footing on Hellenistic soil. Von Allmen therefore proposes to discover 'what were the forces behind this Hellenization of Christianity, and what sort of people were its first exponents'.[34]

Von Allmen distinguishes three movements, almost stages based on three types of people. The *first* is the missionary movement. This explosion came about without the initiation by the Jerusalem 'pillars' (Gal. 2:9); indeed, the Aramaic-speaking apostles were caught unawares by these developments. What happened rather was that 'Philip and his Hellenist brothers saw in the persecution that was scattering them a divine call to preach the gospel outside the limits of Jerusalem'.[35] This was partly because they had the linguistic competence: they were at home in Greek and familiar with the LXX. Even at this stage, however, this Hellenistic 'missionary' movement was not a missionary movement in any modern sense. No one was being commissioned or sent. It was simply 'a work of evangelism undertaken under the pressure of external events (of persecution) that were understood to be providential'.[36] All of this suggests to von Allmen that in this 'first adaptation of Christianity to a new context', although there was a 'missionary thrust' it was not the thrust of people from one culture evangelizing the people of another, but the spread of Christian witness from Hellenistic Christians to Hellenists. In other words:

> No true 'indigenization or contextualization' can take place because foreigners, the 'missionaries', suggest it; on the contrary, true indigenization takes place only because the 'indigenous' church has itself become truly missionary, with or without the blessing of the 'missionaries'.[37]

The *second* movement is that of 'translators'. In one sense, as von Allmen rightly points out, no translation was needed. The 'missionaries' and those being evangelized shared Greek as a common language, and even a Greek Bible, the Septuagint. What concerns von Allmen here is something else: viz., 'the manner in which the Hellenists, who had received the Gospel from the lips of Aramaic Christians, translated it into Greek for the pagans. By Gospel I mean here, therefore, the living preaching'.[38] Von Allmen uses form critical theory and appeals to 1 Cor. 15:3–5, 11 to insist that the Hellenists were not free-lances: there were limits to how far they could digress from the tradition that had come to them. But a telling step came, he says, when the Hellenistic believers chose *kyrios* to render Hebrew *rabbi* and Aramaic *mari*. The result was a title for Jesus that served simultaneously as, among Jews, a Greek transcription of the divine Name, and, among others, as the word used to pay honour to the Emperor. This is the pre-Pauline history of the title. Von Allmen asks:

> Was it a fatal slip? Criminal truckling to the Greeks and Romans? Paul does not look at it in that way, since he makes this very title of Lord the centre of his theology. In any case, there can be no talk of truckling when to confess 'Jesus is

Lord' exposed one to persecution for refusing Caesar the honour he claimed for himself.[39]

What all this assumes, von Allmen argues, is that 'the "native" preachers were bold enough . . . to be themselves, while remaining faithful to the foundations of the faith they had received, to sift critically the received vocabulary in order to express themselves intelligently to their linguistic brothers'.[40]

The *third* movement was the rise, not of theologians, but of poets — i.e. those whose work assisted the church in its indigenous worship. Von Allmen approves the thesis of Schlink, that 'the basic structure of God-talk is not the *doctrine* of God but the *worship* of God'.[41] We may examine this movement, he says, by studying some of the hymns preserved in the Pauline epistles. Von Allmen selects as his test case Phil. 2:6–11. He prints it in poetic format, putting in parentheses the bits that many scholars hold to be Pauline redaction. Von Allmen's chief point with respect to this hymn, however, is that the parallelism between 'taking the position of a slave' and 'becoming like a man' (2:7) is not a Jewish or Jewish-Christian idea at all; for among them a man was not considered to be a slave. 'It is for the Greeks, particularly at this late date, that man is a slave, bound hand and foot in submission to all-powerful Destiny'.[42] Moreover, von Allmen argues, 'it would be possible to find in the hymn a number of other expressions which find their closest equivalent in the Gnostic myths of the Original Man: the 'divine estate', the equal of God'.[43] But none of this is dangerous syncretism, von Allmen argues, for in this hymn the language used decribes not 'a mythical Original Man losing his divine form and assuming a human appearance'; for only the vocabulary remains, and 'it is used to sing the praise of Jesus of Nazareth who entered history as a man of flesh and blood'.[44] 'We must see in this hymn an interesting, and indeed successful attempt to express the mystery of the condescension of Christ in the characteristically Greek vocabulary'.[45]

From this, von Allmen draws a more general conclusion:

The theologian has no right to fear the spontaneous manner in which the Church sometimes expresses the faith. If the apostles had been timorous and shut the mouths of the poets through fear of heresy, the Church would never have found footing on Hellenistic soil. Thus the way things happen in the primitive church teaches us that in the Church the life and faith is [*sic*] the primary thing. Missionaries do not preach a theology but rather the Gospel (the good news). Nor is the response of faith yet theology, but rather worship or hymns proclaiming the mighty deeds of God in Jesus Christ.[46]

It is only following these movements, von Allmen argues, that theologians are wanted, exemplified by Paul. But even here, he points out, Paul is not a systematician in any modern sense. The two functions of theology are the critical and the systematic; and Paul in his writings devotes himself primarily to the former. By this, von Allmen means that before adapting an already coined formula, Paul examines it 'critically'; and his criterion is 'the received faith'.

He does not demand that doctrine should be in literal agreement with the primitive Christian preaching. But whatever may be its formal expression, the doctrine must correspond to the inner thrust of the apostolic faith, and so eschatology is an essential element of Christian theology. Provided one reintroduces this moment of expectation, this eschatological tension, then why not use Greek terminology?[47]

Along this line, von Allmen argues that the church began with the language of master/disciple, and adapted it to the Hellenistic mystery religions of the day to make Christianity over into 'the definitive and absolute mystery religion'.[48] The one limitation Paul imposed on this Greek influence was resurrection language. Christ may be like Osiris or Kore when Paul says 'You died with Christ', but Paul is independent of Greek thought when he says 'You have been raised with him' — especially so when he sets the ultimate raising as a hope for the future.

Along similar lines, Paul in Colossians (whether the epistle was composed by Paul or someone from the Paul school) responds to the strange amalgam of Judaizing and syncretism by setting over against the worship of angels the supreme headship of Christ. Paul begins, von Allmen argues, with the central fact that Jesus is Lord — Jesus as crucified and risen. This central feature of Christianity enables Paul to rebut the Colossians. This is what von Allmen means by the 'ordering function of theology'.

> Even amidst the fiercest polemic, Paul remains firmly rooted in the basis of the Christian faith; Christ who died and was raised. It is only from this centre that one may dare to say anything at all; and all theological statements, whether polemical or constructive, must be set in relation to this centre.[49]

Von Allmen then turns from the New Testament to the problem of how anyone, African or otherwise, must properly set about 'doing theology' in his or her own context. At this point he is building on his biblical analysis in order to address problems of contextualization. Before setting forth his own proposal, he briefly describes three *impasses* that must be overcome.

The first is *paternalism*. Paternalism expresses itself not only in the sense of superiority manifested by Western theologians, but also in the 'colonized' complex of Africans and other victims of colonization. In the first century, the power relationship between the cultures was if anything the reverse of the modern problem: the Jewish-Christians must have felt threatened by the all-pervasive Hellenistic culture, not the other way round. Von Allmen's solution is that Africans become aware of the value of their own culture in its own right, so that they may 'bring to birth an African theology that is more than a theology characterized by reaction'.[50] Moreover, just as the Hellenistic-Christian movement in the first century was the work of Hellenists themselves. In a spontaneous movement, so also must Africans do their own theology; and this means that Westerners cannot without paternalism even *encourage* Africans to get on with it. Rather: 'Once and for all, then, there must be trust'. And clearly this principle must be extended beyond Africa to all missions-receiving nations.

The second *impasse* is *heresy*. Von Allmen says that since 'everyone is a heretic in somebody's eyes',[51] we must tread very cautiously. His study of the New Testament leads him to conclude that at the first stage of indigenization, people are not too worried by dangers of heresy; and in any case, in Paul's writings,

> the heretics are not to be found among the Hellenistic pro-
> gressives but rather among the Judaizing reactionaries who
> feel themselves obliged to denounce the foolhardiness or the
> rank infidelity of the 'translation' project upon which the
> Church has become engaged in Hellenistic territory. But,
> remarkably enough, this very conservatism goes hand in
> hand with a, perhaps unconscious, paternalism. The legalism
> of the Colossian heresy is accompanied by a disproportionate
> respect towards other powers than Jesus Christ.[52]

The third *impasse* is an approach to contextualization that perceives it as an adaptation of an existing theology. The Hellenists, von Allmen argues, simply proceeded with evangelization; and the theology eventually emerged *from within* this Hellenistic world — but as a later step. Von Allmen's conclusion is stunning:

> It must be said with all possible firmness: there can be
> no question, in our days either, of an Africanization or
> a contextualization of an existing theology. Any authentic
> theology must start over anew from the focal point of the
> faith, which is the confession of the Lord Jesus Christ who
> died and was raised for us; and it must be built or re-built
> (whether in Africa or in Europe) in a way which is both
> faithful to the inner thrust of the Christian revelation and
> also in harmony with the mentality of the person who formu-
> lates it. There is no short cut to be found by simply adapting
> an existing theology to contemporary or local taste.[53]

What this means is that so far as it is possible, African Christians, and indeed all Christians, must begin *tabula rasa*. Missionaries should provide working tools and building materials to believers not yet able to train their own people, and then leave them to get on with the task.

> Rather than teach a theology (even a theology that claims to be a 'New Testament theology') what we should try to do is point out what the forces were that governed the elaboration of a theology on the basis of the material furnished by the early church. This is the reason why, in my opinion, the study of the history of traditions in the early church is of capital importance in Africa even more than elsewhere.[54]

In short, what von Allmen proposes is that no one has the right to tell or even encourage Africans to get on with the task, as that would smack of paternalism; and meanwhile no one has the right to provide them with any theology, as this would vitiate the principles of contextualization as he understands them. We must simply let the African church be African; and an African theology will ultimately result.

C. PROBLEMS IN VON ALLMEN'S BIBLICAL EXEGESIS

There are many points of detail in von Allmen's exegesis that could be usefully raised; but I shall restrict myself to four areas. Like him, I shall largely dispense with the clutter of detailed footnotes, and sketch in a response with fairly broad strokes.

1. Von Allmen's reconstruction of the earliest stage of witness is seriously deficient. As we have seen, he denies the influence of the Aramaic-speaking apostles, assigns all credit to the Hellenistic believers who interpreted the outbreak of persecution as a divine call to preach the gospel outside the limits of Jerusalem, and from this deduces that true contextualization takes place not because outsiders (the Aramaic-speaking Christians) suggest it, but because the indigenous church (the Hellenistic Christians) have themselves become truly missionary.

As I have already acknowledged, it is true, as Boer[55] pointed out some years ago, that the church in Acts is not presented as a community of believers with an immediate and urgent sense of commitment to carry out, in an organised and methodical way, the great commission. Nevertheless, the arguments of both Boer and von Allmen could do with a little shading.

First, the church began from a tiny group. It did not begin as a multinational missions agency with boards and head offices and district conferences, plotting the systematic evangelization of the world. It began with a handful of people transformed by the Spirit of God and by the conviction that with the death and resurrection of Jesus the Messiah the promised eschatological age had begun. Immediately there was witness — not the strategic witness of careful planning but the spontaneous witness of irrepressible spiritual life, the most effective witness of all. In this atmosphere of early pulsating beginnings, it was inevitable that each group of early believers shared their faith primarily with those of its own language and culture. But at this very early stage, to draw lessons about the slowness of the Aramaic-speaking community to reach out to the Hellenistic world is no more realistic than to draw lessons about the slowness of the Hellenistic church to reach out to the Aramaic-speaking world. Luke's narrative simply does not address the kind of questions von Allmen seems to be posing.

Second, even at the earliest stages of Christianity, and within the Aramaic-speaking community, there was a consciousness that what was being experienced was the fulfilment of the Abrahamic covenant by which *all* peoples on earth would be blessed (Acts 3:25). And when the Aramaic-speaking church faced the first strong opposition, the believers prayed for holy boldness to speak the word courageously (Acts 4:24–30). It is very difficult to distinguish this from the attitude of the Hellenistic believers when they faced persecution. There is no evidence (*pace* von Allmen) that the latter alone saw in persecution a special divine call to preach the gospel outside the confines of Jerusalem. Rather, the believers scattered, the Aramaic-speaking ones to places congenial to them, and the Hellenistic believers to places congenial to them — *both* groups still boldly witnessing. Even then, the Hellenistic believers spoke, at first, primarily if not exclusively to Greek-speaking *Jews* (Acts

11:19–20) — a point von Allmen finds so difficult he has to say that Luke probably shaded the account here 'to prevent the stealing of Paul's thunder and keep for him the honour he thought his due'.[56] But a simpler explanation lies immediately to hand, provided we are not trying to squeeze the text into a preset mold. The Hellenistic believers were in the first instance themselves Jews; and so quite naturally they witnessed within their own Greek-speaking Jewish environment. In this sense there is no major cross-over of racial and cultural and linguistic barriers by *either* Aramaic-speaking *or* Greek-speaking Christians at this point. And when the Hellenistic believers do begin their witness before Gentiles in Antioch (Acts 11:20–21), the account is placed after the evangelisation of Samaria and of Cornelius, about which more in a moment.

Third, the reticence the Aramaic-speaking believers ultimately displayed was not over the *fact* of evangelism among Gentiles, but over *the conditions of entrance to the messianic community*.[57] Many streams of Judaism were aggressively proselytizing others in the first century; so it is not surprising, even from the perspective of their background, that early Jewish Christians, both Aramaic- and Greek-speaking, did the same. The debates behind Gal. 2 and Acts 15, therefore, do not stem from problems in mere indigeneity or contextualization, still less from carelessness about the great commission (or, in much modern discussion, its inauthenticity), but from a massive theological question: On what grounds may Gentiles be admitted to the messianic community? The answer had to do with the way in which the new covenant could be seen to be related to the old; and the synthesis forged by these debates in the early church was used by God to contribute to the writing of our New Testament documents.

To reduce such complex and frankly unique circumstances to the parameters of the modern debate over contextualization is to distort and trivialize (however unwittingly) the biblical evidence. It is historical nonsense to label the Hellenists 'progressives' and thereby tie them to modern liberal theology, while labelling the Aramaic-speaking Christians 'reactionaries' in order to bracket them with modern evangelicals. Indeed, it is worth observing that according to Luke the first opposition that resulted in a martyr sprang from a 'conservative' *Hellenistic* synagogue (Acts 6:9)! This entire point is so important that I shall return to it from another perspective in the next division of this paper.

Fourth, within the synthesis I am suggesting, the large amount of space Luke devotes to the conversion of the Samaritans (Acts 8) and to that of Cornelius and his household (Acts 10–11) is eminently reasonable — the latter completely unmentioned by von Allmen, and the former barely so. The Cornelius episode is particularly instructive; for here, before there is any record of witness to non-proselyte Gentiles by Hellenistic Jewish believers, an Aramaic-speaking apostle is sent by the Lord to a Gentile who is not, technically, a proselyte. The point of the story, carefully repeated by Peter before a suspicious Jerusalem church, is that if God by pouring out his Spirit on the Gentiles, as on the Jews, has shown that *he* has accepted them, can Jewish believers do any less? This point does not concern the crossing of merely cultural, racial and linguistic barriers, as significant as such barriers are. The 'them/us' dichotomy stems from Israel's self-consciousness as the people of God, and therefore from the clash between God's antecedent revelation in what we today call the Old Testament, and God's revelation in Christ Jesus and all that has come from it. The Jewish believers raise their questions not at the level of contextualization, *but at the level of theology* — indeed, at the level of *systematic* theology, for their question ultimately concerns the way in which the old and new covenants are to be related to each other. But none of this does von Allmen consider.

Fifth, part of von Allmen's arguments about the reticence of Aramaic-speaking apostles stems from silence. The truth of the matter is that Luke does not purport to give us a comprehensive history of the early church, but a highly selective one. After Acts 8:1, we know nothing or next to nothing about the ministries of (say) Matthew or Thomas or Bartholomew or Andrew. Extra-canonical sources are not very reliable in this area; but some of the best of them tell us that Thomas, for instance, proclaimed the gospel as far east as India, where he was reportedly martyred. Von Allmen's sweeping conclusions regarding the Aramaic-speaking apostles are therefore based not only on a rather selective and anachronistic approach to Acts, but even on the book's silences.

Sixth, the above arguments suggest that Luke is less interested in providing us with a merely sociological analysis of how various groups in the early church functioned, than with detailing how the resurrected Christ, by his Spirit, continued to take the initiative in building his church. There are indeed heroes and villains in Acts; but above all there is on display the missionary heart of God himself. Not only does the initiative belong to God in the Cornelius episode, but even in Acts 2 the gift of tongues enables Jews from every linguistic background to hear the wonderful works of God in their own language — not only the principal reversal of Babel but the demonstration of the principial removal, and not by Hellenistic or Aramaic-speaking Jewish Christians *but by God himself*, of the temporary barriers surrounding his old covenant people. The theme of prophecy and fulfilment in Acts is designed to display the inevitability of the dawning of the gospel age — precisely because it is God who planned it and is even now bringing it to pass by his Spirit. To force this magnificent panorama into lesser molds is to fail to understand it. We may learn some useful lessons about contextualization in the pages of the New Testament; but we must not force this book into our preconceived categories, nor compel it to provide detailed answers to questions it scarcely considers.

2. In almost every case, von Allmen's conclusions are not entailed by or even very clearly suggested by the exegetical evidence he presents. To take but one example: After discussing the role of the 'poets' in leading the church in worship, von Allmen, as we have seen, draws 'some more general conclusions. The Theologian has no right to fear the spontaneous manner in which the Church sometimes expresses the faith. If the apostles had been timorous and shut the mouths of the poets through fear of heresy, the Church would never have found footing in Hellenistic soil'.[58] Even if von Allmen's exegesis of Phil. 2:6–11 is basically correct,

there is no way to make it support so broad a conclusion. Von Allmen himself points to areas in which the earliest witnesses and apostles *refused* to follow Greek thought, which implies that the church was *not* willing to give the poets an entirely free hand. In any case, although it is true that a growing church, like the first century church, often produces its own hymnody, it is illegitimate to deduce from Paul's citation of one particular hymn that he had no right to check any hymnodic form of expression. Von Allmen's error in logic immediately becomes obvious when his argument is set out in syllogistic fashion:

1. Poets preceded theologians like Paul.
2. Paul approves a particular poem.
3. Therefore no theologian has the right to call in question the content of any hymn.

In reality, to provide a competent assessment of how far the apostles were willing to step in and question the theological formulation (including the poetry) of others, it would be necessary to examine all that the New Testament has to say about heresy — a point to which I shall briefly return.

Thus to argue that 'the way things happened in the primitive church teaches us that in the Church the life of faith is the primary thing'[59] is to obscure some important distinctions. In one sense, of course, this argument is valid: the early church was little interested in the niceties of theological argumentation for its own sake, but in life lived under the Lordship of Christ. But this life of faith did not perceive 'faith' to be exhaustively open-ended: it had an object, about which (or whom) certain things could be affirmed and other things denied. Indeed, I would argue that the church was interested in theological formulations, not for their intrinsic interest, but precisely *because* it rightly perceived that such formulations shaped and controlled much of the 'life of faith' believers were expected to lead. In any case, von Allmen's conclusions in this regard seem to depend rather more on an existentialist hermeneutic than on his own exegesis.[60]

3. Von Allmen's presentation of the development of Chri-

stology[61] is questionable at a number of points. I shall mention only three. First, the background on which he relies for his judgment reflects only one line of research, that of the history-of-religions school made popular in New Testament studies by such scholars as Reitzenstein and Bousset,[62] and mediated to us by Rudolf Bultmann and others. Not only is this line of scholarship in less favour today than it once was, but also its many intrinsic weaknesses have been made clear by significant publications which a commitment to even-handedness might at least have mentioned. Brown, for example, has shown that the use of *mysterion* in the New Testament finds its closest antecedents not in Greek mystery religions but in a semitic milieu.[63] Again, it is not entirely clear that full-blown Gnosticism, as opposed to neoplatonic dualism, antedates the New Testament;[64] but even if it does, the differences between it and the New Testament presentation of Christ's death are profound. And to what extent may the 'in Christ' language reflect, not Greek mysticism, but *forensic identification* with Christ?[65]

Related to this is a second criticism. To what extent do the demonstrable developments in the ascription of labels and titles to Jesus of Nazareth reflect innovation *removed from the historical actuality*, and to what extent do they merely reflect clarified and growing understanding of what · was in fact *true* — an understanding mediated in part by the pressure of events, including opposition? This sort of question von Allmen does not raise; but it is essential that we consider it if we are to understand what he himself means by developments that remain 'faithful to the foundations of the faith'.[66]

Consider, for instance, his treatment of *kyrios*. There is little doubt that Paul understands 'Jesus is Lord' to be a confession not only of Jesus' 'lordship', i.e. of his authority, but of his identification with Yahweh, rendered *kyrios* in the LXX. Was the apparent development from master-disciple relations ('my lord' meaning 'rabbi' or the like), to full ascription of deity to Jesus, in accord with or contrary to *what Jesus himself was and is?* If von Allmen would respond, 'Contrary to', then certain things inevitably follow: (1) The truth of Christological confessions does not matter, but only the sincerity and naturalness to any culture of its own formulations. (2) Jesus himself should not be identified with Yahweh at any ontological or historical level, but only at the level of confessions which may or may not reflect reality. (3) 'Remaining faithful to the foundations of the faith' can in this case only refer to existential commitment to an empty *dass*, not to 'foundations of the faith' in any propositional or contentful or falsifiable sense. (4) How a culture responds to the gospel, i.e. with what degree of contextualization, is far more important than the content of the gospel proclaimed and believed. If on the other hand von Allmen would respond, 'In accord with', then again certain things inevitably follow: (1) He holds that Jesus really was and is 'Lord' as 'Yahweh is Lord', even though some time elapsed before the disciples fully grasped this. (2) More broadly, he has in this case committed himself to what is sometimes called the 'organic' view of the rise of Christology: i.e. that the full-blown doctrine grew out of the truth dimly perceived but truly *there* in the beginning of Jesus' ministry. The development is one of understanding and formulation regarding what was, not innovation and inventive explanation of what was not. (3) 'Remaining faithful to the foundations of the faith' therefore has objective criteria, rendering some formulations *un*faithful. (4) The gospel itself includes true propositions and historical verities, and at all such points is non-negotiable, even if it clashes with some dearly held cultural prejudices.

Which answer, then, would von Allmen give? I am uncertain, for his essay does not make this clear. Perhaps it is a little troubling, however, to find him asking whether the adoption of *kyrios* was a 'fatal slip'. His answer is that it was not 'truckling' if it exposed believers to persecution. True enough; but was it a fatal slip?

I myself hold to the 'organic' view I outlined above; and elsewhere I have sketched in the kind of growth in understanding that was involved.[67] It is arguable, for instance, that even in the parables Jesus tells in the synoptic gospels, the figure who clearly represents Jesus (in those parables where he is represented at all) is frequently a figure who in the Old Testament metaphorically stands for Yahweh (bridegroom, or farmer, for example — there are eight other examples).[68] Certainly, there is ample evidence that Jesus repeatedly applied to himself passages from the Old Testament that had reference to God. There even appears to be dominical sanction for using 'Lord' in reference to Jesus (Matt. 21:3), even though it is very doubtful that the disciples understood all of this at the time. The question arises therefore whether the shift to Greek *kyrios* was so very innovative after all, or largely the result of increased understanding of who Jesus truly was, in the light of his resurrection and ascension. And in any case, if the gospel was going to be preached in Greek at all, Greek terms had to be used. The crucial question, therefore, is whether the Greek terms used by Hellenistic believers were filled with pagan content, or with Christian content in harmony with the gospel truth transmitted. Von Allmen implicitly recognises this when he points out that the 'man' in Phil. 2:7 is not the 'Original Man' of Gnostic mythology, regardless of the term's provenance. Context is more important as a determinant of meaning than is philological antecedent. Why cannot the same insight be deployed in other cases?

Similar things may be asked about von Allmen's treatment of the slave-man parallel in Phil. 2:7. Apart from the fact that here as elsewhere in his essay von Allmen sweeps the Greeks together into one undifferentiated structure of thought,[69] the question is whether the hymn's formulation says something untrue of Jesus. In fact, it does *not* put him in the condition of a slave 'bound hand and foot in submission to all powerful Destiny'. Although some Greek thought conceived of man's plight in such terms, the word for 'slave' has no necessary overtones of such thought; and *in this context*, the essence of Jesus' 'slavery' is his voluntary refusal to exploit his equality with God[70] in order to become a man, not involuntary submission to inflexible and unavoidable Destiny. In what sense, therefore, has anything of substance in the gospel been changed by this Greek terminology?

Third, von Allmen's use of vague language blurs important distinctions. Paul, von Allmen says, 'does not demand that doctrine should be in literal agreement with the primitive Christian preaching'.[71] What does 'literal' mean in this sentence? It cannot mean 'verbal', since we have crossed from Aramaic to Greek. But what, then? Von Allmen simply says that 'the doctrine must correspond to the inner thrust of the apostolic faith'.[72] Not to the apostolic faith itself, we notice, but to its 'inner thrust'. We may ask how this inner thrust is to be isolated, or, to put it it another way, who is to determine it. Calvin? Barth? Bultmann? Von Allmen? The only answer von Allmen gives here is that since 'new hope is part of the inner thrust of the faith', therefore 'eschatology is an essential element of Christian theology'.[73] But 'eschatology' is a 'slippery word'[74] in modern theology. In Bultmann's thought, it has nothing to do with the return of Jesus at the end of the age, the present inaugurated kingdom then being finally consummated in a new heaven and new earth. Rather, it is reduced to the tension in the existential moment of decision. Does von Allmen follow Bultmann, then, when he rhetorically asks, 'Provided one reintroduces this moment of expectation, this eschatological tension, then why not use Greek terminology?'[75] Why not, indeed — provided it is the same eschatological structure as that of the historic gospel. But if this 'eschatological tension' has been redefined as 'this moment of expectation' by appealing to Bultmannian categories, the 'inner thrust of the apostolic faith' appears to have come adrift. There is no longer any objective gospel at all; and appeals to an 'inner thrust' may simply hide infinite subjectivity. Once again, I am left uncertain where von Allmen stands in all this, or what he really thinks about Bultmann's reinterpretation of Pauline eschatology, because his language is so vague; but I am persuaded his approach would do well to heed the wise assessment of Beker:

> First Corinthians 15 provides us with an impressive example that the coherent center of the gospel is, for Paul, not simply an experimental reality of the heart or a Word beyond words that permits translation into a multitude of world views. Harry Emerson Fosdick's dictum about the gospel as an 'abiding experience amongst changing world views', or Bultmann's demythologizing program for the sake of the

kerygmatic address of the gospel, is in this manner not true to Paul's conception of the gospel. However applicable the gospel must be to a Gentile in his contingent situation, it does not tolerate a world view that cannot express those elements in the apocalyptic world view . . . that to Paul seem inherent in the truth of the gospel . . . And far from considering the apocalyptic world view a husk or discardable frame, Paul insists that it belongs to the inalienable coherent core of the gospel . . . It seems that Paul sacrifices dialogical contingency to dogmatic necessity by imposing a particular world view on Hellenistic believers. And if Paul imposes a dogmatic interpretative scheme on the 'core' of the gospel, he seems to require not only faith as *fiducia* but also faith as *assensus*.[76]

4. Von Allmen's overarching reconstruction of the development of early Christianity depends on a reductionistic schema that runs more or less in a straight line from Judaism to Hellenism. More careful work has shown how misleading this schema is.[77] Judaism was already impregnated with Hellenistic concepts and vocabulary. Almost certainly the apostles themselves were bilingual or trilingual. At the same time, many New Testament documents (e.g. the Gospel of John) that had previously been classed as irremediably Hellenistic have been shown, since the discovery of the Dead Sea Scrolls, to have at least linguistic links with the most conservative strands of Judaism.

The same point can be made by again referring to two observations to which I have already alluded in this paper. First, there is no record of Hellenistic Jews being evangelized by Aramaic-speaking Jews. This is because *the church was bilingual from its inception*. It could scarcely be otherwise, considering that most if not all of the apostles came from Galilee. Even von Allmen's expression 'the Aramaic-speaking apostles' is misleading; for in all likelihood, both the Eleven and Paul were comfortable in both Aramaic and Greek. Of course, many Jews who became Christians during the first weeks and months after Pentecost were from the Diaspora; and presumably most of these would not be fluent in Aramaic, but would be more at home in the Hellenistic world than would those who had spent all their lives in

Palestine, even in Galilee; but it was never the case that a purely Aramaic-speaking church had to learn Greek in order to reach out to Greek-speaking Jews. For von Allmen therefore to distinguish the Hellenistic wing of the church from the Aramaic wing as if the former were the freshly evangelized and therefore the exclusively 'indigenous' church which alone could become 'truly missionary' is to propound disjunctions with no historical base and which offer no direct parallels to modern problems in contextualization, and few parallels to modern problems in crossing the bridge to the third horizon.

Second, we have seen that the really significant movement recorded in the New Testament documents is not from Judaism to Hellenism, linguistically and culturally considered, but from the old covenant to the new. This development had racial and cultural implications, of course, but primarily because the old covenant was enacted between God and one particular race. Profound theological questions therefore had to be faced, in light of the new revelation brought by Jesus and confirmed and clarified by the Holy Spirit in the early church. Modern problems of contextualization cannot in this regard be seen as parallel to the first expansion to Gentiles — unless new revelation is claimed as the basis on which the modern expansion into the new languages and cultures is taking place!

C. BROADER METHODOLOGICAL PROBLEMS IN VON ALLMEN'S ESSAY

There are two methodological problems in von Allmen's article that deserve separate consideration, one relatively minor and the other major.

1. The minor problem is found in the frequent disjunctions that force the unwary reader to 'either/or' reasoning when other options are not only available but arguably preferable. For instance, as we have seen, von Allmen approves the work of Schlink, who by concentrating on the *form* of 'God-talk' argues that 'the basic structure of God-talk is not the *doctrine* of God but the *worship* of God.'[78]

Quite apart from the question as to the relation between form and content (a notoriously difficult subject), this conclusion is far too disjunctive: doctrine *or* worship. After all, even in worship the worshiper has *some* notion of the God he is worshiping; and therefore unless that notion is completely ineffable, he has some doctrine of God. Even the postulate 'God is utterly ineffable' is in fact a doctrinal statement. It is logically impossible to be involved in worshiping God or a god *without* a doctrine of God, even if that doctrine is not very systematic, mature, well-articulated or for that matter even true. Meanwhile von Allmen's approval of the Schlink disjunction has done its damage by giving the impression that so long as there is worship, doctrine really has no importance and can safely be relegated to a very late stage of development. The kernel of truth in his analysis is that it is possible to have doctrine without being involved in worship — a pathetic and tragic state indeed; but that does not mean the converse is possible, let alone ideal.

Or to take another example, von Allmen concludes: 'Even amidst the fiercest polemic, Paul remains firmly rooted in the basis of the Christian faith: Christ who died and was raised. It is only from this centre that one may dare to say anything at all . . .'[79] Now the first of these two sentences is true, even if slightly reductionistic. Indeed, we must insist that Paul's understanding of Christ's resurrection will not compromise over such matters as a genuinely empty tomb and an objective resurrection body. It is certainly true that this is one of the cornerstones of the faith Paul preaches. But it is going too far to use this non-negotiable truth as the *sole* criterion by which all must be judged. True, no aspect of genuine Christianity can tamper with this central truth, or fly in its face; but it is not true that this is *the only non-negotiable* for Paul — as if, provided a person holds to this centre, all else is for the apostle negotiable. That is demonstrably *not* true. The eschatological error in Thessalonica, or the assorted moral errors in Corinth, are not resolved by simple reference to Christ's death and resurrection; yet Paul is adamant about the proper resolution of these matters as well. Indeed, as von Allmen has phrased things, someone might believe that Jesus died and rose from the dead *exactly as Lazarus rose from the dead*, and still be holding to the 'centre'. But Paul would not agree; for Christ's death and resurrection is qualitatively different from all others. If so, we must say in what way it was different (e.g. his was the death of God's Son; it was an atoning death; his body after the resurrection was different from his body before death in ways that Lazarus' body was not; etc); and by saying in what way we are admitting other non-negotiables, other matters essential to Christian faith. The implicit disjunction *only* from this centre, from *nowhere* else suddenly begins to fray around the edges.

2. But there is a far more important methodological problem with von Allmen's work. At the beginning of his essay, he sets out to show that the creation of an African theology is both necessary and possible 'on the basis of a true fidelity to the New Testament'.[80] In a sense that I shall shortly elucidate, I entirely agree that an African theology is both necessary and possible. But von Allmen's way of establishing what is in 'true fidelity to the New Testament' is not the way most readers of the New Testament would judge such fidelity; and therefore it needs to be clearly understood.

Von Allmen does not attempt to justify his position on the basis of what the New Testament documents *say*, but on the basis of his reconstruction *of their development*. The authority lies not in the content of the Scriptures, but in von Allmen's understanding of the doctrinal changes those Scriptures reflect. This is manifest not only in the thrust of von Allmen's essay, but especially in its conclusion: 'Rather than teach a theology (even a theology that claims to be a "New Testament theology")', he writes, 'what we should try to do is point out what the forces were that governed the elaboration of a theology on the basis of the material furnished by the primitive church'.[81] The 'material furnished by the primitive church' can only be a reference to the New Testament documents (and perhaps also to other early Christian literature — though for the earliest period we are pretty well shut up to the New Testament); so von Allmen is saying that we should not attempt to teach the content of these documents, but restrict ourselves only to deductions about the forces that generated the elaborations found in these documents. And what is in conformity with von Allmen's understanding of these forces is precisely what he says is in 'fidelity to the New Testament'! In reality, of course, his theory is not in fidelity to the New Testament but to his deductions about the forces that shaped the New Testament; for as we have seen, these deductions frequently run counter to what the New Testament documents actually *say*.

More troubling yet is von Allmen's confidence regarding the objectivity and reliability of the scholarly reconstruction he sets forward as the core of the new curriculum. But I shall let that point pass for the moment to focus a little more clearly on the cardinal difference between Byang Kato and Daniel von Allmen. In brief, it is the source of authority in Christianity. Both profess allegiance to Jesus Christ as Lord. But *which* Jesus? The Jesus of the Jehovah's Witnesses? The Jesus of von Harnack? The Jesus of Islam? For Kato, it is the Jesus of the New Testament, because for him the New Testament documents are authoritative. Therefore every religious claim or precept must be tested against that standard. For von Allmen, it is not entirely clear how the confession 'Jesus is Lord' is filled with content; and although he appeals to the New Testament, in reality he is appealing to his reconstruction of the forces that shaped it. That reconstruction serves as the supreme paradigm for an endless succession of further reconstructions, and in that sense gains some authority. But the documents themselves, in their actual content, are stripped of authority. A person might therefore confess 'Jesus is Lord' but mean something very different from what Paul or Luke means. Does this not matter? Von Allmen seems to want to defend a core of gospel truth as one of the final criteria; but it is not clear how that core can avoid endless changes in content, making it no core at all but the proverbial peeled onion.

The same sort of problem appears in Kraft.[82] Basing himself on von Allmen's article, Kraft assigns Luther's description of James as an 'epistle of straw' to Luther's 'unconscious ethnocentrism',[83] without struggling with Luther's later growth in understanding both of the gospel and of the nature of the canon.[84] The point, according to

Kraft, is that the Bible is a 'divine casebook' that embraces many different models of appropriate religion, each in its own way reflecting the non-negotiable core. Different cultures will feel most at home with this part or that part of the Bible, and prefer to overlook or ignore other parts. Luther found Paul congenial, and was uncomfortable with James. Well and good, Kraft argues: let each culture choose those parts that speak to it most clearly. This diversity produces many different theologies; and, writes Kraft:

> We need to ask which of these varieties of theology branded 'heretical' were genuinely out of bounds (measured by scriptural standards), and which were valid contextualizations of scriptural truth within varieties of culture or subculture that the party in power refused to take seriously. *It is likely that most of the 'heresies' can validly be classed as cultural adaptations rather than as theological aberrations.* They, therefore, *show what ought to be done today* rather than what ought to be feared. The 'history of traditions' becomes intensely relevant when studied from this perspective.[85]

Note, then, that the 'scriptural standards' to which Kraft refers are not what the Bible as a whole says, but an array of disparate theologies each based on separate parts of the Bible, an array that sets the limits and nature of diverse traditions and their development. In treating the Bible as a 'divine casebook' Kraft is very close to von Allmen in the way he conceives of biblical authority.

At the risk of oversimplification, I would argue that there are five problems in their conception. The *first* raises an historical question. By suggesting that 'most' of the historical heresies of the church ought to serve us today as models for what ought to be done in different cultures, has Kraft reflected deeply enough on the nature of heresy? Certainly ecclesiastical powers have sometimes persecuted groups that were more faithful to the Scriptures than the powers themselves; but that is not quite the spectre that Kraft is raising. He is arguing rather that ecclesiastical powers have persecuted groups with positions that more closely align to certain paradigms found in the Scriptures than do the pow-

ers — while the powers themselves retain a superior fidelity
to Scripture with respect to *other* paradigms found in Scripture. But surely it is the very nature of heresy to grasp a
piece of truth and inflate it out of all proportion. I do not
know of a single heresy where that is not the case. But no
such heresy could Kraft's approach ever detect, since the
very essence of his programmatic call is to foster groups
that adopt parts of Scripture congenial to them. How, for
instance, would Kraft respond to the central Christology of
Jehovah's Witnesses, or to any other Arian group? I am not
asking how he would respond personally, as if his own
Christology were suspect: that is simply not the point. How,
rather, would he approach the question, methodologically
speaking, of their acceptability within a broadly 'orthodox'
framework?

The *second* question is theoretical: namely, is this the way
that biblical authority is to be perceived, on the basis of its
witness? I would answer with a firm negative. Of course
there were cultural forces at work in the development of
the biblical books. But the question is whether God so
superintended those forces that the Bible's documents are
to be read not only as historical documents that reflect the
progress of revelation in redemptive history but also as a
whole, not merely as case studies but as a divinely ordered
progression that results in a unity of thought, a world in
which there is prophecy and fulfilment, type and antitype,
dark saying and clearer explication, diverse styles and genres
and languages but a complementarity of thought — all
resulting in the possibility of finding unambiguous *biblical*
truth for many kinds of doctrinal, ethical and intellectual
matters, not simply disparate and potentially mutually contradictory 'truths'.[86]

The *third* problem concerns the extent to which these
models depend on the paradigm shift theory of Kuhn and
others.[87] Even if he was largely right regarding the substantial incommensurability of competing scientific paradigms,
Kuhn never suggested that there is a *total* change in meaning
when one moves from one paradigm to another. Some things
hold under both Newtonian and Einsteinian physics.
Indeed, one might argue that some elements (e.g. the law

of the excluded middle) are necessary constituents of every conceivable paradigm. More important, recent study has shown that Kuhn's work needs serious revision, and should not be depended on for too great a degree of support.[88]

The *fourth* problem is practical. It is true, as Kraft says, that ever culture finds certain parts of the Bible more congenial than others. On this basis Kraft seems to encourage each culture to operate with its own 'canon within the canon'. But this inevitably means that the final authority rests, not in the Bible, but in the culture. The canon comes to lose all canonical authority. If a society is polygamous, it may follow Abraham or David (Kraft's example); but then why not follow, in some other culture, Mosaic law regarding slaves, stoning, temple ritual and the bitter-water rite? How about wiping out entire peoples? A Hitler might find such accounts and commands very congenial. On the other hand, does any society find the Sermon on the Mount congenial? The problem is not only how the Old Testament passages to which I've just referred relate to later revelation (part of the *second* problem, above), but also how the Bible can ever have any prophetic bite at all. In my understanding of the canon, the preacher who is sensitive to the cultural sensibilities of his hearers will not only exploit their canonical preferences, and seek to relate the parts of the Bible into a self-consistent whole, he will also take extra pains to preach, teach and apply, within this canonical framework, those parts of Scripture his hearers find *least* palatable. This may not be his first step; but it is a necessary step, for otherwise no prophetic word will ever be heard, no correction of culture, no objective *canonical* balance. It appears, then, that advocates of a certain kind of contextualization are aware of the dangers of what might be called 'Scripture plus' (i.e. the distortion of Scripture's message by the dogmatic *addition* of cultural baggage), but are insufficiently sensitive to the dangers of 'Scripture minus' — the distortion of the message by preferential removal of those parts of the Bible's message that seem uncongenial.

The *fifth* problem concerns the nature of von Allmen's appeal to a core gospel which he does not see as culturally negotiable, or, to use Kraft's expression, the 'supracultural truth' of the core. But I shall return to this problem in the next section.

E. REFLECTIONS ON VON ALLMEN'S THREE *IMPASSES*

The first *impasse* to a truly African theology, in von Allmen's view, is *paternalism*. There is real insight here. We have all witnessed or heard about those horrible situations where a Western missionary squelches the honest probing of an African or other student who is questioning the missionary's interpretation of Scripture at some point. The put-down might be in terms like these: 'What right do you have to question this interpretation? This is the product of two thousand years of study and thought. Your business is to go and learn it!' May God forgive all teachers who employ such tactics, especially those who do so in the name of the authority of Scripture while unwittingly elevating tradition above Scripture. Moreover, von Allmen is wise to point out the inverted power structures when we compare the first century with the twentieth.

Nevertheless, von Allmen's solution — simply to let the Africans get on with it, offering neither criticism nor encouragement (because that too is a reflection of paternalism) but simply trust — is in my view not nearly radical enough. Unwittingly it falls into a new kind of paternalism. While theologians in the West are busily engaged in cut and thrust *among themselves* is it not a kind of inverted paternalism that declares a respectful 'hands off' policy to African theologians and biblical scholars? Surely it is far better to enter into debate with them. The real problem lies in heart attitude. The solution is the grace of God in the human life, grace that enables Africans and Westerners and others alike to learn from and criticise each other without scoring cheap shots or indulging in 'one-upmanship'.

The second *impasse* to a truly African theology, in von Allmen's view, is a *fear of heresy*. Certainly there is a great danger in this area, found not least in Western missionaries whose zeal is great but whose knowledge is slim. But von Allmen gravely underestimates the seriousness with which heresy is taken in the New Testament, and overestimates the amount of diversity there.[89] At what point, for instance, can von Allmen sympathize and emphathize with the sentiments expressed in Matt. 7:21–23; John 3:36; Acts 4:12; Gal. 1:8, 9; 2 Tim. 2:17–29; Rev. 21:6–9? Even Paul's famous 'all things to all men' (1 Cor. 9) unambiguously presuppose limits beyond which he is not prepared to go.[90]

Granted the truthfulness of Scripture and the rightness of the canonical approach I have briefly sketched in, Christians have not only the right but also the responsibility to learn from *and to correct* one another on the basis of this agreed standard. This must not be in any witch-hunting or judgmental spirit; but failure to discharge these responsibilities in a gracious and thoughtful way may not only reflect inverted paternalism but a singular indifference to the truth claims of 'the faith that was once for all entrusted to the saints' (Jude 3).

The third impasse in the way of a truly African theology, according to von Allmen, is *the perception that contextualization must be merely the adaptation of an existing theology.* Again, there is considerable insight here. Will that theology be truly African which simply takes, say, Hodge's *Systematic Theology* and seeks to rewrite it for some African (or Burmese or Guatemalan or any other context? Anyone who has thoughtfully worked cross-culturally for an extended period of time knows the answer to that question. There are far too many church clones, extending all the way to the style of buildings. David Adeney in conversation has drawn attention to a sign he saw in Shanghai before the revolution, announcing the presence of the 'Dutch Reformed Church of America in China'.

Nevertheless, von Allmen's solution, to foster a true *tabula rasa* and insist that a truly African theology can only flower when it emerges without reference to any existing theology, is impossible; and even if it were possible, unwise. It is impossible and unwise for four reasons:

(1) It is impossible because a *tabula rasa* is impossible. If the new hermeneutic has taught us anything, it is taught us that. Even if we were to follow von Allmen's suggestion and teach only tools and the history of traditions, we would

still be conveying *some* theological content. Teaching Greek invariably includes Greek sentences from the New Testament; and translating them entails *theological* decisions about the history and development of traditions as well as linguistic expertise. Moreover, one cannot talk about the history and development of traditions without talking about the traditions themselves. Even initial evangelization and church planting could not possibly have been accomplished by conveying no more than 'Christ died and rose again'. And in any case, even what one does *not* teach is teaching something. If a lecturer refuses to discuss, say, the interpretation of Romans or the language used of the atonement, he or she will invariably appear to be hiding something, thus conveying a distasteful impression — e.g. that such matters are religiously unimportant, or frightening, or too difficult.

(2) It is impossible because there is no core of gospel truth in the sense presupposed by von Allmen, no 'supracultural truth' in the sense demanded by Kraft.[91] They both treat the Scriptures as having only casebook authority, examining it for every hint of cultural development, while nevertheless insisting that there is an undissolved core of indispensable gospel truth, a supracultural truth. In one way, this is far too radical; in another, it is not nearly radical enough. It is too radical, I have argued, because it reduces the locus of non-negotiable truth to one or two propositions such as 'Jesus is Lord' or 'Christ died and rose again', when in fact the corpus of non-negotiable truth embraces all of Scripture; that is the data base from which theological reglection must take its substance and controls. But now I wish to argue that in another way the position of these two scholars is not radical enough, in that it seems to think the core or supracultural confessions escape all restrictions of culture; and that is demonstrably untrue.

Consider, for example, the sentence 'Jesus is Lord'. We might all agree that no Christianity is possible where this three-word sentence is denied. But to a Hindu, the sentence might be happily accommodated within his syncretistic framework. In that context the confessin is far from being a *sufficient* test of genuine Christianity. To a Buddhist, it would mean Jesus is inferior to Gautama the Buddha, for it still *predicates* something of Jesus. To a Jehovah's Witness, there is no entailment regarding Jesus' deity. And to an existentialist, the same sentence is a mythological expression designed to call us to the decisions that characterise authentic existence.

My point is that from the perspective of human perception and formulation *there is no supracultural core.* However the heart of the gospel be conceived by human beings, it is conceived in a particular linguistic, cultural, philosophical and religious framework. Only God is supracultural. But this does not relativize the gospel. Far form it; it simply means that the supracultural personal God, in order to communicate with his finite and culture-bound sinful creatures, necessarily had to accommodate the form of his communication to their space-time limitations, their historical contingencies. From God's point of view, of course, truth may be supracultural; and for our part we may cheerfully insist that truth is supracultural in that it can be communicated to many different cultures. But it cannot be communicated to each culture in the same way; it cannot be communicated supraculturally. Thus it is difficult to see how we can determine what the supracultural core really is once we have abandoned the 'given' of Scripture. And even that 'given' comes to us in the garb of culture. None of this entails the relativizing of the truth; but it does mean that if any person is to understand the culturally conditioned Scriptures and apply them aright, he must, as part of the exercise, seek to shape his own horizon of understanding to that of the cultures and languages of Scripture, and then make the transfer of meaning back to his own environment.[92] To put the matter another way, I must find out what 'Jesus is Lord' means in the Greek New Testament, how it functions, how it is coordinated with other truth, and then seek to confess the same truth in my own language and culture — even if it takes a paragraph instead of a three-word sentence, or a complete overturning of my conceptual framework (as, in this case, must happen to, say, the Buddhist). That it is always possible to convey *any* truth in another culture should be obvious to anyone with the most rudimentary knowledge of linguistics: if modern developments in that discipline have taught us anything, it is that cross-cultural communication is possible, even if seldom straightforward.

Thus, although we may wish to speak of a 'core' of truths without believing in which one cannot be a Christian, even this core cannot be approached supraculturally. Someone might object that if everything is embedded in culture, then even the cross suffers the same fate. Does this not suggest, it might be asked, that the cross itself is optional? What would have happened if God had decided to send his Son to New York or Manila in 1985? Should we not try to discern God's purposes *behind* the cross, behind this particular cultural form? But the question itself betrays the problem: it presupposes that we have access to supracultural truth in some direct fashion. Even if we decided affirmatively — that is, that we *should* try to discuss the meaning of the cross apart form the cross itself — we would inevitably couch the principle we thus 'discovered' in some other cultural garb — ours! The truth of the matter is that all we have is the revelation God did in fact give; and it is cast in certain historical and cultural frameworks that cannot be disregarded, for we have no other access to God's truth.

It appears, then, that there is no intrinsic philosophical reason why the *entire* Bible cannot be seen (as it claims to be) as a definitive and true revelation, even if *all* of it is, in the sense just explained, culture-bound. And this suggests that the appeal of von Allmen, Kraft and others is epistemologically and hermeneutically naive.

(3) It is unwise because von Allmen, believing his proposed *tabula rasa* to be possible, and his particular reconstruction of gospel traditions neutral, is in fact promulgating his own brand of theology, while honestly but mistakenly thinking himself above the fray. No blindness is worse than that which thinks it sees (as John 9:39–41 points out). Is it not obvious that even as Western evangelical missionaries try to impose their theological frameworks on their converts, so Western missionaries of more 'liberal' persuasion try to impose their scepticism and relativism on theirs?[93] Far better is it to admit these tendencies, and become aware of the limitations these inevitabilities impose on the cross-cultural missionary.

(4) It is unwise because it fails to grapple with the third horizon. Modern debate over hermeneutics commonly speaks, as we have seen, of the *two* horizons; missiologists force us to think of the third. If the second horizon of understanding is that of the reader or interpreter of Scripture, that horizon of understanding will be at least roughly similar to that of the interpreter's colleague in his own culture; so that when the interpreter has fused his own horizon of understanding with the first (that of the text) so effectively as to have facilitated a true transfer of meaning, he becomes capable of learning to think through the meaning of the text in his own language and cultural framework; and then it is a relatively small step to communicate these findings to his colleague. Of course, the interpreter's own understanding may still need considerable correction, revision, deepening and so forth; but for the sake of simplifying the argument, let us suppose that he is substantially right in his understanding of the text, the 'fusion' operation having been responsibly carried out. If this interpreter now wishes to communicate the truth he has learned to a person of *another* culture, of course, he faces the third horizon, that of the 'target' person or group. To communicate accurately the substance of what he has learned, the interpreter, now a witness or preacher of sorts, must fuse the horizon of his own understanding with that of the hearer — for a start, he must learn a new culture. The truth he wishes to convey must then be passed on in the words and actions and parameters of that language and culture. That is one of the things that makes an effective missionary. In time, the new hearer, now a convert, learns to fuse the horizon of *his* understanding with that of the biblical text; and because he probably knows his own culture better than the missionary ever will, he has the potential, all things being equal, to become a far clearer and more effective witness and theologian in his own culture than the missionary does.

One problem, of course, is that the missionary may unwittingly incorporate a lot of his own cultural baggage into the gospel he is preaching. But that substantial truth *can* be conveyed across cultures is demonstrated by both von Allmen and Kraft themselves: they are read, and understood,

by Africans and Westerners alike. A second problem is that
the new convert may have unwittingly picked up some of
this unnecessary baggage from the missionary. But it is
precisely in fostering the fusion of the convert's horizon of
understanding with that of the biblical text, which both
missionary and convert agree is the basis of authority for
their shared faith, that there is a possibility of the convert's
divesting himself of these unwise and sometimes unwitting
accretions, a possibility of developing a genuinely contextualized theology.

In fact, as I suggested in the introduction, the model can
become far more complex yet, because each generation of
believers tries to grapple with the way the gospel given in,
the Bible has been understood in other ages, branches and
cultures in the history of the church; and this involves still ·
more fusing of horizons if true understanding is to be gained.
That is what makes a competent historian.[94] Moreover, von
Allmen frequently speaks of a genuine *African* theology over
against *Western* theology, as if these two labels represent
undifferentiated wholes; whereas in fact there are many
different Western theologies (not to mention cultures and
languages) and even more African theologies (and cultures
and languages). Why should Byang Kato's theology be criti-
cised as too subservient to Western thought because it is in
line with one form of Western evangelicalism, whereas
Mbiti[95] is praised for his genuine African insights even
though he learned his eschatology in Europe? There is a
double standard afoot here; and it has less to do with
questions of contextualization than with animus against evangelicalism. It is very difficult to see how Mbiti is more
'African' than Kato, or vice-versa, in precisely the same way
that it is difficult to see how Moltmann is more 'Western'
than Carl F. H. Henry, or vice-versa.

In short, reflection on the third horizon, which relates to
the missionary responsibility of the church, sheds light on
the relation between the first two horizons, and renders
invalid all theories that depend on the possibility that
humans locked in space and time can formulate supracultural
truth supraculturally. This means either that there can be
no gospel at all (which of course von Allmen would not say),

or that the locus of revealed and propositional truth must include far more than the restricted core some are advancing.

F. CONCLUDING REFLECTIONS

Where, then, does all this leave us? What is genuinely contextualized theology that is faithful to the gospel preserved and proclaimed in Scripture, and how do we foster it — assuming that we should?

I should first set out what I mean by contextualization. In the past, many missionaries of large spirit and vision spoke of the importance of the indigenization of the church. By this, as we have seen, they meant to sum up the 'three selfs': the church must become self-governing, self-supporting, and self-propagating. 'Contextualization' goes beyond this to include questions of biblical interpretation and theological expression: i.e. the Word of God needs to be 'contextualized' in each culture.[96]

In many ways, this is surely right. Precisely *because* each culture approaches the Scriptures with its own set of prejudices and blinkers, it will be able to see, and (initially at any rate) be prevented from seeing, certain things that another culture might respond to (or fail to respond to) in quite a different way. For this reason, not only every culture, but ideally every generation in every culture (especially in those cultures that are undergoing rapid transition), must get involved in its own Bible study, and learn to express and apply biblical truth in its own context. In this light African theology, indeed, many African theologies, are both necessary and possible — as are, say, Portuguese and Taiwanese theologies.

But from the drift of the argument in this paper, I would delimit that contextualization of theology by five considerations:

First, the 'given' is Scripture. Of course, other things are not less important: prayer, humility, personal knowledge of the Saviour, enthusiastic submission to the Lord Jesus Christ, and more; but the 'given' data on which any truly Christian church must base its theology are the documents

of the Word of God. How this model of theology is related
to the problem of the 'hermeneutical circle' has been worked
out elsewhere.[97] But a truly contextualized theology is, in
my view, one in which believers from a particular culture
seek to formulate a comprehensive theology in the language
and categories of their own culture, *but based on the whole
Bible*. In doing so, they will want to be informed about many
other attempts in other languages and cultures; and they will
struggle with questions such as the relationships amongst the
biblical covenants, the nature of prophecy and fulfilment,
and much more. But the line of control is from the Scripture.
In one sense, therefore, I agree with von Allmen that theology has not been properly contextualized if it simply tries
to take over the effort of some other culture. However, this
does not entail the abandonment of all contact with other
theologies, which would be impossible anyway, but only
that the line of direct control must be from Scripture.

The stumbling block that has tripped up von Allmen in
his understanding of contextualization is his sub-biblical
grasp of the Bible. For whenever there is an attempt to build
a theology on an alleged supracultural core, or on an entirely
non-propositional revelation (the Bible in this case being
nothing more than a faulty witness to that revelation),[98] the
inevitable result is that the *real* line of authority lies elsewhere: in the presupposed philosophy (articulated or otherwise), or in the standards and world-view of the culture, or
in the preferences of the theologian. Western Christendom
has generated its liberal Jesus, its Marxist Jesus, its Mormon
Jesus, its unknown but existentialist Jesus, and so forth; but
from the perspective of the Christian who believes that the
Scriptures are authoritative, the core problem behind these
reductionist and faddish theologies is their abandonment of
the biblical data. Uncontrolled and speculative subjectivity
is the inevitable result, even though each siren theology
proclaims itself as the answer. Similarly, if we now cultivate
various, say, African, Scottish, Indian and Burmese theologies, while abandoning the authority of Scripture, we have
merely multiplied the subjectivity and speculation of the
enterprise; and none of these efforts will prove very enduring, because at no level will they mesh with the central

heritage of biblical Christianity, however expressed in diverse cultures. But if by African, Scottish, Indian and Burmese theologies we are referring to attempts by nationals to work directly from Scripture in order to construct a biblically controlled theology each for its own language, culture and generation, the enterprise cannot be too highly lauded and encouraged; and the result in each case will mesh substantially with other efforts elsewhere, once their respective 'horizons of understanding' have been fused. And where there are disagreements that are not purely linguistic or cultural about what the Scriptures actually say, then at least in this case there is a common, recognised authority that renders further joint study and discussion possible and potentially profitable.[99]

Second, the study of historical theology is a well-nigh indispensable element in the task. As I have already indicated, it strikes me as a kind of inverted paternalism to give Western students substantial doses of historical theology, including the study of theology in many languages and cultures not their own, and then advocate keeping such information from (say) African believers, unless, presumably, Africans are the ones teaching the subject. Yet historical theology should not be taught as if it were normative, but should be constantly assessed both culturally and against the norm of Scripture. In other words, while von Allmen wants to assess streams of *inner* canonical tradition, as he reconstructs them, against the minimalistic, supracultural gospel he judges to be normative, I want to assess *post*-canonical streams of tradition against the 'given' of the canon itself. Such study invariably widens the options, generates care in biblical interpretation, exposes the thoughtful student to his or her own blind spots, and enables the thoughtful person to detect patterns of genuine continuity, frequent doctrinal and ethical sources of contention or objects of disbelief, and so forth.

Third, it follows therefore that a Christian in, say, Lagos, Nigeria and another in Oslo, Norway do not have to pass each other as ships in the night. They will of course construct their theologies along quite different lines, using different languages, metaphors, genres, and so forth. But once the linguistic and cultural barriers between them have been substantially overcome (as is the case when one of the two learns the language and culture of the other), enabling them to communicate fairly freely, there is no intrinsic reason why these two Christians should not sit down and, with patient probing, not only learn from each other but be corrected by each other — precisely because each of them has learned to fuse his own horizon of understanding with that of the Scriptures both hold to be normative. The African, for instance, might expose the unbiblical individualism of his European counterpart, and show how much of the biblical language of the church is 'family' language — points on which the European may have been insensitive. On the other hand, the European may challenge the African to ask if his understanding of family solidarity may not have been carried too far — perhaps by introducing elements of ancestor worship into his theology, even though such worship has no sanction in Scripture.[100] It thus becomes important for *every* cultural group to 'do theology' not only for its own sake but also because each will contribute something valuable to the worldwide understanding of biblical truth. But the exchanges must ultimately be reciprocal; and it must be recognised that the authority that corrects every culture is the Word of God.

Fourth, although the subject cannot be explored here, there are two important theological truths that should be borne in mind in this debate. The first is that the Bible's teaching on the depravity of fallen human nature, a depravity extending even to the natural mind that *cannot* understand the things of God (1 Cor. 2:14), in one sense makes the communication process, the transfer of meaning from the second horizon to the third, far harder than those who focus only on the new hermeneutic can imagine. But conversely, the Bible's own solution to this dilemma — the enabling work of the Spirit of God, is not afraid to bring God into the picture; and is therefore a highly creative and powerful 'solution'. This is most emphatically *not* a surreptitious appeal to mystical and ill-defined knowledge, but an acknowledgement that the Spirit's convicting, transforming, regenerating work changes attitudes and motives and values that had once erected immense epistemological barriers. Failure to wrestle with these two points has led to some serious misjudgments even by those who take a high view of Scripture.[101]

Fifth, pace von Allmen, there is no reason why Westerners should not encourage Africans to develope their own theology — just as there is no reason why Africans should not encourage us to do a far better job of developing our own.

The aim must always be to develop indigenous, contextualized Christianity that is in hearty submission to Scripture, growing in its understanding of and obedience to God's Word. If this means, in the West, that we must re-think our tendencies toward, say, scepticism, individualism, an arrogant sense of racial superiority, and materialism, is Byang Kato so wrong when he warns believers in his own context of their dangers of falling into syncretism, universalism and Christo-paganism? Why should it be thought that the Bible can be wielded as a prophetic sword over Western culture and not over African culture?[102]

The struggle between the views of Kato and von Allmen does not ultimately turn only on the way contextualization should proceed, but even more on the authority of Scripture; and as such, the debate is a reflection of a similar struggle throughout Christendom — one which, ironically, is fuelled even more by the West's rationalism than it is by post-colonial nationalism.

6

Syncretism, Secularization and Renewal

SUNAND SUMITHRA

A. INTRODUCTION

How can we describe the condition of the church in our times? It is a mixed picture, to be sure. One of the most striking parallels in the Scriptures is the state of the people of Israel in the book of Isaiah. The first five chapters depict not just the self-understanding of Israel, but of God's understanding of them, as well as his solution to their problem. God complains that his people do not know him! They are observing the rituals and sacrifices, but he does not delight in them. He accuses them of listening to the diviners from the East and the soothsayers from Egypt, of their adulterous idolatry. The people are more interested in wine and mirth, and in decking themselves out with costly ornaments, than in right and moral relationships. Had God rejected his people? Yes, was his answer, 'because their speech and deeds are against the Lord, defying his glorious presence', and 'they have despised the word of the Holy One of Israel'. Therefore, says the Lord, his anger is kindled against them, to devour them. This, it seems to me, is an accurate picture in general of the church of our time, particularly of the church in India, though, no doubt, there are pockets of God's renewing activity here and there.

This essay attempts to analyse the causes and the conditions of the contemporary Christian church and suggest remedies, all within the scope of the area delimited by the title. I have chosen as the method of study a theological analysis, rather than an historical or exegetical approach, since other essays in this collection deal with these aspects to various degrees.

It is most significant that already at Jerusalem in 1928, at the Second Meeting of the International Missionary Council syncretism and secularization were being discussed as *the* problem of the church. In the light of resurgence of non-Christian religions, and of increasing materialism and secularism in the West, the greatest enemies of Christian progress were seen to be, *not* other religions, but secularism and syncretism. In fighting against these two enemies, Christianity tried to find a solidarity with other religions which had not been found in Edinburgh, at the First Meeting in 1910.

In retrospect, the approach taken by the Second Meeting seems incredibly naive. Precisely because the conference of 1928 saw other religions as co-bulwarks against materialism, secularism and syncretism, the slide was accelerated. There was a gigantic failure to see that the pluralism and syncretism which resulted from the conference's own stance actually aided the rush towards secularism, since spiritual truth itself became thoroughly negotiable.

As late as 1962, we find Hendrik Kraemer writing[1] that syncretism and secularism are the two great problems confronting the contemporary church. No doubt there are others: disunity of the church based on denominational, caste, racial, tribal and other fleshly differences; the need for committed leaders; the great hindrance of not practising what we preach; a dimmed sense and urgency for evangelism, and so on — all these are in themselves big problems. But in one way or another, each of these problems is related to the two stressed by Kraemer; and we will be dealing with them when we in turn deal with these two problems.

Another preliminary consideration must be understood:

here we are talking of syncretism and secularization *in the church*. Syncretism is really a problem of Christianity as a religion, or more exactly, of the truth-claim of all religions. Syncretism attempts to solve the problem of the plurality of truth-claims by relativising them all.

By contrast, secularization challenges the very essence of Christian religion. Secularization itself, of course, is proving notoriously difficult to define; nevertheless, an increasing number of scholars understand it to be *the process by which religion is shoved to the periphery of human concern*. The things that really matter to us, such as education, politics, the natural sciences, sports, economics and the like, outstrip Christianity in importance and thus the secularist simply sidesteps or ignores the claims and proclamations of the church. In any state where secularization has proceeded apace, there may or may not be many Christians; but if there are, they themselves tend to resort to their Christian beliefs only at peculiarly religious moments. Their thinking is not profoundly Christian; and those who are exceptions to this rule will find themselves isolated from the rest of society.[2]

It may be tempting to some to deal with the secularization of Christianity from a strictly ecclesiastical and sociological point of view — that is, without reference to Christianity's historic commitment to truth, a commitment which cannot be negotiated without the loss of essential and vital Christianity. There are good reasons why such an approach may seem to have validity.

For example, in India, modern writers use the term Hindu*ism* less and less, but more and more Hindu*dom* or Hindu-*ity*, thus rejecting the early bias that reduces their religion to a mere system of thought. In fact, they insist, it is really a way of life. K.M. Panikkar never tires of insisting on this point. But surprisingly, when all the various concepts, rituals, world-views or ethical systems and cultural elements are stripped away, Hindus themselves agree that the core of their Hindu religion is in none of them; it is primarily in their sociological structure — of *Varnasharma Dharma* (the caste system and the four stages of Hindu life). In parallel with this approach, thinkers such as Carl H. Ratschow and Lesslie Newbigin declare that the essence of Christianity is, in the long run, concretely in the church. Theology, mission, worship and service are all functions of the church, and so it is quite valid to talk of syncretism and secularism as problems of the church.

But in fact the problem is more complex. If we hastily abandon all essentialist thought in Christianity, there is no stopping point to the ensuing retreat, short of process theology. Even Kraemer does not see the real depth of the problems he highlights, precisely because of his slightly sub-biblical view of Scripture. Although he insists that the vertical makes its impact on man and history, he views the Bible itself as so locked into man's history and church that it cannot be seen as part of the vertical self-disclosure of God, that is, as revelation. Such anomalies present us with a clear conclusion and it is impossible to consider the problems of the syncretism and secularization now endemic to much church life without equally considering the truth-claims of biblical Christianity.

Be that as it may, we shall now consider in turn the three words in the title, bearing in mind that the church claims to be *more* (though certainly not less) than a sociological phenomenon.

B. SYNCRETISM

The word syncretism was first used by Plutarch, and in a political sense. He says that Cretans, though always in a state of internal discord, show a united front against a common enemy; and this he calls *synkretismos*. In the sixteenth century, the word was used to describe Bessarion's attempt to reconcile Plato and Aristotle. During the Reformation, the word retained its original political meaning — in spite of profound differences, to combine forces against a common foe. In the seventeenth century, the term became very common, especially among theologians. Calixtus, who attempted to formulate a common confession of various Protestant lines, was accused of being a 'syncretist', presumably a very bad sort of heretic. Since his time the term has retained, for many, its evil smell! It is only in the nineteenth century, when the History of Religions school monopolised the word, that intensified study led to the discovery of the original connotation of the term. Kraemer defines syncretism as 'a systematic attempt to combine, blend and reconcile inharmonious, even often conflicting, religious elements'. Such an attempt is intentional, made on the basis of reflection.

It is wise to limit the scope of the term syncretism to *illegitimate* mingling of *irreconcilable* elements, as Kraemer does. For in the history of religions there are plenty of examples of spontaneous and unconscious adaptations which are better labelled indigenization. Similarly, adaptation, assimilation, absorption, digestion, accommodation, adoption, acculturation, and scores of other terms are not, strictly speaking, syncretistic processes. If that were so, then not only do world religions like Islam, Buddhism and Hinduism become syncretisms, but also Judaism and Christianity! Gunkel called Christianity a syncretistic religion because he confused the illegitimate process of syncretism with legitimate and inevitable processes of indigenization. Indigenization[3] is a process of showing the relevance and the meaning of the Christian gospel in a given cultural context, without diluting the uniqueness and finality of Jesus Christ as God's revelation, as syncretism does. It may indeed be difficult fully to preserve the finality of Jesus Christ in indigenizing the Christian message, but indigenization itself is inevitable. This does not mean it is necessary to assign positive connotations to the term syncretism on the ground that (as some Indians have argued) the fear of syncretism has come to mean the absolutisation of Western Christianity. In this paper, 'syncretism' will invariably connote illegitimate forms of accommodation.

The early adoption of Greek philosophies to express the Gospel of Christ sometimes proved to be rather bad sorts of indigenization, for in so doing the fulness of the gospel was often truncated; and at best the theologians in question did preserve the finality of Christ as God's revelation. Mithraism did not so preserve it, and became a syncretistic religion. Theosophy, the Baha'i faith, Akbar's *Din-e-Ilahi*, and Manichaeism are examples of syncretism in history. All such attempts to combine diverse influences which damage the uniqueness and finality of the revelation in Jesus Christ are illegitimate indigenization.

As we have seen, syncretism is a problem of religion pluralism. How does the Bible deal with the pluralist question?

Generally speaking, the Old Testament condemns the Gentile religions in strong terms. They are seen as idolatry (often under the metaphor of adultery or fornication), and ignorance. That is why the very first commandment reads: 'You shall have no other gods before me'. The idols were called abominations, wind and confusion. They are nothings, for only Yahweh is the sovereign. Perhaps even more important are the insights of the first eleven chapters of Genesis, before Israel arrived on the scene. Here, the relationship between God and mankind is portrayed in a dialectical manner. Man is created in the image of God, and yet thrown out of his presence; man rebels against God, and yet is sought by him. For our purpose, this means that the world of religions still lies within the compass of God's concern, and that he is not absent from it. Because of creation and the fall, human religions are truth mixed with falsehood — sometimes they are wrong, sometimes partly right, and sometimes really right! This explains why in all religions the noblest as well as the basest elements are to be found. This also explains the necessity of biblical revelation; for God preserved in the Jewish–Christian Scriptures his truth, without contaminating it with falsehood.

But to argue that every religion preserves some good, though true, is simplistic, and overlooks *the tone* with which Old Testament writers approach competing religious claims. The reason lies in the fact that truths may not be judged atomistically. True statements and right practices cannot be added up like a number of independent coins; for they are inevitably reshaped and transformed by the larger system of the religion to which they belong. Religious affirmations are not just so many marbles in a bag, some of them white, some of them black, and some of them grey; they are qualified by the system that stands in rebellion against God. Bavinck has some excellent discussion along these lines;

and ultimately in his view the question returns to this fundamental test: What are you doing with God?[4]

In the New Testament, it is obvious that Jesus was wholly in line with the Old Testament prophets, though he added his own authority to what they said. That in him the Scriptures are fulfilled is Jesus' distinctive. In the Sermon on the Mount, he favours genuine piety as against outward religiosity. On the whole, Jesus was not so much concerned with religions in themselves as with worshippers as religious persons.

It is often argued that the prologue to the Gospel of John demonstrates that all religions find their validity in Christ. The *logos* concept of the prologue, it is claimed, is borrowed from Greek philosophy; and so the light which illumines every man who comes into this world is equated with *logos spermatikos*: that word, like seed, is strewn in mankind in all the religions and philosophies. A closer examination of the concept of *logos* shows that it is Hebrew in origin, not Greek. God created all the universe with his Word; and this divine self-disclosure, mediated through the concept of Wisdom in Prov. 8 and elsewhere, is the background for the Apostle John when he says that in the beginning was the Word, and the Word was with God, and the Word was God.[5] As Kittel's word study shows, the New Testament concept of *logos* is fundamentally different from the Hellenistic *logos*.

As for Paul, it is equally difficult to exegete his speech at Lystra (Acts 14:8–18) to mean that God is revealing himself through all religions, as is often done. Paul is telling the people here that his primary purpose is to convert them from their idolatry to the true and living God, who has abandoned the Gentile peoples to their own ways but all the time has been reminding them of himself, their Creator and Sustainer, through the regular meeting of their needs and the faithful provision of good things. If anything, this passage shows that all religions are in error, in which God-forsakenness manifests itself; yet at the same time God has not left people to themselves. Similarly Paul's speech at the Areopagus (Acts 17:16–34) clarifies that all peoples in their religious attempts have gone astray and are quite oblivious of God; yet in these very attempts they are dimly aware of him, aware as it were of his absence. But God in his mercy and faithfulness has not abandoned them unredeemably; through conversion to one man Jesus Christ, every one can again be reconciled to God. In the first chapter of Romans Paul definitely — indirectly but by implication — includes all religions and philosophies under the category of futile human imaginings, because of which men are entangled in their own foolishness and perversions, so that God had no alternative except to give them up.

In other epistles also Paul thinks of people without Christ as without God and without hope. In Galatians the apostle pronounces a firm anathema on those who proclaim a Christ other than the Christ who is really 'there' — the one whom he himself preaches. In his Epistle to the Colossians, Paul explicitly confronts what appears to be some kind of syncretist melding of Jewish traditions and various Hellenistic influences; and he resolutely sets his face against all forms of religion that call in question the finality, sufficiency, and authority of Jesus Christ. The list could go on.

In short, the New Testament picture of non-Christian religions is not greatly different from that of the Old Testament: they raise questions rather than provide answers concerning God and at best their truth is severely mixed with falsehood. They reveal both the need for God's revelation, and man's incapability of knowing God and his nature as holy love. Christian faith, holding Jesus Christ as the true and sufficient revelation of God, and the cross and resurrection as the supreme revelation of God's love, holiness and power, cannot legitimately be mingled with other religions.

For this reason, religious pluralism should not be a problem for Christian faith. For if God himself chose — indeed, established! — Hebrew-Christian 'religion' to preserve his revelation, so we too must preserve it. Religious tolerance is always the primary defence of the non-prophetic religions — that is, of those religions outside Judaism-Christianity. The axiom behind such a tolerance is that truth is neither monopolised nor preserved fully by any one religion, and so, since the whole is greater than the sum of its parts, each religion must relativize its claims to make room for those of the others.

We have already reflected on the positive elements and successful features within other religions. But what about the lacks or failures within Christianity? Do we not need other traditions to complement Christianity where it is wanting? Our answer can only be this: that according to the Bible, Jesus Christ is the final and sufficient revelation of God, and God's plan for man's salvation; beyond what Jesus reveals, man needs nothing more. If there are any lacks, they should be seen as imperfect understandings of the Jesus of the Bible, and all failures as failures of his disciples to obey him. Resurgence and reformation of non-Christian religions in our time need not mean any threat to Christian faith or the finality of Jesus Christ; for the gospel has within its message the paradoxical effect of waking and maintaining opposition to itself from other religions! Thus Christian missions often provoke counter-missions in other religions as well as the inclusion of Christian elements in them, as Chenchiah and Devanandan have shown.

Swami Vivekananda's principle of the harmony of all religions as India's contribution to the world, Mahatma Gandhi's understanding that all religions ultimately lead to the same goal, or Radhakrishnan's Hindu syncretism of all religions based on his belief that Hinduism is *Sanatana Dharma* (eternal religion) need not shock us — perhaps these are the attempts we can expect from religions like Hinduism, in the long run. But Christian attempts to syncretize should bother us. Consider Vatican II's approach to non-Christian religions as ordinary ways of salvation, while Christianity is the extraordinary way, so that in the scale of religions Christianity is at the centre, with the purest content of truth, while other religions in growing concentric circles contain the gospel in increasing impurity. Such an approach reduces the difference between the Christian Gospel and other religions to a merely quantitative one — which is only one step behind discovering Christ in other religions. This is the implication of Karl Rahner's theory of the'anonymous Christian'. M. M. Thomas' approach, which he calls 'Christ-centred syncretism', is a little different. He holds that, thanks to the impact of Christian missions, Christ is transforming all religions from within themselves (Christ is informing them!), so that we need no longer convert individual human beings, but should concentrate on the conversion of all religions to Christ. But in such an approach the Jesus of the Bible is totally separated from the principle of Christ-hood, which is another way of saying 'cosmic Christ', incognito Christ, undiscovered or acknowledged or unbounded Christ. Obviously, all such Christologies fall short of recognising the Jesus of Nazareth of the Scriptures as the only norm. That the Messiah of the Old Testament became the Jesus of the New Testament, and that the truth of the Jews became the basis of the Christian Gospel is the foundation stone on which alone any Christology can be built. The whole Bible is the norm, not just the New Testament.

Finally, the approach of the WCC's sub-unit, 'Dialogue with Men of Other Faiths and Ideologies' (DFI), also smacks of syncretism; that is, it jeopardizes the finality of Jesus Christ as God's revelation. With its two key concepts, open-ness and commitment, though theoretically commendable (only one who is totally committed to Christ can be fully open to other religions), yet because of its cosmic christology it falls short of the biblical emphases. The later develop-ments, called 'more than an encounter of commitments', go beyond the dialogue concerning truth concepts, but enter into a common understanding of spirituality with other religions. Thus *epoche*, a temporary suspension of faith, worship with other adherents, even using several Scrip-tures — all these replace proclamation by participation as the primary method of Christian missionary task.

What can we say in evaluating such syncretistic tendenc-ies? At least two aspects must be stressed. First, behind all these attempts is the unexpressed postulate that religion is a most potent source of strife in the world, and so must somehow be relativised. In the face of imminent nuclear holocaust, the survival of mankind is the greatest moving force of all human efforts. Mankind can survive only by being united; thus the unity of all humanity is the grand utopian goal towards which all syncretistic movements move. All religions must either give way or accommodate all others as an essential part of each of them in order that there may be peace and harmony, and the human race can continue. Clearly, this is another way of expressing universalism. But the biblical approach is not quite so inclusive. The belief that God is still in control of history (after all, history is His story), and the appropriation of God's offer of salvation of faith in his son Jesus Christ as the only way are by no means universalist. Whatever may be our eschatological picture of heaven and hell, biblical judgmental dualism based on the justice and holiness of God is inevitable.

Second, the concept of unlimited human progress is still dominant in circles which embrace syncretism as the way out. Process philosophy is becoming the one formidable alternative to the biblical revelation. In an approach where the newer is the better, sin is understood as necessary evil or growing pain, God either the goal of the process or the process itself, and authentic humanity becomes the goal of salvation, the borderline between salvation history and secular history is obliterated, and the exclusive claims of the Christian gospel are seen as fanaticism, the absolutization of the historical and empirical. Thus all syncretistic efforts are seen as one step forward in the evolution of mankind. A full evaluation of process philosophy has yet to be made from the evangelical perspective, although some attempts already exist.[6] But the God of the Bible, as the Creator, omnipotent, omniscient, holy and merciful, cannot be equated with any concept in process thinking. He is both the Alpha and the Omega, whose holy will has been revealed from the beginning, and not at the end of the historical events.

C. SECULARIZATION

The etymology of the term 'secular' is most interesting, and is to be found in most of the books in recent times which discuss the question of secularism. The Vulgate uses two words for the one English word, 'world', namely *mundus* (from which we have the word, mundane) whose connotation is limited more or less to the spatial expanse of the world, and *saeculum*, which deals with the temporal aspect of the world. *Saeculum* means age. The septuagintal equivalent for *mundus* is *kosmos*, and the equivalent for *saeculum* is *aiōn*. As John Macquarrie has shown,[7] the term 'secular' gathered several shades of meaning in its development. To begin with it meant 'this age', in contrast with 'the age to come'. Already here there is a sense that to be secular is to be inferior. Later in church history the word secular acquired an anti-religious character. A secular priest was one who was in charge of non-ecclesiastical affairs, and a religious priest was one who could administer sacraments. When a priest was transferred from his religious duties to the secular ones, he was a 'secularized' priest. The separation of Pope from Emperor necessitated the separation also of spiritual from political duties. This process was called the process of secularization. Thus the term 'secular' was used in opposition to the spiritual or the ecclesiastical as well. Still later, the term was used synonymously with positivism, so that secular was equated with all that is based on reason and experiment, and not on faith; and metaphysical structures, on which theology was understood to be based, were rejected as irrational and speculative.

Finally a thoroughgoing secularist was also a completely autonomous person. No higher being than man was acknowledged, no transcendental aspect to human existence; and so man became the measure for everything. Nowadays, when we use the term 'secular', we mean some or all of these connotations — namely, that which is not supernatural or religious, which is not Beyond or transcendental or holy. In any sense of the term, secularism is a way of looking at reality which operates necessarily without God.

D. THE SECULARISM VS. SECULARIZATION DEBATE

If secularism is a closed worldview necessarily without God, what about secularization? Friedrich Gogarten was the first to differentiate between secularism as an outlook and secularization as a process — the former opposing, the latter in harmony with, the biblical message. In the dominant

definition of secularization today, that advanced by the
discipline of sociology, secularization (as we have seen) is
that process which removes Christianity to the periphery of
life. But Gogarten adopted a definition which he thought
made it possible to understand secularization to be in harmony with the biblical message. He defined secularization
as 'Vergeschichtlichung der menschlichen Existenz' (human
existence determined by the dimension of history). T. van
der Leeuwen embraces this definition and says that since
the process of secularization is nothing but the process of
the ripening of the Christian values, it is a result of the
biblical revelation. 'In this age of ours 'Christianization' can
only mean that peoples become involved in the outward
movement of Christian history.' Similarly, Alexander Duff
says that the best result of Christian missions in India can
be nothing more than giving it a secular Government. Har-
vey Cox goes even deeper in finding the roots of secularization: he finds them in the very story of the Israelites. He
says that in creation God reveals himself as the sole Creator,
and thus nature is disenchanted of its swarms of demons
and daemons. At the Exodus, Yahweh humiliated all the
Egyptian gods, and thus desacralised politics, which thus
far was operative only in divine realms. And finally, at the
Sinai covenant, God deconsecrated all values by making the
covenant so human. Secularization is the legitimate goal of
the Christian gospel. Paul van Buren, Bishop J. A. T.
Robinson, Paul Tillich, M. M. Thomas and scores of others
have accepted the process of secularization as the legitimate
consequence of the Gospel. M. M. Thomas of India, for
example, looks at secularization only as a process of liberating all the areas of human life (politics, economics, science,
etc.) from the control of religion — which thus ties in with
the sociologists' definition, except that Thomas might be
accused of making a virtue of necessity. This is typical of
most of the positive assessment of secularization. Nature,
thus far swarming with spirits, became in the process of
secularization man's humble tool so that he could exploit it
at will, or 'hominize' it. Both technological revolution and
the revolt of the oppressed peoples are to be traced back to
secularisation as their primary source.

On the other hand, theologians like Sauerzapf see in secularization the danger of diluting the gospel emphases. He says that it is due to secularization of the gospel that 'the gradual disappearance of absolute values in the field of ecumenics was compensated in an unbiblical and earth-centred way, by a kind of enthusiasm strangely cloaked in eschatological terms.' Joachim Ruff, F. W. Künneth and Peter Beyerhaus also similarly see in the process of secularization the danger of secularism itself, namely, that man is more and more determining his self-understanding and destiny without the hypothesis of God. And between an outlook which is a-theological and one which is anti-theological there is but a short step. Leon Morris speaks of the impossibility of 'religionless Christianity' because it is a man-centred Christianity, lacking in Christian theology, Christian worship and evangelism. For him, a religionless Christianity is not Christian!

I would agree with his conclusion that in the final analysis there is not much difference between secularism and secularization. As a liberating process, secularization is in fact a process liberating man from the control of God's holy will. Every time any area of life is secularized, that is what we are doing. The replacement of the kingdom of God by utopian visions, of evangelization by ideological programmes, revelation by revolutions is the inevitable effect of the secularizing process. For it is not the human being's self-understanding, but God's interpretation of human beings (as found in the Bible), which is the basis for human activity. If the message of the gospel has nullified the power of all idols, it does not mean that it has also nullified the power of the omnipotent God!

What can we say about secularization by way of evaluation? At least three things. First, the real source of secularization goes beyond the secularism of Holyoake — it is rooted in the European enlightenment itself. Man becomes his own norm as reason becomes the supreme authority. All values, all knowledge of truth and all actions must be determined by man alone; man becomes the maker of his own nature and destiny. There is a close parallel between the process of secularization and that of the Fall!

Second, as a corollary of this, human freedom is seen as the essence of humanity. Whatever a person may have, if he or she does not have true freedom, he or she is not considered to be human. Thus liberation of human beings from every kind of oppression is adjudged positively. Secularization, as a process of liberation of man from 'God-oppression', can thus be seen as good. But the biblical standard is not unqualified freedom of man; it is rather freedom 'to do the will of him who sent me' — that is the meaning and purpose of human existence. The former glorifies man, the latter God.

Third, in the process of secularization, the uniqueness of biblical revelation is at stake. Since it is human expertise which is more and more the criterion for human values and goals, the Scriptures become one of the resources for man, instead of being his ultimate authority. Secularization of the Christian gospel cannot but end in the elimination of the *skandalon* of the cross; for in secularization man is the measure, not Jesus Christ.

E. RENEWAL

We have seen that both syncretism and secularization are as thorns in the flesh for the Christian church. More than this, they constitute a disease, a positive menace, not mere undernourishment for the body of Christ. How can the church be renewed, revived and immunised against such diseases?

In the Scriptures, the Christian never renews himself, but is always renewed by God. Thus God is the source of renewal in the church. At the same time, God's renewal is in the spiritual realm; it is a renewal of the human heart, not of structures or ideologies, concepts or activities. Thirdly, it is the Holy Spirit who is always the agent of God's renewal. This mean that the first step in the renewal of the church is the church's conscious waiting upon her Lord in prayer.

The one great need in the Indian Church is the need for God's fresh visitation! Beyond the need for leadership, for apologetic literature and edifying books, we Indian Christians need to see our God afresh as never before. Already there are several cell-groups scattered over the land which are constantly praying for such a wide-spread spiritual renewal. There are several parts of the land which are already experiencing such a reviving of churches, but we long and wait for a visitation of the Spirit in a mighty way!

Along with such expectant prayer, we in India particularly need to recover the biblical picture of God. Amid the syncretizing forces of Hindu pluralism, we seem unconsciously to be thinking of the God and Father of our Lord Jesus Christ as one among the 33 million gods! We have forgotten that he is the sole Creator, all powerful and all knowing. His infinite and perfect goodness, justice, wisdom and power are hardly the basis for our secular lives! There is lacking a boldness in our life and mission which we will find only in such a faith and experience of God.

The third step perhaps would be a determined return to the Bible as the final authority. The whole church needs to be educated to study, believe and obey the Bible as the inspired Word of God.

A fourth step would be living out our lives in obedience to the light we have received. The great hindrance is not in the message but in the messenger, in those of us who are the carriers of the gospel in our day to day life.

Fifth, there is a great need to develop Christian apologetics and train frontline leadership at every level of the church's activity. Christian writing is now beginning to appear, relevant to the problems raised by our neighbours, but it still has far to go. Our theological colleges, mostly dominated by modernist philosophies, can hardly produce leaders who are able to give a reason for their hope in Jesus Christ. We need a vast number of training institutions where such grass-root equipping can be done.

F. CONCLUSION

In concluding the essay, I want to come back to the book of Isaiah with which we started. In the face of the death of the king and the hopelessness of the situation, the prophet Isaiah went to the temple to wait upon the Lord. There, he was given a message, and a commission to go and tell the people. But before he could receive the commission, he was to be cleansed and made ready to receive God's message; and before he could be cleansed, he had to see himself as he really was — as God saw him; and before he could really have a true self-understanding, he had to see what God is like! The renewal both for Isaiah and the people of Israel came only when Isaiah had a vision of God as he is, high and lifted up. This shows that there is no self-understanding without grasping God's understanding of us, and there is no renewal without such a self-understanding. We know ourselves only when we are in the presence of the holy God. Isaiah saw the almighty God as thrice holy, and was convicted of his own — and his people's — unholiness. He confessed his sin, was cleansed and renewed to renew others.

Many movements and theologies of our time have so debased God that we Christians have forgotten that primarily God is a holy God. While in normal times we acknowledge and rejoice in our understanding of God as a loving and merciful Father, in times of renewal we come to tremble before him as the Holy One, as the consuming fire! Perhaps in our time where syncretism and secularism are rampant, there is no better antidote to these 'diseases' than to re-emphasise the holiness of God. May the good Lord grant to each one of us a vision of him like that which Isaiah had, so that we too may be renewed and commissioned to renew our brothers and sisters.

7

The Church and Persecution

DAVID H. ADENEY

The twentieth century opened with the death of hundreds of Chinese Christians and missionaries during the Boxer Rising in China. The next year, 1901, James Chalmers was beheaded by cannibals in the South Pacific Islands. Throughout the years that followed, from Russian and Chinese prisons and labour camps to the jungles of Ecuador, from the borders of Tibet to the villages of Uganda during Idi Amin's reign of terror, faithful believers have demonstrated the truth of Tertullian's saying that 'the blood of the martyrs is the seed of the church'.

During the twentieth century the gospel of Jesus Christ has spread to almost every nation on earth. Only a handful of countries are without any known witness to the Saviour of the world. But this advance of the gospel has been costly. Probably more lives have been laid down and more Christians have suffered imprisonment in the last 100 years than in any other period of church history.

Persecution has been the experience of the people of God down the ages. When a new Chinese believer in Shanghai, just before his baptism was asked, 'Are you prepared to suffer?' he knew perfectly well that great numbers of his fellow believers had already suffered for their faith and he must also be prepared to go the way of the cross.

In the first century, it would be perfectly natural to ask

such a question. The early followers of Christ realized that discipleship would be very costly and they had to be prepared for suffering. Paul reminds Timothy that 'everyone who wants to live a godly life in Christ Jesus will be persecuted' (2 Tim. 3:12). The Lord Jesus himself was criticized, abused, ridiculed, arrested, beaten, and finally put to death on the cross. On numerous occasions, Christ warned his disciples of the suffering that lay ahead of the church. He told his followers that they would be 'betrayed even by parents, brothers, relatives and friends, and they will put some of you to death. All men will hate you because of me' (Lk. 1:16-17).

Immediately after the choosing and commissioning of the Twelve he reminded them of the hostile society into which he was sending them. They would be 'sheep in the midst of wolves'. Persecution involving physical suffering was inevitable (Matt. 10:16-18). Later in his final discourse with the disciples he told them that they must be like their Master: 'If they persecuted me they will persecute you' (Jh. 15:20).

But the warning of impending suffering was accompanied by the assurance of the presence and help of the Holy Spirit who would teach them what to say when they were brought before governors and kings. Twice Christ used the words 'for my sake' when referring to future persecution. When after Pentecost the apostles were arrested and beaten, they left the presence of the council rejoicing that they were counted worthy to suffer dishonour for the name (Acts 5:40). Many years later the apostle John would claim that he was on the prison island of Patmos 'on account of the word of God and the testimony of Jesus' (Rev. 1:9). It was the consciousness that the suffering they endured was for the sake of Christ which enabled the martyrs of the early church to be faithful unto death.

Christ did not however encourage his disciples to seek persecution. He said, in effect, 'when you are persecuted in one place, flee to another. There are still many more towns to be reached with the gospel' (Matt. 10:23). Persecution was indeed used to scatter the early Christians, driving them out from Jerusalem first to Samaria and later to Antioch where the first Gentile church was founded (Acts 8:4, 5 and

11:19). Both in Christ's commission to his disciples and in his discourse concerning the destruction of the temple and the coming of the Messiah, Matthew records Christ's words, 'He who endures to the end will be saved' (Matt. 10:22, 24:13). Jesus placed great emphasis upon the importance of being prepared for persecution, in order not to be overcome in the hour of trial.

As an incentive to faithfulness, Christ spoke of the promise of immortality, telling his followers that they should not be afraid of those who can kill only the body. In the midst of suffering they were to remember that their heavenly Father, who knows even the fall of a sparrow and numbers the hairs of their heads, would be with them (Matthew 10:28–33).

The apostles knew that they would be following in the footsteps not only of their Master but also of the prophets and saints of the Old Testament. Christ called the Jewish leaders of his time 'the descendants of those who murdered the prophets, and shed innocent blood from the time of Abel to that of Zechariah' (Matthew 23:29–35). Stephen during his trial also indicted the members of the Sanhedrin — 'which of the prophets did not your fathers persecute?' (Acts 7:52)

A few of the prophets enjoyed a measure of freedom under God-fearing rulers but many suffered and lived under the threat of their lives when they denounced the sins of the nation and government. During the reign of Ahab and Jezebel many prophets were killed, though some escaped by hiding in caves. Manasseh probably killed many true servants of God and later on men like Jeremiah were imprisoned, ill-treated, and eventually lost their lives. In the letter to the Hebrews we have a graphic picture of the believers of the old covenant who 'suffered mocking and scourging and even chains and imprisonment. They were stoned, they were sawn in two, they were killed with the sword, they went about in skins of sheep and goats, destitute, afflicted, ill-treated — of whom the world was not worthy' (Heb. 11:36–38).

The first time outside the history recorded in the Bible that the Jews as a nation suffered severe persecution for their faith was under the Seleucidae in the second century B.C.

Antiochus IV Epiphanes, in his attempts to unite his empire under one faith and one culture, used cruel force to Hellenize the Jews. He drove out their legitimate high priest, profaned the temple by sacrificing swine on the altar, and decreed that the possession and study of the law, the circumcising of their own sons and other traditions dear to the Jews were offenses against the state punishable with the death penalty. Some of the Jews compromised and cooperated with the Seleucidae while others, like the Maccabees, undergoing intense persecution, resisted, refusing 'to profane the covenant' (1 Macc. 1:62:64).[1]

These stories of suffering on account of the faith undoubtedly inspired the early disciples. They looked upon the Maccabees as 'the forerunners of Christian Martyrdom'. When threatened by the rulers of the Jews they did not ask to be preserved from suffering but rather to be given boldness. Perhaps Peter remembered this experience when he wrote:

> Dear friends, do not be surprised at the painful trial you are suffering, as though something strange were happening to you. But rejoice that you participate in the suffering of Christ, so that you may be overjoyed when his glory is revealed. If you are insulted because of the name of Christ, you are blessed, for the Spirit of glory and of God rests on you (1 Pet. 4:12–14).

Peter and Paul both emphasized the identification of Christ with his church. Peter could never forget the way in which the Lord Jesus turned and looked at him just after he had denied his Lord; and so he tells the scattered believers to whom he is writing that they are not to be ashamed if they 'suffer as a Christian'. Later he rejoiced to suffer for the name of Christ and now is urging them to remember that they too were to share in Christ's suffering. Paul's first glimpse of the identity of the church with their risen Lord came on the road to Damascus when he was confronted by the living Christ and heard the words, 'Saul, Saul, why are not persecuting me?' Immediately there came the realization that when he presided over the execution of Stephen and cast many believers into prison, he was in effect persecuting

Christ himself. From that time onward, he longed to share 'in the fellowship of his suffering'. Generations of Christians have been comforted in their hour of trial by the knowledge that their bodies are the temples of the Holy Spirit. The living Christ was therefore with them in the time of persecution. They were members of his body.

Paul reminded the Corinthian believers that 'if one part suffers, every part suffers with it' (1 Cor. 12:26). This truth is often forgotten by Christians who live in lands that are free from persecution. We have been slow to identify with our brothers and sisters who are suffering in other parts of the world. If we really believed that in their suffering Christ himself was being persecuted we would realize that we cannot separate ourselves from their experience; for we also are members of his body and therefore related to each suffering Christian.

We have a two-fold responsibility: first, to show our love for Christ by being deeply concerned for fellow members of the body who are being persecuted and by doing everything possible to help them; and second, to realize that the persecutors are actually opposing the risen Christ himself and must eventually fail. Not only is the reward 'great in heaven' for those who are persecuted for righteousness' sake (as Jesus promised), but there is also the living hope that the causes for which they suffer will eventually triumph. Peter says 'The spirit of glory and of God rests on you' (1 Pet. 4:14). The reference to the spirit of glory would remind Jewish Christians of the Shekinah Glory which marked the tabernacle as God's dwelling place. Christians who suffered for Christ's sake would be conscious of a special anointing of the Holy Spirit. They would also be aware of the fact that suffering with Christ in the world today would be a preparation for sharing in his glory in the future.

When Christ promised his blessing to those who are persecuted he indicated that persecution refers not only to physical suffering but also to being reviled — 'those who utter all kinds of evils against you' (Matt. 5:11). In the first century Christians were accused of all kinds of crimes. Popular caricatures depicted them as enemies of society and participants in vile behaviour. In recent history Christians have often been wrongfully accused and seen their reputations destroyed just as Christ himself suffered from false accusations. At the end of the last century missionaries in Japan found that a sign had been erected close to the path leading to their home, announcing that 'the evil sect called Christians is strictly prohibited'. Even today Japanese Christians are reminded of the intense persecution that took place in the seventeenth century. Christianity was then called 'the diabolical religion' or 'the evil faith'. False rumours were spread stating that Roman Catholic priests would go to the bedside of dying believers in order to remove their blood. The terrible persecution which followed when hundreds of Christians were crucified or tortured is still remembered today in areas where these events occurred.

In the first century, serious persecution did not take place until almost 30 years after the death of Christ. At first Christians did not face the opposition of the Roman empire. But by the time of Nero, it was quite clear that the church was not just another Jewish sect, and it then became the target for severe attacks. Christians were branded as followers of another king, Jesus (as they had been in Acts 17:7). Persecution continued intermittently until the time of Constantine.

REASONS FOR PERSECUTION

Before thinking of the way in which God has used persecution in the life of the church, we must ask why non-Christians have been so violent in their opposition to the Christian faith.

(a) Religious motivation

Some of the fiercest persecutions endured by Christians have been in the name of religion. Jesus told his disciples. 'They will put you out of the synagogue; in fact, a time is coming when anyone who kills you will think he is offering a service to God'. (John 16:2). The disciples would be persecuted by fellow Jews who were seeking to preserve the purity of their religion. They sincerely thought that they were serving God by persecuting what they considered to be a blasphemous sect.

Saul of Tarsus also persecuted the church because of religious motives. He sincerely believed the truth of Judaism and was convinced that the Christian faith was a threat to the religion he loved. In order to preserve the true religion of Israel he felt that the followers of Jesus of Nazareth, whom he regarded as blasphemers, must be destroyed. He states this very clearly in his testimony before King Agrippa:

> I too was convinced that I ought to do all that was possible to oppose the name of Jesus of Nazareth. And that is just what I did in Jerusalem. On the authority of the chief priests I put many of the saints in prison, and when they were put to death, I cast my vote against them. Many a time I went from one synagogue to another to have them punished, and I tried to force them to blaspheme. In my obsession against them, I even went to foreign cities to persecute them (Acts 26:9–11).

Later Paul himself was persecuted by those who considered that he was betraying the Jewish faith. They could never tolerate the admission of Gentiles into the church on equal terms with Jewish believers.

During the persecutions of the early church in the second and third centuries, Christian martyrs were hated by those who worshipped idols. There was a fear that in some way Christians might triumph over the local gods. Persecutors even burned the bodies of Christians, believing that this would prevent them from having the hope of the resurrection.

In the world today, most persecution of Christians comes from ardent supporters of other religions or ideologies who cannot tolerate a rival faith.

A young man from a Muslim community in an Asian country committed his life to Christ. As a result he suffered intense persecution from his family. He was beaten and hot pepper was poured into his eyes, but still he continued in the faith. Finally his uncles planned to kill him, but owing to the intervention of a sympathetic relative he was rescued. Why should people who claim to worship the one true God plan to murder their own flesh and blood? Basically it is for religious reasons. They believe that a Christian convert will do untold damage to the Islamic community. A Muslim society makes little distinction between the secular and the sacred. Rather, their law is based on their theology. So they can understand the psalmist David when he writes that 'the Law is sweeter than honey, more precious than gold' because it gives order to the chaos of our experience and comes from God himself. Like Moses, Joshua, Eli and Samuel, Muslims equate disobedience to God with sin against the state. Their common faith sets them apart, binds them as a community and governs nearly every aspect of their lives. Psychologically, it gives them an identity, a participation in an enduring significant reality. Ritually, there is power in intoning a creed daily with 700 million others and in the train of myriads who have lived before. Even though some Muslims are becoming more tolerant and many no longer hold fast to every aspect of the Islamic creed, yet there are still many communities where Muslims feel completely justified in persecuting any who change their faith or threaten the stability of the community.

Other religions also attack the Christian faith. Hinduism, which claims to be like a mighty ocean, able to absorb all religious truth, would gladly accept Jesus as one of many deities. I have heard a young Hindu say, 'I love Jesus very much'; and then he goes on to add, 'I also love Krishna'. A Hindu taxi driver carries pictures of Roman Catholic saints because, he says, 'They all can help'. But when Christianity claims to be unique and demands the sole allegiance of its followers, persecution from fanatical Hindus often results.

Even in Thailand where Buddhists seem to be a gentle and tolerant people, persecution has sometimes erupted and missionaries have lost their lives when the local religious community felt that it was threatened because of the number of new converts.

b. Political Motivation

The politically-minded Sadducees persecuted the apostles for reasons of politics. They were concerned lest the spread of the message of the risen Christ might cause trouble with the Roman officials and thus jeopardize their position of leadership. Later on, part of the reason for the bitter attacks on Paul by the Jews was that they regarded him as a traitor to the Jewish nation.

Under the Romans, persecution was also for political reasons. The early missionaries to Thessalonica were accused of 'defying Caesar's decrees, saying that there is another king, one called Jesus' (Acts 17:7). It was only after the death of Paul that the church experienced that full force of persecution by the state which is so vividly portrayed in the Revelation. The Roman Empire, powerful in many senses, exercised one particular power which became a cause of great trial to the early Christians. The growing practice of 'Emperor worship' meant that an increasing number of them were required publicly to make the fateful choice between Caesar and Christ.[2] The letters to the seven churches, indeed the whole message of Revelation, was intended to strengthen the faith of Christians who soon would be facing even greater trials. Paul had been able to rely on Roman law and his status as a Roman citizen to obtain a measure of protection, but by the time that John was imprisoned on Patmos, the state had launched an all-out attack on the church and already 'the souls of those who had been slain for the word of God and the testimony they had maintained, were seen under the altar crying out to God (Rev. 6:9–11).

In the nineteenth and twentieth centuries many Christians have been persecuted because their religion has been regarded as a form of cultural imperialism. In the nineteenth century, Christian missions were linked with western colonialism. The door to China was opened by the bayonet of western soldiers and the unequal treaties that followed victory in the iniquitous opium trade war. Even though missionaries protested against the opium trade and did not seek the protection of government forces, yet they could not avoid the stigma of being related to western nations which were causing so much humiliation to China. Many Chinese Christians suffered persecution because of their association with western missionaries.

Some African Christians have suffered because they were members of a tribe involved in inter-tribal warfare. In Burundi thousands of Christians, including pastors and teachers, lost their lives. Christians should seek to avoid situations which would involve them in persecution for reasons not connected with their Christian faith. But in many parts of the world the followers of Christ have unavoidably found themselves caught up in political conflicts.

In some cases, Christians are persecuted on political grounds when in actual fact their only crime is their faithfulness to their Lord and Saviour. In both Russia and China Christians who refuse to join the State-approved religious organization find themselves in trouble. They are accused of being anti-revolutionary because they are not willing to accept the regulations and restrictions set down by the government. A Marxist totalitarian government can never tolerate any movement which gives allegiance to a power that is above the state. Christians are persecuted because Marxists have another gospel with which the Christian gospel competes, distracting people from pouring all their energies into the revolution and the reconstruction of society along Marxist lines.

Marxist governments recognize that religion cannot easily be destroyed. They have tried to persecute the church and wipe it out by means of brutal oppression; but in every case the seed of the church remains and the witness to Christ grows stronger than before. As a result some Marxist governments now use a double strategy. They authorize an official church which is under government control and is severely limited in order to prevent its rapid growth. At the same time, those who refuse to accept government regulations and cooperate within the official church are persecuted and many of their leaders are imprisoned. We can never expect Marxism as an ideology to accept Christianity. Marxists aim at building a 'spiritual socialist civilization' but the 'spiritual' refers to a Marxist humanistic attitude and has no reference to the spirit of man. Marxism does indeed promote a world view which is completely contrary to that of the Christian. Klaus Bockmuehl comments:

> We are told that Marxism is nothing but an economic system. It has nothing to do with faith. As a Christian one can also be a Marxist. The answer to this must be 'no'. As a Christian one may well be a socialist; that is, one may plead for the common ownership of certain forms of property and production . . . but one cannot simultaneously be a marxist and a Christian, for Marxism stands not only for a certain doctrine of property but also for a comprehensive world view to which atheism is an important presupposition . . . The abrogation of its atheism would necessarily imply the abolition of its historical materialism and thus its anthropology, its eschatology, and its ethics . . . Marxists themselves tell us 'ideological co-existence is as impossible as fried snowballs'".[3]

In China Christians are still persecuted when they do not conform to what is described as legal religious activities. Recently a friend wrote to me telling of a period of questioning and imprisonment after which he was released and ordered not to take part in any illegal activities. When he asked what were illegal activities he was told that any religious activity outside of the government-recognized Three Self Patriotic Movement was illegal.

Both in Eastern Europe and in China, Marxist governments have realized that frontal attacks on the church have failed. They expected that when the old generation of believers passed away, religion would vanish. Josef Ton of Rumania refers to an East German theologian who at a Lutheran convention in 1972 had the courage to comment on this theory, which he described as 'toleration to a vanishing point'. He said Christians had been granted a period of grace until they were snuffed out. Every regulation, prohibition and restriction of religious freedom of the churches was imposed with the purpose of accelerating the hoped-for disappearance of religion in socialism.[4] In China the government has indeed decided that direct persecution will not destroy the church. Christians now have to be prepared for a more subtle type of opposition. The spiritual warfare continues when churches are again opened and pastors are released from prison. The government now seeks to hinder the growth of the church through control, restrictions on evangelism and atheistic education. Religious activities are allowed only within registered church property. The government agrees not to propagate atheism in these areas, but it also insists that the church should not spread the gospel outside of religious institutions. The government is especially sensitive to the undermining of Marxist faith amoung young people. Within the education system only the government's atheistic ideology is permitted to be taught. Membership of the Youth League and the Communist Party is open only to those who reject all religious belief. Religion is still considered to be detrimental to the development of a socialist society, but the government is prepared to wait for its disappearance, recognizing that it may be a long time before religion 'withers away and dies'.

Josef Ton believes that the Communist Party must eventually change its attitude towards this aspect of religion in the individual and social life. He says, 'Socialism is fighting against its own interests when it maintains the war against religion. Socialism needs the new man, the moral man. This new man cannot be created by slogans or moral codes of behavior or laws. Only the Spirit of Christ can revolutionize a man, transform him, and make him a new kind of person'.[5] In a number of Socialist countries the present strategy of the government seems to be to use the church to further its own ends. The church may be useful in international relationships and may also be used in obtaining economic aid. In order to make sure that the church will co-operate with the government the state seeks to influence the appointment of church leaders. Not only the more liberal and politically minded, but even conscientious Christians who will follow the guidelines set down by the government, are chosen. Those older leaders who have been independent and active in evangelism must be replaced by others who will be more cooperative. Patriotism must be strongly emphasized within the church. In the early days, under the plea of separation of church and state, educational and social institutions such as hospitals and orphanages were completely cut off from Christian influence. This is still government policy, but Christians are encouraged to obtain economic support for social projects. At the same time the church is required to indoctrinate its own members and ensure that they fully support the Communist Party. Those who do not accept the guidelines for religious freedom set forth by the government are liable to face persecution. The state sets up its own religious bureau to supervise the activities of the church, and religious leaders are expected to cooperate with this bureau in the suppression of any who are involved in what is described as 'illegal religious activities'. Church leaders will strongly deny that there is any form of religious persecution and will declare that those who are now imprisoned are suffering for some political offence. When the church is controlled by the government, Christians face three dangers:

1) Division among believers

Because government informers are active within the church there tends to be a spirit of mistrust. Some fear the authorities; others seek to gain privileges and power through pleasing the government. Some betray fellow Christians in order to gain personal advantage. During past periods of severe persecutions Christians had been truly united. Often in labour camps they found themselves drawn closer to members of denominations with whom they had previously had no contacts. In Russia it was said that Catholics defend the Orthodox, Orthodox believers defend Pentecostals, and Baptists defend Catholics. Now that the fires of persecution have died down, 'the accuser of our brothers who accuses them before our God day and night' (Rev. 12:10) intensifies his attempts to destroy the fellowship. Barriers are built between those who agree to work within the government framework and those who feel that to do so would lead to compromise. Mutual suspicions tend to hinder the on-going witness of the gospel.

2) Undermined spiritual vitality

In an institutionalized church there is a tendency to follow the pattern of secular organizations. All kinds of committees are formed and much time is spent on discussing relationships with the government. Political studies have to be a part of the programme. Pastoral teams are often made up of people from diverse backgrounds, and frequently tensions arise because of a lack of the true unity of the Spirit.

3) Hindered evangelistic outreach

The main emphasis is now upon educating the believers. Only those authorized by the church committee are allowed to teach and preach. Evangelistic bands are not permitted to visit areas where there is no church. Pastors are allowed to work only within their own district. As government control increases, opportunities for evangelism become more and more limited. In spite of this, wherever there are Spirit-filled men and women, the word of the Gospel will continue to go forth.

The question of the Christian's relationship to the government has brought division among believers in a number of Communist countries. Some believe that Paul's exhortation to be 'subject to the governing authorities' (Rom. 13:1) involves accepting government religious organizations and maintaining a witness within the government-appointed framework. Others, however, insist that Christ's dictum 'No man can serve two masters' is relevant to this situation. If the church is controlled by the government then Christ is not truly head of the church. The leadership will not be appointed by the Holy Spirit and government restrictions may well cause Christians to compromise, obeying man rather than God.

c. Economic Motivation

The silversmiths in Ephesus instigated riots against the Christians because of economic reasons. They saw their trade suffering because so many were becoming Christians and no longer would buy the little silver images of Diana of the Ephesians.

Paul's imprisonment and beating in Philippi owed much to the fact that he cast out an evil spirit in a slave girl, with the result that the owners who had benefitted financially from her ability to tell fortunes brought accusations against Paul and caused the city authorities to take action against the apostles (Acts 16:16–24).

In the jungles of South America, Bobishara, a Christian, was murdered a few years ago because his faith in Christ had led to an improvement in his economic situation. His tribe lived together in communal houses that held about 80 hammocks. They wove cloth, chiseled tools and weapons, and composed songs. They had little contact with the outside world. Some oil company workers had been killed by members of the tribe. After conversion, the Christian Motilones lived peaceably and continued to hunt and fish. But now they also raised cattle, cultivated crops and ran their own health centres and school. They wanted to keep their land and develop it. They had connections with government bureaucracy so as to defend the title to their land. But the government is a long way from the jungle. Settlers are right there. Bruce Olson, who brought the news of Jesus to the Motilones, describes[6] how one afternoon Bobishara was approached by a bulky outlaw, Humberto April:

'I've come to tell you to get off this land,' he said. 'This is my land. I am a Columbian colonist. I have the right to claim land for colonization and I claim this land. You can get off . . .'.

Bobishara interrupted him. 'And I have something to tell you'. He spoke calmly but with great force. 'This is our land. It has always been our land. It always will be our land. We have ceded enough land to you. Six months ago we ceded lands to you, at your demand and what have you done? You have sold them and now you demand more. But we will not give more, we will protect what is ours'.

'Shut up,' Humberto screamed. 'Shut up. You dirty Indian, shut up'. Spittle came out of the corners of his mouth and made little spots on his red face. Then he put his forefinger across the thumb of his right hand so that it made a cross. He held it towards us, his eyes bulged, his hands shook so much he could hardly hold it straight. He kissed his fingers.

'For God,' he said, kissing his fingers again and spitting

on the ground. 'For the saints'. Again he spat, his head
jerking to the side so violently it looked more like a spasm
than a conscious movement. 'For the "virgin mother"'. A
third time he spat. 'And for this cross'. He spat again. Then
looking straight at us he held his thumb and finger to his
mouth and kissed them. His voice grew guttural. 'I'll kill
you'.

Two weeks later, one of the settlers came to the free
medical treatment station of the Motilones and tricked Bobishara into thinking he needed help. Bobishara went with
him and when he beached his canoe he was ambushed. At
his funeral about 200 people held hands in a circle and
thanked God for the model Bobishara had been in life and
in dying for them. It is easy to condemn the settlers who
killed Bobishara, but we must also recognize that there are
poor Christians in lands which are undeveloped who are
sometimes oppressed and suffer greatly because of the
selfishness of so-called Christian regimes and Christian business organizations. The Christian church has often sided
with the exploiters of the poor.

Christians also suffer when they will not take part in
dishonest practices. A group of Christian truck drivers in
India were threatened with dismissal because they would
not join the others in making false reports of the amount of
petrol received for their trucks and so making dishonest
gains. A Christian student in Hong Kong got into serious
trouble with his family because he refused to write down on
his scholarship application form a false figure describing his
father's income. A church which takes a strong stand against
current dishonest practices may well face various forms of
persecution.

d. Social Motivation

The early church was persecuted because its members
refused to participate in many of the social activities of their
day. These activities frequently involved idol worship. In
some cases they were contrary to the moral law of God.
Because of their opposition to the social practices around
them they were regarded as outcasts from society. Many

false charges were levelled against them. Christ had forewarned his disciples that they would be hated by all men, and this prophecy was fulfilled in the days when Christians were regarded as 'atheists' because they would not worship the gods, and as immoral because stories were told about the secret communion services in which it was said they practised cannibalism and other forms of immorality. In Russia today, Christians are frequently charged with crimes against the State which have no basis in reality.

In China in 1984 'The People's Daily' carried an article complaining that many people were praying to God for healing so that they would not have to pay their medical bills. This was described as 'a serious social disorder'. While it is true that Christians may sometimes go to extremes and even engage in superstitious practices, there is no justification for describing prayer for the sick as a serious social disorder!

In Africa the confrontation of Christian belief and ethics with traditional culture and religion has often brought persecution. Missionaries sometimes demanded that African Christians should cut themselves off completely from African culture. A Christian African could be recognized by his wearing foreign clothes, refraining from wearing ear-rings, and refusal to take part in traditional ceremonies.[7] Christians may have to suffer persecution for refusing to take part in ceremonies related to the worship of the spirits but should not renounce customs which have no real religious significance. Some have suffered because they completely rejected their own culture and accepted an alien culture. Others have suffered because, recognizing the ethical distinctiveness of the people of God, they have refused to be sucked into the culture around them. They do not withdraw from their own culture, but there is a sense in which they are bound to be 'counter-cultural' — just as Jesus was opposed to evils in the Jewish culture and for this reason was crucified by a conspiracy of both the religious and political establishments.

Paul faced the same problems. He never compromised in respect to morality and encouraged Christians to hold fast both to their faith and also to the ethical principles of the Kingdom of God. He did, however, warn Christians not to

make an issue of non-essentials. Followers of Christ are not
to judge others on questions of diet or observance of certain
feast days (Rom. 14). If persecution comes it must be on
account of loyalty to holiness and truth causing separation
from that part of the culture which conflicts with Christian
teaching.

Whatever may be the reason for persecution, we must
consider the effect that it has upon the church. For those
who are not directly involved in the persecution, it is fairly
easy to analyse the positive results of persecution. Sometimes
we forget the tremendous cost involved when a church
passes through a time of severe persecution. We often speak
of the martyrs as the seed of the church, and undoubtedly
there are many examples of the church growing following a
period of persecution. But we must never take lightly the
dangers that come through persecution. Intense suffering
has sometimes caused true believers to deny their Lord and
even betray fellow Christians. Some have committed suicide.
One priest in Russia attempted suicide but did not succeed.
When reproached by someone who said, 'How could a priest
commit suicide?', he explained that he had come to a place
where it was a choice of losing his faith and denying his
Lord or of dying and he felt that it was better to die than
to deny his Lord. Persecution does result in casualties and
grievous wounds in the body of Christ. We can be inspired
by the courage of those who have remained true, but we
must never forget the costliness of their witness and the
suffering which they overcame while others succumbed to
the almost unbearable pressures placed upon them.

POSITIVE RESULTS OF PERSECUTION

a. Persecution leads to the purifying of the Church

Peter, who himself had experienced imprisonment and
beating, likened suffering to the process of gold being purified in the fire (1 Pet. 1:7). The genuineness of faith is
revealed in the lives of those who pass through trials. This

has certainly been true in the church in China. After describing the times of ridicule through which she had passed, one lady remarked, 'If you find a Christian in China, usually you will find a real one'. A Christian doctor wrote, 'I do not speak of the suffering of the church but of the purifying of the church'. Another Christian spoke of a time when he was sent to work on a barren patch of ground, pulling out the weeds and stones and thorns. As he was working, it seemed as if the Lord said to him, 'What you are doing now is a picture of what I am doing in the church. You are preparing this barren piece of ground for a harvest. Through suffering I am now preparing the church so that there will be a great spiritual harvest in the days to come'. That spiritual harvest has taken place in the last few years. There has been a separation of the wheat from the tares. Just as the heavier wheat falls to the ground on the winnowing floor while the chaff is blown away, so those with true faith remain and nominal Christians disappear. In the parable of the sower Jesus compares the seed sown on the rocky ground with those who immediately receive the Word of God with joy, but 'when trouble or persecution comes because of the word, they fall quickly away' (Mk. 4:17). In Matthew's version, the superficial hearer of the word, 'since he has no root, . . . lasts only a short while' (Mat. 13:21). Christ's emphasis was: 'He who endures to the end will be saved' (Mat. 24:4–13). Persecution, therefore, reveals those to whom the grace of endurance has been given.

Before 1949 there were many nominal Christians in China. When testing came, in many cases they denied their faith. At that time the church was divided theologically by the conflict between liberals and evangelicals. One prominent church leader in the west admitted that liberal Christian belief was no match for the enthusiasm of young Marxists who believed that they had been sent to build a new society. Many of the liberals rejected their Christian faith. The church was further weakened by denominational divisions. Indigenous groups had often been formed in protest against western domination of the church, but they too were splintered by personality conficts among the leaders and sometimes by doctrinal differences as well. The suffering which started in the 1950s resulted in the overcoming of many of these differences, and through persecution a much purer church evolved. This does not mean that the enemy has ceased to sow different kinds of 'tares' and divisions which weaken the witness of the people of God. But it always seems that during a time of suffering Christians are drawn together and experience much more of the true unity which is in Christ.

b. Persecution leads to a deeper fellowship with God in prayer

The prayer life of the people of God has always flourished during times of persecution. The story of Nehemiah is full of short prayers uttered in the midst of persecution — 'Hear us, O God, for we are despised' (4:4). 'They were all trying to frighten us, thinking, "Their hands will get too weak for the work, and it will not be completed". But I prayed, "Now strengthen my hands"' (6:9).

David when he was pursued by Saul's soldiers prayed, 'I cry to you, O Lord; I say, 'You are my refuge, my portion in the land of the living. Listen to my cry, for I am in desperate need; rescue me from those who pursue me, for they are too strong for me. Set me free from prison, that I may praise your name"' (Psalm 142:5–7).

Jeremiah when he was suffering because of his faithfulness in declaring the word of the Lord cried to God. 'You understand, O Lord; remember me and care for me. Avenge me on my persecutors. You are long-suffering — do not take me away; think of how I suffer reproach for your sake' (Jeremiah 15:15).

When the disciples were ordered not to speak or teach at all in the name of Jesus they returned to their own company of friends. They did not have a committee meeting to discuss what they should do but immediately began to pray (Acts 4:24–31). The result of their prayer was that they were all filled with the Holy Spirit and spoke the word of God with boldness. When Peter was released from prison just before he was due to be executed, he went to the house of Mary where many were gathered together and were praying. At this time of crisis it was natural for the Christians to meet together for prayer.

In the meetings of the house churches throughout China the prayer meeting is central. When a former leader of the house churches was asked how leadership developed, he replied that leadership usually emerges from the prayer meetings. In their services a great deal of time is spent in prayer. It is natural for those who are sick to ask for the prayers of the leaders of the church; and often through these prayer meetings sick people are healed, and the power of God is revealed. As in Acts, God has stretched out his hand to heal through the name of his holy servant Jesus.

Many who have passed through times of suffering and imprisonment have learned new lessons in the school of prayer. Anatoli Levitin was imprisoned for carrying out an informal religious educational programme for young people. During the time that this Russian Orthodox Christian was in an isolation cell he was able to spend much time in prayer. He wrote,

> The greatest miracle of all is prayer. I have only to turn my thoughts to God and I suddenly feel a force bursting into me; there is a new strength in my soul, in my entire being . . .[8]

During his time of prayer he would imagine himself taking part in the Orthodox liturgy.

> At the central point of the liturgy . . . I felt myself standing before the face of the Lord, sensing almost physically his wounded, bleeding body. I would begin praying in my own words, remembering all those near to me, those in prison and those who were free, those still alive and those who had died. More and more names welled up from my memory . . . the prison walls moved apart and the whole universe became my residence, visible and invisible, the universe for which that wounded pierced body offered itself as a sacrifice . . . after this, I experienced an exultation of spirit all day — I felt purified within. Not only my own prayer helped me but even more the prayer of many other faithful Christians. I felt it continually working from a distance, lifting me up as

though on wings, giving me living water and the bread of
life, peace of soul, rest and love.[9]

Paul, when in prison, urged the Ephesian church to 'pray
in the Spirit on all occasions . . . pray also for me, that
whenever I open my mouth, words may be given me so that
I will fearlessly make known the mystery of the gospel, for
which I am an ambassador in chains. Pray that I may declare
it fearlessly, as I should' (Eph. 6:18–20).

c. Persecution in the church brings revival

The persecution of the church in Jerusalem was
accompanied by a movement of the Holy Spirit which created a community in which the love of God was manifest
and the word of God was proclaimed with authority: 'With
great power the apostles continued to testify to the resurren-
tion of the Lord Jesus, and much grace was upon them all'
(Acts 4:33). Luke goes on to say that there 'was not a needy
person among them' because the early disciples shared their
belongings. Later, after the disciples had again been arrested
and beaten we find that 'they never stopped teaching and
proclaiming the good news that Jesus is the Christ' (Acts
5:42). This early Christian society was marked by love, care
for one another, and constant evangelism. These are indeed
the marks of true revival.

Much later, after the gospel had spread to the Gentile
world, the Thessalonian Christians received the word 'in
spite of severe suffering . . . with the joy given by the Holy
Spirit' and as a result the word of the Lord 'rang out . . .
in Macedonia and Achaia'.

Almost 2,000 years later reports are still being received
of revival coming as a result of persecution in the church.
A letter from China written on 6 May, 1982, describes how
a group of young people went out preaching and were
arrested.

For three days they were without food or water. They were
beaten and their hands were tied with ropes, but still they
were singing and praising the Lord. As a result it is reported
that in this area the flame of the gospel has spread every-

where. There had never been revival here before, but through this persecution this place has truly received the seeds of life. May everyone who hears this give thanks and praise for the revival of the church in this area.

Commenting on this situation the writer says:

> But the growth in the life of the church has been promoted even by the servants of the devil. Wherever the church flourishes there are difficulties. The revival of the church here has grown up in this situation. For if Jesus had not been crucified, none today could be saved; if there were no testing by fire, then true faith would not become apparent, and if there were no training we could not become instruments used by the Lord. If the rock is not split open the water of life cannot flow forth. So difficulties are the means for promoting life and revival in the churches.

d. Persecution in the church scatters Christians and spreads the gospel

Following the death of Stephen Luke records that 'a great persecution broke out against the church at Jerusalem, and all except the apostles were scattered throughout Judea and Samaria' (Acts 8:1). In Acts 8:4 and again in Acts 11:19, those who were scattered are described as 'going about preaching the word'. In this way the gospel first spread to Samaria, and later the scattered disciples brought the message to Antioch, which became the base for Paul's outreach to the Gentile world.

In the history of the church there are many records of persecution leading to missionary advance. Because of the persecution of those who would not conform to the state church in seventeenth century England many dedicated Christians left England and founded settlements in the Eastern part of America. Other parts of Europe also contributed devout men and women who were scattered abroad because of persecution. In remote areas of China where formerly there was no Christian witness, today there are strong churches which have arisen among the Christians who were sent to work in labour camps in these isolated regions.

e. Persecution in the church reveals the reality of Christian faith to non-Christians

When Paul urged Timothy to 'fight the good fight of faith' he reminded him 'of Christ Jesus, who while testifying before Pontius Pilate made the good confession' (1 Tim. 6:13). Whenever the followers of Christ have stood before rulers and those responsible for persecuting them, their courage and steadfast faith have made an impression upon the non-Christian world. It was Stephen's courageous witness in the midst of suffering which sowed the seed of conviction within the mind of Saul of Tarsus. The words of the Risen Lord, 'It is hard for you to kick against the goads', may well have referred to the inner conviction received from Stephen's testimony that he was fighting against the truth. He had seen the glory on the face of the dying martyr but he had not realized that the living Christ was present, dwelling by the Holy Spirit in the body of his persecuted servant.

Later during the terrible periods of persecution that took place under the Roman emperors before Constantine, unbelievers were impressed by the willingness to die for Christ which characterized the martyrs. 'His limbs were burning but he continued himself unbending and unyielding, firm in his confession, refreshed and strengthened by the heavenly spring of the water of life which proceeds from the body of Christ'.[10]

The same kind of courage has been demonstrated in the lives of Chinese believers during the Cultural Revolution. A Chinese sister was asked by the judge who was sentencing her why she was smiling, and she replied that she was thinking of another Judge in another court on another day before whom she must stand.

A Christian engineer working in a factory was severely beaten by the Red Guards because he gave thanks at meal times for his food. He was deprived of food for three days. When finally a meal was set before him again it was made up of the dirtiest bits of food that had been swept off the floor. Again he thanked God. He was asked why he thanked God for such filthy food. He replied he was thankful that he could still eat. Again he suffered. One of those who saw his patience under suffering was a girl whose parents were Party members. She returned home and told her brother. Sometime later her brother found himself living with a Christian doctor who is a friend of mine. When he was ill this doctor ministered to him, and one day the brother asked the doctor if he believed in God. On hearing that he did believe in God this young man told the story that his sister had told him concerning the Christian engineer and said that he had been much impressed as he wondered why a Christian would be prepared to suffer in that way. In the end he came to know Christ.

f. Persecution is a witness to the Christian hope

In time of persecution, Christians have always been sustained by the hope of Christ's coming. They have also shown by their faithfulness 'even unto death' that the resurrection of Christ and the hope of his coming are certainties that form the foundation of their lives. Peter reminds those who are being persecuted of 'a living hope through the resurrection of Jesus Christ from the dead' (1 Pet. 1:3). Paul urges Titus to declare the great truths of the gospel with all authority 'while we wait for the blessed hope — the glorious appearing of our great God and Saviour, Jesus Christ' (Tit. 2:13).

The long line of martyrs — from the Colosseum in Rome to those slain by the spears of Auca tribesmen, by the sword of Amin in Uganda, or by disease in the Russian or Chinese prison camps have all looked forward to the coming of the King of glory. In the Colosseum, during the first two centuries of the church's history, large numbers of Christians were torn by wild beasts, nailed to crosses and suffered other forms of cruel death under the Emperor Nero and his successors. In the center of that arena today, surrounded by the crumbling seats of those who once came to mock at the Christians as they went to their death, stands a cross. At its base are inscribed the words *Ave Crux Spes Unica* — 'Hail to Thee, O Cross the Only Hope'.

In countries all over the world a persecuted church has witnessed to the indestructibility of the community of the Risen Lord and has pointed to the great climax in human history when 'every knee shall bow and every tongue confess that Jesus Christ is Lord to the glory of God, the Father.'

For Jesus suffering was the gateway to glory. 'Did not the Christ have to suffer these things and then enter his glory?' (Luke 24:26). Peter reminds persecuted Christians that the same is true for them: 'If you are insulted because of the name of Christ, you are blessed, for the spirit of glory and of God rests on you' (1 Pet. 4:12–13).

If the spirit of glory and of God rests upon the persecuted church we may well ask what kind of image appears in the affluent church of the west which knows little of suffering and persecution.

g. Persecution is an important factor in the growth of the church

There are missiological implications in the record of the amazing growth that has followed the persecution of the church in mainland China. During 30 years when Christians suffered and were deprived of help from the world-wide church, the good seed, 'the sons of the kingdom' (Mat. 13:38), fell into China's soil and 'died'. From that sowing of the seed there has come a great harvest. It seems that the growth of the mainland church has been faster than that of the Taiwan church, supported as it is by missionaries, theological seminaries, and an abundant supply of Bibles and Christian literature. It is true that persecution on the mainland has resulted in some casualties, for some denied their Lord. We remember too that in other parts of the world, such as North Africa, persecution has sometimes destroyed churches. But at the same time there is much to indicate that suffering is a necessary ingredient in the process of healthy church growth.

It is during a period of persecution that the life of the church can shine out most brightly. The church may out-

wardly appear to be weak and rejected but at the same time
its members manifest a world-view and a lifestyle which
non-Christians often envy. It has no earthly power on which
to rely; but the power of God is manifest in answer to prayer
and the healing of the sick. Often as in apostolic times God
'stretches out his hand to heal and performs miraculous
signs and wonders through the name of His holy servant
Jesus' (Acts 4:30). The church is surrounded by falsehood
and hatred, but its members are loyal to the truth and seek
to show the love of God in a society which has become
disillusioned and often cynical. In a society which is characterized by alienation and despair, the church has demonstrated the reality of the hope that comes from the indwelling
Christ. It is because of these qualities in the church that
men and women have been attracted to the Saviour of the
World and rapid church growth has taken place.

The church world-wide has always shown concern for the
persecuted church, and suffering Christians have looked to
the universal church for fellowship in prayer and understanding. We must explore ways in which this communion
between churches can be strengthened. How can the church
that is free from persecution minister to the persecuted
church? Perhaps even more important is the need to learn
lessons from the persecuted church and discern what may
be lacking in the missionary outreach of the prosperous
church in developed and affluent societies.

Persecution has caused Christians to discern between
essentials that must be preserved at all costs and those things
which even though good in themselves are not essential for
the survival of the church. Structures may be changed
and priorities redefined. The church becomes much more
flexible and completely dependent on the guidance of the
Holy Spirit. Public meetings, church organizations, ordained ministry may temporarily disappear, yet the church
continues. Priority is given to the prayer meeting and fellowship between believers. Leaders are chosen on the basis
of their faithfulness during times of trial. The distinction
between professionally trained church workers and working
men and women with the gifts of the Spirit fades away. The

church grows as each member shares in suffering 'like a good soldier of Christ Jesus' (2 Tim. 2:3).

The history of churches in the non-western world shows that few have been established without periods of persecution. Both national Christians and missionaries have suffered for the sake of the kingdom of God. Many people groups in the world remain unevangelized. If the church is to be established among those who are still resistant to the gospel, it is likely that it will require the vision and initiative of men and women who will be prepared to suffer — men and women who, like those before them, are ready to be conquerors 'by the blood of the Lamb and by the word of their testimony; they did not love their lives so much as to shrink from death' (Rev. 12:11).

Bibliography for ch.1 (pp.13-87)

D. Douglas Bannerman, THE SCRIPTURE DOCTRINE OF THE CHURCH. Grand Rapids: Eerdmans, 1955.

James Bannerman, THE CHURCH OF CHRIST. 2 vols. Edinburgh: Banner of Truth, 1960.

G. C. Berkouwer, THE CHURCH. Grand Rapids: Eerdmans, 1976.

Ernest Best, ONE BODY IN CHRIST. London: SPCK, 1955.

Louis Bouyer, THE CHURCH OF GOD. C. U. Quinn, trans. Chicago: Franciscan Herald Press, 1982.

Robert Brow, THE CHURCH: AN ORGANIC PICTURE OF ITS LIFE AND MISSION. Grand Rapids: Eerdmans, 1968.

L. Cerfaux, THE CHURCH IN THE THEOLOGY OF ST. PAUL. G. Webb, A. Walker, trans. N.Y.: Herder & Herder, 1959.

Edmund P. Clowney, TOWARD A BIBLICAL DOCTRINE OF THE CHURCH. Philadelphia: Presbyterian and Reformed, 1969.

Edmund P. Clowney, THE BIBLICAL DOCTRINE OF THE CHURCH. Vol. I. Philadelphia: Presbyterian and Reformed, 1979.

Yves M.-J. Congar, SAINTE EGLISE. Paris: du Cerf, 1964.

Alan Cole, THE BODY OF CHRIST. London: Hodder & Stoughton, 1964.

Oscar Cullmann, PETER. Philadelphia: Westminster Press, 1953.

Avery Dulles, MODELS OF THE CHURCH. Garden City, N.Y.: Doubleday, 1978.

R. Newton Flew, JESUS AND HIS CHURCH. N.Y.: Abingdon, 1938.

J. A. Heyns, THE CHURCH. Pretoria: N.G. Kerkboekhandel, 1980.

F. J. A. Hort, CHRISTIAN ECCLESIA. London: Macmillan, 1900.

George Johnston, THE DOCTRINE OF THE CHURCH IN THE NEW TESTAMENT. Cambridge: Cambridge University Press, 1943.

Alfred Kuen, JE BATIRAI MON EGLISE. Saint-Legier sur Vevey, Switzerland: Editions Emmaus, 1967.

R. B. Kuiper, THE GLORIOUS BODY OF CHRIST. Grand Rapids: Eerdmans, n.d.

Hans Kung, THE CHURCH. N.Y.: Sheed & Ward, 1967.

Ralph P. Martin, THE FAMILY AND THE FELLOWSHIP: NEW TESTAMENT IMAGES OF THE CHURCH. Grand Rapids: Eerdmans, 1980.

E. L. Mascall, CHRIST, THE CHRISTIAN AND THE CHURCH. London: Longmans, Green, 1955.

Paul Minear, IMAGES OF THE CHURCH IN THE NEW TESTAMENT. Philadelphia: Westminster Press, 1950.

Jurgen Moltmann, THE CHURCH IN THE POWER OF THE SPIRIT. London: SCM Press, 1977.

J. Robert Nelson, THE REALM OF REDEMPTION. London: Epworth Press, 1951.

Lesslie Newbigin, THE HOUSEHOLD OF GOD. London: SCM Press, 1957.

Anders Nygren, CHRIST AND HIS CHURCH. Philadelphia: Westminster Press, 1956.

Wolfhart Pannenberg, THE CHURCH. Philadelphia: Westminster Press, 1983.

Lloyd M. Perry, GETTING THE CHURCH ON TARGET. Chicago: Moody Press, 1977.

John H. Piet, THE ROAD AHEAD: A THEOLOGY FOR THE CHURCH IN MISSION. Grand Rapids: Eerdmans, 1970.

Karl Rahner, THE SHAPE OF THE CHURCH. London: SPCK, 1974.

John A. T. Robinson. THE BODY. Boston: Regnery, 1952.

Robert L. Saucy, THE CHURCH IN GOD'S PROGRAM. Chicago: Moody Press, 1972.

Edward Schillebeeckx, THE MISSION OF THE CHURCH. N.Y.: Seabury Press, 1973.

Rudolf Schnackenburg, THE CHURCH IN THE NEW TESTAMENT. W. J. O'Hara, trans. N.Y.; Herder & Herder, 1965.

Hans Schwarz, THE CHRISTIAN CHURCH. Minneapolis: Augsburg, 1982.

Juan Luis Segundo, THE COMMUNITY CALLED CHURCH. Maryknoll, N.Y.: Orbis, 1973.

Howard A. Snyder, THE PROBLEM OF WINESKINS. Downers Grove, Ill.: Inter-Varsity Press, 1977.

Howard A. Snyder, THE COMMUNITY OF THE KING. Downers Grove, Ill.: Inter-Varsity Press, 1977.

Alan Stibbs, GOD'S CHURCH. London: Inter-Varsity Press, 1959.

Thomas F. Torrance, ROYAL PRIESTHOOD. Edinburgh: Oliver & Boyd, 1955.

David Watson, I BELIEVE IN THE CHURCH. Grand Rapids: Eerdmans, 1978.

Claude Welch, THE REALITY OF THE CHURCH. N.Y.; Charles Scribner's Sons, 1958.

Colin Williams, THE CHURCH. Philadelphia: Westminster Press, 1969.

NOTES (pages 13–87)

1. A brief preliminary bibliography accompanies this essay (pp.303–4). See especially D. A. Carson, ed., *Biblical Interpretation and the Church: Text and Context* (Exeter 1984).
2. In spite of his wealth of analysis and perception, Gibson Winter's prescription for the church is sociological, not theological: *The New Creation as Metropolis* (New York 1963). So, too, Marxist presuppositions shape the view of Gustavo Gutiérrez, *A Theology of Liberation* (Maryknoll 1973).
3. J. C. Hoekendijk, 'The Church in Missionary Thinking', *IRM* 41 (1952) 325.
4. Oliver S. Tomkins, ed., *The Third World Conference on Faith and Order Held at Lund, August 15th to 28th, 1952* (London 1953) 22.
5. Alfred Loisy, for example, said that 'Jesus announced the kingdom of God, but what appeared was the church'. *L'Evangile et l'Eglise* (Paris 1902) 11. See the account of the change in scholarly opinion in Oscar Cullman, *Peter* (Philadelphia 1953) 166–167. See also the essay and literature cited by Gerhard Maier, 'The Church in the Gospel of Matthew: Hermeneutical Analysis of the Current Debate; in D. A. Carson, *op. cit.* 45–63.
6. IQS 5:5; 8:1, 2, 5–10; 9:3; 11:8. Ps. 18:17, 32. See Otto Betz, 'Felsenmann und Felsengemeinde . . .' *ZNW* 48 (1957), 49–77. See also E. P. Clowney, *The Biblical Doctrine of the Church* (Phillipsburg, N.J. 1979) 87–107.
7. 1QH 6:24–26.
8. George Johnston, *The Doctrine of the Church in the N.T.* (Cambridge 1943) 36 n.2. J. Y. Campbell, 'The Origin and Meaning of the Christian Use of the Word ECCLESIA', *JIS* 49 (1948) 133.
9. See the discussion of Presbyterianism and Independency in James Bannerman, *The Church of Christ* (Edinburgh 1868) ch. 5, pp. 296–331. See also, for the view of congregational independency, Robert L. Saucy, *The Church in God's Program* (Chicago 1972) 114–119.
10. *The Form of Presbyterial Church-Government, and of Ordination of Ministers; Agreed upon by the Assembly of Divines at Westminster*, etc. (Philadelphia 1745; reprint, New York 1880).
11. E. P. Clowney, 'The Final Temple', *WTJ* 35 (1973) 156–189.
12. W. D. Davies, *Paul and Rabbinic Judaism* (London: SPCK, 1965) 113–114.
13. On the church and the kingdom see Herman Ridderbos, *The Coming of the Kingdom* (Philadelphia 1962) 334–396. R. T. France, 'The Church and the Kingdom of God', in D. A. Carson, *op. cit.* 30–44, emphasizes the dynamic use of the term in relation to God's saving power.
14. C. E. B. Cranfield, 'The Christian's Political Responsibility according to the N.T.', *SJT* 15 (1962) 176–192. Cf. David H. Adeney, 'The Church and Persecution', in this volume, pp.275–302.

15. G. Mendenhall, 'Covenant', *IDB* 1, 714–723.
16. The black obelisk of Shalmaneser III in the British Museum shows Jehu doing obeisance, followed by a caravan of tribute. See R. D. Barnett, *Illustrations of Old Testament History* (London 1966) 48, fig. 25.
17. Ralph D. Winter, 'Churches Need Missions Because Modalities Need Sodalites', *EMQ* 7 (1971).
18. See R. T. France, 'Jesus, l'Unique: Les fondements bibliques d'une confession christologique', *Hokhma* 17 (1981) 43–44.
19. As against John A. T. Robinson, *The Body* (London 1952), who says, 'It is almost impossible to exaggerate the materialism and crudity of Paul's doctrine of the Church as literally now the resurrection body of Christ' (p. 51).
20. See lexicons on *rōš;* Wm. L. Holladay, ed., *A Concise Hebrew and Aramaic Lexicon of the Old Testament* (Grand Rapids 1971) 329.
21. Friedrich Büchsel declares, 'The deepest ground for the fact that we may not represent being-in-Christ in a spatial or quasi-spatial way is that Christ always is and remains the Lord, the Judge, for Paul' ('"In Christus" bei Paulus', *ZNW* 42 [1949] 154). Büchsel and others protest the concept of Pauline mysticism described by Adolf Deissmann, *Die neutestamentliche Formel 'in Christo Jesu'* (Marburg 1892).
22. Friedrich Hauck, '*Koinōnos*' etc., *TDNT* 4, 797–809.
23. James D. G. Dunn, *Baptism in the Holy Spirit* (London 1970) 45.
24. See Eduard Schweizer, '*Pneuma*', *TDNT* 6, 411; Eduard Lohse, '*Pentekoste*', ibid. 48; James D. G. Dunn, *Jesus and the Spirit* (Philadelphia 1975) 140; *Baptism in the Spirit* 48.
25. Rudolf Bultmann, *Theology of the New Testament* (New York 1951) 1, 155–157.
26. See James D. G. Dunn, *Jesus and the Spirit* 322, 323.
27. See Peter T. O'Brien, *Colossians, Philemon* (WBC; Waco, TX 1982) 206–211.
28. Michel de Goedt, 'The Intercession of the Spirit in Christian Prayer (Rom. 8:26–27)', in Christian Duquoc and Claude Geffre, eds., *The Prayer Life* (New York 1972) 26–28.
29. Herman Ridderbos, *Paul: An Outline of His Theology* (Grand Rapids 1975) 429–430.
30. B. B. Warfield, 'God-Inspired Scripture', in S. G. Craig, ed., *The Inspiration and Authority of the Bible* (Philadelphia 1948) 245–296. Cf. J. I. Packer, '*Fundamentalism*' *and the Word of God* (Grand Rapids 1958) 75–114.
31. For this concept of theory and praxis see Gutiérrez, *op. cit.*, 'Theology as Critical Reflection on Praxis', 6–15.
32. Geerhardus Vos, 'Paul's Eschatological Concept of the Spirit', in Richard B. Gaffin, Jr., ed., *Redemptive History and Biblical Interpretation: the Shorter Writings of Geerhardus Vos* (Phillipsburg, NJ 1980) 110.
33. Gene A. Getz, *Building Up One Another* (Wheaton, Ill. 1976).

34. Leon Morris, *Commentary on the Gospel of John* (Grand Rapids 1971) 697–698.
35. Similar arguments have been advanced in support of hierarchical orders of ministry within the Reformed churches. See Thomas Witherow, *The Form of the Christian Temple* (Edinburgh 1889) 326–338.
36. *The Form of Presbyterian Church-Government Agreed upon by the Assembly of Divines at Westminster* 49: 'The officers which Christ hath appointed for the Edification of his Church . . . are, Some extraordinary, as Apostles, Evangelists, and Prophets, which are ceased . . .'.

NOTES (pages 88–119)

1. P. Minear, *Images of the Church in the New Testament* (London 1961), together with his later article, 'Idea of Church', in *IDB* 2.607–617.
2. For further details on *ekklēsia* see, in addition to my *Colossians, Philemon* (Waco, TX 1982) 57–61, K. Berger, 'Volksversammlung und Gemeinde Gottes. Zu den Anfängen der christlichen Verwendung von "ekklesia"', *ZTK* 63 (1976) 167–207; W. Klaiber, *Rechtfertigung und Gemeinde* (Göttingen 1982) 11–21; and G. Maier, 'The Church in the Gospel of Matthew: Hermeneutical Analysis of the Current Debate', in *Biblical Interpretation and the Church. Text and Context*, ed. D. A. Carson (Exeter 1984) 45–63.
3. Note especially Berger, *ZTK* 73 (1976) 171ff.
4. So correctly R. Banks, *Paul's Idea of Community* (Grand Rapids 1980) 43.
5. Cf. Klaiber, *Rechtfertigung* 18.
6. Banks, *Idea* 43.
7. If the plural *hai ekklēsiai* is the correct reading (and it has the attestation of several witnesses of the 'Western' text), it would be consistent with the above-mentioned instances. However, the strongest manuscript support is a favour of the singular *ekklēsia* and it has been suggested the latter may have been changed by early scribes to the plural in order to conform to Acts 15:41 and 16:5; cf. B. M. Metzger, *A Textual Commentary on the Greek New Testament* (London 1971) 367.
8. Cf. Banks, *Idea* 45.
9. Paul's reference in Galatians (1:13; cf. also 1 Cor. 15:9; Phil; 3:6) to his original persecution of 'the church of God' does not contradict our suggestion since the expression may signify the reference to the church at Jerusalem before it was distributed into a number of smaller assemblies in various parts of Judea, or that it was as the believers met together that the arrests were made — their gathering together provided evidence of their Christian association (Banks, *Idea* 44).

10. Concerning the details of these house-churches we know little; note Banks, *Idea* 45–50 and 226–227 for further bibliographical details.
11. *BAG*, 241.
12. See below under 'body' and 'bride'.
13. It is possible to take the reference to *ekklēsia* at Mt. 16:18 as denoting a heavenly gathering. However, since the meaning is disputed we have not included it within our survey; cf. also Maier, in *Biblical Interpretation* 45ff.
14. W. J. Dumbrell, 'The Spirits of Just Men made Perfect', *EQ* 48 (1976) 154.
15. D. Peterson, *Hebrews and Perfection* (Cambridge 1982) 160; I am indebted to his treatment of the section 12:18–24 on pp. 160–167.
16. Peterson, *Hebrews* 161.
17. C. K. Barrett, 'The Eschatology of the Epistle to the Hebrews', in *The Background of the New Testament and its Eschatology. Studies in Honour of C. H. Dodd*, ed. W. D. Davies and D. Daube (Cambridge 1954) 376, cited by Peterson, *Hebrews* 160. Cf. also F. F. Bruce, *The Epistle to the Hebrews* (London 1964) 372.
18. Bruce, *Hebrews* 376.
19. As O. Michel, *Der Brief and die Hebräer* (Göttingen 1975) 464, argues.
20. Bruce, *Hebrews* 377.
21. Bruce, *ibid.*
22. Peterson, *Hebrews* 164. Note his detailed discussion (162–166) in relation to the perfection motif in Hebrews.
23. Peterson, *ibid.*
24. Dumbrell, *EQ* 48 (1976) 159.
25. *Proselēlythate* (of v. 22 a perfect tense; note v. 18 which by means of the negative *ou . . . proselēlythate* reinforces the same point.
26. For a discussion of the hermeneutical issues involved see especially Edmund P. Clowney, 'Interpreting the Biblical Models of the Church: A Hermeneutical Deepening of Ecclesiology', in *Biblical Interpretation and the Church. Text and Context*, ed. D. A. Carson (Exeter 1984) 64–109.
27. *Lumen Gentium*, no. 17, 1.26–29; cited by J. C. Coppens, 'The Spiritual Temple in the Pauline Letters and its Background', *SE VI* (= TU 112 [1973]). 53–66, esp. 53.
28. R. J. McKelvey, *The New Temple. The Church in the New Testament* (Oxford 1969) 92. For further details see O. Michel, *TDNT* 4. 880–890; R. Y. K. Fung, 'Some Pauline Pictures of the Church', *EQ* 53 (1981) 89–107, and M. von Meding, *NIDNTT* 3. 781–785.
29. R. J. McKelvey, 'Temple', *NBD* 1247.
30. McKelvey, *New Temple* 106; and Fung, *EQ* 53 (1981) 101.
31. On the distinction between *naos* ('sanctuary') and *hieron* ('temple precincts') see Fung, *EQ* 53 (1981) 101 n.47.
32. The *kai* ('and') is explicative (cf. McKelvey, *New Temple* 101; Klaiber, *Rechtfertigung* 39).
33. At 1 Cor. 6:19 the temple metaphor is used of the individual, rather

than of the community, as the dwelling-place of the Holy Spirit. C. K. Barrett, *The First Epistle to the Corinthians* (London 1968) 151, aptly remarks: 'There is no inconsistency vetween the two ways of using the metaphor; both are correct, and each is used in an appropriate context'.

34. *New Temple* 101.
35. Cf. especially E. Käsemann, 'Sentences of Holy Law in the New Testament', in *New Testament Questions for Today* (London 1969) 66–81.
36. *New Temple* 94; cf. A. Plummer, *The Second Epistle of St Paul to the Corinthians* (Edinburgh 1915) 208–209
37. Although the alternative reading 'you' (*hymeis*) has good manuscript support and suits the form of address in vv. 14, 17 and 18, it is not as well attested as the first person plural and is very likely due to the influence of 1 Cor. 3:16; cf. especially, Metzger, *Textual Commentary* 580.
38. *New Temple* 95; cf. Fung, *EQ* 53 (1981) 102.
39. McKelvey, *ibid.*
40. The issue regarding the authorship of Ephesians is not significant as far as this point is concerned.
41. A. T. Lincoln, *Paradise Now and Not Yet* (Cambridge 1981) 150. Note especially his treatment, pp.150–154, to which I am particularly indebted.
42. Lincoln's argument, *Paradise* 151, in favour of *tōn hagiōn* referring to angels is fourfold: (i) *hagioi* means 'angels' (rather than Jewish Christians) at Col. 1:12 and Eph. 1:18; (ii) there are close parallels in the Qumran literature where fellowship with angels is linked with the notion of the community as the temple (cf. 1QS 11:7f.; 1QH 3:21–23, etc.); (iii) 'the believers' attachment to the heavenly city' has already been made by Paul in Gal. 4:26; and (iv) the text we have examined in some detail, i.e. Heb. 12:22, teaches the same point about fellowship with angels. Even if Lincoln's arguments about the reference to 'angels' are not compelling, the contextual indicators (vv. 17–18, 20–22) are that a heavenly dimension is in view.
43. Lincoln, *Paradise* 151.
44. For a detailed discussion of this difficult expression see W. A. Grudem, *The Gift of Prophecy in 1 Corinthians* (Washington 1982) 82–105; cf. McKelvey, *New Temple* 112–114; Fung, *EQ* 53 (1981) 102–103.
45. Note the recent defence of this view by McKelvey, *New Temple* 195–204, and Grudem, *Gift* 85–86.
46. J. Jeremias, *TDNT* 1. 792; *TDNT* 4. 275; note also Lincoln, *Paradise* 152–154, and 231 where other supporters of this interpretation are listed.
47. *Paradise* 152–153.
48. *Paradise* 153.
49. H. Merklein, *Das kirchliche Amt nach dem Epheserbrief* (München 1973) 155–156; cf. McKelvey, *New Temple* 116.

50. *New Temple* 117.
51. *Ibid.*
52. For further details see McKelvey, *New Temple* 155-176, and Dumbrell, 'The New Temple'.
53. McKelvey, *New Temple* 187.
54. *Ibid.*
55. W. J. Dumbrell, *The End of the Beginning — A Survey of Biblical Eschatology* (Sydney 1985) — chapter on 'The New Temple'; R. J. Bauckham, 'The Lord's Day', in *From Sabbath to Lord's Day: A Biblical, Historical and Theological Invesigation,* ed. D. A. Carson (Grand Rapids 1982). 240-245, draws attention to the participation by martyrs in the worship of the heavenly sanctuary (Rev. 7:9ff.; 14:2,3; 15:2-4).
56. Although McKelvey, Best and others have argued the case strongly for a temple reference, J. H. Elliott, *The Elect and the Holy* (Leiden 1966) 157-159, and Dumbrell, 'The New Temple', following Schlatter, Vielhauer and Blinzler, claim that the reference is to God's house(hold).
57. For discussions on the origin of the phrase see E. Best, *One Body in Christ* (London 1955) 83-93; M. Barth, 'A Chapter on the Church — The Body of Christ', *Int* 12 (1958) 137-142; E. Schweizer, *TDNT* 7. 1024-94; J. Hainz, *Ekklesia* (Regensburg 1972) 260; and Fung, *EQ* 53 (1981) 92.
58. Cf. F. F. Bruce, *Paul: Apostle of the Free Spirit* (Exeter 1977) 420-421.
59. The parallelism of 'the body of Christ' (v. 16b) and 'the blood of Christ' (v. 16a) would strongly suggest that both refer to Christ, as Fung rightly observes; note his reference *EQ* 53 (1981) 92.
60. For a discussion on the relationship between the physical body of Christ and his body [the metaphorical body of Christ, i.e.] the church, see R. H. Gundry, *Sōma in Biblical Theology* (Cambridge 1976) 223-244; and Klaiber, *Rechtfertigung* 44-46, together with the literature cited there.
61. Note Fung, *EQ* 53 (1981) 93; cf. also Best's appeal (*One Body* 104) to the notion of corporate personality and the incorrect conclusion he draws from this: 'the phrase "the body of Christ" is Christ as a corporate personality, and he is this to the Church as a whole, and not to each of the individual congregations separately'. The phrase 'the body of Christ' is used explicitly here of the congregation of Corinth!
62. Fung, *EQ* 53 (1981) 93.
63. *Ibid.*
64. Best, *One Body* 113.
65. Best, *One Body* 156.
66. Bruce, *Paul* 421
67. The same point is made by the Johannine image of the Vine (Jn. 15:1-11) with the disciples pictured as branches which must abide in jesus as the Vine in order to bear fruit.

68. On the vexed question of the Colossian 'heresy' and its false teacher(s) see my *Colossians, Philemon* xxx-xxxviii.
69. Lincoln, *Paradise* 145.
70. Lincoln, *Paradise* 146. For a discussion of this enigmatic text see M. Barth, *Ephesians* (New York 1974) 154ff.
71. Lincoln, *Paradise* 147.
72. On the alternative interpretations see Barth, *Ephesians* 207–208 and note especially Fung, *EQ* 53 (1981) 95. One must bear in mind that the two senses of the body of Christ cannot be kept entirely separate: 'The man who is united with another by the crucified body is united with him in the body of Christ, i.e., the community', Schweizer, *TDNT* 7. 1078.
73. Fung, *EQ* 53 (1981) 95–96, who in part cites R. P. Martin. See also Fung's lengthy note on the significance of the participles and the interrelationship of the clauses, p.96, n.29.
74. F. F. Bruce, *The Epistles to the Colossians, to Philemon and to the Ephesians* (Grand Rapids 1984) 70–71.
75. For further details see C. Chavasse, *The Bride of Christ* (London 1939); Best, *One Body* 169ff.; R. A. Batey, *New Testament Nuptial Imagery* (Leiden 1971); J. P. Sampley, *'And the Two Shall Become One Flesh'* (Cambridge 1971); Barth, *Ephesians* 668ff.; and Fung, *EQ* 53 (1981) 97–100.
76. The figure of Israel as the wife of Yahweh was presented here and there in Judaism, particularly within apocalyptic eschatology: for details see Batey, *Imagery* 9–11.
77. R. P. Martin, in *NBD* 169. Although there is some difference of scholarly opinion on the matter, in our judgement this picture of the church as the bride of Christ derives from the teaching of Jesus: cf. Mk. 2:19, 20; Mt. 25:1–13; Jn. 3:29.
78. Lincoln, *Paradise* 163.
79. Fung, *EQ* 53 (1981) 98–100.
80. For a fuller exposition see my *Colossians, Philemon* 157–244.

NOTES (pages 120–153)

1. See his booklet, *Worship: the Missing Jewel of the Evangelical Church* (Harrisburg, PA n. d.)
2. B. H. Leafblad, in R. Allen and G. Borror, *Worship: Rediscovering The Missing Jewel* (Portland, OR 1982) 10.
3. L. Ryken points out the significance of the Puritan conception of work as an integration of every honourable vocation with a Christian's spiritual life: 'Puritan Work Ethic: The Dignity of Life's Labors', *CT* (Oct. 19, 1979) 15.
4. Luther said, 'To have a God is to worship God'.
5. D. Macleod, 'Theology Gives Meaning and Shape to Worship', *The Princeton Seminary Bulletin* 68 (1975) 38.

6. See M. L. Loane, 'Christ and His Church', in *Fundamentals of the Faith*, issued by *CT* (Washington, D. C. n. d.) 15 Cf. Hendrikus Berkhof, *Christian Faith* (Grand Rapids 1979) 377.

7. *Worship: The Christian's Highest Occupation* (Kansas City, n. d.) 16.

8. 'Worship in Isaiah 6', *Ref Th Rev* 43 (1984) 16; cited in David Peterson, *Ref Th Rev* 43 (1984) 65.

9. A. F. Rainey, 'Sacrifices and Offerings', *ZPEB* 5.201–202.

10. Cf. R. E. Webber, *Worship Old and New* (Grand Rapids 1982) 163.

11. A. E. Milligram, 'Sabbath, the Day of Delight', *ZPEB* 5.342. Cf. H. H. P. Dressler, 'The Sabbath in the Old Testament', in *From Sabbath to Lord's Day*, ed. D. A. Carson (Grand Rapids 1982) 24.

12. G. H. Waterman, *ZPEB* 5.184.

13. H. H. P. Dressler, *op. cit.* 26. A. J. Heschel, *The Earth is the Lord's, the Sabbath* (New York 1966) 18.

14. H. H. P. Dressler, *op. cit.* 33.

15. G. H. Waterman, *art. cit.* 185. E. Lohse has suggested on the basis of *B.Pes.* 68*b* that compulsory attendance at the synagogue was regarded as part of the sabbath observance, but C. Rowland notes that the reference is not to the Sabbath but to festal days: cf. 'Sabbath Observance in Judaism at the Beginning of the Christian Era', in *From Sabbath to Lord's Day* 51.

16. Note 2 Chr. 36:21; Jer. 25:11f. where the Exile was the consequence of Israel's failure to observe the prescribed seven year rests which God prescribed for the land.

17. Cf. D. Freeman, 'Feasts', *NBD* 420–421.

18. For a definitive statement see O. Cullmann, *Christ and Time*, tr. F. V. Filson (Philadelphia 1964) *passim*.

19. For the Jewish opinion cf. C. Rowland, *op. cit.* 46; G. H. Waterman, *art. cit.* 186; M. M. B. Turner, 'The Sabbath, Sunday, and the Law in Luke/Acts', in *From Sabbath to Sunday* 102. D. Guthrie, *New Testament Theology* (Leicester 1981) 943, notes that there must have arisen many problems for those who sought to maintain the Jewish pattern of seventh day rest in the Gentile world, but that the New Testament provides no guidance on such problems.

20. Cf. P. E. Hughes, *Interpreting Prophecy* (Grand Rapids 1976) 28–29.

21. 'The OT makes it plain that for the godly person of that era, just as for godly persons of any era all activities are to be carried out with an eye toward God. 'In all your ways acknowledge him (lit. 'know him') . . .'. D. G. Mostrom, *The Dynamics of Intimacy with God* (Wheaton, IL 1983) 38. Worship in the OT 'is generally conceived of as a way of acknowledging God's sovereignty', D. G. Peterson, *op. cit.* 65.

22. Cf. W. F. Adeney, in *Hastings Dictionary of the Bible* (1902) 941, 942.

23. T. W. Jennings, Jr., *Life as Worship: Prayer and Praise in Jesus' Name* (Grand Rapids 1982) 6.

24. Cf. D. A. Carson, 'Jesus and the Sabbath in the Four Gospels', *From Sabbath to Lord's Day* 75.

25. According to the Talmud, the Sabbath is 'somewhat like eternity' [or 'the world to come']; A. J. Heschel, *op. cit.* 74. For Christians, however, Jesus as God's representative, 'has himself replaced the codified prescriptions of the Law for the community of Christians and has himself become the embodiment of the divine will' (Hugh Anderson, *The Gospel of Mark* (NCB; London 1976) 111.

26. D. A. Carson, *op. cit.* 75.

27. Cf. O. Cullmann, *Early Christian Worship* (London 1959) 10. 'Prayers', plural, in Acts 2:42 probably means 'periods of prayer'.

28. O. Cullmann, *ibid.* 15. We might compare the weekly vigil of the Korean Evangelical Church in São Paulo. Every Friday night at 9:30 two buses fill with worshipers who are transported about 40 kms. to a 'Prayer Garden'. Prayer, praise, Bible Study and exhortation occupy the hours until 2:00 a.m. After some pumpkin soup, three hours of sleep, the regular 5:00 a.m. prayer service is celebrated. Everyone is back in the city center by 7:00 a.m. to begin their day's work.

29. *Dial. W. Trypho*, in *Ante-Nicene Fathers* 1.199–200 Cf. Clement of Alexandria, in *Ante-Nicene Fathers* 1.481.

30. *Adv. Haer.* 14.16 in *Ante-Nicene Fathers* 3.70.

31. *On Idol.* 14, *Ante-Nicene Fathers* 3.70.

32. Cf. R. J. Bauckham, 'Sabbath and Sunday in the Post-Apostolic Church', in *From Sabbath to Lord's Day*, 277–278.

33. Cf. B. Lindars, *Commentary on John* (NCB; London 1972) 189: 'Jesus brings eschatological prophecy into the present'.

34. See F. F. Bruce, 'Age', in *ISBE* (Grand Rapids 1979) 1.67–68.

35. The only article that touches on worship in the Declaration of Faith of the Baptist Churches of Brazil (with the exception of No. XIV regulating Baptism and the Lord's Supper) states that Sunday is the Christian Sabbath, requiring abstention from secular work and 'the pious observance of all the means of grace'.

36. Is it significant that the crowd that had eaten to their full the day before sought for Jesus again the following day?

37. O. Cullmann, *Worship* 96. Whenever Christ communicates with his church, she is privileged to partake of him. Cf. T. F. Torrance, *op. cit.* 75–76.

38. The Jews used the term 'bread' for the Torah. T. F. Glasson, *Moses in the Fourth Gospel* (London 1963) 47 n.1.

39. O. Cullmann, *Worship* 10.

40. For evidence see R. J. Bauckham, 'The Lord's Day', in *From Sabbath* 221ff.

41. May there be some suggestion of the night meetings in the symbolism of the seven golden lamps to represent the Asian churches?

42. C. F. D. Moule, *Worship in the New Testament* (London 1961) 16.

43. The *Didache* also indicates that the earliest post-apostolic era also celebrated the Eucharist on the Lord's day (14:1). Cf. K. Lake, *Apostolic Fathers* (Cambridge, 1965) 1.331; R. J. Bauckham, *art. cit.* 227–232.

44. Cf. O. Cullmann, *Worship* 31.

45. D. G. Mostrom, *op. cit.* 137.
46. C. F. D. Moule, *op. cit.* 13.
47. J. White sees 1 Cor. 5:7f. as the chief evidence that the New Testament church observed Easter (*Introduction to Christian Worship* [Nashville 1980] 50). Cf. R. E. Webber, *op. cit.* 165.
48. See B. Lindars for views regarding the meaning of the phrase 'innermost being' and the significance of the cry of Jesus on the last day of the feast, *op. cit.* 300 ff. and T. F. Glasson, *op. cit.* 48ff.
49. D. G. Mostrom, *op. cit.* 38. 'Worship is to Christian living what the mainspring is to the watch', said L. R. Axelson, in *Gathered Gold*, compiled by J. Blanchard (Welwyn, Herts, 1984) 340
50. D. G. Peterson, *op. cit.* 65.
51. Cf. T. F. Torrance, *Royal Priesthood* (*SJT* Occasional Papers No. 3; Edinburgh 1963) 1.
52. Cf. O. Cullmann, *Early Christian Worship* 9 n.1. E. Lohmeyer, *Lord of the Temple*, tr. S. Todd (Edinburgh 1961) 38–39.
53. D. A. Carson, 'Jesus and the Sabbath in the Four Gospels', *From Sabbath to Lord's Day* 79. Cf. C. F. D. Moule, *op. cit.* 14.
54. O. Cullmann, *Worship* 117.
55. R. P. Martin, *Worship in the Early Church* (Grand Rapids 1975) 23.
56. Just as there is but one flock and one Shepherd (Jn. 10:16) and one vine but numerous branches (15:1–6). The Father's house *has* many 'rooms', despite the fact that Jesus must go to prepare a place for his disciples. The imagery means that Jesus incorporates in himself the world-wide church, nevertheless the redemption of the church requires that he go to Calvary and return via the resurrection. The idea of the *parousia* is secondary to his purpose in this passage. Cf. R. P. Shedd, 'Multiple Meanings in the Gospel of John', in *Current Issues in Biblical and Patristic Interpretation*, ed. G. F. Hawthorne (Grand Rapids 1975) 253ff.
57. Cf. R. P. Martin, *op. cit.* 23,.
58. The word *en* is missing in the original. 'Spirit' (*pneumati*) should probably be instrumental. We worship 'by the Spirit' in contrast to Jews who continue to practise the rites of the pre-Christian cultus.
59. Cf. J. A. Robinson, *Commentary on Ephesians* (Grand Rapids 1979) 72. J. R. W. Stott. It seems best to see a parallel teaching in Eph. 1:23 where Christ fills the Church by his Spirit: cf. J. R. W. Stott, *God's New Society* (Downer's Grove, IL 1979) 65.
60. See 1 Pet. 2:4f. where the singular 'stone' and plural 'stones' express the total concept. There were no sacred buildings used by Christians exclusively for worship until the end of the second century.
61. Cf. B. Shelley, *The Church: God's People* (Wheaton, IL 1978) 10–12. Rusticus (AD 165) asked Justin Martyr. 'Where do you assemble?' Justin said, 'Where each one chooses . . . because the God of the Christians is not circumscribed by place, but being invisible fills heaven and earth and everywhere is worshipped and glorified by the faithful' (*Martyrdom*, 2).
62. Paul does not state, however, that the immoral person has been lost.

Nor does he tell the Corinthians to turn the offenders over to Satan as in 5:5.

63. Cf. E. Best, *One Body of Christ* (London 1955) 74ff.

64. Paul's chapter on the gifts and worship, followed by his hymn on love, aims at the single purpose of building up the church. Cf. J. White, *op. cit.* 31.

65. T. F. Torrance, *op. cit.* 31, citing I. Muirhead, 'The "Forme of Marriage": 1562 and Today', *SJT* 6 (1953) 331. Roman Catholic theologians have often been inclined to draw the conclusions here opposed.

66. Although the NT knows no sacred hours or places, it by no means diminishes the importance of the gathering, its purpose being 'edification' (cf. 1 Cor. 14:3, 4, 5, 12, 26) and worshiping God (cf. Eph. 5:19, 20; 3:16, 17, Rev. 5:12–14; 14:7).

67. Cf. Exod. 32:11 where to propitiate literally means 'soften the face': cf. F. D. Kidner, 'Sacrifice: Metaphors and Meaning', *Tyn Bull* 33 (1982) 122.

68. T. F. Torrance, *op. cit.* 3.

69. F. D. Kidner, *op. cit.* 130.

70. *Ibid.* 131.

71. *Ibid.* 132.

72. *Ibid.* 133.

73. F. D. Kidner, *ibid.* 134.

74. Cf. *ibid.* 135.

75. Cf. W. Eichrodt, *The Theology of the Old Testament* (ET London 1961) 1.158–165 (esp. 164–165) for the significance of the laying on of hands. Cf. D. Guthrie, *op. cit.* 433 for the significance of the blood.

76. V. Taylor, *New Testament Essays* (Grand Rapids 1972) 49.

77. For the significance of the atonement in the Gospel of John, see G. L. Carey, 'The Lamb of God and Atonement Theories', *Tyn Bull* 32 (1981) 112ff.

78. *Commentary on 1 and 2 Timothy and Titus* (Waco, TX 1974) 64–65.

79. See F. F. Bruce, *The Time is Fulfilled* (Exeter 1978) 83: 'Perhaps it is not accidental that the four words used for sacrifice in Ps. 40:6–8 (Heb. 10:5–7) cover the main types of levitical sacrifice. They are swept aside in the declaration that what God wants is obedient hearts and lives. Preparation for this new covenant outlook can be found in the Old Testament. Samuel's contention that obedience is better than sacrifice (1 Sam. 15:22) finds repeated mention in the prophets (Isa. 1:10–20; Mic. 6:6–8; Hos. 6:6; Amos 5:21–27, etc.).' Cf. R. P. Martin, *The Worship of God* (Grand Rapids 1982) 66.

80. L. Goppelt, *op. cit.* 169.

81. D. Guthrie, *op. cit.* 433–434.

82. L. Goppelt, *op. cit.* 149.

83. Cf. F. F. Bruce, *The Time* 93–94.

84. Cf. T. F. Torrance, *op. cit.* 34.

85. Cf. E. C. Selwyn who takes the phrase *eis christon* (1 Pet. 1:11) to mean sufferings 'for Christ', i.e. Paul's sufferings would have greatly

receded had he not been committed actively to extend the scope of his divinely ordered mission (*The First Epistle of St. Peter* [London 1946] 136–137).

86. *Typos*, tr. D. H. Madvig (Grand Rapids 1982) 151.

87. Cf. K. Munzer, in *NIDNTT* 1. 474–475; and G. R. Beasley-Murray, *Baptism in the New Testament* (Exeter 1972) 203.

88. Indicated by the aorist, *parastēsai*.

89. See BAGD, *s.v.*

90. It may be misleading to afffirm, as E. Käsemann does, supported by T. W. Jennings, Jr., that the meaning of presenting our bodies is, 'our life in the world in all its relationships and connections' (T. W. Jennings, Jr. (*Life as Worship* 6; cf. E. Käsemann, *New Testament Questions of Today* [ET Philadelphia 1969] 135), if no clear distinction is made between the Christian's relationship to the church and his relationship to the world.

91. Timothy is urged to give attention to 'the exhortation' (1 Tim. 4:13). The article indicates that like 'the reading', it was a part of the public worship (cf. Acts 13:15; Cf. Michael Griffiths, *The Church and World Mission* [Grand Rapids 1982] 169).

92. The meaning may be that he has dedicated his whole person to the gospel. Cf. 4 Mac. 1:23ff. where the term is applied to the martyr priest Eleazar. L. Goppelt, *op. cit.* 151 n.92.

93. L. Goppelt, *ibid.* 150–151.

94. Cf. G. R. Beasley-Murray, *op. cit.* 200ff.

95. See R. P. Martin's citation and discussion of Justin Martyr (*Apol.* 67), clear indication that the contributions of the congregation are voluntary: 'Those who prosper, and who so wish, contribute, each one as much as he chooses to' (*The Worship of God* 62).

96. C. F. D. Moule, *op. cit.* 18–19.

97. Cf. C. F. D. Moule, *op. cit.* 11.

98. *Str-B* 1.246.

99. The word *homologounton* (Heb. 13:15) includes proclamation as well as praise.

100. The essence of Christian worship is more or less defined in 12:28–29 as 'a manner of life which is pleasing to God and which is sustained both by gratitude and by a serious sense of responsibility' (D. G. Peterson, *op. cit.* 68).

101. *Op. cit.* 154. 'Obedience is better than sacrifice' (1 Sam. 15:22).

102. Cf. C. F. D. Moule, *op. cit.* 26–27.

103. Note the significance that joy had in worship (Acts 2:46; 5:41f.; Lk. 24: 41, 52).

104. T. F. Torrance, *op. cit.* 1; *TWNT* 3.257ff.; *NIDNTT* 3.33.

105. Cf. J. P. Hyatt, *Exodus* (NCB; Grand Rapids 1971) 200; *NIDNTT* 3.36.

106. Note Ecc. 5:1; Hos. 12:6; Zec. 3:2; Hag. 2:15; Isa. 29:13; 58:2, where all Israel has the privilege of drawing near to God, a right reserved to priests in such passages as Exod. 19:21f.; Lev. 10:33; Ezk. 42:13; cf. D. G. Peterson, *op. cit.* 70.

107. Cf. R. P. Shedd, *Man in Community* (Grand Rapids 1964) 31–32.
108. T. F. Torrance, *op. cit.* 79.
109. Cf. F. F. Bruce, *New Testament Development of Old Testament Themes* (London 1965) 55–56.
110. B. Lindars, *op. cit.* 528; T. F. Torrance, *op. cit.* 80. See L. Goppelt, *Theology of the New Testament* (Grand Rapids 1982) 2.249; *TDNT* 8.82.
111. Cf. R. E. Brown, *The Gospel According to John* (AB; New York 1970) 2.776ff.
112. L. Goppelt, *Typos* 163, 165. The author of Hebrews is concerned to point out the contrast 'between the limited effectiveness of the former priesthood and the absolute effectiveness of the priesthood of Christ to bring a right relationship with God (cf. 7:25)' (D. G. Peterson, *op. cit.* 71).
113. J. Murray, *The Heavenly Priestly Activity of Christ* (London 1958) 7ff.
114. Cf. B. F. Westcott, *The Epistle to the Hebrews*, 3rd ed. (London 1914) 110.
115. Cf. E. P. Clowney, *The Biblical Doctrine of the Church* (Nutley, NJ 1979) 19–20.
116. *Theology of the New Testament* 252.
117. Cf. J. Baehr, in *NIDNTT* .337.
118. E. P. Clowney, *op. cit.* 111; 'Their position is also a calling in the service of God's world-wide dominion.'
119. Cf. B. Shelley, *op. cit.* 79.
120. Paul is referring to public prayers in this text.
121. Cf. E. P. Clowney, *op. cit.* 139.
122. For the OT promises, see *ibid.* 69ff.
123. Cf. E. Schweizer, 'Worship in the New Testament', *The Reformed and Presbyterian World* 24 (1957) 295: 'It is completely foreign to the New Testament to split the Christian community into one speaker and a silent body of listeners' (cited in R. P. Martin, *Worship in the Early Church* 135).
124. *Op. cit.* 72.
125. See A. Kuyper, *The Practice of Godliness* (Grand Rapids 1948, 1977) in his suggestive discussion of 'Man Versus Nature', chap. 3, pp. 27–35.
126. R. P. Shedd, *Man in Community* 114.
127. *The Practice of the Presence of God*, ed. H. Martin (London 1956) 18, 22.
128. Discerning the body (1 Cor. 11:29) refers to believers' consciousness of their mutual interdependence in love. Failure to recognize the sacredness of that relationship was judged by God with sickness and death (v. 30).
129. Clement of Alexandria and Calvin both stressed that prayer is corporate in nature even when said in secret. Cf. T. W. Jennings Jr., *op. cit.* 37; cf. Calvin, *Inst.* III. xx. 39; cf. K. Barth, *CD* III/4, 102.

130. A similar understanding of the nature of Israel as the one Synagogue yet meeting in many synagogues is found in Judaism: cf. R. P. Shedd, *Man in Community* 130.
131. For the OT prophecies, see E. P. Clowney, *op. cit.* 70–71.
132. B. Shelley, *op. cit.* 36.
133. *Ibid.* 36–37.
134. *World Council of Churches Report* (1967) 'The Church for Others'.
135. *Op. cit.* 377.

NOTES (pages 154–212)

1. According to the Editor, in his initial letter of invitation to write this paper.
2. In saying this we have no intention of denying the essential and fundamental nature of the ministry of Christ himself: not only is the Christian ministry continuous with and patterned after Christ's own ministry, but all ministry in the church is the activity of the living Christ himself. Cf. W. D. Davies, *Christian Origins and Judaism* (London 1962) 235–236; E. Schweizer, *Church Order in the New Testament* (ET London 1961) 189–190 (=23b).
3. Cf., on spiritual gifts, R. Y. K. Fung, 'Ministry, Community and Spiritual Gifts', *EQ* 56 (1984) 3–20 (esp. 4–13); and on the question of style, *idem*, 'Function or Office? A Survey of the New Testament Evidence', *EvRevTh* 8 (1984) 16–39; 'Charismatic versus Organized Ministry? An Examination of an Alleged Antithesis', *EQ* 52 (1980) 195–214; 'Spiritual Gifts or Organized Ministry? (1) The New Testament Evidence', *The Harvester* 60/4 (April 1981) 28–29; 'Spiritual Gifts or Organized Ministry? (2) Some Conclusions', *ibid.* 60/5 (May 1981) 34–35. These will be referred to below as, respectively, 'Ministry . . . Gifts', 'Function or Office?', 'Charismatic versus Organized', and 'Organized Ministry? (1)/(2)'.
    For the sake of convenience, we mention here two other articles which will also be referred to below by a shortened title — 'The Nature of the Ministry according to Paul', *EQ* 54 (1982) 129–146; 'Some Pauline Pictures of the Church', *EQ* 53 (1981) 89–107 — as 'Nature of Ministry' and 'Pauline Pictures' respectively. For permission to use material from all the above-mentioned articles (especially in the second section of this paper), grateful acknowledgment is made to the editors of the periodicals concerned: Prof. I. H. Marshall (*EQ*), Dr. B. J. Nicholls (*EvRevTh*), Mr. J. Lamb (*Harvester*).
4. An earlier study was published in Chinese as 'Paul and the Ministry of Women', in *A Life of Ministry*, ed. R. Y. K. Fung and C. T. Yu (Hong Kong 1982) 200–262. It may be observed that the third section of the present paper reaches conclusions which differ in significant respects from those of our previous study.

5. So R. A. Cole, *ZPEB* V 506–507. Cf. A. E. Cundall, *Judges* (TOTC; London 1968) 15–17, 74.

6. J. D. G. Dunn, *Jesus and the Spirit* (London 1975) 206 (printed in italics in the original).

7. For details on the lexical data, cf. 'Ministry . . . Gifts' 4–6.

8. In view of the anarthrous *didaskalous*, we take the expression here to be a hendiadys meaning 'teaching shepherds' (or 'shepherding teachers'), following M. Barth, *Ephesians* (AB; 2 vols; Garden City 1974) 436, 482, who admits, however, that 'the wording chosen is so ambiguous that it is difficult to decide the exact character of the fourth group' (438). Some think that the *poimenas* and *didaskalous* here represent two separate groups: e.g., T. K. Abbott, *The Epistles to the Ephesians and the Colossians* (ICC; Edinburgh 1968) 118; J. Jeremias, *TDNT* VI 497. See also n. 14 and cf. n. 27 below.

9. Recognition of this fact is important because it acknowledges the freedom of 'the sovereign Spirit to fashion new gifts for fresh occasions and special needs as they will arise in the life and service of the church' (R. P. Martin, *The Spirit and the Congregation* [Grand Rapids 1984] 13). It is to be observed also that while these are the only four lists of charismata specifically designated as such, the *fact* of spiritual gifts finds frequent expression elsewhere in Paul; on this cf. R. Banks, *Paul's Idea of Community* (Grand Rapids 1980) 96–97.

10. Cf. S. Schulz, 'Die Charismenlehre des Paulus: Bilanz der Probleme und Ergebnisse', in *Rechtfertigung* (Fs. E. Käsemann), ed. J. Friedrich, W. Pöhlmann and P. Stuhlmacher (Tübingen/Göttingen 1976) 433–460 (446).

11. In line with its usage in the Old Testament (where Yahweh is the Shepherd of Israel: e.g. Gen. 49:24; Ps. 80:1; Isa. 40:11; Jer. 31:10) and elsewhere in the New Testament (where Jesus is the Shepherd or Great/Chief Shepherd of his people: e.g. Jn. 10:11; 21:15–17; Heb. 13:20; 1 Pet. 5:4), the term 'shepherd' in Eph. 4:11 is employed figuratively to denote leaders of local congregations. These spiritual shepherds are to care for (Jn. 21:16; 1 Pet. 5:2) and feed (Jn. 21:15, 17; Acts 20:28) the congregation, to exercise watchful oversight over them (Acts 20:28, 31) and to be an example for them (1 Pet. 5:3). For the 'pastor' to fulfil these functions, the need for teaching is obviously of first importance, both negatively as a means of warning against heresy (Acts 20:29) and positively as a means of feeding; hence the close connection with teachers in Eph. 4:11 — and our juxtaposing of the two terms at this place.

12. With H. B. Swete, *The Holy Spirit in the New Testament* (London 1910) 185, we take *logos sophias* and *logos gnōseōs* as related to teaching. If, with M. Green, *I Believe in the Holy Spirit* (Grand Rapids 1975) 184, the 'utterance of knowledge' is interpreted as 'some revelatory word from God for the benefit of others', 'a God-given disclosure of knowledge that could not normally be available to the recipient' — an understanding that is often found in Pentecostal expositions (on

which cf. Dunn, *Jesus and Spirit* 415 n.107) — then this gift would come under our sub-section D (or conceivably B).

13. That the *pistis* of 1 Cor. 12:9 is not the justifying faith of Gal. 3 and Rom. 3(:25–26) and 4, or the saving faith of Eph. 2 — the two are, of course, the same — is indicated by its being placed in close proximity to the gifts of healing and miracles in the list of special charismata. This distinction is between *Kerygmaglaube* and *Wunderglaube*, mentioned by Martin, *Spirit and Congregation* 44, citing O. Wischmeyer (see *ibid.* 147 n.7).

14. The separate entry of 'pastors' here in spite of n.8 above seems justified by the use of the word *poimenes* in Eph. 4:11. As Barth, *Ephesians* 439, explains, 'Our translation "teaching shepherds" seeks to do justice to the stress laid upon the teaching capacity of a bishop, but it leaves open the possibility that at Paul's time some bishops considered other tasks their first responsibility, e.g. the administrative functions mentioned in 1 Cor. 12 and Rom. 12' — thus taking *ho proistamenos* (number 15, in our list [C]) in the sense of 'he who rules' (differently from us; see next note). The function of shepherding or pastoring is independently attested by other scriptures; cf. n.11 above.

15. Of all the metaphorical meaning of the word *proistanai*, the most important is the sense 'to preside = lead, conduct, direct, govern' (B. Reicke, *TDNT* VI 700), and the word in Rom. 12:8 is taken in this sense in KJV, RV, NEB, NASB, NIV; and by L. Goppelt, *Apostolic and Post-Apostolic Times* (ET Grand Rapids n.d.) 184; H. Ridderbos, *Paul: An Outline of His Theology* (ET Grand Rapids 1975) 455; Barth (as in previous note). The word is placed, however, between two terms which have to do with deeds of love and kindness, and it would have the distinct advantage of keeping intact what appears to be a 'triad' to take it in the sense of 'caring for, assisting, helping' (so Reicke, *op. cit.* 701). Cf. RSV; F. Davidson/R. P. Martin, *NBCR* 1040*b*; C. E. B. Cranfield, *The Epistle to the Romans* (ICC; 2 vols; Edinburgh 1975, 1979) 626–627; Dunn, *Jesus and Spirit* 251.

16. Cf. R. B. Gaffin, Jr., *Perspectives on Pentecost* (Phillipsburg, NJ 1979) 101; Banks, *Community* 98, 99 with n.19; 'Ministry . . . Gifts', 8 n.25.

17. That in these passages the anarthrous *prosētai* refers to New Testament prophets and should not be taken to mean that Paul has in view only 'the apostles who are also prophets' is convincingly argued by Gaffin, *Perspectives* 93–95. Cf. 'Pauline Pictures', 102–103 with n.54.

18. Cf. Gaffin, *Perspectives* 61.

19. For elaboration on these four observations cf. 'Ministry . . . Gifts', 6–11. That the Spirit is not said to be the source of the charismata is rightly emphasized by Banks, *Community* 95, and Martin, *Spirit and Congregation* 36. On the pre-eminence of love in the exercise of spiritual gifts, cf. Schweizer, *Church Order* 100–101 (7k); Martin, *op. cit.* 36, especially 42–46, where love is expounded as the essential accompaniment of all the gifts.

20. Three times in 1 Cor. 12:8–10, 28, 29f. glossolalia and the interpretation of tongues appear at the bottom of the list. It is observable that

prophēteia and *prophētai* occupy different positions in lists (A) and (B); this suggests that it is particularly these two gifts (glossolalia and the interpretation of tongues) that Paul is concerned to put in their proper place.

21. Cf. Dunn, *Jesus and Spirit* 263–264; Gaffin, *Perspectives* 46–48.
22. The expression *metron pisteōs* is fully discussed by Cranfield, *Romans* 613–616. Of the many interpretations that have been proposed, the view which commends itself to us as doing the most justice to the phrase is that which takes *pistis* 'in the restricted sense of the faith that is suited to the exercise' of any particular gift — the faith corresponding to the believer's own measure of gift by which that gift is to be exercised (J. Murray, *The Epistle to the Romans* [NICNT; Grand Rapids 1968] 2.119); cf. C. Hodge, *A Commentary on Romans* (London 1972) 386–387; Dunn, *Jesus and Spirit* 211, 412 n.67; Gaffin, *Perspectives* 62–64.
23. Cranfield, *Romans* 623.
24. Cf. *ibid.* 611, 618 for the insistence that a believer's God-given charisma *constitutes* his divine vocation.
25. The importance of such single-minded devotion to the fulfilment of tasks for which one is equipped by the corresponding spiritual gifts is underlined by M. Green, *To Corinth with Love* (London 1982) 150, where (commenting on 1 Cor. 1:17) he writes: 'Within all Christian ministry there is a crying need for men to find their own particular niche, stick to it and release other people for contributing their gifts to the Body of Christ'. A practical application of this principle to the pastoral ministry is suggested by W. L. Combs, 'Using Your Strengths in Ministry', *Church Administration* (July 1983) 12–14. To the question of how to discover one's spiritual gift(s), Gaffin, *Perspectives* 53, suggests a '*factual* and *situational* approach.'
26. J. N. D. Kelly, *The Epistles of Peter and of Jude* (BNTC; London 1969) 179.
27. Barth, *Ephesians* 436, cf. 482. Cf. also n.8 above.
28. The same general distinction is made by E. Schillebeeckx, *Ministry* (ET London 1981) 34. Cf. Barth, *Ephesians* 477, 481; K. Giles, 'New Testament Patterns of Ministry', *Interchange* 31 (1983) 43–60 (43).

According to R. Schnackenburg, 'Christus, Geist und Gemeinde (Eph. 4:1–16)', in *Christ and the Spirit in the New Testament (Fs. C. F. D. Moule*, ed. B. Lindars and S. S. Smalley (Cambridge 1973), 279–296 (290–291), the *hēmōn* of v. 7 already refers to the office-bearers (*Amtsträger*) of v. 11. Five arguments are given in support of this view. (*a*) *De* shows that v. 7 begins a new section which is marked off from vv. 1–6, so that the *hekastō hēmōn* of v. 7 no longer has in view the *pantes* of the preceding verses. But this seems debatable. We maintain that it is most natural to take the *hēmōn* as referring back to the *pantōn* of v. 6a which, in the light of v. 5, most probably refers to believers. (Cf. 'Ministry . . . Gifts', 9 n.26, where the last word in line 6 should be corrected to read *pantōn*.) (*b*) There is a change from the second person of vv. 1–6 to the first person in

v. 7; only after the exposition on the office-bearers does 'we' (which includes the addresses) appear in v. 13, and there *hoi pantes* is added. But the second person is fittingly used in direct paraenesis (note v. 1, *parakato humas*), while the first person is not inappropriately used in a section (vv. 7–16) in which Paul, having shown the church to be a spiritual unity (vv. 4–6), now goes on to point out the diversity of gifts and functions which exists in the Body and to indicate their relation to God's over-all purpose for the church. It may be doubted that *hoi pantes* in v. 13 is intended to contrast the whole body of believers with the (supposed) office-bearers (*hēmōn*) of v. 7; rather, the phrase — in which the article 'gathers all the particulars under one view' (J. A. Robinson, *St. Paul's Epistle to the Ephesians* [London, n.d.] 182*b*) — simply emphasizes that 'the church as a whole', 'the totality of believers' is to attain to mature manhood (on v. 13 cf. 'Nature of Ministry', 141–142). (*c*) *Charis* in v. 7 refers to the special grace for the exercise of ministry, the nearest parallel being in 3:8. But it may be observed that 3:8 uses the more specific expression *hē autē*, which is further defined by the following epexegetical infinities *charis euangelisasthai . . . kai phōtisai* (vv. 8*b*, 9*a*; cf. Rom. 1:5, where *charin*, if it forms part of a hendiadys with *kai apostoten*, is defined by *eis hypakoēn ktl.*), whereas 4:7 simply has *hē charis*. Schnackenburg also compares the *dōrea* of God in 3:7 with the *dōrea* of Christ in 4:7. Here again, whereas 3:7 contains the specifying words *egenēthēn diakonos*, 4:7 carries no such specification (on our understanding of 4:7*b* cf. 'Ministry . . . Gifts', 7 with n.21). (*d*) 4:7 is supported by the citation in v. 8 (*dio legei*) and the giving of gifts there is explained in v. 11; hence v. 7 is connected with and is to be interpreted by what follows. But it seems obvious that the quotation in v. 8 is made chiefly because the words, *anabas eis hypsos . . . edōken domata* exactly serve Paul's purpose: having stated the general distribution of gifts to all believers as a fact in v. 7, Paul uses the Old Testament quotation in v. 8 to show that 'the distribution of gifts is involved in the very fact of the Ascension' (Robinson, *Ephesians* 179*a*), and then proceeds in v. 11 to give some specific examples. Understood in this way, v. 8 need not be seen as already defining the giving of gifts in v. 7 as confined to office-bearers. (*e*) V. 16, where *en metrō henos nekastou merous* is an unmistakable resumption of v. 7 (and *dia pasēs hapnēs tēs epichorēgias* is to be referred to the office-bearers), confirms the interpretation that *hēmōn* in v. 7 refers to office-bearers. The first observation, however, simply suggests that one's understanding of v. 16 should be consistent with one's understanding of v. 7, while the statement we have put in brackets expresses a view from which we have elsewhere expressed our reason for dissent (cf. 'Pauline Pictures' 96 n.29).

On the basis of the above considerations, we do not find Schnacken- burg's fivefold argument compelling. In addition we submit that the emphatic *heni . . . hekastō* attached to *hēmōn* in v. 7, which is difficult to account for on the view in question but is in perfect harmony with

Paul's clear teaching elsewhere that *every believer* is a recipient of some spiritual gift(s), renders the broader understanding of *hēmōn* the more likely view.

29. What was said in 'Nature of Ministry' 143 n.47, first paragraph, and 144, second paragraph, requires modification inasmuch as in the work of 'showing mercy' (Rom. 12:8d) 'Paul is thinking of service which reaches beyond the limits of the Christian fellowship' (Cranfield, *Romans* 628; there the important place of *diakonia* in the life of the church in its worldward aspect is also emphasized).

30. Cf. 'Nature of Ministry', 139–144.

31. Dunn, *Jesus and Spirit* 254 (put in italics in original); cf. 209, 210, 211, 253, 263, 264 for repeated emphasis on the same point.

32. At the beginning of Rom. 12:6b the versions rightly supply such an expression as 'let us use them' (RSV, cf. NIV), 'let each exercise them accordingly' (NASB). Cf. NEB: 'The gifts we *possess* . . . must be *exercised*' (emphasis added); see also Cranfield, *Romans* 618. Against Dunn, see also the criticism of M. Turner, 'Spiritual Gifts Then and Now', *VE* 15 (1985) 7–64 (30–31, 35).

33. Dunn, *Jesus and Spirit* 254. Glossolalia is omitted here in view of C. F. D. Moule, *The Holy Spirit* (Grand Rapids, 1978) 90, who says of the gift: 'Those who are familiar with it assure us that it is never 'ecstatic', if that word is taken to mean out of the subject's control. . . . It is exercised consciously and controlledly and in such a way that, if the gift is available, the use of it *can be started and terminated at will*' (emphasis added). This indirect testimony is in line with Paul's teaching in 1 Cor. 14:32. Even in the case of prophecy, it is to be observed that some apparently exercised such a frequent or regular ministry with their gift that they came to be acknowledged as 'prophets' (e.g. 1 Cor. 12:28f.; 14:29, 32; Acts 21:10), while others did so only temporarily on particular occasions (e.g. Acts 19:6). Cf. Gaffin, *ibid.* 59.

34. For instance, the gift of 'sharing' (Rom. 12:8b) is probably to be taken as consisting in a person's 'spiritual *capacity*, his god-given *inclination* to give' of what is his own, and in the generic expression *ho eleōn* (Rom. 12:8d) Paul is speaking of 'those who, having a special *aptitude*, are appointed by the church to concentrate upon the work in its name' (Cranfield, *Romans* 625, 628, emphasis added). Cf. Giles, 'Patterns of Ministry', 47; Moule, *Holy Spirit* 86.

35. D. Guthrie, *New Testament Theology* (Leicester 1981) 765.

36. Dunn, *Jesus and Spirit* 255 (put in italics in the original).

37. Cf. Banks, *Community* 100; Martin, *Spirit and Congregation* 36–37.

38. Cf. G. E. Ladd, *A Theology of the New Testament* (Grand Rapids 1974) 535; Green, *Holy Spirit* 195; D. C. K. Watson, 'David Watson on Spiritual Gifts', *Theology, News and Notes* (March 1983) 18–23, 34 (19–20); Guthrie, *Theology* 765–766 with n. 211. Dunn, who takes the view that 'nowhere does charisma have the sense of a human capacity heightened, developed or transformed', concedes that 'charisma may of course chime in with an individual disposition and

temperament, and will certainly make use of natural abilities' (*Jesus and Spirit* 255, 256).

39. Gaffin, *Perspectives* 48. Cf. Turner, 'gifts', 33.

40. On the present infinitive *anazōpurein* in this verse, see J. N. D. Kelly, *The Pastoral Epistles* (BNTC; London 1972) 159.

41. On the distinction cf. 'Function or Office?', 16 with n.3.

42. According to G. V. Smith, 'Paul's Use of Psalm 68:18 in Ephesians 4:8', *JETS* 18 (1975) 181–189, Paul's quotation of the former text in the latter is to be understood as an analogous application or 'remoulding of the thought of Psalm 68:18 on the basis of the Scriptural commentary in Numbers 8:6–19; 18:6 which the Psalmist used. The Levites are described as taken from among the sons of Israel and given as a gift to the sons of Israel' (189, cf. 187). Now if in Ps. 68:18 'both the captives and the gifts are the Levites' (187) and this thought is applied analogously to the church, there is no sharp distinction between gift and person — a fact which would explain why our list (D) is made up entirely of persons. (I am indebted to the Editor for drawing my attention to the article by Gary Smith.) On the combination of persons and gifts in list (B), cf. 'Ministry . . . Gifts', 12.

43. Goppelt, *Apostolic . . . Times* 183, followed by Ladd, *Theology* 535. Cf. Guthrie, *Theology* 566.

44. E.G. Schnackenburg, 'Christus, Geist und Gemeinde', especially 292, 295 (cf. the English summary on 296, last two paragraphs); and the references cited in 'Ministry . . . Gifts', 6–7 n.16.

45. Cf. 'Ministry . . . Gifts', 12–13. In contrast with the scholars referred to in the preceding note, Eph. 4:11 is held to refer to functions rather than offices by Guthrie, *Theology* 566, 762; cf. Dunn, *Jesus and Spirit* 289, who considers that the words 'evangelists' and 'pastors' both denote functions rather than offices. Also in favour of understanding the lists (1 Cor. 12, Eph. 4) of functions is D. G. Stewart, *ZPEB* I 618b.

46. Cranfield, *Romans* 619.

47. Cf. the references cited in 'Ministry . . . Gifts', 13 n.45. Cf. Turner, 'Gifts', 35.

48. See the references cited in 'Function or Office?', 16 n.1.

49. See his *Essays on New Testament Themes* (ET London 1964) 63–94.

50. For more detailed discussions see 'Function or Office?', 'Charismatic versus Organized', 'Organized Ministry?'. Attention may be invited to the footnotes to the first two of these articles, only a fraction of which reappear in the present section of this paper. For some helpful criteria of 'office', see Turner, 'Gifts', 35.

51. Cf. 'Function or Office?', 17. The quotation at the close of this paragraph is from T. W. Manson, *The Church's Ministry* (London 1948) 47–48.

52. Cf. 'Function or Office?', 17–20.

53. The three quotations are taken from, respectively, H. von Campenhausen, *Tradition and Life in the Church* (ET Philadelphia 1968) 131; A. F. Walls, *IBD* I 371b; and R. A. Bodey, *ZPEB* IV 237b.

54. Cf. 'Function or Office?', 21–23; 'Charismatic versus Organized', 196–210; 'Organized Ministry? (1)'.
55. F. F. Bruce, *Paul and His Converts* (London/Abingdon 1962) 60. For a different reading of the evidence, cf. Turner, 'Gifts', 35–36.
56. This generalized description approximates more the situation of Ephesus than that of Crete, judging from the fact that deacons appear as the local church officers only in Ephesus but not in Crete, presumably because in the less developed churches of Crete there was as yet no need for two kinds of officers.
57. With Käsemann cf. e.g. Dunn, *Jesus and Spirit* 347–350; idem, *Unity and Diversity in the New Testament* (London 1977) 351–352.
58. W. Lock, *The Pastoral Epistles* (ICC; Edinburgh 1966) xix.
59. H. W. Beyer, *TDNT* II 617.
60. G. Bornkamm, *TDNT* VI 667. *Contra* H. von Campenhausen, *Ecclesiastical Authority and Spiritual Power in the Church of the First Three Centuries* (ET Stanford 1969) 107 ('monarchical episcopacy is by now the prevailing system').
61. Käsemann, *Essays* 87.
62. I. H. Marshall, '"Early Catholicism" in the New Testament', in *New Dimensions in New Testament Study*, ed. R. N. Longenecker and M. C. Tenney (Grand Rapids 1974) 217–231 (228; cf. 229–230).
63. As by Käsemann, *Essays* 88 (whence the twice-quoted phrase). Positively, cf. Turner, 'Gifts' 36 (in criticism of Dunn, point [4]).
64. *Ibid.* 84 (emphasis added), cf. 88.
65. Cf. 'Function or Office?', 34–35. The quotation at the close of this paragraph is from H. W. Montefiore, *The Epistle to the Hebrews* (BNTC; London 1977) 242.
66. Cf. 'Function or Office?' 31–34.
67. Cf. p. above.
68. Cf. 'Nature of Ministry', 138.
69. So e.g. Kelly, *Peter and Jude* 180–181.
70. Goppelt, *Apostolic . . . Times* 187.
71. G. Bornkamm, *TDNT* VI 664.
72. As Bornkamm, *ibid.*, maintains.
73. So J. B. Mayor, *The Epistle of St. James* (Grand Rapids 1954) 169.
74. On this see *ibid.* 232–233; M. Dibelius/H. Greeven, *James* (ET Hermeneia; Philadelphia 1976) 254b.
75. Cf. p. above; earlier, 'Nature of Ministry', 181.
76. Cf. 'Function or Office?', 35–36.
77. G. Bornkamm, *TDNT* VI 669.
78. Cf. 'Function or Office?', 36–39; 'Charismatic versus Organized', 210–214; 'Organized Ministry? (2)'.
79. Schweizer, *Church Order* 13 (1a), 17 (= 1d).
80. Examples of such are: Galatia (Acts 16:5), Thessalonica (17:4), Corinth (18:8) and Ephesus (19:10, 17–20; cf. 1 Cor. 16:8f.).
81. J. Schneider, 'The Local Church in the New Testament', *The Christian Review* 8 (1939) 13–24 (13). Cf. J. M. Barnett, *The Diaconate* (New York 1981) 8.

82. Campenhausen, *Authority and Power* 80.
83. So e.g. E. J. Forrester/G. W. Bromiley, *ISBER* I 697a. Cf. C. K. Barrett, *The First Epistle to the Corinthians* (HNTC; New York/ Evanston 1968) 295–296.
84. Guthrie, *Theology* 765.
85. Cf. p.oo above.
86. R. P. Martin, *1 Corinthians — Galatians* (London 1968) 32.
87. Cf. Gaffin, *Perspectives* 89–102. In view of the discussion in Turner, 'Gifts', 46–48, we would wish to make a distinction between the association of New Testament prophets as a class who shared the foundational role with the apostles, and the continuance of the gift of prophecy as described by Turner.
88. Cf. n.75 above (with corresponding comment in the text).
89. Cf. 'Ministry . . . Gifts', 11–12.
90. E. M. Howe, 'The Positive Case for the Ordination of Women', in *Perspectives on Evangelical Theology*, ed. K. S. Kantzer and S. N. Gundry (Grand Rapids, 1979) 267–276 (275). Cf. F. F. Bruce, 'Women in the Church: a Biblical Survey', *CBR* 33 (1982) 7–14 (11–12).
91. C. Brown, *NIDNTT* III 1067.
92. This is perhaps an appropriate juncture to mention one or two things. First, a paper on 'Women's Ministry in Paul's Teaching' written specifically for the Cambridge consultation in November 1984 was subjected to rigorous critique; I have derived much profit from the constructive criticisms which that paper received then, and also (and especially) from subsequent correspondence with the Editor. Neither Dr Carson nor any other member of the study unit, however should be held responsible for any weaknesses or mistakes that may be found in the present section of this essay where my views are set forth tentatively. Second, when in nn.241, 242 below reference is made to comments by some members of the consultation (at which I was not present), I owe the information to a report by the Editor on the discussion of my paper.
93. 'Charismatic versus Organized', 197 with n.4; 'Function or Office?', 32–24 with nn.41, 42.
94. Cf. e.g. R. T. Beckwith, 'The Office of Woman in the Church, to the Present Day', in *Why Not? Priesthood and the Ministry of Women*, ed. M. Bruce and G. E. Duffield, rev. and augmented by R. T. Beckwith (Appleford, Abingdon 1976), 26–39 (33). It has even been suggested that Phoebe was in fact the minister of the church at Cenchreae: so e.g. E. M. Howe, *Women and Church Leadership* (Grand Rapids 1982) 31.
95. On the significance of both expressions see Cranfield, *Romans* 785.
96. See e.g. B. M. Metzger, *A Textual Commentary on the Greek New Testament* (London/New York 1971) 539.
97. Cf. e.g. C. H. Dodd, *The Epistle of Paul to the Romans* (London 1970) 241; P. K. Jewett, *The Ordination of Women* (Grand Rapids 1980) 71.

98. In its other three occurrences (1 Cor. 4:12; Eph. 4:28; 2 Tim. 2:6) the word has a physical sense. The cognate noun *kopos*, similarly, is often used of labour in the service of the gospel (1 Cor. 3:8; 15:58; 2 Cor. 10:15; 11:23; 1 Thess. 3:5). Cf. F. Hauck, *TDNT* III 827, who rightly observes that a distinctive New Testament and Pauline use of *kopos* is for Christian work in and for the Christian community.

99. G. G. Blum, 'The Office of Woman in the New Testament', in *Why Not?* 63–77 (66), thinks that there can be no reference to preaching here; cf. D. J. Moo, 'The Interpretation of 1 Timothy 2:11–15; A Rejoinder', *TrinJ* 2 NS (1981) 198–222 (213), who notes that 'the same verb (in its only other pauline occurrence) is used in an exhortation to the Philippian church as a whole (Phil. 1:27)'. Worth pondering, however, is this statement by J. Harper, *Women and the Gospel* (CBRF Occasional Paper No. 5, 1974) 22*b*: 'We should beware of the idea that when men labour in the Gospel, they preach, but when women labour in the Gospel they provide refreshments and accommodation for the man'. Cf. F. F. Bruce, *The Pauline Circle* (Exeter 1985) 85.

100. So e.g. J. B. Hurley, *Man and Woman in Biblical Perspective* (Leicester (1981) 231–233; G. Stählin, *TDNT* IX 464 n.231; K. Hess, *NIDNTT* III 546, 549; C. Brown, *ibid.* 1065. Others think that the masculine noun used of deacons and the setting of verse 11 in a passage otherwise dealing with deacons indicate that the office of deacon can only be filled by men, and that the women are auxiliaries assisting the work of the deacons: so e.g. G. W. Knight III, *The New Testament Teaching on the Role Relationship of Men and Women* (Grand Rapids 1977) 48, 68. But an imperative apparently addressed only to men can be equally applicable to women (e.g. Ex. 20:17), so that *diakonoi* can include women deacons (cf. Rom. 16:1), the more so as the female term *diakonissa* was yet unknown at that time and in order to specify that women could be also be deacons Paul had no alternative but to mention them by their sex as *gynaikes*: cf. S. T. Foh, *Women and the Word of God* (Nutley, NJ 1980) 256–257; Kelly, *Pastoral* 83–84.

101. So A. Oepke, *TDNT* I 788; cf. Beckwith, 'Office of Women', 33.

102. So Kelly, *Pastoral* 115; G. Stählin, *TDNT* IX 455 n. 144; C. Brown, *NIDNTT* III 1065; S. Solle, *ibid.* 1075.

103. Cf. Blum, 'Office of Woman', 66 ('missionary or teaching office'); Knight, *Role Relationship* 47 ('the teaching-ruling offices and functions'); Guthrie, *Theology* 778 ('a position of authority').

104. E. and D. Fraser, 'A Biblical View of Women: Demythologizing Sexegesis', in *Women and the Ministries of Christ*, ed. R. Hestenes and L. Curley (Pasadena, C 1979) 26–36 (32), and E. S. Fiorenza, 'Feminist Theology as a Critical Theology of Liberation', in *Woman New Dimensions*, ed. W. J. Burghardt (New York 1977) 29–50 (41), respectively.

105. R. Scroggs, *IDBS* 966*b*; cf. *idem*, 'Paul and the Eschatological Woman', *JAAR* 40 (1972) 283–303 (291–293).

106. Cf. e.g. W. Grundmann, *TDNT* IX 552 n.377; J. H. Yoder, *The Politics of Jesus* (Grand Rapids 1972) 177 n.23; Hurley, *Man and Woman* 126–127; and especially S. B. Clark, *Man and Woman in Christ* (Ann Arbor 1980) 139–149.

107. Quotations from G. B. Caird, 'Paul and Women's Liberty', *BJRL* 54 (1971–72) 268–281 (272–273); K. Stendahl, *The Bible and the Role of Women* (ET Philadelphia 1966) 34; F. F. Bruce, 'St. Paul in Macedonia: 3. The Philippian Correspondence', *BJRL* 63 (1980–81) 260–284 (283); R. E. Brown, 'Roles of Women in the Fourth Gospel', in *Woman New Dimensions* 112–123 (123); and P. K. Jewett, *Man as Male and Female* (Grand Rapids 1975) 147–148, respectively. Cf. B. Mickelsen, 'Women in Paul's Teaching', in *Women and the Ministries of Christ* 152; B. Witherington III, 'Rites and Rights for Women — Galatians 3.28', *NTS* 27 (1980–81) 593–604 (esp. 600).

108. Cf. Foh, *Women* 141–142 (quotation from 142); Clark, *Man and Woman* 149–163. See also H. C. Cavallin, 'Demythologising the Liberal Illusion', in *Why Not?* 81–94; M. Boucher, 'Some Unexplored Parallels to 1 Cor. 11:11–12 and Gal. 3:28: The New Testament on the Role of Women', *CBQ* 31 (1969) 50–58 (57f.); J. J. Davis, 'Some Reflexions on Galatians 3:28, Sexual roles, and Biblical Hermeneutics', *JETS* 19 (1976) 201–208 (202); R. L. Saucy, 'The Negative Case Against the Ordination of Women', in *Perspectives on Evangelical Theology* 277–286 (281–285).

109. The passage is considered by some as a non-Pauline interpolation either in its entirety (e.g. G. W. Trompf, 'On Attitudes Toward Women in Paul and Paulinist Literature', *CBQ* 42 [1980] 196–215) or with the exception of verse 2 (so L. Cope, '1 Corinthians 11:2–16: One Step Farther', *JBL* 97 [1978] 435–436). Paul's commendation in verse 2 may be more apparent than real: see e.g. F. F. Bruce, *1 & 2 Corinthians* (NCB; London 1971) 102.

110. G. Schrenk, *TDNT* III 49. Cf. W. C. Kaiser, Jr., *Toward An Exegetical Theology* (Grand Rapids, 1981) 118–119, who rightly urges that exegesis of 1 Cor. 11:3–16 'must show a deep respect for the theology inculcated here'. *Pace* A. Padgett, 'Paul on Women in the Church: The Contradictions of Coiffure in 1 Corinthians 11:2–16', *JSNT* 20 (1984) 69–86 (79–80), who takes the clause as introducing the Corinthians' beliefs (vv. 3–7b), with Paul's corrective beginning at v. 7b.

111. E.g. P. J. Sampley, *'And the Two Shall Become One Flesh* (Cambridge 1971) 80, 81; F. Stagg, *New Testament Theology* (Nashville 1962) 297; N. Hillyer, *NBCR* 1065b; W. F. Orr and J. A. Walther, *I Corinthians* (AB; Garden City 1976) 259; G. Taylor, 'Women in Creation and Redemption', *CBR* 26 (1974) 14–28 (24–25); D. M. Lake, *ZPEB* V 954–955. An even more specific rendering — 'the head of a wife is her husband' — is adopted by (among others) Barth, *Ephesians* 614; Ridderbos, *Paul* 381.

112. Cf. e.g. Foh, *Women* 102; J. G. Baldwin, *Women Likewise* (London 1973) 18; Orr-Walther, *I Corinthians* 263.

113. Cf. e.g. D. J. Davies, 'An Anthropological Perspective', in *Why Not?* 141–147 (143–144); G. W. Knight III, 'The New Testament Teaching on the Role Relationship of Male and Female with Special Reference to the Teaching/Ruling Functions in the Church', *JETS* 18 (1975) 81–91 (83). The implication of Jesus' statement in Matt. 5:32a is relevant here.
114. Cf. Clark, *Man and Woman* 181; Hurley, *Man and Woman* 179–181.
115. E.g., on the one hand, E. Schweizer, *TDNT* VII 1076–1077 with n.489; C. Brown, *NIDNTT* II 160, III 1063; F. H. Palmer, *IBD* II 615–616; (involving subordination) C. K. Barrett, *A Commentary on the First Epistle to the Corinthians* (HNTC; New York 1968) 249; M. E. Thrall, *The Ordination of Women to the Priesthood* (London 1958) 31, in agreement with S. Bedale, 'The Meaning of *kephalē* in the Pauline Epistles', *JTS* 5 (1954) 211–215, and, on the other hand, Hurley, *Man and Woman* 165–167; Clark, *Man and Woman* 83–84 with note; J. R. Price, *ISBER* II 640a.
116. See W. A. Grudem, in *TrinJ* 3 NS (1982) 230–231 (in review of Hurley's *Man and Woman*); and especiallly *idem*, 'Does *kephalē* ('head') Mean 'Source' or 'Authority Over' in Greek Literature? A Survey of 2,336 Examples', Appendix 1 in G. W. Knight III, *The Role Relationship between Men and Women* (rev. ed.; Chicago 1985) 43–68 (quotation from 53).
117. So, rightly, Hurley, *Man and Woman* 176–177.
118. Cf. e.g. D. E. H. Whiteley, *The Theology of St. Paul* (Oxford 1964) 121–122; H. Conzelmann, *1 Corinthians* (ET Hermeneia; Philadelphia 1975) 183b. Also note the concession made by Scroggs, 'Eschatological Woman', 300 n.50.
119. So H. Schlier, *TDNT* III 674–675; R. C. Dentan, *IDB* II 541a. It may be worth emphasizing that what is common to the three clauses is chiefly the fact of headship. The order of the original — not: God — Christ — man — woman, but: man — Christ, woman — man, Christ — God (compare and contrast the order in 1 Cor. 3:22f.) — militates against the idea of a rigid ladder-like hierarchy: cf. K. Barth, *CD* III 4:173; M. Bührig, 'The Question of the Ordination of Women in the Light of Some New Testament Texts', in *Concerning the Ordination of Women* (Geneva 1964) 41–56 (45–46); A. Dumas, 'Biblical Anthropology and the Participation of Women in the Ministry of the Church', *ibid.* 12–40 (34). As W. H. Mare, *EBC* X 255, rightly remarks, 'Paul does not mean by the analogy that subordination in each case is of the same completeness'. At the same time, we are reminded that while 'headship' is 'an analogical and not a universal concept [,] . . . neither is it purely equivocal, or there would be no force in making the comparison' (E. L. Mascall, 'Women and the Priesthood of the Church', in *Why Not?* 95–120 [119]).
120. E.g. W. J. Martin, 'I Corinthians 11:2–16: An Interpretation', in *Apostolic History and the Gospel* (Fs. F. F. Bruce), ed. W. W. Gasque and R. P. Martin (Exeter 1970) 231–241 (esp. 233); J. Murphy-

O'Connor, 'Sex and Logic in 1 Corinthians 11:2–16', *CBQ* 42 (1980) 482–500 (esp. 483–490); Hurley, *Man and Woman* 168–171, 179.

121. This is admitted by Hurley, *ibid.* 184. But see also n.142 below.
122. For the dishonoured 'heads' in vv. 4–5 as involving both the physical and metaphorical senses, cf. e.g. Bruce, *Corinthians* 104; C Brown, *NIDNTT* 2. 160. Verse 4 describes a merely hypothetical case, which serves as a foil for the censure on women which follows in vv. 5–6 (cf. A. Robertson and A. Plummer, *The First Epistle of St. Paul to the Corinthians* [ICC; Edinburgh 1967] 229).
123. The reasoning in v. 6 is not strictly logical but based on analogy, as F. W. Grosheide, *Commentary on the First Epistle to the Corinthians* (NLC; London 1954) 254, points out.
124. Cf. e.g. Barth, *Ephesians* 661; R. Kugelman, *JerBC* II 270a (51–69). In the case of an unmarried woman, her metaphorical head would presumably be her father, or some other male figure on whom she was dependent. (We might compare in this connection the classical Chinese saying which speaks of the virtuous woman's dependence on the submission to 'her father before she is married, her husband after her marriage, her [grown] son when she is old [and widowed]'.)
125. See e.g. J. Jeremias, *Jerusalem in the Time of Jesus* (ET Philadelphia 1975) 359–360.
126. So C. Brown, *NIDNTT* II 159–160. Cf., in greater length, Clark, *Man and Woman* 168–170. For a dissenting opinion see J. K. Howard, 'Neither Male nor Female: An Examination of the Status of Women in the New Testament', *EQ* 55 (1983) 31–42 (34–35 n.5). The fact that 'pagan prophetesses in the Graeco-Roman world prophesied with uncovered and dishevelled heads', if known to Paul, would be regarded by him as a further argument for his ruling (Bruce, *Corinthians* 105). Cult prostitution is regarded by some as another relevant factor: e.g. R. and J. Boldrey, *Chauvinist or Feminist?* (Grand Rapids 1976) 59.
127. The close proximity of 'glory' to 'image' suggests that *doxa* here has the sense of 'reflection': so e.g. Conzelmann, *1 Corinthians* 187a; G. Kittel, *TDNT* II 237; H. Schlier, *TDNT* III 679; BAG 230a (*s.v.* 1 c). E. E. Ellis, *Paul's Use of the Old Testament* (Grand Rapids 1981) 63, holds that in 1 Cor. 11:7ff. Paul came into contact with a rabbinic tradition which makes 'the point that "the glory of the Holy One" is derived from the males and woman is the man's glory' — thus using *doxa* in a subjective sense. In the light of this suggestion, it is not impossible that *doxa* in v. 7a may include, besides its primary meaning of 'reflection', the secondary sense of 'that which brings honour': precisely because man bears God's image and reflects his glory, he also brings honour and praise to him.
128. That the woman was also created in God's image (cf. Gen. 1:26f.) is implied by Paul's deliberate avoidance of complete parallelism in v. 7b, where he does *not* say *eikōn kai doxa andros*: so e.g. Jewett,

Male and Female 56. Paul omits mentioning the fact that woman also is in God's image because his present concern with the relation of woman to man (cf. v. 3) rather than to God (Robertson-Plummer, *First Corinthians* 231). On Paul's handling of the Genesis texts (1:26f.; 2:18–23) see Bruce, *Corinthians* 105.

129. Cf. Prov. 11:16 (LXX *gynā eucharistos egeirei andri doxan*); 12:4; 31:10f. In the above exegesis, the word *doxa* acquires a different meaning in each half of v. 7: its primary meaning in 7a is determined by its close connection with *eikōn* its sense in 7b is derived from the explanatory verses (8f.) which follow. J. I. Packer, 'Postscript: I Believe in Women's Ministry', in *Why Not?* 164–174, aptly says that 'the traditional word *subordination*, with its overtones of qualitative superiority and inferiority, is not the clearest term for [the concept of a 'help meet' for the man]: *support* is better' (169). We use the term 'subordination' in this paper *without* any implications of superiority and inferiority. On 'subordination' as a preferable translation for *hypotassesthai* to 'submission', see W. M. Swartley, *Slavery Sabbath War and Women* (Scottdale, Pa./Kitchener, Ont. 1983) 265–266 (citing J. H. Yoder).

130. The opinion of M. D. Hooker, 'Authority on her head, an examination of 1 Corinthians xi.10', *NTS* 10 (1963–64) 410–416 (esp. 411, 415–416), that Paul makes his argument turn on the contrast between two sorts of glory (man as the glory of *God* ought not, but woman as the glory of *man* ought, to be covered in the presence of God), is endorsed by (among others) C. Brown, *NIDNTT* II 161. But see the criticism of Clark, *Man and Woman* 170n. A further objection which might be raised is that if Paul did argue in that way (i.e. that the glory of man [=woman] ought to be concealed in public worship), it is not clear how this argument is to be applied today. If pressed, it would lead to the conclusion that Christian women today should have their heads covered (or some equivalent expression) during worship — a view which few modern scholars would champion (an exception is B. K. Waltke, as reported in *NTA* 22–496).

131. E.g. F. Godet, *Commentary on the First Epistle to the Corinthians* (ET Grand Rapids 1957) 2.122, and Robertson-Plummer, *First Corinthians* 232, respectively.

132. So W. A. Grudem, as in n.116 above (231).

133. I owe this suggestion to Dr D. A. Carson.

134. Cf. Clark, *Man and Woman* 171n. The thought of the head-covering as a sign of dignity protecting the woman from interference — suggested by e.g. *MM* 255a (*s.v. exousia*); O. Rogers, 'The Role of Women in the Church', *CBR* 26 (1974) 6–13 (6) — seems alien to the context of church worship.

135. E.g. H. J. Schoeps, *Paul* (ET Philadelphia 1961) 39. For decisive reasons against this view see Robertson-Plummer, *First Corinthians* 233; Barrett, *First Corinthians* 253–234; Orr-Walther, *I Corinthians* 260–261.

136. E.g. Caird, 'Women's Liberty', 278, and H. Bietenhard, *NIDNTT*

I 102–103; G. Kittel, *TDNT* I 86; J. Ruef, *Paul's First Letter to Corinth* (London 1977) 110, respectively.

137. E.g. Conzelmann, *1 Corinthians* 190a. Others regard vv. 11f. as (a) the first indication of Paul's uneasy conscience, (b) the result of a momentary reassertion of Paul's Christian sense, (c) a conscious correction of what was said earlier, or (d) being alone the true theological climax of the entire discussion. See e.g., respectively, (a) V. R. Mollenkott, *Women Men and the Bible* (Nashvile 1977) 100; (b) J. Moffatt, *The First Epistle of Paul to the Corinthians* (MNTC; London 1939) 153; (c) M. Daly, *The Church and the Second Sex* (New York 1975) 81; (d) Scroggs, 'Eschatological Woman', 300 with n.47, 302.

138. J. H. Thayer, *A Greek-English Lexicon of the New Testament* (New York n.d.) 517a (s.v.).

139. Barrett, *First Corinthians* 177–178.

140. Cf. Hurley, *Man and Woman* 177–178.

141. *Physis* is here taken not in the sense of a 'natural sense, native conviction or knowledge' (Thayer, *Lexicon* 660b [s.v.]), but as referring to the general order of nature as created by God, a sense which reflects its usage in popular Stoicism: so e.g. BAG 877b (s.v.); G. Harder, *NIDNTT* II 661; K. Wegenast, *ibid.* III 764.

142. In *anti peribolaiou* (v. 15) the preposition could mean 'instead of'. This is taken by some as providing a partial basis for the view that what Paul requires of women at worship is not head-covering, but long hair or a particular coiffure (cf. n.120 above); but this view does not accord well with vv. 6f., where *katakalyptesthai* most likely refers to head-covering (cf. N. Weeks, 'Of Silence and Head Covering', *WTJ* 35 [1972] 21–27 [24]). Hence, *anti* is better taken in the sense of 'answering to', as by e.g. F. Büchsel, *TDNT* I 372; A. T. Robertson, *Word Pictures in the New Testament* (Nashville n.d.) 4.162.

143. As taken by Foh, *Women* 116, and Harper, *Women* 28a, respectively. The latter view lays emphasis on the fact that the original says 'such' (*toiautēn*) custom (KJV, RV, NEB) and not 'other custom' (RSV, NASB, NIV). but surely the meaning of 'such' is to be determined from the context.

144. J. P. Meier, 'On the Veiling of Hermeneutics (1 Cor. 11:2–16)', *CBQ* 40 (1978) 212–226, thinks that Paul rests his 'definitive argument' on church tradition (216, cf. 223). But, as already mentioned (n.109 above), Paul's commendation of the Corinthians in v. 2 may be only apparent, not real.

145. E.g. A. Oepke, *TDNT* I 787; H. Schlier, *ibid.* III 680, and W. Michaelis, *ibid.* VI 852–853; Dunn, *Jesus and Spirit* 280, respectively.

146. On the distinction between a basic principle and its cultural expression (in this case 'veiling'), cf. e.g. G. R. Osborne, 'Hermeneutics and Women in the Church', *JETS* 20 (1977) 337–352 (343); C. Brown, *NIDNTT* II 161–162.

147. Hurley, *Man and Woman* 181.
148. 1 Cor. 14:34–36 (or vv. 34–35) is frequently regarded as non-Pauline: e.g. H. Koester, *Introduction to the New Testametn* (ET Philadelphia 1982) 2.125. For a defence of the authenticity of vv. 34–35 see Thrall, *Ordination* 77–79; E. E. Ellis, 'The Silenced Wives of Corinth (1 Cor. 14:34–5)', in *New Testament Textual Criticism: Its Significance for Exegesis* (*Fs.* B. M. Metzger, ed. E. J. Epp and G. D. Fee (Oxford 1981) 213–220.
149. Some (e.g. Barrett, *First Corinthians* 330) would link v. 33b to v. 33a (as in KJV, RV, NASB) so as to avoid the awkward juxtaposition of *en pasais tais ekklēsiais* and *en tais ekklēsiais*. But the result does not yield a satisfactory sense, whereas the inelegant juxtaposition does: the former expression refers to other churches, especially those in Paul's mission field, the latter to all the gatherings (cf. the sense of *ekklēsia* in 11:18; 14:19; 28, 35) of the Corinthian church (so e.g. Godet, *First Corinthians* 2.308). An interesting (but unconvincing) view takes *tōn hagiōn hai gynaikes* as a unit, meaning 'the wives of the saints': G. H. Clark, *First Corinthians* (Nutley, NJ 1975) 245.
150. E.g. L. Morris, *The First Epistle of Paul to the Corinthians* (London 1958) 201; Orr-Walther, *I Corinthians* 312; Ellis, 'Silenced Wives', 214–215 217.
151. Cf. e.g. Harper, *Women* 10a; Clark, *Man and Woman* 187; Packer, 'Postscript' 171. It is noteworthy that the word 'cursed' is used in the Gen. 3 account only of the serpent and the ground (vv. 14, 17), not the woman (or the man, either).
152. E.g. Hurley, *Man and Woman* 192, and D. R. Pape, *In Search of God's Ideal Woman* (Downers Grove 1976) 146, respectively.
153. R. and C. C. Kroeger, 'Pandemonium and Silence at Corinth', in *Women and the Ministries of Christ* 49–55 (51–52).
154. See D. A. Carson, *Exegetical Fallacies* (Grand Rapids 1984) 39–40. Cf. n.171 below.
155. Foh, *Women* 118; cf. Sampley, *'One Flesh'* 99, and (among others) Bruce, *Corinthians* 136; Knight, *Role Relationship* 37, 44, respectively.
156. If this is accepted, it resolves the difficulty of finding 'the appropriate text in the Old Testament' which leads Martin to take *ho nomos*, rendered as 'the ruling' 'the principle' (cf. Rom. 3:27; Gal. 6:2), to be an allusion to Paul's own 'ruling' or 'norm' (i.e. his earlier teaching, picked up in v. 37) (*Spirit and Congregation* 75, 76, 87).
157. E.g. Grosheide, *First Corinthians* 342; R. Kugelman, *JerBC* II 272b (= 51–81).
158. E.g. L. Scanzoni and N. Hardesty, *All We're Meant to Be* (Waco, TX 1974) 68.
159. A. Oepke, *TDNT* I 787; G. Delling, *ibid.* VIII 43.
160. E.g. H. H. Esser, *NIDNTT* II 446; D. Hill, *New Testament Prophecy* (London 1979) 134–135, and Clark, *Man and Woman* 184, respectively.
161. E.g. Kroeger, 'Pandemonium', 51–52; Stendahl, *Role of Women* 30;

F. F. Bruce, *ZPEB* I 970*b*; R. J. Karris, 'The Role of Women according to Jesus and the Early Church', in *Woman and Priesthood*, ed. C. Stuhlmueller (Collegeville, MN 1978) 47–57 (53, in agreement with W. Meeks); K. E. Bailey, 'The Structure of I Corinthians and Paul's Theological Method and Special Reference to 4:17', *NovT* 25 (1983) 152–181 (170, cf. 171).

162. So, rightly, Bruce, *Corinthians* 135–136, and Knight, *Role Relationship* 37; Blum, 'Office of Woman', 67, respectively. For further arguments against this fifth view, see W. A. Grudem, *The Gift of Prophecy in 1 Corinthians* (Washington, D.C. 1982) 248–249 n.24.

163. E.g. Dunn, *Jesus and Spirit* 435 n.115; *idem, Unity and Diversity* 130.

164. Martin, *Spirit and Congregation* 87.

165. Ellis, 'Silenced Wives', 218. Cf. M. Evans, *Woman in the Bible* (Exeter 1983) 99, 100, 107.

166. See our comment immediately following n.155 in the text above. Cf. Clark, *Man and Woman* 187 (wives = the model for all women); and especially Grudem, *Prophecy* 247–248 n.24 (wives = an example to cover most cases).

167. E.g. Knight, 'Role Relationship', 88; *idem, Role Relationship* 36–37.

168. R. K. Johnston, 'The Role of Women in the Church and Home: An Evangelical Testcase in Hermeneutics', in *Scripture, Tradition, and Interpretation (Fs.* E. F. Harrison), ed. W. W. Gasque and W. S. LaSor (Grand Rapids 1978) 234–259 (252).

169. See Hurley, *Man and Woman* 188–192, 247; and especially Grudem, *Prophecy* 242–255. Cf. M. E. Thrall, *I and II Corinthians* (CBC; Cambridge 1965) 102 (cited in Martin, *Spirit and Congregation* 86); Bruce, 'Women in the Church', 10: 'the prohibition expressed in these verses refers to the asking of questions which imply a *judgment on prophetic utterances* (so, at least, their *context* suggests)' (emphasis added). The fact that the silence enjoined in v. 34a is required of 'all the churches of the saints' does not pose a problem for the interpretation here preferred as it does for view (4) above, since prophesying, in contradistinction to glossolalia, was apparently a much more widespread phenomenon in the primitive church (cf., besides the references in Acts and 1 Cor. Rom. 12:6; Eph. 4:11; 1 Thess. 5:20; 1 Tim. 1:18; 4:14).

170. Grudem, *Prophecy* 253. Cf. Hurley, *Man and Woman* 192.

171. In v. 36, the masculine *monous* obviously cannot refer to the women alone, but probably refers to the whole church. Interpreted as a reference to the male members alone, *monous* has been used, together with the sharply disjunctive force of the particle *ē* in interrogative sentences, to support the thesis that vv. 33b–35 represents, not Paul's opinion, but a chauvinist view which Paul refutes by the twofold rhetorical question of v. 36: so D. W. Odell-Scott, 'Let the Women Speak in Church. An Egalitarian Interpretation of 1 Cor. 14: 33b–36', *BibThBull* 13 (1983) 90–93. Against this view it may be said that (i) the alleged quotation is very lengthy compared with

those commonly acknowledged to be quotations of the Corinthians' opinions (e.g. 6:12; 10:23); (ii) v. 33b certainly reads more like the beginning of a directive from *Paul* and its content can be satisfactorily explained (see text); and (iii) the particle *ē* (KJV, RV, RSV: 'What!') should be understood to imply a refutation, not of vv. 33b–35, but of the attitude of the Corinthians which Paul wishes to correct. See Carson, *Exegetical Fallacies* 38–39, for additional arguments (adduced against the similar interpretation of Kaiser, on which cf. n.154 with text above).

172. Martin, *Spirit and Congregation* 86.
173. E.g. Trompf, 'Attitudes', 214–215. Cf. nn.109, 148 above.
174. E.g. Mollenkott, *Women* 96, 103. For criticism see e.g. Davis, 'Reflexions' (n.108 above) 206–207.
175. E.g. Robertson-Plummer, *First Corinthians* 230, 324–325.
176. C. C. Ryrie, *the Role of Women in the Church* (Chicago 1980) 76–78.
177. Ridderbos, *Paul* 462. To be mentioned perhaps under this head is the view of G. L. Almlie, 'Women's Church and Communion Participation: Apostolic Practice or Innovative Twist', *CBR* 33 (1982) 41–55: 1 Cor. 11 refers to the Lord's Supper, 1 Cor. 14 to 'the teaching meeting in which only a limited number of men participated' (44, cf. 41, 43, 51).
178. So J. Héring, *The First Epistle of Saint Paul to the Corinthians* (ET London 1964) 154. Cf. H. Schlier, *TDNT* III 680; P. Richardson, *Paul's Ethic of Freedom* (Philadelphia 1979) 157.
179. E. E. Ellis, *Prophecy and Hermeneutic in Early Christianity* (Grand Rapids 1978) 27 with n.25.
180. The Pastoral Epistles are regarded by the majority of modern interpreters as pseudonymous writings: so e.g. A. T. Hanson, *The Pastoral Epistles* (NCB; Grand Rapids/London 1982) 2–11. In defence of Pauline authorship see e.g. D. Guthrie, *New Testament Introduction* (London 1970) 584–624; idem, 'The Historical and Literary Criticism of the New Testament', in *Biblical Criticism: Historical Literary and Critical* by R. K. Harrison *et al.* (Grand Rapids 1978) 85–123 (esp. 108–109). See also T. D. Lea, 'The Early Christian View of Pseudepigraphic Writings', *JETS* 27 (1984) 65–75.
181. F. F. Bruce, 'All Things to All Men': Diversity in Unity and Other Pauline Tensions', in *Unity and Diversity in New Testament Theology* (*Fs.* G. E. Ladd), ed. R. A. Guelich (Grand Rapids 1978) 82–99, draws attention to 'Chrysostom's understanding that, was the men were to pray with holy hands, so the women were to pray in modest dress' (94); cf. *idem*, 'Women in the Church', 10, where he indicates agreement. The implication of Chrysostom's understanding is that, as in 1 Cor. 11:4f., there is no discrimination between the sexes as regards praying in church.
182. For *manthanō* here in the sense of learning through instruction, see BAG 491a (*s.v.* 1).

336 Notes to page 198

183. For the verb cf. Lk. 14:4; Acts 11:18; 21:14; it is a different sense in Lk. 23:56. For the cognate noun cf. Acts 22:2. The significance of this observation would be increased to the degree that the hypothesis (discussed in Hanson, *Pastoral* 7–10) of Luke being Paul's amanuensis in the writing of the Pastorals (C. F. D. Moule) or their author (S. G. Wilson) is accepted.
184. Cf. e.g. M. J. Harris, *NIDNTT* III 112; H. Bürki, *Der erste Brief des Paulus an Timotheus* (2. Aufl.; Wuppertal 1976) 89.
185. Cf. 1 Tim. 1:10; 2 Tim. 4:3; Tit. 2:1 (*hē hygiainousa didaskalia*; Tit. 1:9 (*hē didaskalia hē hygiainovsa*); 1 Tim. 6:3; 2 Tim. 1:13 (*hygianinontes logoi*); Tit. 2:8 (*logos hygiēs*).
186. According to D. J. Moo, '1 Timothy 2:11–15: Meaning and Significance', *TrinJ* 1 NS (1980) 62–83 (64), *hypotagē* is 'found at the focal point' of vv. 11f., whose apparently chiastic structure supports a dual reference — submission to sound teaching (v. 11) and to men (v. 12). It would appear, however, that by constructing the verses as constituting an ABCBA pattern (in which, one might note in passing, the fourth line is disproportionately longer than all the rest), Moo has over-emphasized the pivotal position of the phrase *en pasē hypotagē* (C). A simpler and more completely chiastic structure would be an ABBA pattern, with the two positive statements flanking the two negative ideas in the middle, thus:

A *Gynē en hēsychia manthanetō en pasē hypotagē*
   B *didaskein de gynaiki ouk epitrepō*
   B' *oude authentein andros*
A' *all' einai en hēsychia.*

On this showing, *en pasē hypotagē* does not occupy a pivotal position at all and the emphasis falls rather on the phrase *en hēsychia* which, in *inclusio* fashion, stands at both the beginning and the end of the period.
187. E.g. N. J. D. White, *EGT* IV 108*b*; Blum, 'Office of Woman' 72. Also see under sub-section F below.
188. This is taken to be part of the meaning of the verb (together with 'domineering over') by Evans, *Woman* 103. See, however, Moo, *art. cit.* 67.
189. E.g. C. Brown, *NIDNTT* III 1066; BAG 120*b* (*s.v.* 2nd alternative); P. B. Payne, 'Libertarian Women in Ephesus: A Response to Douglas J. Moo's Article, '1 Timothy 2:11–15: Meaning and Significance', *TrinJ* 2 NS (1981) 169–197 (175 with n.6). In the light of the context, which deals with church meetings, *authentein* is then understood by some as the opposite of subordination 'to what the men in the congregation teach', and *oude authentein* as not interrupting men who speak in church: so e.g. L. Morris, 'The Ministry of Women', in *Women and the Ministries of Christ* 14–25 (22); M. Dibelius/H. Conzelmann, *The Pastoral Epistles* (ET Hermeneia; Philadelphia 1972) 47*a*. This thought, however, is then already present in v. 11, and it may further be doubted if 'not

domineering over' can thus be attenuated to the sense of 'not interrupting'.

190. E.g. Moo, *art. cit.* 66–67; BAGo 120b (*s.v.* 1st alternative); and, especially, G. W. Knight III, 'AUTHENTEIN in Reference to Women in 1 Timothy 2.12', *NTS* 30 (1984) 143–157. With the NASB rendering cf. Thayer, *Lexicon* 84a (*s.v.*). According to Robertson, *Word Pictures* 4.570, *authentein* was the vernacular term for 'playing the master' for which the literary word was *autodikein*; cf. *idem, A Grammar of the Greek New Testament in the Light of Historical Research* (3rd ed.; New York 1919) 510 (idea = 'be ruler of'); J. H. Moulton and W. F. Howard, in *A Grammer of New Testament Greek* by J. H. Moulton, *Vol. II: Accidence and Word-Formation* (Edinburgh 1968) 278. Differently, Green, *To Corinth* 159–161, offers as 'a serious possibility' the suggestion that *authentein* has here an erotic sense and that Paul is forbidding a woman 'to teach men obscenity and fornication'.

191. E.g. Knight, *Role Relationship* 30, 49, 51, 52; *idem,* 'Role Relationship' 84–85; Foh, *Women* 125–126, 239, 248.

192. Payne, 'Libertarian Women', 175.

193. With the first suggestion cf. 1 Jn. 3:6b, *pas ho hamartanōn ouch heō raken auton oude egnōken auton*; with the second suggestion cf. Jn. 14:17a, *hoti ou theōrei auto oude ginōskei* (*sc. auto*). From the Pauline writings, two of the passages referred to in the next note seem to offer help here: Rom. 8:7 *tō . . . nomō tou theou ouch hypotassetai, oude gar dynatai* Gal. 4:14 *kai ton peirasmon hymōn . . . ouk exouthenē sate oude exeptysate*. While neither of these examples exactly reproduces the structure of 1 Tim. 2:12, in both of them the *ou* clause is complete in itself and the complement or object of the verb after *oude* is to be supplied from the *ou*-clause. With Gal. 4:14 cf. Heb. 10:8, *thysias . . . ouk ēthelēsas oude eudokēsas*.

194. Cf. Moo, *art. cit.* 68 with n.41. See e.g. Rom. 8:7; 9:16; 11:21; 1 Cor. 2:6; 11:16; Gal. 1:1, 16f.; 3:28; 4:14; 1 Thess. 2:3; 5:5; 2 Thess. 3:7f.; 1 Tim. 6:16.

195. Miss Mildred Young, my colleague at CGST and a seasoned teacher of New Testament Greek, has expressed to me her opinion that enclosing v. 12b in parentheses (as I have done) 'makes clearer the direct thought relationship between *didaskein* and *all, einai* — more clearly than, say [the use of] commas [does]'.

196. Hurley, *Man and Woman* 201.

197. As it certainly could — particularly in the light of the observation that 'the connection of clauses negatived by *oute* is close and internal, so that they are mutually complementary and combine into a unity [Gal. 1:12, *oude . . . parelabon . . . oute edidachthēn*, here springs to mind], whereas clauses negatived by *oude* follow one another much more loosely, often almost by accident as it were' (Thayer, *Lexicon* 461b, *s.v. oude*).

198. Cf. R. Scroggs, *IDBS* 968b; M. J. Harris, *NIDNTT* III 112; Moo,

art. cit. 68. In substance, therefore, our conclusion is not in conflict with the position of those mentioned in n.191 above.

199. E.g. Barth, *Ephesians* 661 n.220, 714 n.406; Hanson, *Pastoral* 72; Ellis, 'Silenced Wives', 217 n.15, Cf. E. K. Simpson, *The Pastoral Epistles* (London 1954) 48.

200. BDF 257(3). This suggestion chimes in with the view that 1 Tim. 2:8–15 is one of the *Haustafel* passages in the New Testament: so e.g. Sampley, *'One Flesh'* 18–19, 97; Hanson, *Pastoral* 43; Barth, *Ephesians* 609 n.6. But since the passage does not really talk about the mutual obligations of husbands and wives, etc., it seems preferable to say, with J. T. Sanders, *Ethics in the New Testament* (London 1975) 85–86, that 1 Tim. 2:8–12 is only a *'Haustafel-like'* passage.

201. Quotation from BDF 463. Moo, *art. cit.* 63 n.9, cites 1 Tim. 1:12, 15; 2:3 in support of his statement that 'the asyndeton need not indicate a transition to another . . . topic'. It may be observed that 1 Tim. 1:12 clearly marks the beginning of a paragraph (cf. Nestle-Aland[26], RSV, NEB, NASB, NIV), while 1:15 begins with the formula *pistos ho logos*, which occurs four other times in the Pastorals (1 Tim. 3:1; 4:9; 2 Tim. 2:11; Tit. 3:8 — all of which are asyndetic). Even with 2:3, the asyndeton may not be unrelated to the fact that 'at this point the practical direction seems to be interrupted by a purely theological passage' (E. F. Scott, *The Pastoral Epistles* [MNTC; London 1939] 20). The point we are making is simply that the asyndeton by itself is not a decisive factor.

202. For the above three arguments see, respectively, Knight, *Role Relationship* 30–31; *idem*, 'Role Relationship', 85 Moo, *art. cit.* 64; and D. Guthrie, *The Pastoral Epistles* (TNTC; London 1964) 77 (whence the quotation).

203. On the illative rather than explanatory force of *gar* in v. 13, see Moo, 'Rejoinder', 202–203.

204. Cf. e.g. H. Braun, *TDNT* VI 261; Hurley, *Man and Woman* 207. For a dissenting opinion cf. Bruce, 'Women in the Church', 11. In the view of Evans, *Woman* 104, 'Perhaps this statement of the priority of Adam's creation is not being used as a separate argument at all but merely as an introduction to the argument about the deception of Eve'. But it is difficult to see why v. 14 should need v. 13 as an introduction; could it not have been worded simply as *Adam gar ouk ēpatēthē ktl?*

205. That Paul here as in 2 Cor. 11:3 has altered the simplex form used in Gen. 3:13 LXX may be due simply to the fact that 'the compound verb came naturally to his mind' (N. J. D. White, *EGT* IV 109b). This suggestion is supported by the fact that elsewhere in Paul *exapataō* occurs five times (Rom. 7:11; 16:18; 1 Cor. 3:18; 2 Cor. 11:3; 2 Thess. 2:3), *apataō* only once (Eph. 5:6). The view that *exapatētheisa* refers to sexual seduction (so e.g. Dibelius/Conzelmann, *Pastoral* 47b–48a; H. Seebaas, *NIDNTT* I 85–86) agrees better with Jewish tradition than the biblical evidence; cf. Ellis, *Paul's Use* 61–63.

206. Knight, *Role Relationship* 66.
207. E.g. W. Foerster, *TDNT* V 581; Kelly, *Pastoral* 68; R. Earle, *ExpBC* XI 362.
208. Cf. N. J. D. White, *EGT* IV 109*b*; Pape, *Ideal Woman* 186.
209. The perfect *gegonen* is perhaps best regarded as an instance of 'the Perfect of Allegory', which 'denotes that the event stands recorded in the abiding Christian tradition' as being still relevant (C. F. D. Moule, *An Idiom-Book of New Testament Greek* [Cambridge 1968] 14-15, citing A. H. McNeile); its effect is to point to Eve's failure as a *standing* warning against being deceived by the devil (cf. 2 Cor. 11:3).
210. Hurley, *Man and Woman* 214-216; Moo, 'Rejoinder', 204 (whence the quotation). See also W. A. Grudem, *TrinJ* 3 NS (1982) 229.
211. E.g. Lock, *Pastoral* 33; P. Fairbairn, *Commentary on the Pastoral Epistles* (Grand Rapids 1956) 132; D. Williams, *The Apostle Paul and Women in the Church* (Glendale, CA 1977) 113.
212. Cf. e.g. Kelly, *Pastoral* 69; Guthrie, *Pastoral* 78. The cognate verb *teknogoneō* (in the New Testament only in 1 Tim. 5:14) likewise refers to 'bearing children' (cf. KJV, RV, RSV, NASB) or, more correctly, 'having children' (cf. NEB, NIV).
213. Boldrey, *Chauvinist* 65.
214. Cf. e.g. W. Foerster, *TDNT* VII 995 with n.131. The same criticism would apply to the interpretations of Hurley, *Man and Woman* 223; Martin, *Spirit and Congregation* 76.
215. E.g. NASB; Bürki, *Timotheus* 93 n.35; Moule, *Idiom-Book* 56; N. Turner, in *A Grammar of New Testament Greek* by J. H. Moulton, *Vol. III: Syntax* (Edinburgh 1963) 267.
216. Kelly, *Pastoral* 69. Hanson, *Pastoral* 74, notes that the view in question is 'difficult to extract from the Greek'; cf. his earlier work, *The Pastoral Letters* (CBC; Cambridge 1966) 38. Pape, *Ideal Woman* 108, raises a further objection from the angle of actual experience.
217. Scott, *Pastoral* 27.
218. W. Hendriksen, *A commentary on I and II Timothy and Titus* (London 1964) 111. Cf. E. M. Blaiklock, *The Pastoral Epistles* (Grand Rapids 1972) 33.
219. N. J. D. White, *EGT* IV 110*a*.
220. E.g. A. E. Humphreys *Timothy and Titus* (CBSC; Cambridge, 1901) 100; A. Oepke, *TDNT* II 67 (also V 649); W. Foerster, *ibid.* V 581; Hanson, *Pastoral* 73, 74; Moo, '1 Timothy 2:11-15', 71-72; *idem*, 'Rejoinder', 204-206. M. J. Harris, *NIDNTT* III 1177, apparently holds that *dia* here has both local and instrumental sense.
221. E.g. Lock, *Pastoral* 33. 'Children' is considered the subject by Barth, *Ephesians* 617 n.32, as also, apparently, by O. Procksch, *TDNT* I 113.
222. Cf. e.g. Kelly, *Pastoral* 69. For various suggestions as to how the change came about, see e.g. A. J. B. Higgins, *PCB* 1003 (=874h); Hanson, *Pastoral* 74; G. A. Denzer, *JerBC* II 354*a* (57-19).
223. U. Luck *TDNT* VII 1103.

224. Cf. Scott, *Pastoral* 28–29.
225. J. G. Sigountos and M. Shank, 'Public roles for Women in the Pauline Church: A Reappraisal of the Evidence', *JETS* 26 (1983) 283–295 (quotation from 289 n.38, and 293, respectively); C. R. Taber, 'Hermeneutics and Culture — An Anthropological Approach', in *Down to Earth*, ed. J. Stott and R. T. Coote (London 1981) 79–94 (esp. 91). Cf. G. Fee, 'The Genre of New Testament Literature and Biblical Hermeneutics', in *Interpreting the Word of God* (*Fs.* S. Barabas), ed. S. J. Schultz and M. A. Inch (Chicago 1976) 105–127 (113–114); G. D. Fee and D. Stuart, *How to Read the Bible for All Its Worth* (Grand Rapids 1982) 68.
226. E.g. R. A. Ward, *Commentary on 1 & 2 Timothy & Titus* (Waco, TX 1978) 51–52; Bürki, *Timotheus* 92–93, 219–227 (esp. 225–227); Payne, 'Libertarian Women' (esp. 185–190), which was the object of Moo's 'Rejoinder'. Cf. Fee-Stuart, *How to Read the Bible* 69 (see also previous note).
227. Kelly, *Pastoral* 12 (details on 10–12).
228. Cf. Martin, *Spirit and Congregation* 88, and especially 151 n.26.
229. Bürki, *Timotheus* 226–227 *Planaō*, when it means 'deceive' (BAG 671a, *s.v.* 1 b), is synonymous with *(ex)apataō*.
230. Cf. Moo, 'Rejoinder', 215–218.
231. *Ibid.* 220–221 (quotation from 221). Cf. Grudem, in *TrinJ* 3 NS (1982) 229–230; *Ordination: Its Meaning, Value and Theology* (Sydney 1981) 19. (The latter is a report to the Sydney Diocesan Synod submitted by a study committee whose membership included [among others] D. W. B. Robinson [chairman], P. T. O'Brien [secretary] and R. A. Cole. It is to Dr O'Brien that I owe my acquistion of a copy of the report.)
232. In *Ordination* 18, it is pointed out that the basic question concerning the ordination of women arises precisely in connection with '[the] teaching office (*magisterium*) of the leader of the congregation'.
233. Cranfield, *Romans* 623. Cf. Grudem, *Prophecy* 139–144 (esp. 142–143); Ridderbos, *Paul* 453; Gaffin, *Perspectives* 72; Green, *To Corinth* 75; *idem*, *Holy Spirit* 171; Turner,'Gifts', 13–14. Some maintain that prophecy involves teaching: elg. E. M. Howe, 'Women and Church Leadership', *EQ* 51 (1979) 97–104 (101–102); Hill, *Prophecy* 126–127. This position would be considerably strengthened if it could be demonstrated that the work of the prophet included the interpretation of Scripture, as is maintained by E. E. Ellis, 'The Role of the Christian Prophet in Acts', in *Apostolic History and the Gospel* 55–67 (58–62); but D. E. Aune, *Prophecy in Early Christianity and the Ancient Mediterranean World* (Grand Rapids 1983) 345, for one, is led to conclude that 'exegesis of the Old Testament . . . was the primary province of the teacher'. Now Paul's discussion of glossolalia *vis-à-vis* prophecy in 1 Corinthians 14 appears to suggest a certain overlapping of prophecy and teaching, with its reference to 'instruction', 'learning' and 'knowledge' (vv. 19, 31, 6); but these words can be satisfactorily explained in their

contexts without an element of teaching being involved in prophecy (see e.g. Grudem, *op. cit.* 185 [on v. 32], 139 [on v. 6]; in v. 19 the word *katēchēsō* is not brought into explicit relation with prophecy), and we may hold to the basic distinction as defined in the text as valid.

234. Apropos of the basic thesis of Grudem's book that unlike Old Testament prophecy, prophecy in the New Testament is not invested with a divine authority of actual words, but only a divine authority in general content, D. G. McCartney, in *WTJ* 45 (1983) 191–197, raises a pertinent question: 'If prophecy in the New Testament is of such relative value, what made it so much more desirable than *teaching . . .* or *pastoring . . .?*' (195). An opposite position to that of Grudem on the issue is expressed by Gaffin, *Perspectives* 68, 70 (cf. 66, 100). Cf. the discusion in Turner, 'Gifts', 15–16.

235. So Moo, 'Rejoinder', 207. For a dissenting opinion see Sigountos-Shank, 'Roles for Women', 285–286.

236. I am indebted to Dr D. A. Carson for suggesting this balanced approach.

237. *Ordination* 23.

238. Clark, *Man and Woman* 135–136. If, as some maintain (e.g. Sampley, *'One Flesh'* 97–98), in all the three classic passages Paul has in view the relation of wives to their husbands and not the relation of women to men in general, then a case can be made out for the position that apparently 'the pivot point with Paul, never clearly spelled out but always assumed', is that a woman in ministry should avoid being in a position of authority over her husband (C. E. Cerline, Jr., 'Women Ministers in the New Testament Church?', *JETS* 19 [1976] 209–215 [212–213]). But in our exegesis of 1 Cor. 11 we have seen reason for not restricting the male-female references to the husband-wife relationship.

239. Cf. *Ordination* 24.

240. Quotation from Packer, 'Postscript', 172; cf. *Ordination* 23. See, on the other hand, W. A. Grudem in *TrinJ* 3 (1982) 231–232.

241. Cf. R. T. Beckwith and G. E. Duffield, 'Towards a Better Solution', in *Why Not?* 153–163 (157), who list four special cases: charismatic exceptions, exceptions due to necessity, exceptions due to God's uncovenanted mercies, and secular exceptions. At the consultation at Cambridge, David Adeney told moving stories of churches in China where all the male leadership was imprisoned or banished, leaving women alone to lead: who would throw the first stone?

242. This seems the appropriate place to reflect something of the diversity of the cultural contexts of the study unit which met at Cambridge. thus, Satoru Kanemoto observed that in Japan the function of women as school teachers is fairly readily transferred to the church without much thought one way or the other, and that the economics of the situation — not profound theological reflection and conviction — dictate that there are very few women in senior posts in urban

areas (where most of the men go for the better-paying positions) but
that they sometimes secure posts of ministry in rural areas. Pablo
Pérez commented that although Latin American society is patrilin-
eal, it is in certain respects matriarchal and matrifocal, largely owing
to Roman Catholic influence in its elevation of Mary. Especially
among the Pentecostalists, women certainly preach and teach. Yet,
because of the Roman Catholic Church's restriction of the *priestly*
role to *men*, there are no women who are senior pastors. Sunand
Sumithra, from an Indian perspective, has no problem whatever in
seeing women being saved in connection with child-bearing: that is
their primary and God-given role! Moreover, a woman is 'married
by definition', since in Hindi the word 'woman' means something
like 'she whose womb is open'; and so until a woman is married she
just naturally is associated with her father's or her brother's house —
as one who is not considered a full mature person at all.
243. Cf. Grudem's 'further plea' in *TrinJ* NS 3 (1982) 232.

NOTES (pages 213–257)

1. Alan Race, *Christians and Religious Pluralism; Patterns in the Christian Theology of Religions* (London 1983).
2. Gerald H. Anderson and Thomas F. Stransky CSP, *Christ's Lordship and Religious Pluralism* (Maryknoll London 1983).
3. Few conservatives, for instance, would disagree with more than the odd detail of the book by M. Warren, *I Believe in the Great Commission* (Grand Rapids 1976).
4. The point recurs in Rahner's writings; but cf. *Theological Investigations* XIV (London 1976) 180–294.
5. Donald Senior and Carroll Stuhlmueller, *The Biblical Foundations for Mission* (London 1983). Cf. also Donald Senior, 'The Struggle to be Universal: Mission as Vantage Point for New Testament Investigation', *CBQ* 46 (1984) 63–81.
6. S. G. Wilson, 'Paul and Religion', in *Paul and Paulinism: Essays in Honour of C. K. Barrett* (ed. M. D. Hooker and S. G. Wilson; London 1982) 339–354, esp. p.349. See further the helpful articles by Dewi Arwel Hughes, 'Christianity and other religions: a review of some recent discussion'. *Themelios* 9/2 (1984) 15–21; and Christopher J. H. Wright, 'The Christian and other religions: the biblical evidence', *Themelios* 9/2 (1984) 4–15.
7. E. Best, 'The Revelation to Evangelise the Gentiles'. *JTS* 35 (1984) 1–30.
8. Charles H. H. Scobie, 'Jesus or Paul? The Origin of the Universal Mission of the Christian Church', in *From Jesus to Paul: Studies in Honour of Francis Wright Beare* (ed. Peter Richardson and John C. Hurd; Waterloo 1984), 47–60.
9. Harry R. Boer, *Pentecost and Mission* (London 1961).

10. E.g. Johannes Blauw, *The Missionary Nature of the Church: A Survey of the Biblical Theology of Mission* (Grand Rapids 1962); J. H. Bavinck, *An Introduction to the Science of Missions* (Philadelphia 1960); J. Herbert Kane, *Christian Missions in Biblical Perspective* (Grand Rapids 1976); Ian Hutchinson, 'What is Mission?' in *Faith active in Love* (ed. John Diesendorf; Sydney 1981) 159–172; Peter Cotterell, *The Eleventh Commandment* (Leicester 1981).

11. Harvie M. Conn, *Evangelism: Doing Justice and Preaching Grace* (Grand Rapids 1982). Many other works that treat a similar theme are of much more mixed worth: e.g. the *Theological Fraternity Bulletin* and the book edited by Tom Sine, *The Church in Response to Human Need* (Monrovia, CA 1983).

12. Dean S. Gilliland, *Pauline Theology and Mission Practice* (Grand Rapids 1983).

13. William Paul Bowers, 'Studies in Paul's Understanding of His Mission' (unpublished Ph.D. dissertation, Cambridge University, 1976).

14. Wolf-Henning Ollrog, *Paulus und seine Mitearbeiter: Untersuchungen zu Theorie und Praxis der paulinischen Mission* (WMANT 50; Neukirchen-Vluyn 1979).

15. John B. Polhill, 'Paul: Theology Born of Mission', *RevExp* 78 (1981) 233–247.

16. Harvie M. Conn, 'The Missionary Task of Theology A Love/Hate Relationship?' *WTJ* 45 (1983) 1–21.

17. The most important work on this complex subject is that of Anthony C. Thiselton. *The Two Horizons*; but cf. also Hendrik Krabbendam, 'The New Hermeneutic', *Hermeneutics, Inerrancy, and the Bible* (ed. Earl D. Radmacher and Robert D. Preus; Grand Rapids 1984) 533–558, and the equally important 'Responses' by J. I. Packer and Royce Gruenler (pp. 559–589); J. I. Packer, 'Infallible Scripture and the Role of Hermeneutics', *Scripture and Truth* (ed. D. A. Carson and John D. Woodbridge; Grand Rapids 1983) 321–356. Broader treatments that shed considerable light on the topic include Richard E. Palmer, *Hermeneutics* (Evanston 1969), and Roy J. Howard, *Three Faces of Hermeneutics: An Introduction to Current Theories of Understanding* (Berkeley 1982).

18. Cf. the excellent article by David J. Hesselgrave, 'Contextualization of Theology', in *Evangelical Dictionary of Theology* (ed. Walter A. Elwell, ed.; Grand Rapids 1984) 271–272.

19. To give but one example, cf. Carl F. H. Henry and W. Stanley Mooneyham, ed., *One Race, One Gospel, One Task*, vol. 2 (Minneapolis 1967).

20. E.g. most recently N. E. Allison, 'Make sure you're getting through', *EMQ* 20 (1984) 165–170.

21. E.g. Charles H. Kraft, *Christianity in Culture; A Study in Dynamic Biblical Thologizing in Cross-Cultural Perspective* (Maryknoll 1980); David J. Hesselgrave, *Communicating Christ Cross-Culturally; An Introduction to Missionary Communication* (Grand Rapids 1978); idem, *Planting Churches Cross-Culturally: A Guide for Home and*

Foreign Missions (Grand Rapids 1980); and the short-lived but influential journal, *Gospel in Context*.

22. E.g. Don Richardson, *Peace Child* (Glendale 1976); idem, *Lords of the Earth* (Glendale 1977).

23. E.g. J. R. W. Stott and Robert Coote, ed., *Down to Earth: Studies in Christianity and Culture* (London 1981).

24. E.g. Eugene A. Nida and Charles R. Taber, *The Theory and Practice of Translation* (Leiden 1974).

25. To name but three of the better known ones: Kosuke Koyama, *Waterbuffalo Theology* (Maryknoll 1974); Gustavo Gutiérrez, *A Theology of Liberation: History, Politics and Salvation* (tr. and ed. by Sister Caridad Inda and John Eagleson; Maryknoll 1973); John S. Mbiti, *New Testament Eschatology in an African Background: A Study of the Encounter between New Testament Theology and African Traditional Concepts* (Oxford 1971).

26. E.g. see the unpublished paper of Lois McKinney, 'Contextualizing Instruction: Contributions to Missiology from the Field of Education', delivered at Trinity Evangelical Divinity School on March 19, 1982.

27. Daniel von Allmen, 'The Birth of Theology: Contextualization as the dynamic element in the formation of New Testament theology', *IRM* 64 (1975) 37–52. This work has been frequently mentioned or discussed by missiologists, and has appeared as well in important reprints: e.g. see Charles H. Kraft and Tom N. Wisbey, ed., *Readings in Dynamic Indigeneity* (South Pasadena, CA 1979).

28. The bulk of the rest of this essay was first published in *East Africa Journal of Evangelical Theology* 3 (1984) 16–59, and is here reprinted with permission. A few significant changes have been made.

29. Byang Kato, *Theological Trends in Africa Today* (WEF Theological News, Monograph 6; April, 1973).

30. Others such as Drs. Adeyemo, Tiénou and Paluku doubtless exert similar influence; but Kato stood out as primarily a specialist in biblical studies.

31. *Ibid.* 1.

32. Von Allmen, 'Birth', 37 (emphasis his).

33. *Ibid.* 38.

34. *Ibid.*

35. *Ibid.*

36. *Ibid.* 39.

37. *Ibid.*

38. *Ibid.* 40

39. *Ibid.* 41

40. *Ibid.*

41. Edmund Schlink, 'Die Methode des dogmatischen ökumenischen Dialogs', *KD* 12 (1966) 209.

42. von Allmen, 'Birth', basing himself on P. Wendland, *Die hellenistisch-römische Kultur* (Tübingen 1912) 104–106.

43. *Ibid.*, referring to J. Gnilka, *Der Philipperbrief* (Freiburg 1966) 131–147.
44. *Ibid.*
45. *Ibid.*
46. *Ibid.* 44.
47. *Ibid.* 46.
48. *Ibid.* 45.
49. *Ibid.* 47.
50. *Ibid.* 48.
51. *Ibid.* 49.
52. *Ibid.*
53. *Ibid.* 50.
54. *Ibid.* 51.
55. Boer, *Pentecost and Missions, op. cit.*
56. Von Allmen, 'Birth', 39.
57. For general discussions on Jewish proselytizing in this period, see B. J. Bamberger, *Proselytism in the Talmudic Period* (Cincinnati 1939); W. G. Braude, *Jewish Proselytizing in the First Five Centuries of the Common Era* (Providence, RI 1940); F. M. Derwacter, *Preparing the Way for Paul: The Proselyte Movement in Later Judaism* (New York 1930); D. Georgi, *Die Gegner des Paulus im 2. Korintherbrief* (Neukirchen-Vluyn 1964); and on this particular point, see especially the doctoral dissertation by W. Paul Bowers, 'Studies'.
58. Von Allmen, 'Birth', 44.
59. *Ibid.*
60. See the assessment of von Allmen by Bruce J. Nicholls, *Contextualization: A Theology of Gospel and Culture* (Outreach and Identity: Evangelical Theological Monographs No. 3; WEF Theological Commission; Exeter 1979). Rather telling is the typology of Bong Rin Ro, 'Contextualization: Asian Theology'. *What Asian Christians Are Thinking: A Theological Source Book* (ed. Douglas J. Edwood; Quezon City 1976) 47–58, who categorizes modern attempts at contextualized Asian theology under four approaches; (1) syncretistic theology; (2) accommodational theology; (3) situational theology; and (4) biblically oriented theology relevant to Asian needs.
61. Von Allmen, 'Birth', esp. 40–46.
62. Esp. R. Reitzenstein, *Der hellenistischen Mysterien-religionen nach ihren Grundgedanken und Wirkungen* (2nd ed'n; Leipzig 1920); Wilhelm Bousset, *Kyrios Christos: Geschichte des Christusglaubens von den Anfängen des Christentums bis Irenaeus* (2nd edn; Göttingen 1921).
63. R. E. Brown, *The Semitic Background of the Term 'Mystery' in the New Testament* (Philadelphia 1968).
64. Cf. Edwin M. Yamauchi, *Pre-Christian Gnosticism; A Survey of the Proposed Evidences* (London 1973); idem, 'Some Alleged Evidences for Pre-Christian Gnosticism', in *New Directions in New Testament Study* (ed. Richard N. Longenecker and Merrill C. Tenney; Grand

Rapids 1974) 46–70; idem. 'Pre-Christian Gnosticism in the Nag Hammadi Texts?' *CH* 48 (1979) 129–141.

65. See the discussion by Peter Stuhlmacher, *Gerechtigkeit Gottes bei Paulus* (2nd ed'n; Gottingen 1966).

66. Von Allmen's expression, 'Birth'. 41.

67. Cf. D. A. Carson, 'Understanding Misunderstandings in the Fourth Gospel', *TynBull* 33 (1982) 59–91; *idem*, 'Christological Ambiguities in the Gospel of Matthew', in *Christ the Lord* (*Festschrift* Donald Guthrie; ed. Harold Rowdon; Leicester 1982) 97–114.

68. Cf. Philip Barton Payne, 'Jesus' Implicit Claim to Deity in His Parables', *TrinJ* 2 (1981) 3–23.

69. There were, of course, many quite different positions or schools of thought in the Graeco-Roman world. Lucretius, for instance, was a thoroughgoing materialist, and was in turn heavily dependent on Epicurus.

70. See especially the frequently overlooked article by Roy W. Hoover, 'The Harpagmos Enigma: A Philological Solution' *HTR* 64 (1971) 95–119.

71. 'Birth', 46.

72. *Ibid.*

73. *Ibid.*

74. The expression is that of I. Howard Marshall, 'Slippery Words: I. Eschatology', *ExpT* 89 (1977–78) 264–269.

75. Von Allmen, 'Birth', 46.

76. J. Christiaan Beker, *Paul the Apostle: The Triumph of God in Life and Thought* (Philadelphia 1980) 170.

77. Cf. *inter alia* I. Howard Marshall, 'Palestinian and Hellenistic Christianity: Some Critical Comments', *NTS* 19 (1972–73) 271–287; and esp. Martin Hengel, *Judaism and Hellenism: Studies in Their Encounter in Palestine during the Early Hellenistic Period* (London 1974).

78. Von Allmen, 'Birth', 41.

79. *Ibid.* 47.

80. *Ibid.* 37.

81. *Ibid.* 51.

82. Charles H. Kraft, *Christianity in Culture*, op. cit., esp. pp. 232–233, 286–287, 295–297.

83. *Ibid.* 32.

84. On recent treatemnts of Luther's attitude to the Scriptures, cf. esp. Eugene F. Klug, 'Word and Scripture in Luther Studies since World War II', *TrinJ* 5 (1984) 3–46.

85. Kraft, *Christianity in Culture* 296 (emphasis his).

86. Charles H. Kraft, 'Cultural Anthropology: Its Meaning for Christian Theology', *Theology Today* 41 (1985) 393 draws attention to Thomas S. Kuhn, *The Structure of Scientific Revolutions* (Chicago 1970) and to Ian G. Barbour, *Myths, Models and Paradigms* (New York 1974).

87. Cf. especially Frederick Suppe, ed., *The Structure of Scientific Theories* (2nd ed'n; Urbana 1977); Gary Gutting, ed., *Paradigms and*

Revolutions; Applications and Appraisals of Thomas Kuhn's Philosophy of Silence (Notre Dame 1980).

88. Cf. D. A. Carson and John D. Woodbridge, ed., *Scripture and Truth* (Grand Rapids 1983), esp. the essay 'Unity and Diversity in the New Testament: The Possibility of Systematic Theology'.

89. *Ibid*; and cf. I. Howard Marshall, 'Orthodoxy and Heresy in earlier Christianity, *Themelios* 2/1 (1976) 5–14.

90. Cf. D. A. Carson, 'Pauline Inconsistency: Reflections on I Corinthians 9.19–23 and Galatians 2.11–14', *Churchman*, 100 (1986) 6–45.

91. *Christianity in Culture* 296–197.

92. For the best discussion, cf. Anthony C. Thiselton, *The Two Horizons* (Exeter 1979).

93. Many examples could be cited. For instance, one major brand of liberation theology has strong roots in Marxism — originally a European philosophy.

94. There is of course a small but vocal minority of historians and philosophers of history who appeal to the new hermeneutic in defence of the 'new history' — which not only insists, rightly, that no history is ever written absolutely '*wie es eigentlich gewesen war*' (to use von Ranke's celebrated expression), but that all history-writing is so subjective that even to speak of accuracy is inappropriate. 'Truth' in history-writing has nothing to do with correspondence. The debate is extremely important, but cannot be entered into here.

95. I am thinking in particular of John S. Mbiti's thoughtful work, *New Testament Eschatology in an African Background: A Study of the Encounter between New Testament Theology and African Traditional Concepts* (Oxford 1971).

96. I here follow one common use of 'contextualization', recently and ably discussed by Martin Goldsmith, 'Contextualization of theology', *Themelios* 9/1 (1983) 18–23.

97. Cf. Carson, 'Unity and Diversity', *art. cit.*.

98. E.g. V. E. Devadutt, 'What is an Indigenous Theology?' in *Readings in Dynamic Indigeneity* (ed. Charles H. Kraft and Tom N. Wisbey; South Pasadena, CA 1979) 313–324.

99. For further reflections on the connections between a high view of Scripture and problems of contextualization, cf. David J. Hesselgrave, 'Contextualization and Revelational Epistemology', in *Hermeneutics, Inerrancy, and the Bible* (ed. Earl D. Radmacher and Robert D. Preus; Grand Rapids 1984) 691–738.

100. See the important discussion by Tite Tiénou, 'The Church in African Theology: Description and Hermeneutical Analysis', in *Biblical Interpretation and the Church: Text and Context* (ed. D. A. Carson; Exeter 1984).

101. E.g. Don Richardson, *Eternity in Their Hearts* (Ventura, CA 1981).

102. See especially Andrew F. Walls, 'The Gospel as the Prisoner and Liberator of Culture', *Faith and Thought* 108 (1981) 39–52.

NOTES (pages 258–274)

1. Hendrik Kraemer, *Religion and the Christian Faith* (London 1956/ Philadelphia 1957).
2. See especially Peter Berger and Thomas Luckmann, *The Social Construction of Reality* (Garden City, New York 1966). At a more popular level, see Os Guinness, *The Gravedigger File* (Downers Grove, IL 1983).
3. The term 'indigenization' will not please all readers; but after (or perhaps despite) prolonged discussion in our study unit, this term seems to me less objectionable than 'contextualization'.
4. J. H. Bavinck, *An Introduction to the Science of Missions*, translated by David H. Freeman (Philadelphia 1960).
5. See especially *TDNT*, *s.v. logos*.
6. Carl F. H. Henry, 'The Reality and Identity of God: A Critique of Process Theology' (*CT* 13/12 1979) 3–6; 13/13 (1979) 12–16; and especially Royce Gordon Gruenler, *The Inexhaustible God: Biblical Faith and the Challenge of Process Theism* (Grand Rapids 1983).
7. John Macquarrie, *God and Secularity* (Philadelphia 1967).

NOTES (pages 275–302)

1. See Saphir P. Athyal, *The Gospel in a Hostile Environment* (ATA 4th Theological Consultation).
2. Michael Wilcock, *I Saw Heaven Opened — the message of Revelation* (Leicester) 22.
3. Klaus Bockmuehl, *The Challenge of Marxism: A Christian Response* (Downess Grove 1980) 53–54.
4. From Josef Ton's paper 'The Christian in Socialism' which was widely distributed in Rumania in 1974. See also idem, *Marxism: The Faded Dream* (Basingstoke 1985), a revision of the earlier paper.
5. *Ibid.*
6. See Bruce E. Olson, *For this Cross I'll Kill You* (Carol Stream, IL 1973) 12–13.
7. See David M. Gitari and Stephen Kaman Gitumbi, 'The History of Persecution in Eastern Africa,' (W.E.F. Consultation: High Leigh, England 1980).
8. Michael Bourdeaux, *Risen Indeed — Lessons in Faith from the USSR* (London 1983) 59.
9. *Ibid.*
10. Eusebius v.1, 21–22.

INDEX

Index of Names

Index of Biblical Passages
Discussed